*The Funding of Scientific Racism*

# The Funding of Scientific Racism

## *Wickliffe Draper and the Pioneer Fund*

WILLIAM H. TUCKER

*University of Illinois Press*

URBANA AND CHICAGO

∞ This book is printed on acid-free paper.

Library of Congress Cataloging-in-Publication Data
Tucker, William H., 1940–
The funding of scientific racism : Wickliffe Draper and
the Pioneer Fund / William H. Tucker.
p.   cm.
Includes bibliographical references and index.
ISBN 0-252-02762-0 (cloth : alk. paper)
1. Draper, Wickliffe Preston.
2. Pioneer Fund (Foundation)—History.
3. Eugenics—Research—United States—History.
4. Eugenics—Research grants—United States—History.
5. Racism—United States—History.
I. Title.
HQ755.5.U5T82     2002
363.9'2'072073—dc21     2001008659

*For Monica*

# Contents

# Acknowledgments

LIKE THAT FAMOUS fictional Southerner, I have relied on the kindness of strangers to complete this work. Because the most important members of the Pioneer Fund, including its founder, have deliberately concealed many of their activities from the public, it was necessary to piece together much of their story from the archival correspondence of various other people who have been involved in these surreptitious projects. I am thus particularly indebted to the numerous archivists and staff members of the facilities listed in the Appendix; although in most cases I don't even know their names, this book would not have been possible without their assistance.

The research for this book was also assisted by my own university, both through a grant from the Rutgers University Research Council and by the energetic efforts of the library staff. In particular, I am grateful to Libby Hart at Rutgers-Camden's Robeson Library, who helped me locate and obtain all sorts of obscure materials.

I owe a special debt of gratitude to a number of friends and colleagues. My long-time, close friend Shep Nachbar took an early interest in this project and visited Hopedale to help me track down the details of Wickliffe Draper's family background; it was also through Shep's diligent work that I obtained an interview with William F. Draper, Wickliffe's second cousin. Barry Mehler, the director and founder of the Institute for the Study of Academic Racism at Ferris State University, generously opened both his files and his home to me. Keith Hurt shared his encyclopedic knowledge of right-wing activists, as well as the transcripts of his interviews with a number of important sources of information. I also benefited greatly from Andrew Winston's expertise on right-wing social scientists. Although all these friends have encouraged and assisted me with this work, naturally the responsibility for the opinion and the analysis is mine alone.

At the University of Illinois Press, Richard Martin has encouraged this project since I first mentioned it to him, and I feel fortunate to have him as an editor. Carol Anne Peschke's meticulous editing of the manuscript has done much to improve it.

My family has been an extraordinary source of encouragement over the three years it took to complete this book. My beloved Uncle Phil was particularly interested in the project and sent me a number of useful articles; I am saddened that he died only months before the manuscript was finished. My son, Tommy, has not only taken an interest in the work but allowed me to use his name and address to order some materials from one supposedly academic source, which led to the fascinating revelation of its connection to David Duke; my fondest hope is that some day Tommy's daughter, Lainey, will read this book and at last understand why Popi's office was always filled with piles of paper.

Finally and most important, I owe an enormous debt of gratitude to my wife, Monica, who provided tangible assistance on a number of trips to archival repositories and whose incredible patience and unwavering support make all things possible. It is to her that I dedicate this book.

*The Funding of Scientific Racism*

# Introduction: Keepers of the Flame

IN THE FALL of 1994 the national obsession with the murder trial of a legendary athlete was temporarily interrupted by a controversy over a book—not a juicy, tell-all, unauthorized biography of a pharmacologically challenged entertainer or a sexually predatory politician but an 845-page tome, authored by a Harvard research psychologist and an American Enterprise Institute policy wonk. Despite its more than 100 pages of appendices on logistic regression and other technical issues, *The Bell Curve* became an instantaneous cause célèbre, providing its junior author, Charles Murray (Professor Richard J. Herrnstein having passed away only weeks before the book's appearance), with much more than his Warholian fifteen minutes of prominence and leading a reporter for the *New York Times Magazine* to designate him "the most dangerous" conservative in the country.[1] Reactions to *The Bell Curve,* with its hereditarian explanation for the relationships between IQ, income, and race, were as diverse as they were predictable—from the *Forbes* reviewer who claimed, in a passive voice conveniently lacking an agent, that the book was being "seriously compared" with Darwin's *Origin of Species* to black intellectuals who labeled it "hate literature with footnotes" and "not simply . . . reactionary but . . . utterly racist."[2]

Although *The Bell Curve*'s fifty-seven-page bibliography listed many studies from mainstream scientific journals, Murray frankly acknowledged that "some of the things we read to do this work, we literally hide when we're on planes and trains."[3] This allusion to a less respectable scholarly subculture was quickly made more explicit by the book's critics. In the *New York Review of Books* Charles Lane referred to *The Bell Curve*'s "tainted sources," noting that seventeen researchers cited in the book's bibliography had contributed articles to, and ten of these seventeen had also been editors of, the *Mankind Quarterly,* "a notorious journal of 'racial history' founded, and funded, by men who believe in the genetic superiority of the white race." Lane went on to identify the *Quarterly's* financial benefactor as the Pioneer Fund, a New York foundation established in 1937 by textile multimillionaire Wickliffe Preston Draper, who had "advocated the 'repatriation' of blacks to Africa." Now headed by New York attorney Harry F. Weyher, who, according to Lane, had proposed that integration be abandoned, the fund also provided millions of dollars in research grants for the *Quarterly's* contributors, a number of whom "were alleged to have pro-Nazi affiliations," as well as for the journal itself. In a later exchange with Murray himself, Lane called the Pioneer Fund and *Mankind Quarterly* "scientific racism's keepers of the flame."[4]

Other comments on Pioneer shared Lane's harsh judgment. An article in *Rolling Stone* titled "Professors of Hate" called the fund "an organization with a terrible past" and described in detail the alleged Nazi sympathies of Pioneer's secretary, John B. Trevor Jr., as well as some of its grantees. Leon Kamin, professor of psychology at Northeastern University and a well-known critic of hereditarian studies, observed that Herrnstein and Murray, in their discussion of race and IQ, had turned for assistance to Richard Lynn, whom they described as "a leading scholar of racial and ethnic differences."[5] "I will not mince words," wrote Kamin, calling it a "shame and disgrace that two eminent social scientists . . . take as their scientific tutor Richard Lynn . . . an associate editor of the vulgarly racist journal *Mankind Quarterly* . . . [and] a major recipient of support from the nativist and eugenically oriented Pioneer Fund." As newspapers, both general and specialized, also began to report on the fund, Pioneer suddenly found itself the object of more adverse publicity in the ten weeks after the appearance of *The Bell Curve* than in the previous fifty-seven years of its existence.[6]

Though not nearly as broad in scope, there had been some earlier controversy involving the fund. In 1977, the *New York Times* reported that Pioneer had been subsidizing work by the two most well-known exponents of genetic differences in intelligence between the races: Berkeley educational psychologist Arthur Jensen and Stanford physicist and Nobel laureate–turned–behavior geneticist William Shockley. In addition, the *Times* described the work of two lesser-known grantees: Ralph Scott, a professor of education at the University of Northern Iowa who had used the money not only for research but also for "anti-school busing, anti-integration seminars" around the country, and Roger Pearson, a British-born social scientist who had been the editor of a far-right pro-apartheid magazine and a pamphleteer for similar causes. An Internal Revenue Service spokesperson interviewed for the story stated that

Scott's off-campus activities "might put the fund's tax-exempt status in jeopardy" under federal law prohibiting the use of such grants for "carrying on propaganda or otherwise attempting to influence legislation."[7] However, when the *Times* phoned Weyher, who even then was president of the fund, to ask about the tax issue, he refused to comment and abruptly hung up.

Articles critical of Pioneer in the 1980s by historian Barry Mehler were also largely ignored by Weyher. In 1983 Mehler revealed that, in addition to funding research, much of Pioneer's money was spent on publishing and disseminating materials supporting hereditarian conclusions. The Foundation for Human Understanding, an organization created by Pioneer grantees and dependent on the fund for resources, sent out unsolicited reprints of an article by Herrnstein to 8,000 newspapers and distributed thousands of free copies of a book by Jensen to admissions officers and college presidents throughout the country in what Mehler characterized as an apparent attempt "to raise questions about the admission of black students." Then, in 1988, Mehler discussed the neo-Nazi associations of some of the fund's grantees and revealed that, ironically, Ralph Scott had been appointed by the Reagan administration to a state Advisory Commission on Civil Rights. And in 1989, Mehler charged that Pioneer's creators—not only Draper but also the fund's first president, well-known eugenicist Harry H. Laughlin—had been Nazi sympathizers, noting that the fund's very first project in 1937 had been the distribution of a Nazi eugenic propaganda film in the United States.[8] To all these accusations Weyher made little public response, perhaps unconcerned because they had appeared in publications with small circulation.[9]

In November 1989, however, a controversy at the University of Delaware forced Weyher to abandon his previous reticence and play a more active, public role in defending the fund. The university's president asked the Faculty Senate Committee on Research to make a formal recommendation on whether the school should accept Pioneer money awarded to Linda Gottfredson, a professor of education who had received $174,000 ($244,000 adjusted for inflation) in support of research arguing that socioeconomic inequality was the *expected* outcome of blacks' genetically lower intellectual ability.[10] Actually, a grant had been declined in 1975 by the University of Louisville's School of Medicine because, as its director wrote to Weyher, "there appears to be a slant towards . . . ethnic differences in intelligence," but Pioneer had not protested, probably because the incident remained private.[11] But now faced with the prospect that a grant might be *publicly* rejected—an undesirable precedent that might be emulated elsewhere[12]—Weyher appeared before the Senate Committee, although his defense of the fund obviously did not allay their concerns. In its formal report the committee recommended that the university "neither seek nor accept any further financial support from the Pioneer Fund" and called it "a mistake for the University to have solicited financial support from the Pioneer Fund . . . in the past." The report found that Pioneer had engaged in a "pattern of activities incompatible with the University's mission" and that its selection of studies to support indicated an attempt "to influence public policy according to a eugenic program." At the same time, the committee emphasized its vigorous support for the full protection of Professor Gottfredson's academic freedom, noting that the content of her work had in no way been the focus of investigation. That is, Gottfredson was free to pursue her research but, in doing so, could not commit the university to accept Pioneer's money.[13]

Although the decision by Delaware's Faculty Senate Committee was eventually reversed after Gottfredson, with assistance from the American Association of University Professors, appealed the dispute to an external arbitrator, the incident appeared to have persuaded Weyher to respond to critics. In any event, adverse publicity was no longer ignored. In fact, in the summer of 1994, the reclusive attorney gave a personal interview to a reporter for the first time in his many decades as Pioneer's president, inviting the writer for lunch to his private, very exclusive Park Avenue haunt, the Racquet & Tennis Club. Though probably motivated by the appearance of a book a few months earlier that repeated a number of Mehler's charges about Pioneer's history, the interview was published, conveniently, within weeks of Lane's charge of "tainted sources" in the *New York Review of Books* and the "Professors of Hate" article in *Rolling Stone*.[14]

By this time, Weyher was in a rapid response mode, quickly submitting letters to the *New York Review of Books,* the *Wall Street Journal,* the *New York Times,* and many other publications that made any critical reference to Pioneer or to Draper, its founder. Indeed, the fund's president announced, newspapers that were initially reluctant to publish his statements—such as the *Sacramento Bee* and London's *Independent on Sunday*—were brought into line after some "prodding by Pioneer's lawyers."[15] In addition, Pioneer's Web site featured a lengthy response to "False Charges" and a sixty-four-page outraged denunciation of ABC News by Robert A. Gordon, a grantee and sociologist at Johns Hopkins, after two four-minute segments on human intelligence, the second of which was devoted partly to Pioneer, appeared on *World News Tonight with Peter Jennings.* This new, aggressive campaign on the fund's behalf culminated in the publication by Weyher, an attorney, of two articles in scholarly journals in psychology, in each case defending Pioneer against what he called "the media's false stories." (Actually, much of the second article to appear was a verbatim but unacknowledged repetition of portions of the first.)[16]

These various responses emphasized a number of common themes. First and most important was Weyher's constant claim that Pioneer's "sole activity" had been to support "empirical research" of high quality, conducted only by "the top experts" at "the best universities and research institutions."[17] As evidence for this assertion Weyher could legitimately point to a number of grantees who, though highly controversial, had won academic honors for their work, were fellows in their respective scientific organizations, and served on the editorial boards of academic journals in their field. In addition, according to Weyher, Pioneer had "no political agenda" and was interested only in scientific excellence: It "has never taken, and will never take, a position on any political . . . issue"; it has "never 'recommended' any policy" and, in particular, has never proposed that "America abandon integration." Indeed, the latter assertion, made in Weyher's letter to the *New York Review*, elicited an apology from Charles Lane, who conceded that it would have been more accurate to state that Pioneer had made "a case for abandoning compensatory education and other programs aimed at helping blacks, as opposed to criticizing integration per se."[18]

Weyher also defended Wickliffe Draper, whom he knew personally and greatly admired, against charges that Pioneer's founder had advocated "repatriation" of blacks to Africa. "I never heard Draper say any such thing, and he denied a printed rumor to the same effect," wrote Weyher in his response to Lane. However, Pioneer's Web site acknowledged that "a small magazine about 35 years ago purported to quote anonymous sources as having heard a now deceased Pioneer director, in private conversations occurring probably 50 years ago, express approval of repatriation programs." The "small magazine" was undoubtedly *The Nation*, which had reported in 1960 that Draper was attempting to interest university geneticists in investigations of racial inequality. One geneticist interviewed for the story had stated that Draper "wished to prove simply that Negroes were inferior . . . and . . . to promote some program to send them all to Africa." Nevertheless, Pioneer's Web site insisted, whatever interest Draper may have expressed was only his suggestion of "black-led voluntary repatriation" as "a subject worthy of study, apparently by another foundation."[19]

Finally, Weyher vigorously rejected any taint of Nazi sympathy on the part of Draper or the fund's other early directors, a charge that, he claimed, had originated with Mehler, whom Weyher characterized as a "swastika painter," Marxist, and "long-time anti-hereditarian activist"; other writers, "seeking sensationalism without ethical concern for the truth," had only recycled "Mehler's innuendo and falsehood." Weyher insisted that Draper had never expressed any support for Nazi policies "in my years of association with him,"

and although Weyher acknowledged that the fund's original five incorpora-
tors had been "interested in the eugenics movement," he pointed out, correctly, that many "left-of-center thinkers" had supported eugenic policies in
the 1930s as a method for "the improvement of the hereditary qualities of the
human race."[20] Presumably, Pioneer's distribution of the Nazi film reflected
this motive, a conclusion also promoted by Robert Gordon's open letter to
ABC, which insisted that the film was not a propaganda document but a
presentation of "the appalling nature of incurable mental retardation and . . .
mental illness" that raised the "possibility of prevention" on a "genetic basis." Both Weyher and Gordon also emphasized that John Marshall Harlan
had been one of Pioneer's five founding directors, a fact not mentioned by
any of the fund's critics. Later named a Supreme Court Justice, Harlan was a
strong supporter of civil rights, according to Pioneer's two defenders. It was
just not possible, suggested Weyher, that two such men as Draper and Harlan could have "founded an organization with Nazi and racist leanings."[21]

What is the truth about Pioneer? Taken at face value, Weyher's defense raises
some important points. If the fund has done no more than provide resources
to universities for scientific research of high quality, then Pioneer may have
been victimized by an intellectually stultifying pressure to conform to political orthodoxy. On the other hand, if the many grants made by Pioneer—not
only to a number of well-known scientists but also to a host of obscure academics who similarly maintain that blacks are intellectually inferior to
whites—mask other, less laudable goals, then the fund may be hiding an oppressive political agenda behind the protection of academic freedom.

Even before looking at the evidence, however, it is clear that Pioneer is not
a typical foundation. Its original certificate of incorporation, drafted in 1937,
listed two "charitable purposes" on which resources were to be expended.
First, the fund was to provide financial aid "for the education of children of
parents . . . of unusual value," and in deciding who should benefit from such
assistance, "consideration shall be especially given to children who are
deemed to be descended predominantly from white persons who settled in
the original thirteen states prior to the adoption of the Constitution . . . and/
or from related stocks." That is, not only was it assumed that certain "stocks"
were ipso facto more likely to be of value than others, but the actual selection of children meriting assistance was to be made by scrutinizing their
parents. The intent, the charter noted, was to encourage such parents to have
more children, "and in so far as the qualities and traits of such parents are
inherited, to aid in improving the character of people in the United States."[22]

The fund's second purpose was to support "study and research into the
problems of heredity and eugenics" and "into the problems of race better-

ment" in the United States, the latter phrase clearly referring to race in the generic sense: the "human race." Also as part of the second purpose, the fund was to aid in the "dissemination of information . . . in general with respect to heredity and eugenics."[23] It was apparently under this provision that Pioneer has frequently subsidized not only research but also the distribution of many books, pamphlets, and reprints in what is essentially a lobbying effort for its grantees' conclusions about race—an activity not mentioned by Weyher in his description of Pioneer's achievements. Although only one project, involving eleven children from nine families selected in 1940, ever received money from Pioneer as aid for education, the fund's first purpose provides an interesting perspective from which to view the second. That is, Pioneer was chartered to support research into heredity, eugenics, and "race betterment," having determined, in advance of any data, that "white persons" descended from the original colonists were of greater value than other citizens.

In 1985, Weyher, Pioneer's president, and Trevor, its secretary, filed an amendment to the charter, making two cosmetic changes. The word *white* was deleted from the description of parents whose children were presumptively of greater value, although the rest of the definition was left intact: Descendants of the colonists would remain the preferred recipients, making the change of questionable significance, were aid ever again to be offered. And the word *human* was inserted before *race betterment,* thus making explicit what was originally perhaps vague but no doubt intended. Asked about the deletion during his appearance before the University of Delaware's faculty committee, Weyher indicated that the fund remained faithful to the original wording but had been pressured into the change only "because of the fact that Mehler and these other people have been making tabloid newspaper stories."[24]

Pioneer's administrative procedures are as unusual as its charter. Although the fund typically gives away more than half a million dollars per year, there is no application form or set of guidelines. Instead, according to Weyher, an applicant merely submits "a letter containing a brief description of the nature of the research and the amount of the grant requested."[25] There is no requirement for peer review of any kind; Pioneer's board of directors—two attorneys, two engineers, and an investment broker—decides, sometimes within a day, whether a particular research proposal merits funding. Once the grant has been made, there is no requirement for an interim or final report or even for an acknowledgment by a grantee that Pioneer has been the source of support, all atypical practices in comparison to other organizations that support scientific research. In the competitive academic environment, where external support for research is both a source of professional pride and sometimes even a reason to expect an increase in salary, it is particularly unusual that a number of recipients have chosen not to acknowledge grants from Pioneer.

Finally, in accord with the tax regulations governing nonprofit corporations, Pioneer does not fund individuals; under the law only other nonprofit organizations are appropriate grantees. As a consequence, many of the fund's awards go not to the researchers themselves but to the universities that employ them, a standard procedure for supporting work by academically based scientists. However, in addition to these awards to the universities where its grantees are based, Pioneer has also made a number of grants to other nonprofit organizations, essentially dummy corporations created solely to channel Pioneer's resources directly to a particular academic recipient—a mechanism apparently designed to circumvent the institution where the researcher is employed.

Before examining the record on Pioneer, one other point merits particular emphasis. I vigorously support the right of scientists to pursue the research of their choice and to announce their results without fear of threat or harassment. Universities and other research institutions are, properly, sanctuaries for the exploration of unpopular ideas and the pursuit of knowledge, no matter how controversial the effort; intellectual freedom must allow what the Yale University code calls "the right to think the unthinkable, discuss the unmentionable and challenge the unchallengeable."[26] My commitment to the right to unfettered research is not diminished one iota by my contention, described in detail elsewhere, that research into racial differences in intelligence has provided no results of any scientific value and that it has been used primarily, if not exclusively, to legitimate racist ideology.[27] In the same spirit of inquiry, of course, I also believe that the policy agenda motivating the support for such research is certainly an appropriate subject of academic inquiry.

The analysis in this book is thus concerned primarily with Pioneer's claim that Draper's money has been disbursed solely for the support of daring, politically incorrect research that could not be conducted without the fund's assistance. Archival records indicate that a different, much less commendable purpose has informed Pioneer's activities from its inception to the present. During the 1930s, Draper was indeed the principal source of financial support for a Klansman's crusade to have blacks repatriated to Africa. And in the 1960s Draper, Weyher, and Trevor—Pioneer's creator and its two officers—were at the core of a number of attempts to preserve Jim Crow laws in the South, providing large amounts of money to organizations opposing equality for blacks on the grounds that they were genetically inferior. They also participated in efforts to inform the nation of the more serious problem underlying the civil rights movement: Jewish control of public discourse. Although all these activities were conducted in utmost secrecy, they provide an important context for any consideration of Pioneer's claims, naturally raising the question whether the same people who had committed themselves and their resources so wholeheartedly to the struggle for American apartheid could then credibly maintain that their support for research on racial differences has had no purpose other than the advancement of scientific knowledge.

Although the record is not complete—and no doubt will remain so, absent the unlikely event that Weyher decides to release the details of the numerous projects surreptitiously funded by Draper—the evidence available now strongly indicates that Pioneer has indeed been the primary resource for scientific racism.

# 1  Our Northern Friend:
   A Tale of Two Colonels

TO EARNEST SEVIER COX, the removal of blacks from the American continent was, in his own words, "a holy cause." Born in Blount County, Tennessee in 1880, Cox had been a newspaper reporter, schoolteacher, minister, and graduate student in sociology, all before turning thirty. The better part of the next decade he spent traveling extensively through Africa, the Philippines, Panama, and South America and then serving with the American Expeditionary Forces at Bordeaux before turning to the obsession that would dominate the last half of his life.[1]

At first, "Colonel Cox," as he was regularly addressed, labored in vain. Both before and after his military service he had worked on a lengthy book manuscript fervently arguing for the repatriation of blacks to Africa, only to find that no publisher would accept it—not even with Cox's assurance that Madison Grant was willing to write an introduction promoting the work;[2] Grant was the author of *The Passing of the Great Race,* a best-selling nativist tract that had been praised by Theodore Roosevelt and cited by legislators during congressional discussions on immigration. Nor was Cox's promise of such prominent support an overstatement; even after the book was privately published, Grant would lobby his own publisher—Scribner's—to reissue it "in a more dignified form," only to be told by well-known editor Maxwell Perkins that Cox "does not know well enough how to write."[3] Originally titled *Decay of Culture: A Study of the Negro in Civilization,* Cox's book eventually appeared in 1923 as *White America,* under the imprint of an identically named organization he had created. In the next few years the White America Society released two additional tracts on race authored by Cox: *Let My People Go* and *The South's Part in Mongrelizing the Nation.*

In *White America* Cox viewed all history and culture exclusively through the prism of race, and his conclusions were unequivocal. "The white man is the sun that lights the world," he declared; "all . . . works . . . worthy of record have, with few or doubtful exceptions, emanated from . . . [his] brain." All civilization thus depended on white superiority, according to Cox; its "every pulse-beat is Caucasian, . . . its source is in the white race, and it cannot continue apart from the white race." Without the presence of white superiority, he concluded, "civilization, as we know it, would perish."[4]

Although Cox acknowledged that signs of civilization had appeared in Asia and in Central and South America, closer scrutiny invariably proved them a product of Caucasian influence. The "earliest inhabitants of Japan," the origin of "the 'fine' type of the aristocracy" in that country, were of "an undoubted white strain, . . . the most truly Caucasian people in eastern Asia." In China, "early records . . . refer to blond tribes," the "Caucasic element" that constituted "the upper class" and the source of "Chinese higher culture," and it was the elimination of that Caucasian influence, according to Cox, that accounted for the decline of Chinese civilization. And when he considered · the great stone structures of Mexico and Peru, Cox was certain that these civilizations, too, must have had Caucasian origins because no other race could have been capable of such architectural achievements. *That the colored races do not originate,*" he concluded in italics, "*is the most solemn fact of human history.*"[5]

The problem, as Cox described it, was that throughout history the white race had been able to retain its remarkable progress and to safeguard civilization only by maintaining its ethnic purity; "civilization," he observed, "has never survived intimate and prolonged contact with the colored race." In Egypt, for example, a Caucasian people had produced a "period of greatness" lasting for thirty centuries, but when "negro blood made the proud Egyptian a mongrel" and a mulatto inherited the throne of the Pharaohs, "three thousand years of progress" were followed by "three thousand years of stagnation." The protection of "blood integrity" was thus imperative, not just out of white self-interest in promoting its own progress but in order to "impart its achievements to the backward races." All races thus had a stake in white purity, insisted Cox: "The cultural debit of the colored peoples to the white race is such as to make the preservation of the white race the chief aim of the colored, if these latter but understood their indebtedness. By keeping the white man white, the colored may look forward to a future in which they are to enjoy cultural surroundings far superior to the works of their own brains and hands."

In the United States, of course, the chief threat to white purity, and hence to civilization, came from blacks. "The white world," wrote Cox, had done "the negro a great service by bringing him from savage Africa" and conferring on him the benefits of progress. However, much to Cox's dismay, instead of realizing their own interest in preserving the racial integrity of their benefactors, many blacks demonstrated an "insane desire . . . to blot out the color line," further proof to Cox that "their inferiority . . . in cultural attainments extends to their rational processes in general."[6]

Although Cox complained of white "negrophilists"—neurotic apostles of miscegenation—his much greater fear was the "touchy mixbreed," who had been transformed into "the bitterest enemy" because denied "full and unrestricted access to the white man's homes and daughters." And everywhere he looked—"the North, the South, the East and the West"—he saw "a cancer that will eat deeper and deeper into the white race": "aggressive negroids," bent on revenge for their enslavement, attempting to "inject the blood of Africa into Caucasian circles." Obsessed by the thought of such contamination, Cox described the prospect of a dusky future in what he clearly considered to be horrifying detail:

> Imagine the mulattoes and the nearer whites of the United States to be greatly augmented in numbers. Suppose they constitute two-thirds of the population. They possess the ballot. . . . Caucasian ideals would assert a dwindling influence in politics, economics, and social aims. No white could hold high office without mongrel support, and the prospective officeholder could not obtain such support without special concessions to the mixbreed element. White politicians would vie with each other in making promises which sooner or later would have to be fulfilled. Eventually the nation would cease to reflect Caucasian ideals and cease to represent Caucasian culture. The pall of Africanism would settle on the land. Mulatto senators! Revolutions! Creativity, ingenuity gone, the arts and sciences would decay, sky scrapers would crumble, plantations would be weed-grown. . . . The halls of the national capitol, once familiar to the noblest of the Saxons, would echo to the tread of mulattoes, and a mixbreed would sit as President.[7]

To this unappealing scenario Cox saw but one possible alternative: repatriation. Nor was such a process to be "left to the negro's decision, any more than the removal of the Indian was left to the choice of the Indian." When the latter people were "in the way of the advancement of civilization," Cox observed, they "were made to move" in order to leave the "Caucasian unhindered in his progress." Could anyone doubt, he inquired rhetorically, that "American civilization was endangered by the Indian as it is by the negro?" Besides, he argued, with no sense of irony, *"if the negro is not of a mettle to redeem"* his homeland, then *"surely he is not a fit associate for that race"* that had just "subjugated a continent and [was] seeking wider activities." Blacks' reluctance to return to Africa was thus the best evidence that they were not fit to stay.[8]

His firm conclusion that the removal of blacks was essential to preserve the nation from "mongrelization" and decline led Cox to a monomaniacal view of the world in which all events, historical or political, were interpreted by their relevance to his obsession. An underlying cause of the American revolution, he explained, was "the British attempt to make the colonies negroid." The real importance of the both the Civil War and the Thirteenth Amendment, freeing the slaves, was to "loosen . . . the arm of the lustful slave owner from the body of his black mistress" and thus to reduce miscegenation, which had found a sanctuary under slavery. On the other hand, the Fourteenth and Fifteenth Amendments, granting full citizenship to blacks and guaranteeing their right to vote, tended to promote the mixing of the races and thus constituted what Cox called "Congress's ideal of a mongrel race in a mongrel nation." However, feminism and woman suffrage, though unpopular with many other white supremacists, drew his enthusiastic approval because no "white Southern politician with a black mistress or a mulatto family will have the courage to run for office" now that white women, the trustees of racial purity, could exercise the franchise. And anyone who did not support repatriation—not just those who opposed it but also those who failed actively to assist the cause—was, ipso facto, an "adherent of . . . amalgamation," an ally of the effort "to secure a mongrel race."[9]

Although throughout his life Cox concentrated on the presence of blacks as the greatest menace to the nation, this practical focus did not suggest an insensitivity to other threats to racial purity. If the "Asiatics of the Western States" continued to proliferate, then it would be necessary to "colonize" them as well, but at the time, he warned, it was "the 'black peril' rather than the 'yellow peril,' with which we are primarily concerned." Indeed, Cox readily acknowledged, not even all members of the white race were "of equal value." The founders of the nation, the superior Teutonics from Northern Europe"—referred to interchangeably by Cox as "Nordics" or "Aryans"—were also threatened by millions of "Caucasic mongrels from South and Southeastern Europe," and the immigration laws were in need of immediate reform to prevent further contamination by these "inferior race stocks."

In the 1920s, at the height of the eugenics movement, questions of racial policy often were considered a "scientific" issue, properly to be resolved in accord with the latest findings of the life sciences, and leading eugenicists offered praise for *White America.* William McDougall, the prominent professor of psychology and chair of the department at Harvard, endorsed Cox's work, calling a separate territory for blacks, preferably in Africa, "the only sound" policy.[10] E. A. Ross, a well-known sociologist at the University of Wisconsin and one-time president of the American Sociological Association, also provided a statement of support for the book; a year later, after a lengthy trip through Africa, Ross wrote to Cox, agreeing that "African territory to which American negroes might be deported should be governed not by the inhabitants but from this country." And the *Eugenical News,* in its review of the book, declared that Cox "will be a greater savior of his country than George Washington" if he could save America "for the white race" by bringing about the expatriation of blacks—the only real solution to what the *News* called "the worst thing that ever happened to the . . . United States, . . . the bringing of large numbers of the Negroes, nearly the lowest of races, to our shores."[11]

With such enthusiastic endorsements, Cox was soon accepted as a fellow expert by those who sought a "scientific" solution to racial issues, someone to whom they could turn for advice on translating science into policy; indeed, his stature among eugenicists increased significantly in the 1930s as many respectable scientists, who had earlier been attracted to eugenics, abandoned the movement, leaving it primarily in the hands of scientific racists and Klan sympathizers. Cox provided expert assistance to Dr. W. A. Plecker, Virginia's state registrar, in crafting an amendment to the state's Racial Integrity Act that would prevent "near-white negroids" from passing as white or claiming to be "Indian" in order "to marry into the white race." When Plecker was invited to read a paper before the International Eugenic Conference in 1932, he merely restated *White America*'s argument that separation was the only alternative to eventual intermarriage, embellished by some details of Virginia's local effort to prevent "amalgamation." Cox's work also came to the attention of foreign experts interested in race. Madison Grant requested that Cox send a copy of *White America* to Professor Hans Günther, "one of the most distinguished anthropologists of Germany," who "is in accord with all our views"; appointed by the Nazis to a major professorship over the local faculty's opposition, Günther provided the theoretical foundation for the regime's racial theory and was regarded as its official ideological spokesperson on race.[12]

The recognition of Cox's expertise produced an opportunity to speak to the Eugenics Research Association (ERA) at its annual conference in New York in 1936, where he met, for the first time, with a benefactor who would solve the financial problems that had hindered his campaign. In early March, Cox received a letter from the association's president, Clarence G. Campbell, agreeing that "repatriation is the only true solution of the Negro problem," and within weeks an invitation to speak on that topic arrived from biologist Harry H. Laughlin, a long-time activist in the eugenics movement; as editor of the association's official organ, the *Eugenical News*, Laughlin had earlier written its highly favorable review of *White America.* Cox quickly sent Laughlin a copy of the talk he intended to give: the usual diatribe against the presence of blacks in the United States, which noted that the "white man's" meager support for repatriation was being interpreted in some quarters as an indication of his "assent to a final solution of the race problem by amalgamation."[13]

However, one particular white man saw Cox's words and vowed not to assent to such an odious prospect. In the week before leaving for the conference, Cox learned from a number of sources that a wealthy New Yorker was looking forward to meeting him. "One of our colleagues, Colonel W. P. Draper, is particularly interested in your work," wrote Laughlin. As editor of *Eugenical News* and someone who knew of Draper's interest in the evils of miscegenation and his willingness to provide resources to oppose it, Laughlin had informed him of Cox's imminent appearance in New York and the substance of his speech, recommending that the two colonels "meet . . . personally." A biology professor at the University of Virginia, who had been offered financial assistance by Draper, also notified Cox that "Draper is seriously interested in the probable solution of the negro problem. . . . He believes that repatriation is the only satisfactory solution and I believe will be able to support you in your work."[14] Draper did indeed share Cox's obsession with repatriation, but—more important—he would provide the resources Cox lacked, making it possible for him to reach a much broader audience and acquire some influential political support. Cox's holy cause was about to become Draper's holy cause as well.

\* \* \*

Burdened with three last names as a constant reminder of his illustrious ancestry, Wickliffe Preston Draper was raised in a family where being "well bred" was not just a figurative expression for good manners. His given names were indications of the Southern aristocracy on his mother's side. Draper's maternal grandfather, General William Preston, could trace his family's history back to ownership of Craigmillar Castle outside Edinburgh, where James V and his daughter Mary, Queen of Scots, were frequent visitors. Educated at Yale and Harvard Law School, General Preston had fought in the Mexican War and been a member of the Kentucky legislature and the U.S. Congress before being appointed ambassador to Spain by President James Buchanan; when Lincoln came to office, he returned to Kentucky to assist the rebel effort, serving first as a command officer in the Confederate Army and then, after being appointed the Confederacy's ambassador to Mexico, as a diplomat. Draper's maternal grandmother, Margaret Wickliffe, also came from a prominent Kentucky family that lived in antebellum splendor on their Lexington estate, owned by Margaret's father, "Old Duke" Robert Wickliffe, the wealthiest planter and largest slaveholder in the state. And in one of the leading eugenics texts, both the Prestons and the Wickliffes were named as examples of "the Kentucky Aristocracy," families of statesmen and generals, in which "the men were brave and gallant, the women accomplished and fascinating and incomparably beautiful."[15]

But just as illustrious, and even more important in determining the material advantages of Draper's life, was the New England Puritan background on his father's side. In the community of Hopedale, Massachusetts, in which he was raised, being a Draper was synonymous with wealth, privilege, and power. Indeed, according to one nineteenth-century observer, if not for an accident of history, the town would have been called Draperville.[16]

Wickliffe Preston Draper arrived in the world on August 9, 1891, just in time to receive his own entry in *The Drapers in America,* a hagiographic genealogy published the following year by a member of the family whose work had been subsidized by Wickliffe's paternal uncle. Proud of their colonial roots dating back to James "the Puritan" Draper, who had left the village of Heptonstall in Yorkshire, England and settled in the New World in 1648, the "Draper men," according to the genealogy, "have ever been to the front in all emergencies . . . have held offices of all kinds in the village, town, city, county, or country . . . have been soldiers, sailors, statesmen, lawyers, doctors, engineers, authors, merchants, farmers, manufacturers, in the church and school, and have brought to each and every one of these occupations an earnestness and steadfastness of purpose and success of the highest order."[17] Nine towns or counties in the United States, and one in the United Kingdom, had been named after the family.

The line leading directly to Wickliffe Draper was particularly distinguished. His great-great-grandfather Abijah Draper had fought at Lexington and Concord and commanded a company of minutemen under Washington at Roxbury. Abijah's son Ira invented the rotary temple, a device for keeping the cloth extended in weaving that doubled output by allowing a single weaver to attend two looms; by the time Wickliffe was a teenager, the business built around his great-grandfather's invention was the largest manufacturer of textile machinery in the world.[18]

The rights to the loom temple were passed on to Ira's son, Ebenezer D. Draper, Wickliffe's great uncle and an ardent believer in the "Practical Christianity" of Adin Ballou, a local religious leader. In 1841, Ballou and a small group of followers, including Ebenezer Draper, purchased a large tract of land in a secluded valley surrounding the Mill River—an area known as "the Dale" within the limits of the town of Milford, Massachusetts—to form a religious community, which they named Hope Dale. Although the land and the few buildings on it had been long neglected, a twenty-four-foot fall in the river could supply the waterpower for small local manufacturing. Amid mid-nineteenth-century America's frenzied economic growth, in which enrichment for the few was creating impoverishment for the many, Hopedale promised a more humane, cooperative society, organized on principles of Christian socialism, abolitionism, temperance, nonviolence, and racial and sexual equality; in fact, well-known abolitionist William Lloyd Garrison sent his eldest son to the Hopedale school to be educated by "those who are virtuous, upright, kind, and loving."[19] In an effort to reconcile individual property rights with greater economic equity, the community offered the sale of shares in a Christian joint stock enterprise that would own and manage residential properties and productive facilities, thus ensuring collective control of property while providing individual profit in proportion to the number of shares held. One of Hopedale's most important economic assets was its small temple manufacturing plant, based on the technology now controlled by Ebenezer Draper and powered by the river. As one of the community's founding members, Draper became a major shareholder, its treasurer, and then its president.

Although the Hopedale community prospered for a time, growing in size and value and returning a small profit to its shareholders, by the mid-1850s it began to experience serious financial difficulties, a problem that, according to historian Edward K. Spann, resulted in substantial part from Ebenezer Draper's managerial shortcomings; although he was a devout believer and an active abolitionist, his major asset as a businessperson was the patent inherited from his father, and his subsequent venture outside the Hopedale community failed.[20]

But the financial problems for Ebenezer Draper and Hopedale constituted an entrepreneurial opportunity for his brother George, Wickliffe's grandfather, who joined the community in 1854, despite having no interest in the principles of Practical Christianity. Where Ebenezer had seen faith and brotherhood, George saw the possibility of wealth. Indeed, Spann's study of Hopedale concludes that George Draper carried out a "coup" against Christian socialism, exploiting the fact that, because of the community's aversion to government, the joint stock arrangement had never been legally incorporated and was simply a matter of conscience and honor between its residents. Persuading Ebenezer to join him, George withdrew their investment, which comprised three-quarters of the shares, blatantly ignoring the provision in the bylaws restricting such redemption to no more than 4 percent of the stock per year. This action precipitated a crisis, which was resolved by allowing the community to retain the school, public square, and cemetery, and three houses to be sold to individuals. The Drapers took everything else—the land, mill, streets, shops, houses, and other buildings; in 1873 they even took possession of the cemetery.[21]

George Draper quickly took control of affairs from his less worldly brother, who retired from the business and left Hopedale in 1868. By acquiring the patents on the various inventions involved in textile manufacturing—the high-speed spindle, improved temples and looms, spoolers, spinning rings, thread guides, and even machinery screws—George Draper virtually monopolized the production of textile machinery in the United States. In addition to the firm that bore his name—which eventually became George Draper & Sons as, one by one, his three sons joined the business—he also became the owner of a complex that included Hopedale Machine Company, Hopedale Furnace Company, Hopedale Machine & Screw Company, and the Dutcher Temple Company. In 1886, Hopedale was officially incorporated as a separate entity from Milford, but it was now "Draperville" in all but name.[22]

Aided by discriminatory tariffs against foreign competition and by control of a whole network of patents guaranteeing exclusive production rights, the next generation took up where George left off, continuing the expansion and amassing even greater wealth, which they used to construct huge mansions in the community that had been founded to reduce economic inequity. William F. Draper, George's oldest son, had enlisted in the Massachusetts Regiment at age nineteen and fought at Antietam, Fredericksburg, Vicksburg, and other campaigns, sustaining serious wounds on two occasions and rising through the ranks to brigadier general "for gallant and meritorious services in the field." After his father's death in 1887, William became president of the firm, which, a decade later, he reorganized, consolidating the various Hopedale plants into one large corporation, the Draper Company, whose capital stock was worth $8 million—hundreds of millions adjusted for inflation (AFI). In 1892, he was also elected to Congress and later appointed ambassador to Italy, where he lived at the Piombino Palace among Roman aristocrats (one of whom his daughter Margaret married, becoming Princess Boncompagni).[23]

But while William Draper was in Italy, his two brothers, annoyed that he was enjoying such a large share of the company's profits as an absentee owner, carried out their own coup, maneuvering him out of the business, which fell to George Draper's youngest son, Eben Sumner Draper.[24] A graduate of the Massachusetts Institute of Technology and a board member of various banks and manufacturing corporations, Eben Draper eventually turned to politics, winning election for one term as lieutenant governor and two terms as governor before returning to management of the Draper Company after a loss in his bid for a third term. When he died suddenly in 1914, the company wound up in the hands of the third son, Wickliffe's father, George Albert Draper, treasurer of the family's corporation as well as president and director of a number of railroads, banks, and other textile mills. At the time, the Draper company was at the height of its corporate strength, supplying most of the textile machinery in the United States and worth tens of millions of dollars; the company's housing stock alone, a majority of the town's 462 dwellings, was valued at almost $2 million (35.5 million AFI).[25]

During Wickliffe Draper's formative years at the beginning of the century, Hopedale was, through and through, a company town—not a tenement-ridden slum associated with many of the era's factories and sweatshops but a rural textile community totally under the paternalistic control of the Draper company, which offered job security, medical aid, and low rent in company houses for its employees in an effort to promote unity of interest between labor and capital at a time of increasing labor unrest. Indeed, unlike owners of many other industries, who typically lived far from their plants and factories, the Drapers lived in and were active members of the Hopedale community, although they lived on elegant estates. To preserve the town's rural character, the Draper Company prohibited fences, street signs, and mailboxes and created an extensive system of parks and gardens. When in 1896 and again in 1904 the company decided to enlarge the town, it hired landscape designers who had apprenticed with Frederick Law Olmstead—a founder of the American profession—to create a functional and naturalistic site plan and prominent Boston architects to design housing for these new areas. However, there were limits to the Drapers' paternalism: ignoring professional advice, they insisted on building high-density housing, forcing the architects to design "box-like duplexes that destroyed the subtlety of the land planning." Nevertheless, three major studies of industrial housing projects in the first decade of the century all named Hopedale as an outstanding American example of workers' housing, although it ranked far below the best western European examples, and exhibits of Hopedale housing won awards at expositions in Louisiana, Paris, Liège, and Milan.[26]

The Drapers' paternalism eventually proved no deterrent to militant labor activity. During Wickliffe's junior year at Harvard, the International Workers of the World began its campaign to organize the company, and then, in the spring of his senior year, led the mostly immigrant workforce in a bitter four-month strike involving fights with police and scabs. (Anarchist Nicola Sacco, wrongly executed along with Bartolomeo Vanzetti in 1927, was a regular on the picket line, having worked at the Draper Company four years earlier.) Although the strike was nominally about demands for a shorter work week and an increase in wages, it was also directed personally at Eben Draper, head of the company at the time, who had represented big business interests during his tenure as governor, vetoing such initiatives as the eight-hour workday.[27] Uncompromising, Draper refused to negotiate, and the strike was broken.

Wickliffe Draper himself was raised in a fashion befitting a member of what Nicholas Lemann has aptly called "the Episcopacy." As a youth, he attended Saint Mark's, the private school of choice for many New England Brahmins, where students were not educated but "prepared." A dismal academic record at St. Mark's, where a lone B in English was his highest grade, proved no barrier to acceptance at Harvard, which, at the time, was more interested in an applicant's pedigree than his intellect. After an equally undistinguished first year, Draper's performance steadily improved, and during his last three semesters he earned mostly B's and a few A's; despite taking a leave of absence for the second half of his senior year, he graduated with his class in the spring of 1913.[28]

At Harvard Draper displayed the proper interests of the patrician outdoorsman—captain of the Freshman Shooting Team, member of the Aeronautical Society, Shooting Club, and Yacht Club, among others—presaging an adult life that would be spent largely on activities such as travel, hunting, and exploration. Perhaps also of significance to the class-conscious Draper, he was not invited to join a "final" club, one of the quasi-fraternities at Harvard that presumed its stamp of approval to preclude interest in joining any other club. At the time such distinctions were much more important than they are today; as novelist Sarah Payne Stuart was told "with a sigh" by her great-aunt Sarah Winslow Cotting, a grande dame of New England "aristocratic lineage," "'I prayed and prayed I would marry a Porcellian man but Cot was only in A.D.'"[29]

In the fall of 1914, only months after hostilities began in Europe but still before America entered World War I, Draper enlisted as a lieutenant in the British Royal Field Artillery, serving in France, Greece, and Belgium until, in 1917, he sustained a shrapnel wound in the shoulder.[30] George Albert Draper immediately traveled to Europe to bring his son home, and, after recuperating, the young Draper applied for and received a commission in the U.S. Army, spending a year as an instructor for trainees. Discharged at the rank of major in 1919, he remained a member of the Cavalry Reserve, where he was eventually promoted and, even as a civilian, liked to be addressed as "Colonel Draper." During World War II, his commission was reactivated, and he served as a "senior observer" in India for the United States. Enamored of his military experience, for the rest of his life Draper dated his handwritten notes in day-month-year army style.[31]

Aside from his brief periods of military service, Draper never pursued a profession or held a job of any kind, his will noting the decedent's occupation as a retired "Lieutenant Colonel, U.S.A."; indeed, Draper was referred to as "the Colonel" by acquaintances, including those who were career officers themselves. In 1923, his father died, leaving an estate of $10.7 million, the bulk of which—after a few donations to hospitals and community organizations—was left in equal shares to Wickliffe Draper and his sister, Helen Draper Taft, recently divorced from a nephew of former President William Howard Taft. A year later she married Nathaniel F. Ayer, another socially prominent New Englander, whom she also divorced in 1930. When Helen died childless in 1933, Draper acquired her share of the estate as well. The portfolio that his father had so shrewdly accumulated and managed Draper now left to the equally sensible stewardship of Guaranty Trust, later to become Morgan Guaranty.[32]

Supported by this inherited wealth, Draper led a globe-trotting life. In response to the inquiry for Harvard's "Twenty-Fifth Anniversary Report" on the activities of the class of 1913, he noted "a dozen years of travel. Shooting jaguar in Matto Grosso and deer in Sonora; elephant in Uganda and chamois in Steiermark; ibex in Baltistan and Antelope in Mongolia. Climbing in Alps and Rockies. Pigsticking in India and fox-hunting in England. Exploring in West Sahara with French Mission."[33] In the United States, Draper's principal residence was one of New York City's most fashionable addresses— 322 East 57th Street, a building whose board later rejected Rush Limbaugh's application to buy a unit there—where he owned the top three floors, filling them with military weapons, trophies acquired on his exotic hunting trips, and a personal gymnasium; the Colonel's sword collection alone was appraised at $54,700 in 1972 ($233,600 AFI). Fanatic about his convenience as well as his privacy, Draper tipped the staff lavishly to ensure that an unoccupied elevator was ready when he was. Visitors he typically met in the Harvard Club, a gathering point for members of the Episcopacy, where generals mingled with business executives and government leaders.[34]

Yet behind this privileged and apparently frivolous lifestyle Draper clearly harbored an ardent desire, perhaps motivated by his forebears' accomplishments, to use his wealth for some loftier purpose—to make some significant social contribution that would reflect his own values and interests. This desire must have grown steadily stronger with advancing age, as Draper, who never married and was not particularly close to any of his numerous relatives, realized that he would leave no direct heirs to his fortune. To promote the physical and military skills for which he had such high regard, for a time the Colonel provided generous cash prizes for an annual "cavalry leadership test" in which soldiers were rated for their physical fitness, equestrian skills, and proficiency with pistol and sabre.[35] But as satisfying as he must have found sponsorship of this award, it lacked the potential for the larger impact on the well-being of the society that Draper wanted to leave as a legacy. To achieve the latter goal, in the mid-1920s he began to devote his resources to the cause of eugenics and racial purity. And although his contributions were but one of many sources of support at the time—and a minor one, at that—by the time of his death in 1972, Draper's money had become the most important and perhaps the world's only funding source for scientists who still believed that white racial purity was essential for social progress.

Of course, in Draper's youth eugenic concepts in general, and ethnic essentialism in particular, were a part of the intellectual zeitgeist. From his undergraduate years through the following decade, the eugenics movement—that deformed child of the Enlightenment—was enjoying its heyday, the elite institutions of the Ivy League were taking the lead in teaching eugenic concepts, and well-educated, proper New Englanders were learning that a distinguished pedigree also had *scientific* significance. Of particular importance, scientists and racists became frequent traveling companions in the eugenics movement, the former perhaps distinguishable from the latter by their more technical training but certainly not by any difference in their conclusions about racial differences or the social policies that they advocated as a consequence: opposition to political equality for blacks and—the much more pressing issue at the time—restriction of immigration from southern and eastern Europe, in the latter case stopping the influx of Jews in particular. The scientists' role in this alliance was to transform virulent racism into rational ideology by providing the authority to justify nativist beliefs in the innate superiority of "Nordics" in both intellect and character and the threat to their greatness posed by any interbreeding with their racial inferiors.

Harvard, the institution of choice for New England patricians, was at the forefront of the movement, offering four different courses in the details of eugenics.[36] Charles William Eliot, who, as president from 1869 to 1909, had overseen the university's transition from a small New England college to an institution of national and international reputation, was one of the vice presidents of the first International Congress of Eugenics in London in 1912, and many Harvard scientists were active in the movement. William McDougall, probably the best-known psychologist in the United States in the 1920s and chair of the department at Harvard, proclaimed blacks and non-Nordic immigrants a biological threat to American civilization and their presence in the country incompatible with a democratic system of government. He also proposed various solutions to this problem, ranging from systematic disenfranchisement of the inferior groups and restrictions on intermarriage with their racial betters to provision of an "ample territory" where all blacks would be confined in "thoroughgoing segregation"—a policy that was implemented in South Africa half a century later.[37] Although McDougall saw the fine Nordic specimens in the United States being converted into a "race of submen" through mixture with alien blood, he saw a ray of hope in the South, where "the good sense of the southern white man forbids him to obey" the federal government's insistence on political equality for blacks and where the Ku Klux Klan—a group of "solid, serious minded, pious and patriotic Americans"—was taking action to oppose the power and influence of the Catholic church.[38]

The most important single figure in the field of eugenics was Charles Benedict Davenport, who would become the first scientist to enjoy Draper's generosity. Referred to by one historian as eugenics' "scientific pope," Davenport had received his undergraduate education and his doctorate in genetics at Harvard, and had taught there and at the University of Chicago before becoming secretary of the Eugenics Research Association (ERA), a role in which he quickly established himself as the recognized head of the movement.[39] Davenport was obsessed with the biological threat of blacks and immigrants. One of his earliest reports on eugenics, in 1910, recommended study of the "mongrelization . . . proceeding on a vast scale in this country." A year later he warned that the United States was being threatened by "blood-chaos": the "aryo-germanic race"—the "carriers of culture and civilization," whose "unparalleled successes" and "dominance in world affairs" had resulted from the qualities "bred into its protoplasm"—was now "in danger of being mixed with the blood" of immigrants "from southern and southeastern Europe and from Asia minor." In a widely cited paper in 1917, Davenport provided the scientific underpinning for this ominous prediction, explaining that genetic disharmonies were being produced by the "racial intermingling" of dissimilar groups. The child of a union between, for example, a Scot and an Italian might inherit the former parent's large stature but the latter's small internal organs, resulting in an unfortunate hybrid, according to Davenport, with "large frame and inadequate viscera—children of whom it is said every inch over 5'10" is an inch of danger; children of insufficient circulation." The opposite combination, of course, would result in "children of short stature with too large circulatory apparatus." One of the worst disharmonies, he observed, occurred in the mulatto, who inherited "ambition and push," presumably from the white parent, "combined with intellectual inadequacy" from the black, resulting in an "unhappy hybrid dissatisfied with his lot and a nuisance to others." A "hybridized people," Davenport concluded, were inevitably "badly put together . . . dissatisfied, reckless, ineffective," yet "this country," he warned, "is in for hybridization on the greatest scale that the world has ever seen" unless immigration was restricted.[40]

And even when the more recent immigrants were not threatening the Anglo-Saxon stock with the dangers of intermarriage, Davenport found them a genetically unappealing group that would change the character of the country. "The great influx of blood from South-eastern Europe," he wrote in one of the most important textbooks of the time, would cause the population of the United States to "become darker in pigmentation, smaller in stature, more mercurial, more attached to music and art, more given to crimes of larceny, kidnapping, assault, murder, rape and sex-immorality," and more prone to insanity. The "Hebrews" he found a particularly offensive group. "There is no question," Davenport observed, "that, taken as a whole, the hordes of Jews that are now coming to us from Russia and the extreme south-east of Europe, with their intense individualism and ideals of gain at the cost of any interest, represent the opposite extreme from the English and the more recent Scandinavian immigration with their ideals of community life in the open country, advancement by the sweat of their brow, and the uprearing of families in the fear of God and the love of country."[41] In private correspondence Davenport complained that "our ancestors drove Baptists from Massachusetts Bay in to Rhode Island but we have no place to drive the Jews to. Also, they burned the witches but it seems to be against the mores to burn any considerable part of our population."[42]

The conclusions of eugenic authorities such as McDougall and Davenport found a particularly receptive audience among many members of the two overlapping circles in which Draper traveled and with which he most closely identified: Ivy League, Anglo-Saxon patricians and the Army officer corps, both of whom were pleased to find their own long-cherished nativist and anti-Semitic beliefs confirmed by the latest teachings of science. Members of both groups considered Nordics the modern equivalent of Plato's men of gold, innately suited for leadership as a result of their inherited racial traits. These superior specimens, as one noted scion of a colonial family described Nordics in a best selling book, were blond, blue-eyed conquerors, "the white man par excellence, . . . all over the world, a race of soldiers, sailors, adventurers, and explorers, but above all, of rulers, organizers, and aristocrats . . . domineering, individualistic, self-reliant, and jealous of their personal freedom, . . . and as a result they are usually Protestant." Only the heroic Nordics lived by the Anglo-Saxon ideals of sportsmanship and fair play, a gentleman's code of honor in which one was gracious in victory, uncomplaining in defeat, and always true to one's word. "It was an article of faith" among army officers, observed one historian, "that only their race created and maintained higher culture and advanced civilizations. Its decline imperiled an entire array of cherished values, creations, and institutions of Western civilization, not the least of which were democracy, science, technology, and even rational thought."[43]

There was no doubt among many of the bluebloods in Draper's milieu that the Nordics would continue to decline in the United States unless the tide of undesirables from abroad could be stemmed. To preserve the United States as a Nordic civilization, even before the turn of the century two recent, wealthy Harvard graduates—Prescott Farnsworth Hall and Robert DeCourcy Ward, the latter a Saltonstall on his mother's side—had founded the Immigration Restriction League (IRL). When Davenport began to create a structure for the eugenics movement, he organized a special committee on immigration, naming his old Harvard classmates, Hall and Ward, to head the group. The new associations with eugenics added the imprimatur of science to the IRL; Ward could now claim, in a professional journal, that "biological studies" of the "crossing of different types" had demonstrated the risk posed by the melting pot to the Nordics, "a race of acknowledged superiority," and Hall even attempted to change the IRL's name to the Eugenics Immigration League but was unable to obtain approval from the organization's board.[44] The IRL later colluded with Earnest Sevier Cox to distribute copies of *White America* to members of congress, and Draper eventually became a vice president.[45]

To the public, the best-known member of the IRL was Madison Grant, a personal acquaintance of Draper and in many ways the model for his life. A wealthy New York socialite, proud descendant of a family that had lived in the city since the colonial period, and member of all the right clubs, Grant had been educated at Yale and held a law degree from Columbia, although he never actually entered the profession. "Finding it unnecessary to earn a living," as his obituary in the *New York Times* put it, he spent much of his life as an outdoorsman, big-game enthusiast, and conservationist who was credited with the discovery of a number of North American mammals—one of which was named after him—and worked on projects such as preservation of the redwood trees and establishment of the Bronx Zoo.[46]

In addition, Grant waged a lifelong campaign against immigration; one historian called him "the nation's most influential racist." A vice president of the IRL since its inception, he quickly became an ardent eugenicist, dabbling in anthropology and presenting himself as a self-styled scientist in support of his claim that non-Nordics, and particularly Jews, were inferior.[47] As an official of numerous eugenic organizations—president of the ERA for a year, chair of its Committee on Selective Immigration, chair of an identically named committee of the American Eugenics Society, and treasurer of the Second and Third International Congresses of Eugenics, among other positions—Grant hobnobbed with prominent scientists and, despite having no scientific training, was regarded by them as a peer. When Davenport was planing the Second International Congress of Eugenics, he stressed the importance of keeping out crackpots, insisting that only scientific men such as Grant be permitted to speak. Indeed, as a cofounder, along with Davenport, of the Galton Society, the select inner circle of the eugenics movement that included its most eminent researchers, Grant insisted that only racially and politically reliable scientists be invited to join; as he wrote to another of the organization's original members, the society was to be "confined to native Americans, who are anthropologically, socially and politically sound, no Bolsheviki [i.e., Jews] need apply."[48]

Grant's best-selling book, *The Passing of the Great Race,* described a Nordic "native American aristocracy resting upon layer after layer of immigrants of lower races," the latter increasingly composed of "the weak, the broken and the mentally crippled" from the Mediterranean and the Balkans, together with the "hordes of the wretched" from the Polish ghettos, an allusion to Jews. In the same way that the United States had learned, during the half century since the Civil War, "that speaking English, wearing good clothes and going to school and to church does not transform a Negro into a white man," declared Grant, "Americans will have a similar experience with the Polish Jew, whose dwarf stature, peculiar mentality and ruthless concentration on self-interest are being engrafted on the stock of the nation." And the result of intermarriage, he explained for the genetically unenlightened, always produced a reversion to the "lower" race: "The cross between a white man and an Indian is an Indian; the cross between a white man and a Negro is a Negro; the cross between a white man and a Hindu is a Hindu; and the cross between any of the three European races and a Jew is a Jew." In addition to preventing the immigration of yet more racial undesirables, Grant looked hopefully to state-mandated sterilization as a solution to the problem of so many "worthless race types." Popular not only in the United States, *The Passing of the Great Race* was also highly regarded by the Nazis, and Grant liked to show visitors a copy of a letter from Hitler, in which the Führer thanked Grant for writing the book, calling it "his Bible."[49]

The professional officer corps, the other group with which Draper closely identified, was even more exercised that the "real Americans" were losing control of their own country; as one officer wrote to another in 1920, "the

'Master Race' is . . . gradually ceasing to be master in its own house; it is being swamped by . . . Mongrels, greasers, whelps, and hounds." Such opinions
were part of an official, institutional culture in the military at the time, per-
vasive among officers who began their careers at the same time as Draper's
service. The Army War College, which prepared selected officers for positions
of high command, invited scientists such as Davenport and McDougall to
lecture on race, and Earnest Sevier Cox's *White America* was assigned as part
of the coursework. Another regular visitor, even well into the 1930s, was
Madison Grant's protégé, Harvard-educated T. Lothrop Stoddard, whose
books were recommended reading.[50] In *The Rising Tide of Color against White
World-Supremacy,* for example, prospective command officers could learn of
the need to maintain "white political domination" in the face of the colored
threat—not so much from blacks, who were dismissed as inferior savages,
but from "Asiatics," the yellow race, who, according to Stoddard, constituted the main danger in an impending struggle for control of Africa and "mon-
grel-ruled" South America. Up until the outbreak of war, Stoddard continued to lecture on "World Affairs" at the college, praising the racial policies
of the Third Reich and encouraging similar, legally mandated measures for
segregation and antimiscegenation in the United States, based on "increasing knowledge of the true nature of race by modern sciences."[51]

The inner circles of the officer corps were particularly concerned over the
threat to Nordic culture posed by the influx of Jews. As Joseph Bendersky has
recently demonstrated in *The "Jewish Threat,"* during the teens and twenties
racial anti-Semitism among military leaders was "not only prevalent and
open but considered morally, politically, and even scientifically warranted."
This military culture adhered strongly to every anti-Semitic stereotype: Jews
were physically weak, cowardly, and incapable of loyalty to anyone but themselves—"a disgrace to the flag," according to one Colonel in 1918, and the only
people in the "world without moral honor or character." In addition, they
were the controlling force behind every movement for world domination,
from Bolshevism to international finance. Predicting "such massacres of the
Jews . . . as have never been even thought possible" by Russians after World
War I, one officer observed that "nothing they can do [to the Jews] is bad
enough to fit the case." These views became common at the highest levels
through the next three decades, as midlevel officers in the World War I era
assumed upper-echelon positions. In 1940, recently retired deputy chief of
staff General George Van Horn Moseley offered to join the America First
Committee only if it first agreed "to eliminate . . . all Jews and Jewish influences" from the organization and to "come out before the nation with a
definite statement against the Jew and all he stands for"; after the war, he

called for a policy to "give the Jews a limited time in which to close their affairs and leave our shores." In 1945, General George S. Patton did not consider "the displaced person . . . a human being," especially "the Jews, who are lower than animals."[52] And in 1951, a former intelligence officer published the most viscerally anti-Semitic book since the war, a work enthusiastically endorsed and promoted by three generals and an admiral: *The Iron Curtain over America,* still offered by neo-Nazi groups a half century later as an indispensable primer on the Jews. *The Iron Curtain* described a conspiracy to dominate the world in which the "Judaized Khazars" behind Bolshevism had infiltrated the U.S. government and fostered the war not to end dictatorship but to kill Aryans and "annihilat[e] . . . Germany, the historic bulwark of Christian Europe."[53]

Draper came of age at a time when, among officers and Anglo-Saxon gentlemen, the ideas of McDougall, Davenport, and Stoddard were at the height of their popular appeal and when Grant's paean to Nordic superiority was praised by presidents, highly recommended by the press, and quoted in congressional discussions of immigration.[54] In addition, Draper was personally associated with many of the activists among both the established elites and the military personnel. Like them, he believed fervently in the eugenic creed, especially in the threat to Nordic genes and culture posed by blacks and undesirable immigrants, particularly Jews. And even though subsequent generations would abandon eugenic thought in both science and politics, Draper's faith never wavered. Like a hippie still preaching flower power at the end of the century or a McCarthyite still warning of foreign agents in Washington long after the demise of the Soviet Union, Draper spent the rest of his life fixated in the zeitgeist of his youth, both its bizarrely oversimplified genetics and its resulting oppressive social policies. Through the civil rights era until his death in 1972, he provided the resources for the tiny handful of scientists who were still pursuing the obsessions of Grant and Davenport: racial superiority, racial purity, rigid segregation, and immigration restriction. And even in the post–civil rights era, Harry Weyher, his chosen successor, used Draper's money to carry on the tradition.

At first, Draper apparently desired to conduct research himself. Letters from Davenport to Draper often alluded to the "lines of work in practical and applied eugenics you might personally engage in" and "[your] intention of carrying on some investigation." But the closest Draper came to participation in any scientific work was his effort as the "assistant leader" of a French geographic expedition in Africa, a role for which his chief qualification was an unquestioning readiness to write a check for all expenses; the expedition resulted in the discovery of the Asselar man skeleton, which Draper subsequently donated to the French Institute of Human Paleontology.[55] One obstacle to his scientific ambitions was a lifestyle centered primarily on travel and outdoor recreation and thus not particularly conducive to disciplined research; Davenport and other correspondents would write to Draper about some urgent matter only to find that he was unreachable for months at a time. Also, he was not much of a writer: Multipage letters from others typically received in response but a few handwritten lines on his blue three- by five-inch personal stationery, and three sentences from Draper constituted a lengthy communication. Finally, Draper was painfully shy and reclusive; according to a relative, "he kept *completely* by himself," and an unexpected greeting could cause him to turn "bright purple, as if he were reading pornography."[56] Although he became a vice president of the IRL, Draper generally shunned any public attention, preferring to pursue his agenda by putting up the money for research that would support it.

In early spring 1923, Draper wrote to Davenport for the first time, describing his interest in a "bequest for the advancement of eugenics," and the very next day the two men had a meeting in which Draper outlined his plan for an endowment of more than $1 million ($10.5 million AFI), producing an annual income of some $60,000 for research ($620,000 AFI), but he wanted to know how the money would be spent. At a time when a middle-class salary was $3,000 or $4,000 a year, this was an enormous sum, and an understandably eager Davenport immediately drafted an ambitious list of projects for his prospective patron's approval, only to receive a tepid response: Draper was about to leave for India but would give the geneticist's proposals "my most careful consideration."[57]

More than two years and numerous attempts later by Davenport to reach the peripatetic millionaire, Draper, while on yet another hunting trip in India, arranged for his bank in New York to send a check for $1,000 ($10,000 AFI) to the ERA, hardly the windfall Davenport had anticipated. When Draper returned, however, he again requested that Davenport submit to him an outline of research plans—an indication that further contributions would be forthcoming—and once again, Davenport proposed a program, focusing primarily on the inheritance of "the native capacities of the individual," a necessary prerequisite to "the investigation of racial capacities."[58]

Although Davenport did not have to wait long for a response this time, he found that Draper had very specific ideas of his own for the use of his money. The geneticist's suggestions "are not quite in line with my thoughts," wrote Draper, who preferred instead to fund "research work on the effect of miscegenation" in countries such as Haiti and Brazil, as well as the United States. Davenport was delighted—this was a topic "of the greatest possible importance." He had himself been obsessed with the dangers of "hybridiza-tion," and finally he would have the opportunity to gather systematic evi-dence for the existence of genetic disharmonies. Davenport proposed that the study be conducted in Jamaica, where "there is a larger proportion of mulattoes and other grades of mixtures" so that he could "test the hypothe-sis that the products of miscegenation are less capable of developing and maintaining a proper social organization than the parental stocks."[59] The $10,000 donation to support this research ($99,000 AFI) was referred to—at both the ERA and the Carnegie Institution, which would publish the study—as the Draper Fund.

Anticipating results "of great scientific and practical utility," Davenport accompanied Morris Steggerda, a young researcher completing his doctor-ate at the University of Illinois, to Jamaica to make the necessary introduc-tions to government officials and generally ensure that the project got off to a smooth start. A diligent data gatherer, Steggerda spent almost thirteen months in the field, submitting 8,000 pages of reports on blacks, whites, and "hybrids" that included not only psychological test scores but also seventy-eight different anthropometric and physiological measurements on such obscure variables as tongue furrows or the ratio of interpupillary to face breadth. Corresponding regularly from his Cold Spring Harbor office in New York, Davenport tried to keep his young associate focused on the study's "main problem, namely, the capacity of the negro to carry on a white man's civilization," reminding him that "anthropometry, no matter how precise, does not bear much upon this question." It was not that he was recommend-ing any reduction in the data being collected, Davenport emphasized, merely that Steggerda pay more attention to certain crucial psychological traits, such as "rating[s] of honesty, thrift and foresight," the characteristics on which "a white man's civilization" is largely based.[60]

Given the high expectations for some definitive evidence of both black inferiority and miscegenation's additional disadvantage, the results must have been a major disappointment for Davenport, and especially for his patron. Although white subjects attained higher average scores on a number of the mental tests, blacks performed better than whites at "complicated directions for doing things" as well as "in simple mental arithmetic and with numeri-cal series," a result for which Davenport offered an interesting explanation: "The more complicated a brain, the more numerous its 'association fibers,' the less satisfactorily it performs the simple numerical calculations which a calculating machine does so quickly and accurately." The data collected on "hybrids" also failed to reveal any significant intellectual disharmonies caused by miscegenation despite Davenport's creative efforts at interpretation. Although he grudgingly acknowledged that "on the *average* the Browns did not do so badly" on the mental tests, there were more of them "than . . . either Blacks or Whites, who were muddled and wuzzle-headed." Blacks were of "low intelligence," he concluded, "but they generally can use what they have in fairly effective fashion"; a number of the "Browns . . . seem not to be able to utilize their native endowment."[61]

The anthropometric data did provide one consolation for Davenport, who claimed at last to find empirical evidence of a physical disharmony: a low correlation between arm and leg length in "hybrids." Blacks, he noted, had "longer" arms and "much longer" legs than whites. Thus, the unfortunate "hybrid" who inherited the black parent's long legs and the white parent's short arms would be put at a disadvantage in retrieving an object from the ground, not to mention the aesthetic considerations in such a disharmoniously constructed person—a "physiological embarrassment," as Davenport called this mismatch between upper and lower extremities.[62]

Despite Davenport's vigorous attempts to make the best of the results, Draper could not have been particularly pleased with the meager return on his investment, although he had certainly not lost his desire to demonstrate the evils of race mixing. Indeed, he apparently still harbored the intention to conduct racial research himself while in Europe, which he shared with Davenport, who responded by offering to appoint Draper a member of the Committee on Race Crossing of the International Federation of Eugenic Organizations, where he could meet such experts as German anthropologist Eugen Fischer; later to become one of the leading contributors to Nazi race science, Fischer had already conducted research on the inferiority of the "Rehoboth bastards"—Dutch-Hottentot crosses—in German southwest Africa. But despite his interest in the topic, Draper was not inclined to spend any more money on Davenport's research on "hybrids," a decision that made the geneticist feel "quite sick." Davenport did his best to persuade the Colonel to "continue the racial studies," proposing that Draper and Steggerda conduct "racework" together, but not even the prospect of personal collaboration with a scientist was sufficient to change his mind.[63]

However, Draper had every intention of continuing his substantial contributions to the ERA but, once again, insisted on imposing his own instructions for use of the funds. Instead of continuing support for the fruitless study of miscegenation, he donated $5,000 ($51,000 AFI) to be used as prize money for a pair of essay contests on the threat to the Nordic population worldwide, an idea that had obviously emanated from Grant's *Passing of the Great Race* and one that Grant himself thought "splendid," expressing his "inclination . . . to add to the gift personally."[64] The first of these two contests, announced in 1928 in the *New York Times* and in eugenic publications, was to focus on birth and death rates to demonstrate that Nordics suffered from a severe disadvantage in comparison to the fecundity of non-Nordic races; the second contest, predicated on the presumption that the first would yield the expected outcome, was to explore the causes of this disadvantage. Interestingly, of the ninety-six essays submitted for the second contest, only five came from the United States; of the remaining ninety-one essays, sixty-seven came from Germany and fourteen from Austria. As usual, the publicity-shy Draper was not mentioned by name in any of the official announcements of the contests, the ERA noting only that the prizes had been offered by "a friend of eugenics." In fact, in addition to contributing the prizes, the Colonel also paid for the winning entries to be published—an additional $3,000 ($31,000 AFI) for both essays.[65]

Draper contributed another $5,000 ($64,000 AFI) to the ERA as prize money for a third contest on one of two possibilities. His first suggestion was that the money be awarded for the best work on the effect of cash bonuses in contrast to preferential taxation as a method for encouraging fertility, an idea that Davenport discouraged on the grounds that it would probably be dysgenic, providing the greatest assistance to poor families, who have "the smallest proportion of gifted children."[66] As an alternative topic, Draper suggested the investigation of the incidence of mental disorders within families—a question that Davenport considered "one of the most important you could propose"—and in 1933 the *Eugenical News* formally announced a contest for original research on the "probability of commitment for a mental disorder of any kind, based on the family's history." Once again, public announcements noted only that "$5,000 in cash . . . had been generously presented by a patron" of the ERA.[67]

Draper's contributions to the ERA were about to come to an end, to be replaced by his contributions to other organizations with even more overt political goals. Eugenics had been developed as an applied science, and no one wanted to apply it more than Wickliffe Draper. Definitive scientific evidence for the importance of genetic influence, the intellectual inferiority of blacks, or the disastrous effects of racial mixtures was only the preliminary step to the more important goal: a social policy based on that knowledge.

\* \* \*

Earnest Sevier Cox and Wickliffe Preston Draper met for the first time on June 7, 1936, at Draper's New York apartment, beginning an association that lasted until Cox's death in 1966 and one based on the two Colonels' sincere admiration for each other's contributions to their common cause. Cox was genuinely grateful for Draper's generosity and Draper equally appreciative of Cox's tireless efforts to create an America for whites only; in fact, in addition to subsidizing the publication and distribution of Cox's writing, during the ensuing two decades Draper occasionally sent him outright gifts of $50 to $1,000 in recognition of his work for the cause.[68] According to Virginia state registrar W. A. Plecker, who had relied on Cox's expertise in crafting the state's Racial Integrity Law a decade earlier and now accompanied his mentor to the meeting, "Colonel Draper showed great interest in the undertakings of Colonel Cox and voluntarily expressed his willingness to help him make a start," indicating the "possibility of aiding further" if there were "evidences of success." In any case, Draper wanted his "gifts spent in such manner as to check upon their value"; as always, continued donations on his part, even for a cause as appealing to him as repatriation, were contingent on tangible results. Draper also made clear that strict anonymity was a condition of his assistance, and in correspondence with allies in the repatriation movement Cox typically referred to his unnamed benefactor as "our Northern friend."[69]

Although there had been hints that a substantial contribution would follow, Draper said nothing specific about its form during his first meeting with Cox. Three months later, much to Cox's surprise, he received an order for 1,000 copies of *White America,* a book that had previously attracted little attention and sold few copies despite the efforts of the Immigration Restriction League to publicize it; indeed, the unknown purchaser had had to pay for a special edition of the work to be reprinted. At first mystified by this sudden, renewed demand, Cox quickly learned that the purchaser was his new, wealthy ally, who wanted 800 copies of the book to be sent directly from the publisher to whomever Cox suggested and the remaining 200 to go to the author for "personal distribution." Cox decided that the books should go to members of Congress and to state legislators in North Carolina and Mississippi; he had just persuaded the Virginia General Assembly to "memorialize the Congress . . . to make provision for the colonization of persons of African descent" and viewed the state's action as the beginning of a groundswell of support for repatriation from Southern legislatures.[70]

It did not take long for Cox to be able to report encouraging results to his benefactor: the recruitment of Mississippi senator Theodore Gilmore Bilbo as a powerful new spokesperson for the cause. One of the most ardent racists ever to serve in the upper house, Bilbo declared that whites were "justified in going to any extreme to keep the nigger from voting," routinely dismissed his critics as "dagos" or "kikes," and referred to blacks as "nigger[s] . . . from the jungles of Africa," where it was their "delight to cut . . . up some fried nigger steak for breakfast."[71] Informed by an outraged Southern citizen that "young, White, student nurses . . . have been nursing nigger patients," Bilbo suggested that the white women in such hospitals "either go . . . on a strike or resign . . . outright." And in his own book on repatriation a decade later, the senator noted that he "would rather see his race and civilization blotted out with the atomic bomb than to see it slowly but surely destroyed in the maelstrom of miscegenation, interbreeding, intermarriage, and mongreliza-tion."[72] A colorful rabble-rouser, Bilbo had formerly been a two-term governor of his home state, after launching his initial candidacy for the office from the yard of a prison from which he had just been released. In 1932, he had retired from the governor's office, personally impoverished and politically discredited after leaving the state in a huge financial hole requiring his successor to impose a host of new taxes and slash the budgets at state institutions, only to make a truly miraculous political comeback. Recently elected to the senate and searching for an issue to call his own, Bilbo read *White America* and "made up my mind," as he wrote to Cox, "to specialize on the repatriation of the negro."[73]

Unveiling this newfound interest during his filibuster in opposition to a proposed federal antilynching bill, Bilbo quoted from Cox at great length, blaming "friction" between the races entirely on "disgruntled and touchy mixed breeds" and "supersensitive mongrels"; the "pure-blood Negro," explained the senator, caused no trouble "because he understands his place . . . and is willing to occupy his place uncomplainingly, mindful of his limitations and inferiority." Instead of the "unconstitutional, un-American, and insulting" antilynching proposal, he declared that the only real solution to "the presence of 12,000,000 Negroes in the United States," as well as the measure "essential to the perpetuation of Anglo-Saxon civilization" and "white su-premacy," was the "deportation or repatriation of the entire . . . race to its native heath, Africa." Even by the standards of a time when Klan membership numbered in the millions, Bilbo's senate speech was intemperate. Referring to a journalist for the *Washington Afro-American* who supported the bill, for example, the senator threatened that "if this anthropoidal ape were to rear up on his hind legs" and dare to pen such lines in a Southern state, "his mongrel carcass would mar the beauty of a southern magnolia tree before the ink upon his damnable sheet had time to congeal."[74]

Cox was delighted, both at this important new ally and at the opportunity to tell Draper that his contribution had already made an impact. "It gives me pleasure to inform you," he wrote to his fellow Colonel, that "we will have representation in Congress as a result of the assistance you gave to the cause." The movement's "chief trouble has been that we had no one . . . to advocate Negro repatriation" at the federal level, but now "Senator Bilbo has asked me to

come to Washington, and that he will do anything he can for us." Pleased to
see that his initial contribution had swiftly produced "progress," Draper now
had good reason to provide further assistance. "If . . . I can be of help, pray let
me know," he responded to Cox; "I shall always be glad to consider . . . any
proposal along the same lines" as the distribution of *White America*.[75]

Within days, Cox took Draper up on his offer. He had sent Bilbo a manuscript on the history of the repatriation movement, which the senator found
"a knock-out," reading substantial portions of it into the record as part of
his continuing filibuster against the antilynching bill.[76] Believing that the
manuscript, which had already been rejected by a mainstream magazine,
could be useful in generating support, Cox saw another possibility for Draper's money to make a difference, and Bilbo—who by now had not only
linked his own political identity to repatriation but was relying on Cox as his
main source of expertise—thought his new advisor's "suggestion to have our
Northern friend to publish and circulate the document . . . a great idea."
Upon hearing the new proposal, Draper was prepared to pay for 10,000 pamphlets, but Cox recommended 3,000 as a more practical number.[77]

The resulting work, "Lincoln's Negro Policy," outlined the history and
benefits to both races of repatriation, noting that eminent statesmen from Jefferson to the Great Emancipator had favored the resettlement of blacks in their
homeland and claiming that abolitionists and slaveholders had "much in common" because they both opposed colonization. As always, any opposition
among blacks, observed the pamphlet, came only from "Negroes [who] openly
advocate amalgamation of the races." As an expression of gratitude to his
Northern friend, Cox had a special copy of the work printed for Draper, certi-
fying that it was "the first copy of the first edition . . . and . . . a gift to the gentleman who had assisted the publishing."[78] The political strategy crafted by Cox
was to time distribution of the pamphlets—sent once again to members of
Congress and to state legislators in Virginia, North Carolina, and Mississippi—
to coincide with Bilbo's eventual introduction of a bill for repatriation.[79]

In the meantime the senator offered an amendment to a public works bill,
calling for the establishment of a "Repatriation Commission." Intending only
to increase interest in the topic in anticipation of the more serious, independent piece of legislation to follow some months later, Bilbo withdrew the
amendment immediately after introducing it, but the ploy allowed him to
make a lengthy speech in support of repatriation, which Cox forwarded to
his patron as further evidence that Draper's money was being well spent.
Again maintaining that blacks were "biologically unfit to associate" in any
way with their superiors, Bilbo once more invoked the image of the magnolia tree as the appropriate fate for racial transgression—this time to be ap-

plied to the Washington functionary who had had the temerity to invite "a most highly efficient, educated and cultured woman from the State of Mississippi" to a "social gathering of employees and officials of the W.P.A." without telling her that she would be "thrust into this motley melee of miscegenated mongrels and full-blood Ethiopians." He also discoursed at length on the science of "hybrids," explaining that the hereditary characteristics from different races, when "chained together within a single individual," produced "the greatest biological monstrosity that the human mind can conceive of." And to demonstrate that his opinion indicated no ill will toward blacks, Bilbo compared it to Hitler's attitude at the time toward *his* country's racial minority: The German leader "did not dislike Jews as Jews," but he realized that they were constitutionally different from Germans, and Hitler appreciated "the importance of race values."[80]

After receiving a copy of the senator's speech, the normally reserved Draper replied with what was for him great enthusiasm, asking Cox to let him "know of the progress of the movement and of anything I can do to help," and—again in contrast to his typical desire for anonymity—he suggested a meeting with Bilbo, who still had not learned the identity of "the Northern white man" from whose generosity he was benefiting. Clearly hopeful that legislation would finally be enacted ridding the United States of its black citizens, Draper also requested that appropriate practical steps be taken, and Cox dutifully informed Bilbo and other key supporters of repatriation that "a wealthy Northern man" and benefactor of the movement now wanted to "send . . . agents to Liberia to look over the land" and to discuss the imminent migration with the Firestone group, owners of the large rubber plantations that would employ many of the newcomers; careful planning was necessary to ensure a smooth exodus.[81] Indeed, Draper even insisted that a book agent locate the obscure work *Unknown Liberia,* published in England two years earlier but withdrawn from circulation, and send it to Cox, presumably so that the activist would be prepared for the practical difficulties of repatriation. Calling Liberia "the most primitive country in the world," the book offered a depressingly hyperbolic picture of "jungle dwellers" who supposedly exhumed freshly buried bodies in order to eat them, made human sacrifices to pagan gods believed to live in the banana trees, and held funereal rites for village chiefs in which dozens of writhing boys and girls were interred along with the deceased ruler.[82]

Amid the usual rhetoric on the need to prevent "amalgamation," on April 24, 1939, Bilbo introduced the "Greater Liberia Act." Although the intention of the act was to mandate removal of every single black person from the United States "within a generation or so," Cox suggested to Bilbo that, to avoid arousing opposition, "we make provision for . . . complete race repatriation . . . but say but little about it." The two Colonels played an important role in preparing for this moment. Both had journeyed to Washington a few days earlier to discuss last-minute strategy with the senator; Cox's pamphlet "Lincoln's Negro Policy," paid for by Draper, had been sent to every member of Congress; and Draper sent Cox an unsolicited contribution—which turned out to be unnecessary and was returned in full—to assist people "who should have to reside in Washington, in support of the bill."[83] Within days of the act's introduction, Draper also sent Bilbo a check for $2,000 ($25,000 AFI) to print and distribute 100,000 copies of the bill and the senator's speech in its support.[84]

This initial enthusiasm was dashed when the bill failed to make it out of committee. In addition to the opposition it might have faced under any conditions, the onset of hostilities in Europe in September 1939 was a major deterrent to an international initiative of such magnitude, and Draper saw "little to do during the present war, but to keep the repatriation ideal alive among the negroes and perhaps to bring it before the whites."[85]

The next opportunity to promote the "ideal" did not arise until well after the war and from an unexpected source. In the summer of 1949, two years after Bilbo's death, a surprised Cox notified his long-time Northern friend that William Langer, a senator from North Dakota, "without my knowledge," had introduced a slightly altered version of the Greater Liberia Bill—its major difference being the omission of the original act's provision for acquiring additional land—and once again there was reason to be optimistic, especially in view of Cox's prediction that "race discord . . . will lead to a sustained migration." Although it took some four years for the bill to receive a hearing, Draper's enthusiasm was undiminished by either the delay or the first signs of the second reconstruction: The four cases soon to be consolidated as *Brown vs. the Board of Education* were working their way through the lower courts. Still eager to support repatriation, he again provided the resources for the strategy crafted by Cox, working with Langer: to have the bill, together with a brief account of the movement's history, printed and distributed to a "select list of individuals," among them newspaper editors, "with a definite request that they write editorials" on the issue.[86]

But in addition to the traditional tactic of appealing to the influential and the powerful, this time Draper wanted to pay more attention to the other end of the spectrum: poor southern working people and sharecroppers, especially blacks. Believing that only the press's silence about repatriation had prevented them from expressing enthusiastic support, Draper sought Cox's advice on the best means "of getting colonization information" to these common folk.

Instead of offering assistance to efforts initiated by others, Draper himself now wanted to "set . . . up a permanent aid for the colonization movement."[87]

Cox suggested working through Southern preachers, both black and white. Although in the rest of the nation the church favored "the Mulatto led movement of integration and miscegenation," he believed that Southern clergymen would actively support repatriation if only they were aware that "the Movement is alive." Draper approved this strategy and authorized Cox to begin preparing a pamphlet that would contain his own analysis of "Lincoln's high ideals," together with a contribution by "one . . . of the Negro leaders" and an introduction by Senator Langer. The finished work was to be sent, according to Draper's instructions, "to a select list . . . of Southern white and colored clergy, teachers, etc."[88]

But just as the pamphlet was ready to be printed, Draper, expressing high praise and "sincere appreciation" for Cox's "splendid work" on behalf of colonization, nevertheless withdrew his support. Although the Northern Colonel's belief in the importance of racial purity—and thus the necessity of racial separation—was as strong as ever, he was suddenly "of the considered opinion that further efforts to successfully accomplish [repatriation] . . . are not propitious" and was thus "disinclined to extend any further financial assistance." Only weeks earlier, the Supreme Court had issued the *Brown* decision, rejecting the myth of separate but equal public education and pointing the way toward a desegregated future. Perhaps at some later date it would again be desirable to urge the physical removal of blacks from the United States, but at the moment the struggle to maintain racial separation within the country would have to take precedence. Although Cox immediately produced his own tract in opposition to *Brown,* Draper would direct his generosity toward other, more powerful defenders of Southern apartheid.[89]

Even after Cox's death in 1966, his wealthy Northern friend wanted to make one last contribution to the dissemination of his thought: "a modest memorial," Draper called it, "to a zealous defender of our race and nation." As an appropriate gesture on behalf of his long-time friend and comrade in the movement, Draper decided to have reprinted as a hardcover book "Lincoln's Negro Policy," Cox's pamphlet that had been so useful in the campaign to support Bilbo's repatriation bill, and he asked Harry Weyher to work out the details of publication; by this time Weyher, as both Draper's attorney and president of the Pioneer Fund, was disbursing Draper's money to numerous opponents of equality for blacks.[90]

Pioneer's president paid to have the work republished as a "memorial to Earnest Sevier Cox" by Willis Carto, the most influential neo-Nazi in the United States, who considered Hitler's fall "the defeat of Europe and America," caused by the "propaganda, lies and demands" of "international Jews." Carto had founded the Liberty Lobby based on a view of the Jews as "culture distorters," conspiring to destroy the racial basis of Western civilization; "if Satan himself had tried to create a . . . force for destruction of the nations," wrote Carto to a friend, "he could have done no better than to invent the Jews."[91] Seeking an issue to energize the movement, he came across *White America* and decided to organize around repatriation; calling for the resettlement of blacks in Africa would not only combat what Carto called the "niggerfication of America" but also exert "the strongest blow against the power of organized Jewry."[92] In Carto's foreword to the new edition of "Lincoln's Negro Policy," he saw "our Nation slid[ing] toward a chaos made inevitable by the cowardly refusal of whites in America to face up to racial realities" and recognize "the one and only responsible solution of America's greatest problem." In addition, the foreword recommended *White America,* which Carto was also republishing at the time, "as one of the best studies of the race problem in America ever written." Both works appeared under the imprint of the Liberty Lobby's Noontide Press, which also distributed such books as *The Hoax of the Twentieth Century,* a debunking of the Holocaust "myth," and *The Iron Curtain over America,* an exposé of the "traitorous conspiracy" between the Russians and the Jews, who "controlled . . . the machinery of the United States government."[93]

Of course, Draper was even less eager to have himself publicly associated with Carto and the Liberty Lobby than with Cox, and extensive precautions were taken to ensure his anonymity. The funds for the new edition of "Lincoln's Negro Policy" were described merely as donated "by a long time friend and associate of Colonel Cox who wished to establish this type of memorial to him."[94] The actual payment was funneled through an intermediary, the "Virginia Education Fund"—itself created to oppose integration—which received $2,400 ($13,000 AFI) from Weyher and dutifully forwarded a check for that amount to C. M. Tribble, one of the two executors of Cox's estate. "Please be assured," Tribble wrote to Weyher after receiving the money from R. B. Crawford, an official of the Virginia Education Fund, "that this donation . . . will be treated as anonymous."[95]

Although Cox's almost lifelong efforts to repatriate blacks to Africa enjoyed little practical success, it was not for lack of support from his anonymous benefactor, who remained devoted to the cause, funding every one of the Southerner's proposals until faced with a more immediate threat: not only that blacks would remain in the United States, but that they would finally be granted the full rights of citizenship. But despite the negligible impact of his assistance, Draper's collaboration with Cox was noteworthy for its implications for the fund he would establish. First and most important, it indicated that the Pioneer Fund was created and endowed by someone whose opinion about blacks was indistinguishable from that held by Klansmen and other unapologetic racists. The fact that Draper regarded Cox—a man pathologically obsessed with white racial purity and the threat that the very presence of blacks supposedly posed to the existence of civilization—as a "zealous defender of *our* race and nation [emphasis added]" strongly suggested that his purpose in establishing a fund for the study of eugenics was not simply to promote the advancement of science but to provide results that would prove useful as support for a more practical agenda.

An additional indication of the true purpose of the fund Draper would create was his insistence on anonymity for the contributions to Cox's campaign—an unwillingness to put his mouth where his money was, at least in public. Indeed, any indication of a breach in "security" immediately produced a fearful response. When Cox once requested a picture of his benefactor, he had to explain to an anxious Draper that he had no intention "to use it now" but wanted only to leave it along with other personal papers, as part of his will, to the University of Virginia. Cox did not get the picture.[96]

Although Draper had generally avoided public recognition for his previous philanthropic activities, his earlier reticence stemmed more from a characteristic shyness and desire for privacy than from any reluctance to be associated publicly with the object of his generosity. For example, he was unperturbed when Davenport and Steggerda acknowledged him, in the introduction to *Race Crossing in Jamaica,* as the source of both the idea and the funds for their study, and, again without objection on his part, the *Eugenical News* occasionally noted the latest financial status of "the Draper Fund."[97] But Draper instinctively appreciated the importance of drawing a line between Davenport's "respectable" scientific work, no matter how transparently political or prejudicial its motivation, and the somewhat less subtle attempts by Cox and Bilbo to justify oppressive racial policies. Of course, the difference was more of style than of substance; neither the geneticist nor the political activists had any real doubt that blacks were inferior to whites or that "miscegenation" was biologically and socially catastrophic. But where Davenport sought to study "the capacity of the negro to carry on a white man's civilization," Cox and Bilbo eschewed any pretense of uncertainty over the results of such research, preferring to proceed directly to their political application. Although Draper's interest in achieving the latter's goals—if possible, removing blacks from the country; if not, keeping them separate and unequal—was the motivation for his support for the former's research, he realized that association with an overtly political agenda would cast doubt on his claim to be interested purely in subsidizing scientific progress.

This dualism continued to characterize Draper's contributions after Pioneer's formation, especially during the civil rights era, when he provided lavish, anonymous support for Southern efforts to oppose equal rights for blacks. Like Cox's campaign for repatriation, the undisclosed donations to these racist political projects represented Draper's real agenda and the true purpose that the studies conducted by Pioneer's openly acknowledged grant-ees were expected to serve.

First, however, there was a less contentious period in which the Pioneer Fund was organized and, at least initially, undertook a small number of un-controversial projects.

## 2 Somebody Whose Views He Could Not Approve: The Formation and Re-formation of the Pioneer Fund

IN MARCH 1937, the Pioneer Fund was incorporated in the State of New York for two "charitable purposes." First, according to the Certificate of Incorporation, the fund was to assist "in providing for the education of children of parents deemed to have such qualities and traits of character as to make such parents of unusual value as citizens." In selecting the recipients of this assistance, stated the certificate, "consideration shall especially be given to children who are deemed to be descended predominantly from white persons who settled in the original thirteen states . . . and/or from related stocks." The point to such contributions by the fund was not only to ensure that the children of these presumptively superior parents did "not lack an adequate education or start in life" but, more important, by allaying concerns about the cost of education, "to encourage an increase in the children of such parents" and thereby "to aid in improving the character of the people of the United States."[1] In practice, however, only a single project of this type, designed during Pioneer's earliest years, was ever funded.

Pioneer's second purpose was to provide aid for "study and research into the problems of heredity and eugenics in the human race . . . and . . . into the problems of race betterment with special reference to the people of the United States, and for the advancement of knowledge and the dissemination of information with respect to any studies so made or in general with respect to heredity and eugenics."[2] This broadly stated charge would allow not only for subsequent grants to scientists conducting research but also for what would become a host of efforts to inform the public about putatively scientific findings "in general with respect to heredity and eugenics," especially concerning racial differences, and to encourage their application to social policy. In effect, the language of the incorporating certificate would allow Pioneer to become a eugenics lobby.

According to the fund's bylaws, the organization was to be managed by a board of directors consisting of five members, three of whom would also be officers of the corporation—either president, treasurer, or secretary. Draper was one of the original members and remained on the board until his death in 1972, but in keeping with his desire to avoid the spotlight, he was not one of the officers. Nevertheless, he clearly exercised final authority on whether to fund a proposal because the money came out of his private coffers, and Pioneer had no other resources. For the few official grants made by Pioneer during the Colonel's lifetime, the board's role was thus reduced to a pro forma resolution to approve funding for projects that Draper wanted to finance; if he decided not to put up the money, the rest of the board was powerless. In theory, of course, the board could reject proposals that Draper favored, but when, in the 1950s, such differences in direction actually threatened to occur, he merely changed the board's composition. As one of the original officers commented about Pioneer many years later, "It was Wyckliffe [sic] Draper's Fund," and, in fact, the organization was sometimes referred to in exactly that manner—as the "Draper Fund."[3]

For Pioneer's first president Draper selected Harry H. Laughlin, a history teacher turned plant and animal biologist, long-time editor of the *Eugenical News,* and the person who, only months before creation of the fund, had brought Earnest Sevier Cox's work to Draper's attention and facilitated the first meeting between the two Colonels. Laughlin had earlier authored the review of *White America* in the *News,* predicting that its author would be considered "a greater savior . . . than George Washington" if he could actually implement a solution to the presence of blacks, "the worst thing that ever happened to the . . . United States." Laughlin also shared Cox's obsession with "race crossing" and had proposed a research agenda to assist in the enforcement of Southern "race integrity laws" by developing techniques for identifying the "pass-for-white" person who might "successfully hide all of his black blood." Indeed, "because of its . . . traditional racial attitude," Laughlin saw the South as the source of "leadership in Americanization during the next generation" and had even suggested to Draper that his fund be an institute associated with the University of Virginia.[4]

In addition, Laughlin had been eugenics' most energetic legislative activist, spearheading the campaigns that had produced the movement's two major policy achievements: the immigration restriction law of 1924 and the statutes permitting involuntary sterilization that were passed by more than thirty state legislatures. A long-time supporter of the theory of Nordic superiority, Laughlin had been called to testify before the House Committee on Immigration and Naturalization during hearings on the proposed act, where he lectured the legislators on the "biological aspects of immigration," impressing the committee's chairman, Albert Johnson, who favored not only the immediate cessation of new immigrants but also the denial of citizenship to many of their children. Happily finding his own prejudices in accord with the latest scientific conclusions, the congressman appointed his witness the committee's "expert eugenics agent," a capacity in which Laughlin returned at regular intervals to warn the committee, first of the "inborn social inadequacy" among new arrivals—their high rates of crime, insanity, feeblemindedness, and epilepsy—and later of the threat that Americans might be "supplanted by other racial stocks" that were "not assimilable," a prospect he judged worse than military conquest.[5] Even after passage of the law, which had the practical effect of terminating most immigration from southern and eastern Europe, Laughlin continued to lobby the government to ensure that "the racial status quo of the country be maintained" because "without such basic homogeneity, . . . no civilization can have its best development."[6]

Laughlin was particularly concerned with preventing any further Jewish immigration. When there were attempts to waive some restrictions in response to refugees from the Third Reich, Laughlin submitted two new reports to the Chamber of Commerce of the State of New York. In 1934, he opposed any "special . . . provisions for . . . Jews persecuted in Germany," despite the fact that immigrants from Germany, which had an annual quota of almost 26,000 under the 1924 law, numbered less than 1,000 per year at the time. He also recommended that no immigrant should be admitted whose ancestors were not "all members of the white . . . race," no matter the country of origin; policymakers should admit only immigrants that they would allow "to marry their own daughters," he explained.[7] Then in 1939, he recommended a substantial reduction of immigration quotas, together with procedures to denaturalize and deport some immigrants who had already obtained citizenship; this time Laughlin singled out Jews as a group "slow to assimilate," a problem related to his doubts that their loyalty was directed primarily to "American institutions and people" rather than to "Jews scattered through other nations." "No alien should be naturalized whose racial or individual make-up tends to hinder his Americanization," he declared, and to strengthen the safeguards against such untrustworthy immigrants, a candidate for citizenship should be "required to swear both racial and national loyalty . . . above loyalty to any alien race-segregate." In private correspondence with Madison Grant, Laughlin considered but rejected any attempt to apply to "the Jewish problem" the solution intended for blacks. "The deportation of four million Jews," he wrote, "would be many times more difficult than the repatriation of three times as many Negroes." Thus resigned to the fact that "the Jew is doubtless here to stay, . . . the Nordics' task," he concluded, "was to prevent more of them from coming."[8]

Laughlin was even more involved in the campaign for involuntary sterilization, drafting a model law that provided the basis for many of the state statutes and proposing an ambitious schedule for sterilizing the least capable 10 percent of the population during the next few decades—those people "so meagerly endowed by nature that their perpetuation would constitute a social menace."[9] When Virginia's statute was challenged in court, Laughlin testified as an expert witness at the circuit level, providing key evidence on the mental defectiveness and sexual immorality of the sixteen-year-old plaintiff and her mother and concluding that these putatively hereditary traits made the girl "a potential parent of socially inadequate offspring," the statutory definition of a person who could be subjected to involuntary sterilization; the Virginia law was subsequently upheld by the Supreme Court in *Buck v. Bell*.[10]

As editor of the *Eugenical News*, Laughlin also fawned over the Third Reich, filling the journal with praise for a government with the good sense to translate eugenic science into state policy. In emulation of the German term *Rassenhygiene*, which was used more frequently in the Nazi movement than *Eugenik*, he added the phrase *Race Hygiene* to the masthead of the *News* even before Hitler's seizure of power. When, shortly after the Nazi takeover, Germany enacted the Law for the Prevention of Genetically Defective Progeny— its own sterilization measure, patterned after Laughlin's model—the *News* was exultant. An unsigned editorial—unmistakably recognizable as Laughlin's work, however, from both the substance and the stilted prose—noted with obvious pride that "the text of the German statute reads almost like the 'American model sterilization law'" and extolled the Nazi regime for leading "the great nations of the world in the recognition of the biological foundations of national character. It is probable that the sterilization statutes of the several American states and the national sterilization statute of Germany will, in legal history, constitute a milestone which marks the control by the most advanced nations of the world of a major aspect of controlling human reproduction, comparable in importance only with the states' legal control of marriage."[11]

As the Third Reich moved further toward becoming the eugenic state, Laughlin's journal followed the advancements with undisguised admiration, devoting an entire issue in 1934 to accounts of progress in Germany. As he explained to Madison Grant, Laughlin selected a speech by Reichminister of the Interior Wilhelm Frick—later tried at Nuremberg and sentenced to death by hanging—to be "the leading article," because it "sounds exactly as though spoken by a good American eugenist in reference to 'what ought to be done'"; in addition to calling it "an offence against Christian . . . charity" to allow "hereditary defectives" to reproduce, Frick's address also warned of the "racial deterioration" in the German people caused by miscegenation with other groups, especially Jews, and he called for "the courage to rate our population for its hereditary value." The speech, declared Laughlin, "marks a milepost in statesmanship," a pronouncement not by a "mere scientist" but by a powerful minister in a government "which is getting things done in a nation of sixty million people."[12] At the end of Hitler's second year in power, the *News* summarized his regime's accomplishments as a triumph of "biological thinking," placing national policy on a firm scientific basis: "In no country of the world is eugenics more active as an applied science than in Germany. The state has taken over the responsibility for building up the German population, in both numbers and quality. . . . As practical statesmanship for effecting the announced ideals, Germany is the first of all the great nations of the world to make direct practical use of eugenics."[13]

Nor did more even radical measures by the Reich diminish Laughlin's enthusiasm in the slightest. In 1935, the Nazi government enacted the Nuremberg Laws, depriving Jews and other "non-Aryans" of citizenship, forbidding their marriage to Germans, and excluding them from various positions in government, education, and health care. Eleven months later Laughlin wrote to an official at the University of Heidelberg, which had awarded him an honorary doctorate, observing that the United States and the Third Reich shared "a common understanding of . . . the practical application" of eugenic principles to "racial endowments and . . . racial health." Indeed, Laughlin seemed to obsess over Jews. His personal papers contained page after page of handwritten, numbered lists labeled "Jews" or "Jew traits," containing almost every known anti-Semitic stereotype, including "chisel," "dishonest," "lie," "steal," "persecution complex," "intellectual freedom (for me not for you)," "hypocritical," "bore within," "other fellow fight your battle for you," and—the Nazis' favorite characterization—"parasite." When a story in the *New York Times* announced establishment by the Nazis of a German "race bureau," which would help administer the laws against "alien races," the article was filed at the Eugenics Record Office, where Laughlin was in charge, with a handwritten notation in the margin that Hitler "should be made honorary member" of the Eugenics Research Organization.[14] To Laughlin, the Nazi regime provided a beacon, lighting a path that he hoped the United States would follow.

Informed of Draper's intent to create a fund for the promotion of eugenics, Laughlin was naturally enthusiastic, viewing the organization as an opportunity to achieve "the most patriotic development of racial ideals" through "conservation of the best racial stocks" and prevent "increase of certain of the lower stocks and unassimilable races."[15] To the man who regarded Earnest Sevier Cox as the nation's savior and looked to Nazi Germany as a role model, there was little doubt which racial groups would be considered the "ideals" and which the "unassimilable."

A more moderate eugenicist, and the man who would soon succeed Laughlin as Pioneer's president, was named as the fund's original secretary. Frederick Henry Osborn was the son of a prominent New York family that counted J. P. Morgan among its relatives and Franklin Delano Roosevelt as a friend and neighbor; his father had been president of the Metropolitan Museum of Art and his uncle, Henry Fairfield Osborn, was a well-known professor of paleontology at Columbia University, head of the Department of Anthropology at the American Museum of Natural History, and an ardent eugenicist who had contributed the preface to an edition of Madison Grant's *Passing of the Great Race*. After earning a fortune in railroad and investment banking before his fortieth birthday, in 1928 Frederick Osborn retired from business, devoting the rest of his life to eugenics and public service and becoming arguably the most well-known and highly respected member of the movement. Shortly before the U.S. entry into World War II, Osborn headed to Washington as one of FDR's dollar-a-year men to be appointed the first head of the Selective Service Committee overseeing implementation of the draft. During the war, despite having no military experience, he received a temporary commission as brigadier general—eventually promoted to major general—and chief of the Morale Branch of the War Department, a position in which he was responsible for educational programs, vocational training, recreation, USO clubs, the publication of magazines and newspapers for the troops, including *Stars and Stripes* and *Yank,* the Armed Forces Radio Service, and even the production of films, where he relied heavily on Frank Capra. Immediately after the war, Osborn served on the United Nations Atomic Energy Commission and the Commission for Conventional Armaments, often engaging in highly publicized confrontations with then–deputy Soviet foreign ministers Andrei Vishinsky and Andrei Gromyko.[16]

More than any other person, Osborn labored to rescue eugenics from its long association with bigotry and discrimination. Interviewed in 1967, he recalled the beginning of his own involvement with eugenics, a time when Grant, Laughlin, and H. F. Osborn, his uncle, were important figures in the movement and declared that "these very respectable gentlemen were all racists." Furthermore, according to Osborn's reminiscences, he had been "full of righteous indignation" in the 1930s upon realizing that the Eugenics Record Office at Cold Springs Harbor, where Davenport had been the director and Laughlin his deputy, was a "fake little institute" involved in "pseudo-science and propaganda," especially in connection with the material Laughlin had prepared for the congressional deliberations on the immigration act.[17]

In fact, this harsh and indisputably appropriate judgment of his former colleagues was more evident to Osborn in 1967 than it had been thirty-seven years earlier. His first public statement on eugenics had referred respectfully to Davenport's research and had offered Laughlin's efforts as the ultimate proof that eugenics could have practical application to public affairs. "The most effective work of this sort ever done," wrote Osborn in 1930, "were the studies and papers of Dr. Laughlin reporting on the effect of immigration into the United States which so greatly influenced Congress in the passage of the acts restricting immigration . . . findings [that] were generally accepted because they were based on carefully gathered and carefully analyzed data." And in a confidential memorandum written in 1933, he referred to Laughlin as "a thoroughly competent man of real ability."[18]

Nevertheless, it is undeniable that before the end of the decade, Osborn began to distinguish himself from earlier eugenicists in very important ways. First, and most significant, he maintained that there was no evidence for "superiorities or inferiorities of a biological nature" between races or social classes. And even if differences existed, he observed, in what has become the almost universally accepted scientific position, they would be "small compared to the much greater differences existing between individuals." As a consequence, in Osborn's view, eugenics had to be concerned always with "individual selection"—with encouraging the best individuals and the best families from every race and class to have more children. A eugenic program based on belief in the superiority of a particular race or social class, he concluded, ran "contrary to . . . scientific knowledge" and "to human ideals which are widely held in the United States."[19]

Osborn also insisted on social and economic improvements for the entire population as necessary for eugenic progress. Dismissing Davenport's oversimplified claims of genetic influence and declaring, instead, that "we are all environmentalists" as well as "hereditarians," he called for a series of measures that, even if proposed sixty years later, would still be considered a liberal activist agenda: increased school and college scholarships, "cheap and speedy" mass transportation, better housing for "skilled and unskilled urban labor," "elimination of slums" in both urban and rural areas and "improved playground facilities," "day nurseries" for all children, and "insurance for medical and maternal care."[20] Osborn's aim was to make it easier for parents in all classes to provide better homes and environments for their children, a goal in direct opposition to the standard eugenic wisdom of the previous three decades.

Finally, in what seemed like an additional attempt to separate his "reform" approach from previous eugenic thought, Osborn emphasized his vigorous opposition to "coercive measures" and "arbitrary control over births," which he considered inappropriate in a democratic society. In his view of the "eugenic ideal," the most "eugenic selection of births" would occur "as a natural process," in which parents would enjoy individual freedom to decide on the size of their family in accord with their own values and uninfluenced by official attempts "to define the 'fit' or the 'unfit.'"[21]

This apparently ringing endorsement of democratic ideals never appeared in Osborn's work without an immediate exception noted for the case of "hereditary defectives," however. "All known carriers of hereditary defect" were to be prevented from reproducing through "absolute segregation, during their entire period of child-bearing age . . . the only alternative to be voluntary sterilization before release." This unappealing choice—essentially confinement or surgery—was to be mandated not only for individuals who were themselves afflicted with such "genetic abnormalities" as deafness, feeblemindedness, and mental illness but also for "normals" who had been identified as "carriers" because they had already produced a "defective child." And it would affect a substantial portion of the population: In 1936 Osborn estimated that there were between 700,000 and 2 million "certain" and another 2 to 3 million "probable" carriers of serious hereditary defect—between 3 and 4 percent of the nation at the time.[22] Although he never engaged in the kind of legislative campaign for sterilization conducted by Laughlin, the two men were not that ideologically distant from each other when Pioneer was created.

As the fund's treasurer Draper chose Malcolm Donald, one of Boston's leading attorneys and a long-time trusted friend of the family; along with Wickliffe Draper, Donald had been named as an executor of George Draper's will and as trustee of the family fortune, should neither Wickliffe nor his sister outlive their father. Even before the fund's creation, Donald had managed Draper's finances.[23] As a Pioneer director, he continued to perform this function, successfully applying for a ruling from the federal Treasury Department that the organization was "exempt from filing returns of income" and from filing "capital stock tax returns." The ruling also meant that Draper's contributions to the fund would be deductible from his own income tax, a benefit that was often a consideration in the Colonel's donations.[24]

The last member of the original board, John Marshall Harlan, grandson of an identically named Supreme Court justice, seemed somewhat of an afterthought as he was the only director whose name had not appeared in the incorporation papers. Where Laughlin and Osborn had been selected to give Pioneer scientific credibility and Donald to provide financial management, Harlan's major assets were his breeding and his British style, both characteristics of some significance to the class conscious Draper; in addition, he was a member of the law firm of Root, Clark, Buckner, and Ballantine, which performed legal work for Pioneer. Descended, like Draper, from a prominent Kentucky family on one side and a wealthy Northeastern family on the other, Harlan had been educated at exclusive private schools in Chicago, Toronto, and Lake Placid before attending Princeton, where his closest friends were the scions of the rich and powerful—names such as Scribner and Firestone. An outstanding academic and extracurricular record, including the presidency of his class for three of his four undergraduate years, earned Harlan a Rhodes Scholarship, and he spent three years at Oxford, becoming, according to his biographer, "a confirmed Anglophile" who even adopted British spelling in his prose.[25]

At the time of his appointment as a Pioneer director, Harlan was a rising star in the legal field, a U.S. attorney in New York who later became chief counsel of the New York State Crime Commission before being named, first, to the federal bench and then by Eisenhower to the Supreme Court. Although this illustrious future was unpredictable in 1937, the decision to appoint Harlan to Pioneer's board turned out to be a remarkably fortuitous choice, allowing Harry Weyher to defend the fund against charges of racism many decades later by pointing out that the "original board of directors included U.S. Supreme Court Justice John Marshall Harlan, . . . who sided with every civil rights plaintiff who came before him on the court."[26]

In fact, Weyher's claim was far from accurate. As legal scholar Tinsley Yarborough has noted, Harlan was a moderate on the Warren court, supporting a number of civil rights plaintiffs but opposing many others and often reluctant to overturn state authority even in the face of substantial evidence of discriminatory intent. In *Swain v. Alabama,* for example, he favored denying certiorari to a case protesting an Alabama prosecutor's use of peremptory challenges to keep blacks off a jury in the trial of a black man accused of raping a white woman; when the case was finally heard by the Supreme Court, Harlan not only upheld the state's position but also rejected a finding of systematic discrimination in jury selection, even though not a single black had served on a jury in that county in the previous fifteen years. He was also extremely reluctant to interfere with discriminatory behavior in the private sector, eventually finding the public accommodations provisions of the Civil Rights Act to pass constitutional scrutiny not because discrimination was a violation of the equal protection guarantees of the Fourteenth Amendment but because it was harmful to commerce.[27]

However, it is undeniable that Harlan did support some of the most significant civil rights decisions of the Warren Court, contributing, according to Yarborough, "the most forceful sentence in *Brown* II" and joining a unanimous court to strike down state antimiscegenation statutes in the appropriately named *Loving* case.[28] Of course, had Draper been able to foresee Harlan's concurrence in these two decisions, the eventual justice, no matter how prominent his background or promising his future, would have been as welcome on Pioneer's board as Martin Luther King at a meeting of the Klan.

In any event, neither Donald nor Harlan played a substantive role on Pioneer's board, both men content to let Draper and the professional eugenicists decide on the merits of a project. Asked by Osborn for his opinion on a report submitted by the first applicant for a Pioneer grant, Donald wrote to the secretary that he had not yet read it but that "very probably my judgment would not be very good when I had." Harlan was no less candid, replying to the same request from Osborn that "I am frank to say that I feel that the 'lay' members of the Board will necessarily have to be guided very largely by your . . . advice."[29]

In fact, little judgment was needed by anyone on the board for Pioneer's first two projects, which Draper already had in mind when the fund was created. Indeed, during the first year of the fund's activity Laughlin made frequent hints that pet projects of his own be funded, all of which Draper politely ignored, thanking Laughlin for the suggestions but noting that his financial "interest will be restricted" to his own ideas.[30] In 1935, Draper had traveled to Berlin, where the International Congress for the Scientific Investigation of Population Problems was being held, to learn first hand what sort of eugenic measures were being enacted by the Nazi government. To facilitate his contact with officials and scientists in the Reich, Laughlin had written to Eugen Fischer, president of the International Congress and an important scientific authority for the Reich, naming Draper as one of the two official delegates from the Eugenics Research Association (ERA) and commending him as "one of the staunchest supporters of eugenical research and policy in the United States"; though unable to make the trip to Germany, Laughlin himself was an honorary vice president of the congress. From Berlin, Draper reported to Laughlin that he had met "several Germans who may be able to give me the information I seek, and which I look forward to discussing with you on my return."[31]

Pioneer's first project, undoubtedly the result of the information Draper had obtained while in Berlin, was the distribution of a German film with

English subtitles called *Erbkrank* (*The Hereditary Defective*), which he had acquired before the fund's creation from the Nazi government's Office of Racial Politics (Rassenpolitisches Amt). Issued originally by that office's predecessor, the Office of Education on Population Policy and Racial Maintenance (Aufklärungsamt für Bevölkerungspolitik und Rassenpflege), the film had been used, with Hitler's support, as part of a major propaganda campaign in Germany.[32] In the *Eugenical News* Laughlin described the film's concern with "the problem of hereditary degeneracy in the fields of feeblemindedness, insanity, crime, hereditary disease and inborn deformity" and its depiction of the enormous expense of these genetic defectives, housed in "costly modern custodial institutions" much finer than "the squalid living conditions of normal children in certain German city slums." The movie indicated, he concluded, that in the "field of applied negative eugenics" Germany had made "substantial progress in its intention to act fundamentally, on a long time plan, for the prevention, so far as possible, of hereditary degeneracy"—no doubt a reference to the Nazi sterilization program for which Laughlin had such high regard.[33] Although ambitious plans were formulated at Pioneer to advertise the film to the biology teachers in 3,000 high schools throughout the country, producing an estimated 1,000 "immediate applications" for loan, the mass mailing never took place, and the film was actually shown in 28 schools in 1937 and 1938, as well as a handful of times to state welfare workers in Connecticut.[34]

Interestingly, Laughlin's published description of the film in *Eugenical News* included a brief section that had not appeared in his original draft, observing that "there is no racial propaganda of any sort in the picture." In fact, the late insertion was false: According to German scholar Karl Ludwig Rost, one subtitle in the film stated that "the Jewish people produce an exceptionally high percentage of mentally ill," followed by depiction of what another subtitle called a "55-year old Jew. Deceitful. Rabble-rouser."[35] The denial of a racial element in the film probably was an attempt to make the Reich's eugenic practices more palatable to those who were repulsed by its anti-Semitism, although Laughlin himself had no such objections. There was no doubt that Draper shared Laughlin's admiration for Nazi racial policies; no one who thought otherwise would have been selected to represent the ERA in Berlin. Indeed, Draper's meeting with officials behind the scenes in Berlin had been facilitated by the connections of his codelegate from the ERA, Clarence G. Campbell, the organization's president and the Nazi press's favorite non-German eugenicist, who appeared before the International Congress as a "champion of Nazi racial principles," according to the *New York Times*, praising the Führer and his scientific advisors for "a comprehensive racial policy . . .

[that] promises to be epochal in racial history." The Reich had set "a pattern," Campbell declared, "which other nations and other racial groups must follow if they do not wish to fall behind in their racial quality, in their racial accomplishments and in their prospects for survival." At the congress's concluding banquet, Campbell gave the toast: "To that great leader, Adolf Hitler!" Elsewhere he observed that "the difference between the Jew and the Aryan is as unsurmountable as that between black and white."[36] Draper, as well as Laughlin, certainly shared these sentiments, which were close to official doctrine among the ERA leadership in 1935; in fact, a year later Draper chose Campbell as one of the judges, along with Davenport and Laughlin, for his third essay contest. Any implication that "race propaganda" would have been a disincentive to distribute *Erbkrank* was purely disingenuous.

Naturally, it was not possible at the time to foresee the mass of corpses at the bottom of the slippery slope down which the Nazi regime was rapidly descending. But the racial policies that had already been enacted against Jews, pointing toward the abyss to come, were identical to those that Draper and Laughlin sought against blacks in the United States: prohibition of their intermarriage and official measures to minimize their contact with the rest of the population.

Pioneer's other initial activity, much more ambitious than the distribution of a film, had also been conceived before the fund's creation by Draper, who wanted to investigate whether an increase in income would produce larger families among members of the "Army Flying Corps." If this question were answered in the affirmative, he was prepared to provide cash grants directly to aviators—in particular for the education of their children—to encourage "high fertility" on the part of these people with presumably superior genes. It was probably because Draper already had this project in mind that Pioneer's Certificate of Incorporation listed as one of its purposes the education of children whose parents were "of unusual value." In fact, the anticipation of assisting aviators even played a role in deciding on the fund's name, which at one point was going to be "The Eugenics Fund" but was changed to the "more colorless . . . 'Pioneer'" because Malcolm Donald, Draper's attorney, was concerned that "some ridicule might interfere with the investigation," should it be known that the aviators' families had been selected "for eugenics purposes."[37]

When a preliminary survey indicated that aviators were particularly concerned over the cost of educating their children, Pioneer's board decided that such families met the language in the charter: "The officers of the Army Air Corps, and their wives, are a class having such qualities and traits of character as to make them of unusual value as citizens; and . . . a majority of children of such parents would be descended predominantly from white persons who settled in the original thirteen states prior to the adoption of the Constitution . . . and/or their related stocks"; financial assistance for the education of their children would "thus encourage an increase of the number of such children." Consequently, pledging up to $230,000, Draper guaranteed scholarship payments for any child born to an officer of the United States Regular Army Air Corps in 1940, providing that the family already had at least three other children. The grants were funded through the purchase of an annuity for each eligible child at a cost of $2,713 ($32,900 AFI). Eleven children from nine families qualified for the award, totaling $29,843 ($362,400 AFI).[38] (In 1999, Douglas Blackmon, a reporter for the *Wall Street Journal,* tracked down a number of the families, finding that although the fathers had in most cases achieved real distinction in the military and other fields—including one general whose life was in part the basis for the 1943 movie *Bombardier*—the children had become average adults, certainly respectable and productive people but hardly the citizens "of unusual value" expected by the fund; among them were two appliance repairers, a home builder, an electrician, a nurse practitioner, and an assembly line worker in a photo-processing plant.[39])

Although this project appeared benign, albeit naive, it probably was informed, in Draper's thinking, not only by his life-long admiration for the military but also by the association, common at the time, of aviation with Nordic racial superiority and, in particular, with the development of air power by the Nazis, who were widely acknowledged as leaders in the field before the war. Charles Lindbergh, the blond prince of the air and a fervent believer in eugenics himself, visited the Reich often in the late 1930s, where he found "youth, hope and vigor" under Hitler, who "has done much for Germany"; particularly impressed by the Nazi aircraft industry, he judged the Reich to have "supremacy of the air" and personally received from Hermann Göring the Service Cross of the German Eagle for his contributions to aviation. Upon his return to the United States in 1939, in an article in *Reader's Digest* titled "Aviation, Geography and Race," Lindbergh urged the country to avoid any conflict with Germany in order "to preserve that most priceless possession, our inheritance of European blood" from the threat of "dilution by foreign races." Aviation, he declared, was a product of western European civilization, "borne on the crest of its conquest, developed by the spirit of its adventure, typical of its science, its industry, its outlook." It was, Lindbergh continued, "a tool specially shaped for Western hands, a scientific art which others only copy in a mediocre fashion, another barrier between the teeming millions of Asia and the Grecian inheritance of Europe—one of those priceless possessions which permit the White race to live at all in a pressing sea of Yellow, Black, and Brown."[40] Naturally, from Draper's point of view, a program to encourage the proliferation of those genetically capable of wielding this "Western" tool would help the racial barrier to endure.

Pioneer undertook little else of significance before the war, which then prevented the two most important board members from any activity on the fund's behalf until well after the cessation of hostilities. Osborn, who took over as Pioneer's president in 1941 when Laughlin died, was occupied with his many responsibilities as a major general in charge of the War Department's Morale Branch, and Draper spent the war years as an observer in India, where the highlights of his service "range[d] from assisting our Commissioner to present his credentials in a décor of white marble and scarlet guards" to watching the tribesmen conduct a "river crossing, complete with all except an enemy." Between 1943 and 1947, no meeting of the Pioneer board was held nor money expended on any project.[41]

With the war over, the fifty-six-year-old Draper was ready to commit himself and his substantial fortune more energetically than ever to the cause of eugenics. As Malcolm Donald, Draper's attorney and confidant, explained to Osborn, the Colonel was interested not in science but in policy; he wanted "to do something practical," such as "moving the colored race to Liberia" or "strengthening State laws to prevent the unfit from producing children." He was "not . . . concerned with research in human genetics since he felt that enough was known on the subject and that the important thing was to have something done." And in personal discussion with Osborn, Draper's list of priorities included not only "colonization of the colored minorities" but also the "reconstruction of American political parties."[42]

Ironically, however, in late 1947, at almost exactly the same time that Draper was searching for ways to translate genetic knowledge into political action, he also began to employ Bruce Wallace—a doctoral student at the time, later a well-known geneticist—as a personal tutor in genetics. Recalling his experience with the "wealthy Manhattanite" some decades later, Wallace said he found his pupil's "intended use of . . . genetic knowledge . . . abhorrent. . . . Criminality . . . was uppermost in his mind as a genetic trait. Needless to say, racial differences, in his opinion, were both hierarchical and genetically based," and Draper became "visibly agitated" when Wallace tried to disabuse him of these notions.[43] The scientific facts were clear and indisputable to the Colonel, who wanted to devote his resources not so much to finance studies that would demonstrate white, northern European genetic superiority but to support projects that would use this presumptive fact as a point of departure and encourage policies to prevent the contamination of this superior group by inferior races, especially blacks.

Pressed to respond to Draper's policy goals, Osborn always expressed "sympathy with his views," agreeing in principle with both colonization and political party reconstruction but finding these ambitious projects "ahead of their time"—too unrealistic at the moment, too difficult to carry out, and, "at any rate, quite out of my experience." In keeping with his reform view of eugenics, Osborn preferred that Pioneer take a more moderate approach, relying on a committee of highly respected scientists to advise the fund, supporting research in psychology, genetics, and differential fertility, developing a "Hall of Human Genetics" in the American Museum of Natural History, and providing support for the American Eugenics Society (AES), of which he was also president at the time.[44]

Although Draper quickly rejected any thought of an advisory committee—no one was going to tell him how his own money should be spent—he was willing to coexist with Osborn as president of the board, ignoring their differences as long as blacks were kept largely separate and subordinate, presenting no serious threat to white racial purity. Indeed, the Colonel even continued to provide annual grants to the AES from 1951 through 1954, for which Osborn was appropriately grateful.[45] But after the *Brown* decision threatened the principles to which Draper had dedicated his life and fortune, it was no longer possible to tolerate, from the president of his own board, any hesitation to join wholeheartedly in the impending struggle against integration and civil rights for blacks. When, less than three months after the Supreme Court's ruling, Osborn next sought assistance from Pioneer for the AES, Draper generously offered even more than the requested amount but also proposed some "suggestions" for amending the Society's "credo" to accord more with his own beliefs, implying an association between acceptance of these changes and receipt of the money. He also noted his fear that the AES "might fall into the hands . . . of somebody whose views he could not approve," apparently another attempt to encourage a favorable view of his proposed amendments.[46]

Draper's suggestions, as always, were concerned with racial purity. "I believe," he stated, in "measures to promote considerable ethnic homogeneity. . . . Hence I should examine any concrete action suggested with this in mind." Furthermore, he continued, if it were possible to obtain results "in line with above, . . . I should assist anyone who seems likely to achieve them." In research in general, the Colonel concluded, "I should be reluctant to assist investigators whose personalities and view points were markedly alien to my own."[47] In other words, Draper wanted the AES to emphasize practical measures resulting in ethnic segregation; research and researchers unlikely to produce conclusions pointing in this direction would not receive support from Pioneer.

These unsubtle hints of a quid pro quo were made explicit at the end of 1954, when Osborn was invited to Draper's plush New York residence for a private meeting. Asked whether Pioneer would continue its support, the Colonel replied bluntly, according to Osborn, that "if the [AES] would take a strong public position along the lines of his thinking, he would not only renew the grant but would be willing to guarantee full support of the Society over at least a five year period. But if they did not want to take a strong position along the lines of his ideas, he would not make any more contributions." Believing that Draper's proposals had "no basis in scientific findings," Osborn replied that "the Society would look elsewhere for its funds."[48]

Although it was clear that the president of Draper's own fund had become "somebody whose views he could not approve," the axe did not fall until seventeen months later, in 1956, when the Colonel informed Osborn that their "values and aims" were "so different that further meetings might not be mutually advantageous or agreeable." Osborn responded by immediately offering his resignation as an officer of the fund, although an official end to his association with Pioneer did not occur until 1958.[49]

Finally unencumbered by any moderating influence, even one as sympathetic to his aims as Osborn's, Draper began to select individuals for the board who would help him to seek out and fund—in small part through official Pioneer grants but even more through the usual anonymous contributions on the Colonel's part—people with "personalities and viewpoints" similar to his own and eager to take the "concrete actions" to achieve "ethnic homogeneity" that had been resisted by the previous president. The re-formed Pioneer board would share Draper's desire to use his vast resources as a weapon against the Second Reconstruction.

To replace Osborn, Draper chose Harry Frederick Weyher Jr., a New York tax attorney—originally from North Carolina and educated at the University of North Carolina and Harvard Law School—who had previously been a member of John Marshall Harlan's staff when the future justice had served as chief counsel to the New York State Crime Commission. It was probably through Weyher's association with Harlan that he had been introduced to Draper.[50] Weyher would make Draper's cause his own, heading the Pioneer Fund through the rest of the century, disbursing his mentor's acknowledged and unacknowledged donations to the campaign against equality for blacks, organizing many of these efforts, monitoring their results, and becoming the heir not just to much of the Colonel's fortune but also to his social policy agenda. If Pioneer was originally "Draper's Fund," it was to become Weyher's.

Pioneer's founder and his chosen successor were, in many ways, kindred souls. Though not as reclusive as Draper, Weyher cherished his privacy, avoiding all attempts by journalists to speak with him until 1994, when he finally granted an interview to a magazine writer. Also like his mentor, Weyher was particularly interested in good breeding. In a work that had much in common with *The Drapers in America,* he compiled and published his own family genealogy (before the Web made such a task much easier), tracing his roots to Austria, where his great-grandparents were "leading residents of aristocratic Vienna," members of the Weyher von Weyherfels nobility; his grandfather moved to the United States, settling in the tobacco farming community of Kinston, North Carolina, where Weyher was raised.[51] The genealogy also documented Weyher's eager attempts to find family links to eminent people. From the General Douglas MacArthur Foundation he learned that the military commander was a very distant relative. An inquiry of Prescott Bush, once a senator from Connecticut and father and grandfather of presidents, was not as productive: No connection between the two families could be found. And for someone who married one of Weyher's children, the genealogy provided not a family background but a "pedigree."[52]

But the most important similarity between Weyher and Draper, and obviously the one that would make the Colonel comfortable leaving the attorney in charge of his fund, was their common attitude toward race. In addition to being a history of his family, Weyher's genealogy also offered sympathetic portrayals of a heroic Southern struggle to maintain white supremacy, including an excerpt reprinted from the autobiography of Thomas Dixon, whose novel *The Clansman,* a glorification of the Ku Klux Klan, had been made into the film *Birth of a Nation.* The excerpt described how the Confederacy won the peace after losing the war: "The children of Shakespeare and Burns . . . [who] would no longer submit to Negro rule" were able to "destroy the tyranny of Scalawag, Carpetbagger and Negro"; although the Republicans "stole the election" of 1876, nevertheless "the conspiracy . . . to destroy the Southern States and build on their ruins black territories . . . failed," and "our people, once more, could smile."[53] More contemporary correspondence in the genealogy indicated that even in the 1990s, in the clubby atmosphere characterizing the exchanges between North Carolina political insiders, Weyher and his friends—Senator Jesse Helms and fellow Pioneer board member Marion Parrott, a relative of Weyher's—still referred to white Southerners who voted for a black candidate as "scalawags" and, only partially in jest, joked about how "the Indians didn't get enough of them."[54]

Like Draper, Weyher also supported the repatriation movement, but where the Colonel offered money and encouragement, the attorney provided assistance of a more strategic nature, suggesting various sources to strengthen Cox's case that blacks should be sent back to Africa. After Cox's death, his estate hired Louisiana attorney Drew L. Smith to complete the activist's latest, unfinished manuscript on his life's obsession; Smith was an appropriate choice to act as Cox's surrogate, having just authored the elegantly titled pamphlet "Details How to Ship Negroes Back to Africa" for the National States Rights Party, a Nazi-style political group supporting passage of a law that, "due to the Negroes' failure to adapt to our American civilization," would strip all blacks of their citizenship and forcibly deport them.[55] To assist with the completion of Cox's manuscript, Weyher recommended a book written by a Northern general because, as one of Cox's executors wrote to Smith, Weyher had been "very much impressed with the recorded interviews this General had with President Lincoln, shortly before his death clearly and specifically stating his intentions of the repatriation of the Negro back to his homeland. . . . If you cannot get a copy he can get one for you. Some of the statements made by the General seemed proof positive that President Lincoln never changed his mind about the separation of the races as the mulattoes and northern dissenters are so feverishly trying to prove." "Since you know Mr. Weyher personally," the executor noted to Smith, "you may wish to communicate with him directly about the book." In addition, when the estate also had *White America* republished by Willis Carto's Noontide Press, three copies were sent fresh from the printer to Cox's executor, who informed Carto that two of them were reserved for Weyher.[56] Whatever might happen to Draper, he could now be certain that the fund was in trustworthy and sympathetic hands.

Shortly after Weyher began his association with Pioneer, another new and equally reliable person was appointed a board member and secretary of the fund: John B. Trevor Jr. would also serve through the rest of the century, the two men thus making up the core of the board for more than four decades. Trevor's father, a Harvard-educated lawyer and industrialist descended from a signer of the Declaration of Independence and, like his close friend Madison Grant, a member of New York's social elite, had served as an officer in military intelligence just after World War I, a role in which he "made his own rules, gave himself his own assignments," according to a colleague at the time. For example, Trevor Sr. developed a plan to suppress a mass uprising of Jewish subversives in New York City, going so far as to order 6,000 rifles and a machine gun battalion for deployment in Jewish neighborhoods in anticipation of a disturbance that never took place. Keeping secret ties to military intelligence even after his return to civilian life, the elder Trevor became, according to one historian, "one of the most influential unelected individuals affiliated with the U.S. Congress," testifying in the hearings that led to the Immigration Restriction Act of 1924 and crafting its plan to designate national quotas for each country based on the number of its residents in the United States in 1890, before the bulk of the immigration from southern and eastern Europe. To defend the quotas, in 1929 Trevor founded the American Coalition of Patriotic Societies, which quickly became an umbrella organization for numerous far-right groups; later named as the coalition's "honorary president" was C. M. Goethe, a president of the ERA who strongly recommended the "marvelous eugenics program of Hitler" as a model that the United States must adopt if it were to have any chance of becoming "Germany's successful rival."[57]

When there were last-ditch attempts in the late 1930s to waive some of the restrictions in the 1924 Immigration Act in order to grant asylum to a few victims of Nazi oppression, Trevor, together with Grant, Laughlin, and Draper, planned the strategy that led to Laughlin's 1939 report. In his position as chair of the Immigration Committee of the Chamber of Commerce of the State of New York, Trevor requested that Laughlin author the report recommending a reduction in quotas as "a new paper which his committee can use in presenting their arguments to Congress." As Laughlin confided to Draper, this was a sound tactic: The Chamber of Commerce was "a better 'sponsor source' . . . than . . . even a patriotic organization."[58] Also before the war Trevor, as head of the American Coalition, collaborated on a number of projects designed to distribute Nazi propaganda, and in 1942, according to investigative journalist Adam Miller, the coalition "was named in a U.S. Justice Department Sedition indictment for pro-Nazi activities." In a particular irony, Trevor and the coalition (as well as T. Lothrop Stoddard) were investigated by military intelligence.[59]

Trevor Jr. grew up surrounded by his father's friends in military intelligence, men still accustomed to operating by their own rules in a James Bond world. "Isn't there some way that the long arm of an organization you and I know can reach out [and] restore McGovern to permanent residence on his native heath," suggested one of these officers to his old colleague's son in 1969, after the senator from South Dakota suggested that the United States pull out of Vietnam.[60]

Upon his father's death in 1956, Trevor Jr. took control of the coalition. Despite its own indictment for sedition during the war, the organization was concerned about a long list of "subversive" institutions and activities. In regular resolutions, which were read into the *Congressional Record* and used in attempts to influence national legislation, the coalition expressed its opposition not only to any attempts to "undermine" the immigration laws by admitting more "aliens" or relaxing the requirements for deportation but also to arms negotiations, membership in the United Nations and its very presence on "American territory," diplomatic relations with the USSR, NATO-sponsored conventions to promote "greater political and economic cooperation," display of the Panamanian flag in the Canal Zone, fluoridation of public water supplies, the National Council of Churches, and the World Federation of Mental Health, whose purpose was the destruction of "our form of government and our American Way of Life." One of the coalition's official spokespersons who presented its resolutions to the House Committee on Foreign Affairs was General Pedro del Valle, a member of the Liberty Lobby's advisory board, who professed "the instinctive distrust which is natural in all Christians for all Jews, diluted or pure"; Jews "cannot also be good Americans," he wrote to a fellow officer, because "all Jews are hostile to the kind of America that anybody but a Jew desires."[61] Del Valle was also a co-owner of the biweekly paper *Common Sense,* which claimed that Mao Zedong was a "front . . . for New York Jews," and was considered a member of "our . . . inner circle of top people" by George Lincoln Rockwell, "Commander" of the American Nazi Party, one of the faithful few who donated to Rockwell's campaign to "nail the nigger and Jew *LEADERS*" behind "Martin Luther Coon."[62]

Not a totally contrary organization, the coalition did find some positions it could enthusiastically support. It commended the Republic of South Africa for "its well-reasoned racial policy," urging Congress to "ferret out" critics of the apartheid regime in both government and the media so that they might receive "their due and proper repudiation." And it called for "an immediate amnesty" for any Nazi war criminals "still . . . suffering imprisonment" as a result of the Nuremberg trials, which it called a "dreadful retrogression into barbarism" and "a form of vengeance antagonistic to Western civilization." Of particular concern to the coalition was the fate of Major Walter Reder, then incarcerated in an Italian military prison although, according to the resolution calling for his release, he had "acted in accord with the highest traditions of military service" in "the encirclement and destruction" of a group of Communists. In fact, Reder had been convicted for his role in the massacre of 1,830 Italian civilians—most of them elderly people, women, and children—in a town in which a few Communists had been elected to the local council.[63]

In 1961, as the nation began taking judicial steps to dismantle the legal superstructure systematically excluding black citizens from the full benefits of citizenship, the coalition added the Supreme Court to its litany of evils, warning that the court's "long train of illegal, unconstitutional rulings . . . will result in the overthrow of . . . constitutional government." Equally objectionable, of course, was the introduction two years later of a landmark civil rights bill—banning discrimination in employment, places of public accommodation, and federally funded institutions—which, according to the coalition, would cause the "destruction of civil and property rights of all citizens to curry the favor of organized minorities."[64] The coalition also began to pressure a university press to republish "two important works" by the "celebrated authorit[y]" Earnest Sevier Cox: *White America* and *Teutonic Unity.*[65] Though originally self-published by the author in 1951, the latter book had actually been written early in the war, motivated by Cox's sense that the allies might be defeated. "If Hitler should have won and had gained control of Africa," explained Cox after the war to C. M. Goethe, the coalition's honorary president, then by stressing the racial kinship between the victors and the United States, "I sought the aid of Germany in removing the African blood from America." Cox's account of Teutonic racial history and the importance of racial unity in the face of the Slavic threat in Europe and the presence of blacks in the United States was quickly circulated among ex-Nazis throughout the world, and requests for copies, together with praise for the work, soon arrived from former Reich notables such as Grand Admiral Karl Dönitz, Hitler's chosen successor recently released from prison; Johann von Leers, a member of "Hitler's body-guard SS" who escaped from "vindictive Jews" after the war and lived underground in Germany before making his way to Argentina; and Nazi social anthropologist Hans F. K. Günther. Cox was also invited, expenses paid, to coalition events featuring segregationist scientists financed by Draper.[66]

During this period, all the coalition's activities probably were funded largely by Draper. In its financial report for the first half of 1964, the coalition reported contributions of $35,750 ($203,000 AFI) from the Colonel, accounting for the organization's entire income for those six months. Although the reports for other years are not available, it appears that Draper was the coalition's chief, and perhaps its only, source of support at the time. Indeed, given his long association with Trevor père and his admiration for Nazi eugenics, Draper may well have been funding the coalition during its opposition to Jewish refugees in the 1930s and its prewar distribution of Nazi propaganda. According to Marshall Ravnitzky, a reporter for the National Law Journal, the Federal Bureau of Investigation has been withholding records on Draper's involvement with the Reich under an inappropriate application of classification rules to files more than fifty years old.[67]

With Draper, Weyher, and Trevor on the board, Pioneer was firmly controlled by virulent opponents of civil rights and Nazi sympathizers. During the next decade, the Colonel provided clandestine funding for a series of organized assaults on attempts to obtain equality for blacks, in which his two co-conspirators would play significant but similarly surreptitious roles. These efforts would be based on claims of white racial superiority and the threat of intermarriage to white racial purity, and hence civilization, thus establishing a direct connection between the ideology of the latest recipients of Draper's generosity and Earnest Sevier Cox's similar obsessions. Once again putatively scientific pronouncements would be exploited as a tactic to attain repugnant political ends: the denial of constitutional rights to citizens because of their skin color. Nor did this campaign to preserve segregation lose sight of what Trevor euphemistically referred to as "the broad spectrum of problems facing us," and there were frequent attempts to accuse Jews of controlling the civil rights movement for their own ulterior purposes. Although these many activities would not be officially acknowledged as Pioneer grants, they were projects supported by the fund in all but name, the money coming from Draper, Pioneer's creator and the sole source of its resources, and Pioneer's president and secretary being extensively involved in their planning and organization. According to the scientists funded by the Colonel, realistic solutions to "the problems of human betterment"—the stated purpose in Pioneer's Certificate of Incorporation—would necessarily preclude the full participation of blacks in the nation's society and polity.

# 3 Our Source of Funds: The Campaign against Civil Rights

FOR ALMOST a century after emancipation, segregated education for blacks in the South had been based on the doctrine of "separate but equal," a bipartite principle whose first condition was enforced as vigorously as its second was ignored. But on the third Monday of May 1954, Supreme Court Chief Justice Earl Warren, speaking for a unanimous court, announced that "separate educational facilities are inherently unequal."[1]

Correctly perceived by both its supporters and its opponents as an arrow, pointing away from the Jim Crow past toward a more egalitarian future, *Brown v. the Board of Education* produced furious vows of "segregation forever" among many Southern state officials and staunch resistance in the courts, the legislatures, and the streets. Nineteen senators and eighty-one congressional representatives from the South signed the "Southern Manifesto," commending "those states which have declared the intention to resist forced integration" and pledging to "bring about a reversal" of the decision. To emphasize its opposition, Maryland, one of the three states never to have ratified the Fourteenth Amendment, confirmed its eighty-eight-year dissent in a new vote. Rather than submit to integration, a number of states passed amendments to their state constitutions abolishing the public school system and replacing it with corporate ownership of private, segregated schools whose students would then receive grants from state and local funds to pay their tuition.[2] Probably the most thoroughgoing official defiance of the ruling, ranging from the governor's office and the courts to the local communities, issued from Mississippi, where, only two days after the *Brown* decision, Congressman John Bell Williams branded May 17 with the South's label: "Black Monday." Only weeks later in Mississippi, the Citizens' Councils movement was formed, the largest and most powerful organization dedicated to preserving white supremacy; within two years there were more than 200,000 members in 600 council chapters throughout the South, half of them in Mississippi alone.[3]

Official intransigence was followed by an outpouring of hatred, as some of the first actual attempts to integrate schools produced acts of savagery. In North Carolina a black student was spit on, full in the face, while the surrounding mob sang "We don't want her, you can have her, she's too black for me." In Tennessee, rocks were thrown at black students, and a school where a single five-year-old black girl had registered was rocked by a dynamite blast. In Alabama, after a mob attempted to stone Autherine Lucy, the first black student ever to attend the state university, she was suspended from class to prevent further public disorder, and the state legislature subpoenaed her to testify on communist influence in the National Association for the Advancement of Colored People (NAACP), the plaintiffs in the *Brown* decision. In Little Rock, Governor Orval Faubus, in an act perilously close to armed rebellion, deployed the Arkansas National Guard to prevent execution of a federal court order, forcing President Eisenhower to federalize the National Guard and call in troops from the 101st Airborne to escort nine black children past furious mobs of taunting whites. And even eight years after *Brown,* in the most explosive conflict between state and federal government since the Civil War, the National Guard and Regular Army were called out to help federal marshals ensure the safety of the first black student to enroll at the University of Mississippi after violent riots and sniper fire resulted in two deaths and scores of injuries.[4]

Desegregated education was the wedge of the Second Reconstruction, opening the way for demands to dismantle the other elements of American apartheid and grant blacks' long-deferred aspirations for equal rights. A year and a half after the Supreme Court ruling, a private citizen performed an act perhaps second only to the *Brown* decision in its eventual impact on the nation's race relations: On a segregated Montgomery, Alabama bus, Rosa Parks, a black seamstress, refused to relinquish her seat to a white person. She was arrested and fined.[5] Within forty-eight hours, a boycott of the city bus system began that lasted for 381 days, producing not only desegregation of the buses but also the emergence of a black minister of immense moral stature as leader of the civil rights movement. During the next decade, other courageous individuals would risk, and sometimes sacrifice, their lives to obtain the right to vote and to receive equal treatment in public accommodations.

For Wickliffe Preston Draper, the goals of the civil rights movement posed a profound threat to his most cherished beliefs. Undoubtedly horrified at the prospect of social and political equality for blacks, the Colonel opened wide his pursestrings between the late 1950s and his death in 1972, pouring huge amounts of money into various anti-integration projects conducted by some of the most ardent racists.

Although the more scientifically oriented initiatives would come later, it is highly probable that Draper provided funding for the first attempt to co-ordinate resistance to *Brown* throughout the South, the short-lived Federation for Constitutional Government, which brought together on its Advisory Committee extremists from eleven Southern states. Many of these activists were soon involved in other projects funded by the Colonel: James Eastland, Theodore Bilbo's understudy and successor in the Senate as Mississippi's chief defender of separatism, served on a committee that distributed Draper's money to worthy scientific recipients; Robert B. Crawford, president of Virginia's Defenders of State Sovereignty and Individual Liberties, coop-erated with Harry Weyher to launder Draper's contribution for the republi-cation of "Lincoln's Negro Policy" as a memorial to its deceased author, Earnest Sevier Cox; Watkins M. Abbitt, a congressman from Virginia, later was a direct recipient of political contributions from Draper; and William J. Simmons, organizer and chief administrator of the Citizens' Councils, not only participated in many projects funded by Draper but also inherited con-trol of a substantial portion of the Colonel's resources. In addition, Weyher sent a $500 ($3,000 AFI) contribution from Draper, "at the recommenda-tion of John U. Barr," to the segregationist North Carolina Defenders of States Rights. Barr was chair of the federation's Executive Committee; if he was encouraging the Colonel to make donations to other organizations, it was probable that his own group was a recipient.[6]

Then, too, the federation embodied the two concerns that were of partic-ular interest to Draper and that he had tried to persuade Frederick Osborn to embrace: the reconstruction of political parties and racial homogeneity. There were hints from Barr that the federation might lead to creation of a third party dedicated to segregation, state sovereignty, and free enterprise, all principles dear to the Colonel.[7] Even more important, the federation's newsletter reflected Draper's obsession with race, not just in the parochial context of Southern resistance to integration but also as the underlying fac-tor in civilization. Indeed, regularly written by Weyher's acquaintance Drew L. Smith—who completed Earnest Sevier Cox's unfinished memoirs and wrote the pamphlet "Details How to Ship Negroes Back to Africa" for the neo-Nazi National States Rights Party—many of the newsletters seemed tak-en directly from Cox's writing, constantly emphasizing the need to protect "Caucasian civilization and white racial integrity." One of Smith's articles opposed Hawaiian statehood because we would be admitting into the nation "an Oriental State" whose "people would be as foreign to us as are the inhabitants of Siam"; there was "reliable evidence," he claimed, that the admission of Hawaii was part of the communist objective "to swamp this country with an immigration of the worst description, so that the American way of life can be undermined and expunged." Smith also regularly repeated Cox-style warnings that "negro mental inferiority" had caused the destruction of "every white civilization" of which they had been a part and that integration and its inevitable consequence—"racial amalgamation"—would only hasten the process in the United States. And naturally he dedicated one issue of the newsletter to "Colonization: The Solution to the Negro Problem."[8]

The federation soon dissolved, and whatever assistance Draper might have rendered, he would have to find other sources of resistance to civil rights. Although Smith's diatribes against both external and internal threats to white racial purity cited all the appropriate scientific authorities in the eugenic canon, he was not himself a scientist, and Draper was anxious to recruit to the cause people who could add impressive academic credentials and scholarly records to their opposition to integration. Whether they looked to religion, law, or custom as justification for their views, all factions among the segregationists agreed on the racial inferiority of blacks and the danger of miscegenation to white purity, which, like Smith and Cox, they all considered essential for the survival of civilization. In addition, they were all certain that "amalgamation" was the true, if unacknowledged, goal of the civil rights movement. As circuit judge Tom P. Brady maintained in his "Black Monday" address, the founding document of the Citizens' Councils, blacks were unwilling to take the "tedious and slow" route to evolutionary advancement, preferring the "inter-marriage turnpikes" as "a much shorter detour." But, warned Brady, "whenever and wherever the white man has drunk the cup of black hemlock," destruction of all "intellect and culture" had been the inevitable result. Thus, all opposition to integration was, in some sense, based on the quasiscientific assertions about black inferiority and white purity that Draper wanted to place explicitly at the center of the controversy. As Carleton Putnam, an activist in a number of the projects supported by Draper, put it, instead of harping on states' rights, southerners "should be talking anthropology."[9]

An additional incentive for segregationists to focus on science was the fact that scientists had testified for the plaintiffs in the lower court hearings culminating in the *Brown* decision, claiming that separation based on race was harmful to "the educational and mental development" of black children and reduced their motivation to learn. And although the Supreme Court's opin-

ion was clearly based not on expert testimony but on constitutional guarantees of equal rights, some of these expert witnesses had immediately trum-
peted their own testimony as the key factor in persuading the court to ignore
its own prior support for the "separate but equal" fiction. If, as the plaintiffs'
experts themselves now maintained, *Brown* had been informed by "evidence"—scientific data of some sort—rather than principle, then the segregationist scientists could claim, with some logic, that they too had scientific
evidence to present, evidence that had not been previously heard by the
courts but that suggested a different conclusion about the source of educational problems for black children.[10]

One of the first attempts by Draper to solicit scientific assistance specifically against integration occurred in 1956 after Weyher received two pamphlets written by Wesley Critz George, professor of anatomy at the University of North Carolina and that state's leading defender of segregation even
before the *Brown* decision; the pamphlets probably were forwarded to Weyher by Thomas F. Ellis, counsel to the North Carolina Advisory Committee
on Education, whom Weyher later appointed to Pioneer's board. In "Race,
Heredity, and Civilization" and "The Race Problem from the Standpoint of
One Who Is Concerned with the Evils of Miscegenation," George opposed
the "protoplasmic mixing of the races" on the grounds that blacks were "genetically unacceptable" and would "destroy our race and our civilization."[11]
The product of a recognized scientist, these works were clearly the sort of
response to the civil rights movement that Draper was seeking. Though not
yet president of Pioneer, Weyher responded to George on behalf of his "client"—Frederick Osborn having been found untrustworthy in matters of race
by this time—asking the professor to recommend an organization that would
distribute the pamphlets so that the unnamed client could "make some
modest contribution toward that end." "He prefers," wrote Weyher, "to make
any such gifts to well-established and reputable organizations for their use
and not to directly finance such projects as an individual." (Weyher later sent
George a check for $500 [$3,000 AFI] from the Colonel to be used to distribute "Race, Heredity, and Civilization.") Weyher also asked whether George
could supply "the names of any professors or other personnel at any university" who might provide assistance to the cause.[12]

This search on Draper's part for additional expertise eventually produced
a dedicated group of activists to work with Pioneer board members Weyher
and Trevor in the campaign to use science in opposition to civil rights. Although most members of the group were academics, there were two notable
exceptions: retired airline executive Carleton Putnam, who, though not
trained in anthropology, claimed to speak on behalf of "a muzzled group of

scientists" in the field; and arguably the most influential single opponent of civil rights in the country, Citizens' Councils chief William J. Simmons, referred to as "Dixieland apartheid's number-one organization man" by one journalist and called "extremist . . . even by Mississippi standards" by the *New York Times*.[13]

Everyone in this group—scientists and nonscientists alike—would certainly have met Madison Grant's criteria for approval: They were "anthropologically, socially and politically sound." All of them were vehemently opposed to integration, which they viewed as merely the first step toward the civil rights movement's ultimate goal: "mongrelization." Most also saw Jews and Communists—a pairing often considered redundant in this circle—as the masterminds and the more dangerous enemy behind the civil rights movement, cynically manipulating blacks for their own purposes; some were seeking to restore to respectability the sort of "racial science" that had characterized scientific thought in the Third Reich; and a number were overt neo-Nazis, open admirers of Hitler and eager to establish a Fourth Reich.

When Draper's quest for "well established and reputable organizations" proved unsuccessful, members of this group formed their own organizations, which he then funded lavishly. From the Colonel's point of view, this preference for setting up a conduit to channel his money to approved projects had two important advantages. First, it provided further protection for his anonymity by interposing an intermediary between him and the project receiving his money. And because the receiving organization typically was created as tax exempt, it ensured that he would be able to deduct the contribution, a matter that was always significant to him. Indeed, aware of this concern on the Colonel's part, George proposed "a possible solution" to "the matter of tax exemption for his contribution in case Mr. Draper were inclined to contribute any money for printing and distributing" the scientist's pamphlets: George recommended that Draper should donate the money to the State of Georgia, which would then distribute the writing through its "educational commission."[14]

Draper provided substantial funding for at least five major projects, often organized and managed by Weyher on the Colonel's behalf, that opposed equal rights for blacks:

—The International Association for the Advancement of Ethnology and Eugenics (IAAEE), which published and distributed a series of reprints and monographs as well as an edited collection of works on race and science and sponsored the journal the *Mankind Quarterly*, from which most of the reprints were taken

—The publication of Carleton Putnam's books and a series of pamphlets by George, Putnam, and others, along with the distribution of these works by the National Putnam Letters Committee and the committee's successor, the Patrick Henry Group

—An attempt to reverse the *Brown* decision through two court cases in which the segregationist scientists were expert witnesses

—A campaign by the Coordinating Committee for Fundamental American Freedoms (CCFAF), closely allied with the Mississippi Sovereignty Commission, to stop passage of the Civil Rights Act of 1964

—The campaign by the Citizens' Councils to organize a system of racially segregated private schools as an alternative to the public school system

Draper and Weyher took extensive precautions to keep the Colonel's contributions to these efforts secret, and only in the last two of these cases does a record exist—a "smoking gun"—specifically linking Draper's money to the projects. Nevertheless, the circumstantial evidence pointing to Draper in the other three cases is overwhelming, leaving no doubt that he was the source of their funds.

## The "Money Bags" and His Attorney: The Evidence

First of all, both the earlier exchange with Osborn that led to his resignation as Pioneer's president and the correspondence with George indicated that Weyher's "client" was eager to provide resources for organized, scientific opposition to integration. Indeed, before the formation of his clique of scientific allies, Draper had personally approached a number of mainstream scientists with offers of assistance, only to be rebuffed. Interviewed by a reporter for the *Nation,* one "well-known geneticist" who had rejected the money called Draper "a racist of the usual type . . . [who] wished to prove simply that Negroes were inferior . . . and wished to promote some program to send them all to Africa," a sentiment echoed by three other researchers to whom the Colonel had made overtures.[15]

To augment these personal efforts Draper also created two committees that began, in the late 1950s, to disburse his money surreptitiously for what Weyher, who administered the funds, called "worthy [scientific] projects." The first of these "Draper Committees"—concerned with "population problems, quality, quantity, and homogeneity," according to Weyher—included Mississippi Senator Eastland, who had accused the Supreme Court of intending to "use force to completely mongrelize the American people," and Henry E. Garrett, a psychology professor who led the scientific campaign against integration and eventually became one of Pioneer's board members.[16]

Serving on the second committee, which specialized in immigration and race, was a congressman and chair of the House Un-American Activities Committee (HUAC), Francis Walter, to whose election campaign Draper had been the largest contributor. Created by Representative Hamilton Fish, the most ardent Nazi sympathizer in the House, who had used his office for the mass distribution of speeches by an eventually imprisoned Nazi agent, HUAC quickly became the gathering point for every Klan supporter and fascist collaborator in the lower chamber, entertaining witnesses such as the general who recommended in 1939 that any Jews "affiliate[d] with organized World Jewry . . . be denied office-holding, suffrage and all other citizenship rights."[17] Another member of the second "Draper Committee" was Anthony Bouscaren, a political scientist and consultant to HUAC, whose books on immigration were published through subsidies from "the Draper Fund," that is, with money from the committee on which he served; among other restrictive measures, Bouscaren sought to have investigated the backgrounds and beliefs of all prospective tourists to the United States before allowing them entry.[18] Richard Arens, staff director for HUAC whose anti-immigrant address was reprinted in the Federation for Constitutional Government's newsletter, served as a paid consultant to the second committee, receiving a $3,000 annual stipend ($18,400 AFI) to find recipients for research grants on "immigration and genetics" (that is, Arens, a congressional staff member, was also being employed by someone with an interest in legislation, a conflict of interest that eventually forced him to resign). One right-wing activist, hoping to obtain support for a project, referred to Arens as "apparently . . . in charge of the studies relating to immigration which Colonel Draper finances."[19]

Yet despite all these strenuous efforts to spend Draper's money on what Garrett described as "unbiased work on racial matters," the Pioneer Fund itself made only five small grants between 1954 and 1971.[20] Thus, when a campaign to oppose integration on largely scientific grounds was finally launched, it was highly probable that Draper had funded it. Having conducted such a frantic search for sympathetic researchers and having had his offers of generosity rebuffed by the mainstream geneticists, it would be only natural for Draper to turn to the scientists who shared his views; he wanted to fund scientific racism, and they were the scientific racists.

Moreover, as Weyher had written to George, his client wanted to finance an organization that would distribute the professor's scientific polemics against integration. The distribution of literature to members of selected groups, long Draper's preferred method for attempting to influence policy and public opinion, was the principal tactic used by both the IAAEE and the National Putnam Letters Committee, the two operations sharing the same "basic mailing list" of some 16,000 names, most of them academics. Indeed, after Princeton sociologist Melvin Tumin published an "examination" by a number of "authorities," who concluded that there was no scientific evidence to support the claims of the segregationist scientists, Garrett wrote to George that the Colonel "thought we should answer Tumin, that he would pay for the printing of the Reply," and that it should be sent out to the "mailing lists." The reply, including contributions by Garrett, Putnam, and George, eventually appeared as a pamphlet published by the Putnam National Letters Committee.[21]

In addition, Draper, always generous to those who told him what he wanted to hear, made regular and substantial personal gifts to many of the scientists involved in the campaign. From 1962 until the Colonel's death in 1972, George received a $1,000 check forwarded by Weyher every Christmas "as a token of [Draper's] appreciation of your scientific efforts during the past year." According to Draper's estate papers, which were required to report any gifts during his last three years, a number of other scientists enjoyed even more generous annual presents during that time period, including zoologist Robert Kuttner, psychologist R. Travis Osborne, and Garrett, all of them members of the IAAEE's Executive Committee and involved in its journal, the *Mankind Quarterly;* altogether Draper gave more than $20,000 ($92,000 AFI) in Christmas gifts to scientists between 1969 and 1971.[22] And although only George left an archive of personal papers demonstrating that the gifts were a practice that had begun a decade earlier, it is fairly certain that the others also had been receiving tokens of appreciation for some time. If Draper, who was always eager to ensure that his generosity provided tax advantages, gave, as is likely, hundreds of thousands of dollars (AFI) to scientists during the 1960s as *personal* (i.e., nondeductible) presents in appreciation for their efforts, then he doubtlessly made even more lavish, tax-deductible contributions to the organizations within which those efforts took place.

Yet another indication of Draper's role can be found in Carleton Putnam's observation, in a letter in spring 1964, that "Dr. Garrett has received an appeal from Dr. Gayre asking *him* to appeal to our source of funds for $10,000" for a "cruise along the north coast of Africa to ascertain whether the North Africans are Caucasians."[23] Although Robert Gayre of Gayre and Nigg, a Scottish anthropologist, was a member of the IAAEE's Executive Committee and editor in chief of the *Mankind Quarterly,* Garrett was personally much closer to the Colonel, receiving $50,000 ($214,000 AFI) in Draper's will in addition to the regular annual presents, and of all the scientists in the campaign against civil rights, he enjoyed the most influence with their benefactor. Garrett headed one of the committees disbursing Draper's funds, publicly acknowledging that "I have placed several grants myself" for research on race, and Garrett was the natural choice, Gayre accurately reasoned, to request the Colonel's support for a newly conceived project.[24]

At first "our source of funds" appeared to approve funding for the expedition, which Gayre arranged to have conducted "nominally" under sponsorship of Duquesne University's Institute of African Affairs, where director Geza Grosschmid was a personal friend and fellow member of the Order of St. Lazarus. According to Gayre's proposal to the institute, "A Study of the Racial Drift of the African Littoral," an investigation of the races along the coastlands, was intended "to prove . . . that there occurred a drift of White Genes from the Mediterranean down both the West and East coasts of Africa," thus accounting for "allegedly native African high civilizations at Zimbabwe and elsewhere."[25]

The initial proposal noted that an unnamed "friend of Duquesne University"—no doubt the same person who had been Earnest Sevier Cox's "Northern friend"—would contribute $10,000 ($59,100 AFI) toward the excursion, although a more detailed, subsequent description specified the source as the "Human Genetics Fund," which appeared to be merely the "Draper Committee" on which Garrett served, embellished with a title that created the illusion of a truly scientific organization and distanced the Colonel from the ultimate recipient of his money. In Gayre's correspondence as editor of the *Mankind Quarterly*, he had earlier advised Nathaniel Weyl, a frequent contributor to the journal who needed a paid assistant for some routine clerical work, that money for the purpose might be available from the Human Genetics Fund, "with which Professor Garrett is connected," again strongly indicating that the fund originated with Draper.[26] And in 1958, Audrey Shuey, professor of psychology at Randolph-Macon Women's College in Lynchburg, Virginia noted that the "Human Genetics Foundation" had provided a grant for the printing, and was going to offer additional funds for the advertising, of her book *The Testing of Negro Intelligence*, which concluded that blacks were intellectually inferior to whites; Garrett had contributed the book's preface and would recommend it in the ad campaign.[27] Interestingly, one of Pioneer's few grants before 1971 went to Randolph-Macon—undoubtedly for Shuey's work—suggesting that there was not a very clearly defined line between projects enjoying Pioneer's officially acknowledged support and those financed by the "Human Genetics Fund" or "Foundation," whatever name was used by the "Draper Committee" headed by Garrett; of course, in any case, the money always came originally from the Colonel.

Duquesne eventually withdrew its sponsorship of Gayre's project shortly after the university president received a letter, sent also to the local media, from an African physicist at the nearby University of Pittsburgh, maintaining that the expedition had "nothing else for its purpose other than promoting racial hatred" and calling it particularly "unfortunate that a Catholic Institution . . . is the sponsor."[28] Six months later, when Gayre was planning a trip to the United States for which he again needed funds, he explained to Weyl that Garrett had approached "Draper to see if he would pay, and he is apparently unwilling to do so," a reluctance that Gayre attributed to the Colonel's dissatisfaction with the "African trip." Although, according to Gayre, the other segregationists decidedly favored his presence in the United States, they were "afraid to offend" Draper by pushing the issue because "the financing of Putnam and . . . Garrett's work comes from that source."[29]

A final indication of Draper's role as financier of the scientists' campaign is the fact that all the segregationists' projects intersected on Harry Weyher's desk. Indeed, the flow of correspondence indicated that everyone else looked to the Colonel's attorney and the president of his fund as both clearinghouse and locus of the final decision on a whole host of matters that certainly seemed like strange concerns for a partner in a New York City law firm. For example, Weyher solicited suggestions for research projects to bolster the segregationist case, probably so that they could be presented to the Colonel for funding consideration. He also circulated the draft of scientific papers that, though apparently intended for publication in the *Mankind Quarterly,* had been sent to *him,* and scientists such as George submitted their comments to the attorney. An analysis of "The Factor of Race on Human Infection" by a professor at the University of Southern Mississippi, for example, considered whether there might be disease germs benign to one race but malignant to the other. In his response to Weyher concerning the paper, George wrote that, although "not many disease entities" fit such a model, he nevertheless thought the work contained "a fine idea that might be very useful," noting that "the venereal disease situation" could produce "the greatest alarm" for parents whose children attended integrated schools.[30] In another instance, Weyher sent Garrett, an associate editor of the *Mankind Quarterly,* the draft of an article, noting that it would be "much edited before publication, but I thought you might like to glance at it now." And when George submitted an article to *Reader's Digest,* Weyher assured him that if the popular magazine rejected the piece, the *Quarterly* "would like to have it." The New York attorney seemed to have at least as much influence at the journal as its editors.[31]

When George was working on *The Biology of the Race Problem,* a scientific attack on integration written at the request of the State of Alabama and then distributed by the National Putnam Letters Committee, behind the scenes Weyher played a major role at every stage of the document's preparation. He circulated a preliminary draft of the report to his fellow board member Trevor and a number of the scientists, all of whom then submitted their comments and corrections to the New York attorney to be passed along to George.[32] When a first printing was ready, it was Weyher, again, who solicited reactions from the usual participants, informing George that, in the opinion of "numerous persons," there ought to be a foreword, much of which the attorney himself then wrote. A grateful George actually wanted Weyher to sign his contribution, declaring that "few people have been more intimately or helpfully involved" with the project, but Weyher, who guarded his privacy almost as much as Draper, declined. In addition, Weyher informed George that there were "a number of errors" in the report and sent the manuscript back to its author, instructing the scientist to "send me a fully corrected copy" so that "any future printings will be better."[33] The final report bore only George's name, but there was no doubt who had supervised the project. Indeed, Weyher also made decisions about the number of copies to be printed, monitored the costs of the process, and then provided instructions to the printer for the bulk distribution of copies, most of which were sent to him and Citizens' Councils chief William Simmons, with lesser numbers to Garrett, Putnam, and George. And finally, when interested parties were informed that copies of the report were available from the National Putnam Letters Committee's New York post office box address, a copy of the notification went to Weyher.[34]

Little else escaped the attorney's input. He forwarded Draper's money—anonymous gifts of stock—to Mississippi's official anti–civil rights organization and played a major role in planning the strategy for lawsuits seeking to prevent integrated education in Georgia and Mississippi, although his own firm had no official role in these proceedings.[35] When the scientists involved with the IAAEE wanted to publish a collection of essays on race, the project had to be subjected to "discussion with Mr. Weyher," and until he made a decision, wrote the prospective editor, "we do not know exactly how much material we can publish." When Princeton sociologist Melvin Tumin published his attack on the segregationists' scientific evidence, Putnam asked for Weyher's permission to compose the "symposium of replies" from Garrett, George, and himself that was eventually financed by Draper and distributed by the National Putnam Letters Committee. Putnam also consulted with the New York attorney on the best choice of administrator for the committee.[36]

Weyher even contemplated funding—no doubt with Draper's money—a motion picture made from the book *White Teacher in a Black School,* a first-person account of a teacher who chose to ignore his family's sensible warning that "the Negroes have become a menace to decent society" and that it was not possible "to educate a bunch of young savages who hate your guts just because you're white," only to find their words confirmed when his charges respond to good intentions with relentless hostility, cursing at him, threatening him, and slashing his tires. The teacher finds degradation ubiquitous in the black community: One student offers him sex in exchange for a passing grade, another student's mother does the same and then charges him with racism, and local gangs demand the beating of a "blind or crippled person" as an initiation rite. Issued by a publisher specializing in far-right literature, the book claimed to be based on actual incidents in "regular everyday public schools," although the language attributed to streetwise urban teenagers sounded more like a lampoon of middle-class notions about ghetto slang; for example, one student wanted to "get me . . . a snazzy car and a sassy chick."[37]

In addition, Weyher obsessively monitored public reaction to the segregationist campaign. When the Citizens' Councils ran an advertisement in newspapers throughout the country, declaring that Lincoln's real "Hopes for the Negro" were complete separation and preferably colonization abroad, Weyher collected "far in excess of one thousand" editorials and articles on the ad. And, noted the attorney approvingly, "Billy Simmons" reported receipt of almost 30,000 replies to the council, which had included a tearsheet in the ad for readers to request additional information. After Putnam's book, *Race and Reason,* was published, opposing racial equality on the basis of blacks' intellectual inferiority, Weyher hired a clipping service to collect any references to the work in the daily press—which he supplemented with items, missed by the service, that he had found on his own—and then issued a regular monthly tabulation of the cumulative results, noting, with satisfaction, that clippings with a "favorable attitude" constituted an overwhelming majority.[38] The Colonel, it is important to remember, always insisted on evidence that his contributions were having an effect.

Weyher also monitored hostile newspaper articles, organizing responses by the scientists. In one case he instructed George to craft a reply, which was then first sent to Weyher for scrutiny before being returned to the anatomist for mailing so that it would not bear a "suspicious" New York postmark;[39] in another, he circulated the description of a study demonstrating that an enriched environment increased brain size and weight in mice, asking the scientists to explain why these results should not change the conclusion that black intellectual inferiority was unalterable.[40]

Well-informed members of the public might have been aware of the anti-integration efforts of Garrett, Putnam, George, Simmons, and the many other activists who eagerly sought the media's attention for their efforts. Particularly sharp-eyed readers of segregationist literature might even have noticed the contributions of Pioneer board member Trevor, who authored articles on Africa in the Citizens' Councils publication, the *Citizen,* during the height of the civil rights movement. In a "Special Report" in late 1962, for example, he described the rigid tribal segregation observed in his own travels in Kenya, noting that "advocates of race-mixing" in the United States should learn from "what the native African has found works best . . . among his own people. Crosses between tribal groups usually show up quite poorly when compared to the really splendid physical specimens . . . among . . . the comparatively pure-bred tribes." Trevor also quoted an anthropologist with experience in Kenya, who found it no more possible to "alter a man's racial characteristics" than to train a Pekingese to act like a bloodhound.[41]

But aside from the very brief flap in early 1960, when the existence of the two "Draper Committees" was reported in a few small publications, neither Weyher's activities nor even his name was mentioned in any news report. Like a Professor Moriarty of scientific racism, the Colonel's attorney and president of the board of his fund lurked constantly behind the scenes, planning and orchestrating strategy, evaluating tactics, but always careful not to let his own presence, nor that of his "client," reach public awareness.

This extensive involvement on Weyher's part in so many different projects, not to mention the extraordinary deference paid to him by all the other participants in the campaign against civil rights, is understandable only if he had the keys to the safe—if he was, as George so succinctly put it, the "attorney for . . . [the] money bags."[42] The evidence leaves little doubt that Weyher was carrying out, enthusiastically, the wishes of his client and mentor, "our source of funds" for the scientists and their associates. Just as Morgan Guaranty managed the finances of Draper's investments, Harry Weyher managed the finances of his politics.

## The IAAEE: A Free and Open Discussion

The most scientifically ambitious project to enjoy Draper's support was the International Association for the Advancement of Ethnology and Eugenics, incorporated in 1959 for two purposes, according to its secretary, A. James Gregor. First, the association would seek to restore "an intellectual climate in the United States, and throughout the Western World, which would permit a free and open discussion of racial . . . problems"; second, it hoped to "re-open the American academic world to the current of European ideas."[43] Combining the Colonel's two main interests, these twin goals reflected, respectively, the organization's desire to provide a scientific argument in opposition to the civil rights movement and to resuscitate the ideology of racial hygiene, which had lain lifeless since being discredited by exposure of the Third Reich's atrocities. Also in keeping with its dual purposes, the IAAEE brought together on its Executive Committee scientists from both sides of the Atlantic. However, geographic location did not suggest any diminished enthusiasm for either of these aims, the Americans being strongly supportive of the larger issues of racial hygiene, as were the Europeans of the resistance to equality for blacks. Indeed, both groups saw the Southern struggle as a part of a larger movement for white supremacy, seeking to keep blacks segregated and powerless not just in the Southern United States but also in South Africa and what was then Rhodesia (now Zimbabwe).

Although the IAAEE eventually boasted an Executive Committee listing thirty-five scientists from the United States and Europe—every one a firm believer in the rigid separation of races—a much smaller group made up the association's core, four insiders who had been named among the original directors in the Articles of Incorporation and who continued to plan and administer the organization's activities. The most important of the four, and certainly the Colonel's favorite, was Henry Garrett, the recipient of regular cash presents from "our source" as well as the $50,000 ($214,000 AFI) from his will. Arguably the most eminent of the scientific segregationists, Garrett was near the end of a lengthy professional career in which he had been president of the American Psychological Association in 1946, the Eastern Psychological Association in 1944, and the Psychometric Society in 1943, a fellow of the American Association for the Advancement of Science, a member of the prestigious National Research Council, editor for a decade of the American Psychology Series, and chair of the Psychology Department at Columbia University for sixteen years before returning to his home state in 1955 to accept a visiting professorship in the Department of Education at the University of Virginia.[44]

After the *Brown* decision, however, Garrett abandoned any pretense at scientific detachment, becoming a tireless polemicist for segregation; in letters to scientific journals and in articles in the IAAEE's house organ, the *Mankind Quarterly,* he constantly sought to portray blacks as "savages"—the "blood brothers" of Africans, who lacked "towels, handkerchiefs and toilet paper"—and, of course, unfit for association with whites. "No matter how low . . . an American white may be, his ancestors built the civilizations of Europe," Garrett declared, "and no matter how high . . . a Negro may be, his ancestors were (and his kinsmen still are) savages in an African jungle." And the reason for their backwardness, he explained, was physiological: The "normal" black resembled a white European after frontal lobotomy.[45] It was thus "unsound," Garrett concluded, to treat "persons . . . strictly as individuals"; racial separation was necessary both to protect the inferior blacks, so many of whom were still "only a cut above savagery" and, more importantly, to

prevent the civil rights movement from attaining the "widespread amalgamation" that he maintained was their real goal. "Should American whites under the emotional goading of various pressure groups" actually "absorb"
blacks through intermarriage, he warned, "our country would inevitably
deteriorate intellectually, morally, and materially," and, as an understandable
consequence, he observed in *U.S. News & World Report,* white parents would
"teach their children to hate Negroes."[46] Not reluctant to follow his own prediction, in private correspondence Garrett suggested that "our best bet" to
prevent implementation of the *Brown* decision was to "make the white
schools so unpleasant for them that the Negroes withdraw."[47]

Though unelaborated in his prediction of national decline, the reference
to "pressure groups" was clarified in Garrett's manifesto in the *Mankind
Quarterly,* "The Equalitarian Dogma," in which he named as the culprits
"oversensitized" Jews, whose "preoccupation . . . with racial matters . . . is
evident in the activities of various Jewish organizations." Interestingly, when
the "Dogma" was reprinted in more widely read publications, including *U.S.
News & World Report,* Garrett excised all references to Jews.[48]

However, this deletion did not suggest any change in Garrett's thinking.
Indeed, he soon became a contributing editor of *Western Destiny,* a magazine descended from a series of neo-Nazi publications. In 1958, Roger Pearson, an Englishman residing in Calcutta, who later moved to the United States
and received more than $1 million in grants from Pioneer, founded the
Northern League in Britain as a postwar gathering point for Nazis; dedicated to Teutonic unity and preservation of the superior Nordics from the threat
of "infection" by "unhealthy stock" (i.e., intermarriage with non-Nordics),
the league published the journal *Northern World,* based largely on the writing
of the Third Reich's most important expert on "race science," Hans F. K.
Günther, a founding member of the league. The new organization soon attracted the attention of neo-Nazis in the United States, and Pearson eventually joined Willis Carto in California, who was publishing the anti-Semitic
*Right,* the alliance producing a merger of their respective publications into
*Western Destiny,* which listed the two men as associate editors, each under a
pseudonym: Carto was "E. L. Anderson, Ph.D.," a name under which he had
already authored articles for *Right,* and Pearson was "Edward Langford," one
of a long list of aliases he used over the next four decades.[49] *Western Destiny*
combined the Englishman's pseudoscientific Nordicism with the Californian's obsession with the Jewish Culture Distorter, "inherently unable to be
in tune with . . . Western Culture and Spirituality."[50]

Garrett remained a contributing editor when, after only two years, publication of *Western Destiny* was "suspended" and replaced by the "new" *Amer-*

*ican Mercury,* which Carto's Liberty Lobby had just acquired, turning the magazine founded by H. L. Mencken and later controlled by the John Birch Society into what one historian has called a "blatantly Hitlerian" periodical.[51] This was no hyperbolic description. Among many expressions of adulation for the Nazi regime, *Mercury* published an article by Manfred Roeder, an official in the Third Reich later jailed for the terrorist bombing of immigrant hostels in West Germany, praising Hitler as "the most popular statesman of all history." In addition, the magazine provided excerpts from notes it claimed that the Führer had dictated during his final days, insisting that "without the Jews and without this lackey of theirs [i.e., FDR], things could have been quite different": The naturally harmonious relationship between Germany and the United States would not have been "poisoned" by the decision of "world Jewry . . . to set up its most powerful bastion" in Washington. *Mercury* also frequently praised Nazi Colonel Otto Skorzeny as "a great soldier who dedicated his life to the survival of the West"; probably the most famous member of the Waffen SS, and Hitler's personal favorite, Skorzeny, according to the Führer, had "saved the Third Reich" by his immediate and brutal crushing of the 1944 coup attempt by a group of high-ranking military officers.[52]

Unsurprisingly, Garrett also became the favorite scientist of the Citizens' Councils, contributing a column to their monthly, the *Citizen,* in which he regularly preached to the converted on the "immature and essentially savage nature of the Negro," the evils of "mongrelization," and the danger that "race mixing" in the early grades will quickly "produce a Negroid culture." Interviewed on the "Citizens' Councils Forum," the organization's television program, Garrett told the viewing audience that the United States "is a European civilization, a white man's civilization . . . where the Negro is considered to be more or less guests."[53]

A second particularly influential member of the IAAEE's Executive Committee was zoologist Robert Kuttner, a founding director and president of the association, and another scientist with a long history of involvement with neo-Nazi groups. Unlike Garrett, however, who apparently gravitated toward Carto's Liberty Lobby network late in his life as a result of shared opposition to the *Brown* decision, Kuttner was a youthful true believer and an energetic participant in neo-Nazi groups even before obtaining his doctorate from the University of Connecticut in 1959. In the mid-1950s and not yet thirty years old, he was already the associate editor and a regular contributor for the *Truth Seeker,* a virulently anti-Semitic publication dedicated to the belief that the demand for racial equality was being used by Jews as part of their "wish to destroy" white civilization. Gentiles in the United States had been—in *Truth Seeker*'s favorite verb—"Jewized" into abandoning the "eternal truths of Nature" offered by the "racist" in favor of "false slogans" of equality that would foolishly extend the "democracy of Nordics . . . to . . . include Mongols and Negroes."[54] Internationally, Kuttner explained in the journal, it was "only a matter of time before the non-European races dispute with us for the regions we have reserved for our own future expansion, . . . lands . . . needed to rule the world of tomorrow." If the white race was to prevail, if it was to be "our star of destiny which shines over this planet," he emphasized, then racial solidarity was a biological mandate: "Loyalty to race is the patriotism of Nature."[55] While an editor of the *Truth Seeker,* Kuttner also contributed articles to Pearson's *Northern World* on the importance of Nordic purity and to the fascist *South African Observer* on the "wisdom of apartheid."[56]

Kuttner's contributions to these journals naturally brought him to the attention of Carto, who enthusiastically recommended his "wonderful work" to Earnest Sevier Cox, praising the young zoologist as an "extremely valuable man for our side, and a racist to his toes."[57] Kuttner soon became a prominent member of the Liberty Lobby and a contributor to *Right,* the American predecessor of *Western Destiny,* similarly based on the belief that "the Jew" was the cause of "every vile thing," the source of all contemporary "anarchy, chaos, ruin, perversion and . . . filth." Indeed, unlike many other right-wing publications, which typically welcomed anyone vigorously opposed to communism, *Right* actually maintained that, just as Jews had created communism, they were now leading the *war* on communism, both movements intending to achieve the same goal: "Jewish Conquest." When *Northern World* and *Right* ceased publication, Kuttner, like Garrett, became an editor and frequent contributor to their successors—first *Western Destiny* and then *American Mercury*—explaining in the latter that, unlike European whites, who had "earned" their own freedom "by merit or by valor" in the face of brutal oppression, blacks "enjoyed a slavery unparalleled in history for mildness and humanity" yet were unable to set themselves free until liberty "was handed to the Negro . . . at little cost to himself."[58]

Carto's trusted associate, Kuttner appeared as a representative of the Liberty Lobby before a House Subcommittee in 1963 to testify against impending civil rights legislation, accompanied by an attorney for the lobby, who added that the zoologist was also president of the IAAEE. Kuttner's statement to the subcommittee stressed two points. In response to the legislation's assumption that discrimination was economically inefficient, he noted that the Germans, "who had a reputation for efficiency," nevertheless "exiled and executed scores of thousands of talented . . . members of a minority group . . . against whom they entertained prejudices," thus demonstrating that the refusal to provide commercial services to blacks would do no harm to the economy; obviously this argument was formulated long before the Liberty Lobby began its campaign to deny existence of the Holocaust. Offering his second observation as the "viewpoint of a scientist," Kuttner explained that a legal requirement for blacks to be permitted the same public accommodations as whites would inevitably produce hostility because of the "element of compulsion," a situation that he again compared to the treatment of "minorities" in Germany, where "racial wars" had developed because the majority were resentful at being compelled to tolerate the presence of racial groups that they otherwise would have accepted with only "minor . . . hostilities." And "perhaps we should consider," Kuttner concluded, "that they had justice on their side." His point was unmistakable: By being too pushy, Jews had provoked their own fate in the Third Reich, and if blacks, similarly, continued to demand equality, they too risked converting benign neglect into justifiably violent retaliation.[59]

But all these detestable pronouncements seemed almost moderate in comparison with the fulminations that Kuttner regularly delivered on the actual results of "Integrated Living." Calling "race mixing" an obstacle to "upward evolution," he noted that only in a zoo does one find such abnormal behavior among animals, yet it was currently "fashionable" among young white women, he observed, "to have an interracial bastard and a heroin habit instead of a college diploma." In the *Citizen* he provided lurid stories of white girls "brainwashed" by liberalism to "accept rape from Negro thugs" uncomplainingly as an understandable consequence of slavery and oppression.[60] Invited to address the annual Leadership Conference of the Citizens' Councils, Kuttner raised the central question for the "average Southern champion," the issue that captured the argument over integration "in a nutshell": "Do you want your daughter . . . to marry a Negro?" But as a Northerner who claimed to have lived in "the ghetto," he ridiculed the notion that black men had any intention to *marry* Southerners' daughters: Their real objective was to place "white girls" on "Ho' Row,'" not with "rings on their fingers," but with "needle scars on their arms." Thus the true purpose of integration, Kuttner explained to his Southern audience, was to facilitate the use of *"white girls . . . [as] the major economic resource"* of black men:

> If you have a drug habit costing $60 or $80 a day, you can survive only if you catch a white girl. And if you want to keep her, you better put her on a habit too, because when she wakes up, she'll run back to mother with her brown baby, if mother will take her. . . . Believe me, no black male can steal enough color TV's out of hotels to support a drug habit. You can't rob pension checks off senior citizens except once a day a month, . . . and it is too small to last you more than one good "high." You can't rob liquor stores and grocery stores

forever. . . . The only answer is to catch a white girl, and integration makes that much easier today.[61]

Like Garrett, Kuttner regularly received substantial checks from the Colonel each year at Christmas as recognition for his efforts.

Easily the most sophisticated member of the IAAEE's inner circle was A. James Gregor, one of the founding directors and the organization's secretary, who eventually became a prominent political scientist at Berkeley and the Hoover Institute. As the secretary, it was Gregor who had announced the association's desire to "re-open the American academic world" to European thought. Of course, the notion that the academic world had been "closed" to ideas from abroad might seem a dubious assumption—especially at a time when the intellectual influence of European émigrés such as Theodore Adorno was at its peak in the United States—unless properly decoded as a reference to discredited fascist ideology. Indeed, at the time, Gregor was extolling the brilliance of the "last phase . . . [of] National Socialist race theory," based on principles advanced by Hitler and developed into a "scientifically sound and emotionally satisfying" philosophy, "little . . . known outside the immediate intellectual circle which fostered it." This was a "far more profound theory," argued Gregor, than the "tragi-comic image . . . of hysterical Nordicism"—a more mature approach eschewing the earlier obsession with coloration, stature, and cephalic, facial, and nasal indices in favor of Hitler's emphasis on deeds and achievements. Thus, Gregor concluded, Nazi policy on race had nothing to do with hierarchical judgments or comparative intrinsic worth but was concerned only with the scientific recognition of differences, the members of each group developing according to their racial "archetype": Nordics, for example, treasured a Nordic ideal, Mediterraneans a Mediterranean one. No mention was made of Jews or Gypsies.[62]

Among the IAAEE members, Gregor also had the most nuanced position in opposition to the *Brown* decision, insisting that even "compelling evidence of Negro biological inferiority" would be irrelevant to the issue of school segregation, which always denied access to "an individual . . . not the abstract collective Negro." Thus it was illogical, he argued, to exclude "the intelligent, moral, clean and enterprising Negro" from a school because of the lower average test scores or behavioral standards of "his *group*." This seemingly more liberal position was not to be mistaken for a belief on Gregor's part that the integration of *some* black students might be permissible if they met the appropriate standards but rather reflected his contention that the segregationists could prevail legally only by making "*race, in and of itself, . . . a relevant fact.*" This he proposed to do by demonstrating that even the most highly qualified blacks suffered "psychodynamic impairments" and "serious inferiority feelings" as a result of contact with whites during their formative years. The putative desire to protect black children by mandating their insulation from whites not only would be a more effective strategy in the courts, according to Gregor, but would provide a "morally 'attractive'" argument for a public that valued such matters.[63]

Indeed, Gregor had already authored an article that would be widely distributed as part of the IAAEE's reprint series, arguing that "what passes as 'race prejudice'" was really a natural preference of all social animals for their own kind and an inevitable disposition to discriminate systematically against individuals who exhibited gross physical differences from one's own group. The more permanent the physical difference and the higher its social visibility, the greater was the tendency to discriminate, and race, of course, was a prime example of both criteria. Thus, any attempt at integration, he concluded, would invariably result in "tensions and disharmonics which it is almost beyond the power of men to resolve."[64]

To this contention—that racial prejudice was "rooted in normal social behavior"—Gregor soon added the other element necessary for his preferred strategy to overturn the *Brown* decision. In conjunction with clinical psychologist Clairette Armstrong, he claimed that segregation protected black children from the "psychic tensions" caused by their inevitable rejection by whites; Armstrong was another member of the IAAEE's Executive Committee, who, as part of Trevor Sr.'s campaign in 1939, had opposed sanctuary for refugee children fleeing Nazi persecution, because of the "large proportion of . . . delinquencies, feebleminded, . . . school retardates . . . insanity and crime" among eastern European immigrants.[65] Indeed, Gregor and Armstrong maintained, "the delusional systems of adult Negro schizophrenics" showed striking similarities to the "behavior of Negro children . . . exposed to protracted contacts with whites." Not only did this argument make race itself the issue, as Gregor had desired, but it suggested that segregation was necessary to preserve black children's mental health.[66]

The last of the association's insiders was its treasurer, Donald A. Swan. Probably the most important person in the actual administration of the organization's activities, Swan functioned more like an executive director, although he was not even a member of the Executive Committee, having never completed his doctorate, a deficiency of some significance to the credential-conscious IAAEE. Born in New York to English parents, Swan was a brilliant child and, according to his mother, had been something of a minor celebrity as a member of radio's "quiz kids," a group of precocious know-it-alls. Completing high school at age fifteen, he began undergraduate work at

Queens College, where he attempted to found a "Nordic League" and was involved in a number of racist and anti-Semitic incidents, as a result of which he was granted "a leave of absence at the request of the college"; though distressed by his prejudice, Swan's mother acknowledged that her son "hated Jews and . . . the coloreds." Eventually completing his studies at Queens, he began graduate work in economics at Columbia University but was expelled, after two years, when his theft of books from the university's library was discovered; Swan later claimed that his treatment at Columbia stemmed from political persecution.[67]

In 1954, the obscure magazine *Exposé* published an unrepentantly confessional article titled "I Am an American Fascist" written by Swan's close friend H. Keith Thompson, who had been a special agent of the Nazi Overseas Intelligence Unit during the war and, as the registered U.S. agent of the Socialist Reich Party, had continued in the postwar period to provide assistance to Major General Otto Remer, formerly Hitler's personal bodyguard and one of the most important figures in the attempt to resurrect Nazism after the war. Announcing his "deep . . . admiration" for the Third Reich and its Führer, whose signed photograph adorned his desk, Thompson expressed particular outrage over the "vicious and vilely dishonorable" post war trials of Nazi "leaders and heroes," instigated "by the Communists and world Jewry."[68] In the next issue, Swan, only nineteen years old at the time, responded to Thompson's article with his own passionate declaration of like-mindedness. Praising Thompson as "a fearless American patriot [who] has spoken out against the smears of the Jewish 'gestapo'" and the Yiddish stooges in Moscow . . . intent on preventing the Nordic Peoples from realizing their rightful aspirations," Swan proclaimed,

> Despite our relatively small numbers, we, the Nordic people, have been responsible for almost all the scientific, literary, artistic, commercial, industrial, military, and cultural achievements of the world. The other races can merely imitate, without any contributions of their own. The world we live in today is a product of Nordic inventiveness, and genius. Only the unfortunate spectacle of Nordic fighting Nordic in the 1st and 2nd World Wars has produced the chaos of today, and prevented the millennium of a "Pax Nordica." I too am an American fascist.[69]

Although Gregor was officially the IAAEE's secretary, it was typically the energetic Swan who carried on the association's correspondence, compiled its "basic mailing list," wrote letters of solicitation to likely new members, sent out notification of meetings, and performed much of the tactical paperwork.[70] In preparation for the scientists' legal assault on *Brown*, for example, he organized the expert witnesses, compiled and abstracted the many studies on "race and cerebral morphology" presented by the segregationists, and wrote substantial portions of the brief himself. (Indeed, Swan and George S. Leonard, a member of the legal team, had a falling out because, according to one of the expert witnesses, "Swan felt that he did all of the work and George got all the money.")[71] Exceptionally bright, totally dedicated to the racist cause, and multilingual to boot, Swan also coordinated the work when different authors contributed to an IAAEE publication and, when necessary, translated articles submitted to the *Mankind Quarterly* by European authors from French or German into English.[72]

In 1966, Swan was arrested and indicted on twelve counts of mail fraud stemming from his use of more than 100 fictitious names to order various products, from which he had made an estimated $100,000 ($551,000 AFI); subsequently convicted, he received a three-year sentence. (According to one acquaintance, the judge was particularly harsh after Swan addressed him with an ethnic slur.) Apparently embarrassed by his criminal behavior, the IAAEE temporarily severed Swan's name from any affiliation with its projects, although the association seemed less troubled by other materials discovered in his home by U.S. marshals at the time of his arrest: an arsenal of weapons, photographs of Swan with members of the American Nazi Party, a "cache of Nazi paraphernalia, including swastika flags . . . and hundreds of anti-Semitic, anti-Negro and anti-Catholic tracts."[73]

Indeed, upon his release Swan remained one of the most important members of the inner circle close to Weyher and Draper, reemerging as a contributor to IAAEE publications and later receiving a number of Pioneer grants. Even more noteworthy as an indication of his significance, after Draper's death Swan was given the prestigious task of determining the disposition of the Colonel's library, a portion of which probably wound up in his own extensive collection of Nazi literature, which H. Keith Thompson called "one of the best on the subject." When Swan died in 1981, Pioneer provided a grant to purchase his entire library from his mother; according to May Swan, there were some 20,000 volumes, requiring four truckers for their removal.[74]

The other initial members of the IAAEE, though not as active as those in the group's nucleus, had similarly unsavory backgrounds. Charles Callan Tansill, for example, a well-known historian at Georgetown University, had been an outspoken defender of Hitler both before and after the war and a member of the "Viereck circle" along with Thompson, the Nazi agent essentially operating behind enemy lines, and Francis Parker Yockey, whose notion of the Jews as "Culture Distorters" had furnished the basis for Carto's Liberty Lobby. George Sylvester Viereck was a poet and novelist, dubbed

"Hitler's prostitute" for his work as head of a Nazi propaganda network in the United States, who served time in prison for the mass distribution of pro-Nazi materials during the war. Before the war, Tansill spent a year in Germany, delivering an address in support of Hitler on Berlin radio among other activities; after the allied victory, he blamed Roosevelt for the foolish opposition to the Nazis and claimed that the postwar Far Eastern Military Tribunal should have been convened in Washington, the location of the *real* culprits. Before the *Brown* decision, on Jefferson Davis's birthday, Tansill had given a speech to a group of confederate loyalists with such a vigorous denunciation of Abraham Lincoln as an unprincipled enemy of the valiant Southern "struggle for freedom" that even die-hard segregationists were embarrassed; after the decision he publicly encouraged officials to "defy the Supreme Court."[75]

Another initial IAAEE member, Herbert C. Sanborn, chair of the Department of Philosophy and Psychology at Vanderbilt University for the three decades before 1942, had also been a long-time Nazi sympathizer, blaming the International Jewish banking conspiracy for World War II and then participating in the postwar campaign, orchestrated by Thompson, for the release of Hitler's chosen successor, former chief of the German navy Grand Admiral Karl Dönitz. Desegregation, according to Sanborn, was "the first step toward national suicide," leading to the destruction of "the racial qualities of the leading peoples of the world" in the attempt to improve to "some uncertain degree the quality . . . of inferior stocks."[76] As a group, the original American directors of the IAAEE represented probably the most significant coterie of fascist intellectuals in the postwar United States and perhaps in the entire history of the country.

Despite their political orientation, however, the members of the IAAEE shared one belief with Karl Marx: They were not so much interested in interpreting the world as in changing it. Indeed, at its inception the IAAEE seemed indistinguishable from another activist organization, the Association for the Preservation of Freedom of Choice (APFC), which filed a Certificate of Incorporation signed by substantially the same group of activists, including Garrett, Kuttner, Gregor, and Swan, a few months before incorporation of the IAAEE; listed as attorney for both groups was Alfred Avins, who also served as counsel for the Liberty Lobby. The APFC was itself the outgrowth of a local New York City group, the Emergency City-Wide Citizens Committee for the Preservation of Freedom of Choice, organized by Gregor and Swan to oppose the city's Sharkey-Isaacs-Brown bill outlawing racial discrimination by landlords against tenants and by real estate developers against buyers. The first attempt ever to bring the IAAEE core together resulted in a joint assembly of the two essentially identical organizations, announced by Swan as "The First General Meeting of: The International Society [*sic*] for the Advancement of Ethnology and Eugenics and The Association for the Preservation of Freedom of Choice."[77]

The purpose of the latter group, according to its Certificate of Incorporation, originally filed in New York City, sounded in part similar to the IAAEE's goal: to conduct scientific research into the problems of intergroup relations in a multiracial society. But in addition, the APFC frankly acknowledged its intention, before actually conducting any research, to resolve those problems and provide for the "fullest development" of different groups by promoting "the right of the individual to associate with only those persons with whom he wishes to associate." Appearing, as it did, five years before passage of the Civil Rights Act of 1964 and at a time when blacks were still struggling for equal access to housing and public accommodations, this language was unmistakably intended to protect and encourage discrimination, and it was recognized as such by the judge before whom the incorporation papers were filed. Referring to the group's purpose as "the negation of a whole series of fundamental and basic rights . . . vouchsafed to *everyone* by the United States Constitution," the Queens County Supreme Court Judge J. Irwin Shapiro suggested that the language of the charter was "but a cloak" for the real aim, "which is to say to certain segments of our population: 'You can't enter . . . ride . . . work . . . play . . . study . . . eat . . . walk . . . [or] worship here," and he denied approval for the certificate. As the APFC's attorney, Avins submitted a response, noting that only *"unreasonable"* discrimination was offensive to public policy; the refusal to rent an apartment was an example of racial discrimination both "reasonable" and "desirable," according to the attorney. Citing Avins's own example as decisive proof for his earlier, tentative conclusion, Shapiro, in a final pronouncement, pointed out that although the APFC was free to speak out in favor of racial discrimination, there was "no constitutional or statutory requirement that a 'hate group' be given a corporate charter." Carto's *Right* called Shapiro's ruling "another sordid example of Zionist perversion of traditional Nordic-American concepts" as well as "legal discrimination against the White Christian in his 'own' country."[78]

Although the APFC was soon successfully incorporated—by applying in Washington, D.C., where Avins and Tansill were residents—the organization's primary activities were a string of bizarre legal actions brought by Avins, including a discrimination suit alleging a conspiracy between the mayor of New York City and four city council members to elect "a member of the Negro race to be the President of the Borough of Manhattan," and a libel suit against a magazine that had quoted Swan's description of himself as "an American fascist."[79] Perhaps the APFC's single notable accomplishment, in keeping with the particular interest that had led to its formation, was a "symposium on anti-discrimination legislation, freedom of choice, and property rights in housing." Featuring contributions by many members of the IAAEE's Executive Committee, the "symposium"—actually a collection of solicited essays and comments—was a relentless attack on open housing laws as a violation of the "fundamental human right" of individuals to live only among "people of their own race, color, religion, or national origin." As the project's organizer, Avins had originally intended to publish the collection in the *Chicago-Kent Law Review,* for which he was the faculty editor, but the school's administration objected to his use of the journal as a platform for his views on race. The papers were published instead by the Liberty Lobby, which then distributed the resulting book to members of both the House and Senate Judiciary Committees when Avins appeared before each of those bodies as part of the Lobby's campaign against the Civil Rights Act of 1966.[80]

In contrast to this short-lived attempt to defeat equal rights by counterposing the right to "freedom of choice," the IAAEE approach, based primarily on "scientific" evidence of white supremacy and the importance of racial purity, proved much more enduring. Using the Colonel's preferred weapon, the printer, the IAAEE produced a steady stream of publications for years, all arguing the impossibility of blacks and whites existing on equal terms in the same society.

The most important of these works was the journal, the *Mankind Quarterly.* Although, strictly speaking, the *Quarterly* was not a publication of the IAAEE and thus did not receive Draper's money directly, it was clearly created to serve as the house organ of the group that was funded by the Colonel and as a vehicle through which the members of the association, many of whom also enjoyed his individual financial support for their work, could express their views. "The purpose of the M.Q.," acknowledged its editor in private correspondence, "was to provide our small group with the opportunity of being published," especially because "our views" were no longer tolerated in other outlets.[81] Moreover, the IAAEE's official "Statement of Aims and Objectives" noted that "the Association is . . . actively engaged in promoting and distributing the new scientific journal, the *Mankind Quarterly,*" and for a time membership in the association automatically entitled one to receive the journal. "Dear friend" solicitations to prospective subscribers were mailed out on IAAEE letterhead, and the association even sent "2,000 *MQ* sample copies to a list of conservatives" as part of an attempt to generate interest in the journal.[82]

In addition, everyone involved in producing the journal was also a prominent member of the IAAEE—Garrett functioning as an associate editor, Kuttner, Gregor, and eventually Swan as assistant editors, and the two most important European members of the association also in editorial roles. The editor-in-chief, Scottish anthropologist Robert Gayre of Gayre and Nigg—the name a reminder of his baronial title and long list of heraldic associations—had also been editor of the German journal *Folk* during the early years of the Reich and was a disciple of Hans F. K. Günther, the Nazi social scientist obsessed with determining intra-European racial composition from the shape of the skull. In the midst of World War II, Gayre had authored a book filled with photographic examples of racial "types"—Nordic, Alpine, Baltic, Sudetish, and Dinaric—taken directly from "Professor . . . Günther's authoritative work on . . . racial science" so that national boundaries could be properly revised "to achieve *racial* stability." While the allies fought Nazi aggression, Gayre explained that the real problem in Europe was a lack of "racial homogeneity" within nations, and, after analyzing the "cephalic index," the width of the face, the "nasal form index," and the proportion of "pointed faces" in central Europe, he proposed that Germany's eastern border be redrawn to make the "Slav states . . . basically more Alpine . . . [and] the Germans . . . considerably more Nordic." After the war, he was a close associate of Pearson's Northern League, and when Pearson translated Günther's writing on "Aryan religion," in the *Mankind Quarterly* Gayre offered enthusiastic praise for the work, boasting of his own prewar acquaintance with the great German "expert."[83]

Believing, as he did, in the importance of racial homogeneity, Gayre was horrified by the miscegenation he saw taking place throughout the world. Although he certainly would have agreed with the APFC that the freedom to choose the race of one's neighbor was a basic human right, to marry someone of a different race was "no more a right of . . . choice" to Gayre "than . . . to go round shooting policemen." In language reminiscent of Charles Benedict Davenport's bizarre notions of genetic disharmonies half a century earlier, he maintained that miscegenation produced "instability" in races whose "inherent" temperaments differed from each other and "many physical as well as mental disturbances": "crowding of teeth, for example, . . . where one stock has naturally large teeth and the other small jaws."[84]

In addition, Gayre maintained that the world was experiencing "the genetic collapse of the Caucasoids"—especially the superior Nordics, the only group he believed capable of democratic government—while "the Negro . . . is breeding like rabbits, because all his natural predators have been removed." The result, he wrote to a frequent contributor to the *Quarterly,* was the "ugly phenomenon" in which arts "suited to the Negroid level" were becoming popular with whites.[85] Only in the white supremacist societies of South Africa and Rhodesia did Gayre see some hope for "evolutionary advance," and he was a frequent contributor to one of apartheid's strongest defenders, the fascist *South African Observer,* passing on articles on black inferiority that had originally appeared in the *Quarterly.* In fact, because of his own country's "anti-White stand," Gayre seriously contemplated renouncing his British nationality in favor of South African citizenship.[86]

The other prominent European member of the IAAEE originally involved in the *Mankind Quarterly* was, like Garrett, an associate editor: R. Ruggles Gates, a British geneticist who had contributed to the prewar Nazi literature on racial hygiene and a friend of the Colonel's to whom Draper had turned for suggestions on how to spend his money. Though well respected for his research in cytology, Gates had squandered much of his career on a misguided attempt to persuade his discipline that different races of human beings were actually five separate species; one review of his book noted dryly that Gates's views on this issue were "unique" among all physical anthropologists and geneticists.[87] Ironically, the standard criterion for distinguishing species is that they not be interfertile, exactly the characteristic that so distressed Gates; like Gayre, he opposed race crossing, maintaining that it caused "physical disharmonies" and "social failure of adjustment" and was cited during the 1930s as the scientific authority for "biology's warning against intermarriage between Jews and those of Germanic . . . race."[88]

As he recounted in a letter to George, behind every setback in his career, behind every professional disappointment and disagreement, Gates saw the malevolent hand of a Jewish conspiracy. While on an honorary fellowship in biology at Harvard just after the war, he expressed disagreement publicly with a Jewish professor in another department, an act that, he was certain, had led to the termination of his fellowship by Jews, who were secretively manipulating the system at Harvard "for their own purposes." Moving across the street to the university's Peabody Museum, he also found well-known anthropologist "Prof. [Earnest A.] Hooton playing the Jewish game": blocking publication of Gates's reply to criticism of his work by a Jewish scientist, the same scientist who "got . . . an English Jew to write an attack" on someone who agreed with Gates. Invited to Washington for a semester as a visiting professor at the traditionally black school, Howard University, he "found a little coterie of foreign Jews directing things behind the scenes"; when one of them circulated a paper on primitive races that Gates had written more than a decade earlier, "the University had the cheek to appoint a Faculty [Committee] to decide whether I was fit to teach these ignorant Negroes, very few of whom were fit to be in any university." Moreover, he complained, his work had been rejected by four scientific journals in the United States, "2 of them edited by Jews and the other two acting under pro-Jewish" influence. "I regard the combined propaganda of Jews and Negroes," Gates concluded, as "the greatest present menace to this country."[89]

Although its subtitle described the *Mankind Quarterly* as a "journal dealing with Race and Inheritance in the Fields of Ethnology, Ethno- and Human Genetics, Ethno-Psychology, Racial History, Demography, and Anthropo-Geography," instead of the scholarly attitude suggested by this impressive list of academic disciplines, editorial discussions revealed a desperate lobbying campaign, a beleaguered effort to win support for racism at a time when the society was finally realizing its moral bankruptcy. In keeping with his desire to use the journal to proselytize, the editor-in-chief often was interested not so much in the usual editorial decisions but in tactical maneuvers to convert conservatives, reluctant to support prompt implementation of court decrees, into full-blown bigots, opposed entirely to civil rights for blacks. "We should try to win over Prof. Dwight Ingle . . . the one person who is nearest to us in point of view," Gayre suggested, referring to the chair of the Department of Physiology at the University of Chicago, who had called integration an infringement on the right to "freedom of association" and had allowed Garrett to publish, in the prestigious *Perspectives in Biology and Medicine,* which Ingle edited, a slightly less mean-spirited version of "The Equalitarian Dogma" than the one that had appeared in the *Mankind Quarterly.* "If by writing for the M.Q.," Gayre schemed, "it closed other journals to Ingle, . . . that . . . would throw him right into our camp." (Ingle was eventually invited to contribute some observations on brain physiology and race to the *Quarterly,* but on almost every page any deviation on his part from the segregationists' position was annotated by cranky editorial insertions, like a teacher making comments on the paper of a misguided student.) William F. Buckley was another conservative whom Gayre judged "very close to our position" and whom he was "prepared to publish," even though "being [a Roman Catholic] he must deviate somewhat."[90]

Anyone actually supporting equal treatment for blacks was regarded as the enemy by the journal, to be attacked by one of the *Quarterly*'s editors. For example, when historian I. A. Newby authored a work critical of the scientists' defense of segregation, Gayre suggested to an IAAEE staff member—no doubt so that the idea could be forwarded to the attorney for the money bags for consideration—that the group "produce another *Mankind* monograph in which his book is torn apart. . . . Gregor is the best person to do this."[91]

Believing that science really did justify discrimination, the *Quarterly* had no sense that the former could or should be separated from the latter. Asked, early on, to participate on the journal's "Honorary Advisory Board," George naively declined the invitation. Not only did he acknowledge a lack of expertise in any of the appropriate fields, but feared he had been "an active partizan [*sic*]" in opposition to "race mixing," which "might detract from the Quarterly's . . . reputation for objectivity"; Gayre assured him that "partizan activities on the racial question" would not be a "particular disability."[92]

Indeed, partisanship on race was regarded almost as a prerequisite at the journal, with prospective contributors evaluated more on political correctness than professional expertise. When Gayre asked George to recommend a scientist knowledgeable on the differences between "Negro, Caucasoid and Mongoloid brains," the anatomist suggested the one person he knew to be "qualified" to prepare such a paper: J. C. Carothers, a research psychiatrist who had made "original observations" in Africa and written a well-known monograph surveying much of the literature on "the African Mind." In a World Health Organization publication Carothers had characterized blacks as "lacking in spontaneity, foresight, tenacity, judgment and humility; inept for . . . logic; and . . . unstable, impulsive, unreliable, irresponsible, and living in the present without reflection or ambition." Only six weeks later, however, George frantically wrote to Gayre that his earlier recommendation had been a dreadful error. Although the parts of the monograph that he had read himself had raised no concern, George had heard from a friend that other sections of this work on neurology were "heavily tainted with . . . WHO propaganda": Among other flaws, Carothers's study had failed to conclude that blacks were "vastly different *structurally*" from whites. Gayre himself contacted Carothers, finding George's friend was indeed correct: The psychiatrist "was quite out of sympathy with us." But perhaps, the *Quarterly*'s editor inquired of George, "your friend could send us a paper?"[93]

Efforts to publicize the *Quarterly* made no attempt to conceal its agenda, a reluctance to resort to euphemisms being an intentional element of the appeal to its target audience. "You have heard again and again that Negroes differ from Whites only in the 'color of their skin,'" observed the association's "Dear Friend" letter to prospective subscribers, promising that the *Quarterly* "brings you the other side of the story." Another letter from an IAAEE official, "hoping for good results" in response to the journal, pointed out that "the Republic was as sick with Negroism in the Reconstruction period as it is today, but the white people finally recovered their sanity." The IAAEE was inclined neither to pretense nor subtlety: This was going to be a publication frankly written *by* racists *for* racists.[94]

As the first issue demonstrated, the *Mankind Quarterly* would deliver everything it had promised. Gayre's introductory editorial noted that the journal was a necessary corrective to the tendency "during the last two decades . . . to neglect the racial aspects of man's inheritance" (i.e., since the Nazi writings on race). One article explained that racism was an "instinctive feeling . . . rooted in man's nature" and served "a biological function." Thus, when members of different races were "mixed together in the same community," hostility was an inevitable result because "each group is endangering the genetic integrity of the other"; in the South, for example, "Whites . . . tend to go berserk against . . . negroes . . . suspected of physical relations with Caucasoid women." The only solution, the article concluded, was to prevent the establishment of any multiracial community in the future and to resolve "existing communities . . . into separate societies on a racial basis."[95] This argument became a core theme in the *Quarterly*, to be repeated regularly during the next forty years in almost identical terms.

Another article in the first issue was a reprint of a work originally published fourteen years earlier at the end of the war by zoologist E. Raymond Hall, an instructive decision by the *Quarterly* because normally a scientific journal would never waste valuable space republishing a paper that had already appeared elsewhere; the article probably was brought to the journal's attention by Kuttner, who had earlier recommended the original version to readers of the *Truth Seeker.* In an analysis that, for the rest of the century, would be regularly cited as authoritative by Pioneer grantees—especially anti-immigration activists—Hall called it a "biological law" that *"two subspecies* [i.e., races] . . . *do not occur in the same geographic area";* even "to imagine" otherwise "is but wishful thinking and leads only to disaster or oblivion for one [race] or the other." For the country to protect itself, Hall found it "necessary to grant citizenship rights to one subspecies only" and to "deport . . . 'invaders' . . . of another subspecies." In particular, Hall was concerned that, in violation of "every biological law," United States citizenship was being granted to "Orientals," threatening the "survival of Caucasians in North America."[96]

Soon after the journal's appearance, a European anthropologist, who had agreed to let his name appear on the *Quarterly*'s "Honorary Advisory Board" before the initial publication, submitted his resignation, explaining that the journal's abuse of his discipline to support racism was offensive to him both as a scientist and as a former prisoner at Dachau. In a revealing comment on the attitude behind the scenes at the *Quarterly*, Gates accepted the resignation, replying to the anthropologist that he would never have been considered for board membership had the editors been aware of his "harrowing experience," which "naturally had such an effect on [his] mental outlook."[97] This was not a journal expected to be palatable to victims of Nazism.

For years the *Mankind Quarterly* would continue to spew out a relentless stream of scientific racism in articles that, for example, called blacks a "misfit in white society" or found them genetically inferior, but "even if . . . of adequate intelligence," undeserving of the benefits of citizenship. Although the journal was vigorously anticommunist, it was also sympathetic to the remnants of the Third Reich who sought to resurrect a Nazi movement based on white racial unity on both sides of the Iron Curtain, producing a white power bloc that would stretch from London to the Urals. The major obstacle to creating this consolidation of the vast "White forces" in Europe necessary to confront the threat of the "Yellow race," observed one article, was the "selfish minority interests" (i.e., Jews) standing in the way of German reunification.[98]

Of particular importance to the neo-Nazi movement was the journal's book review section, which, in addition to excoriating anyone who suggested the possibility of equal rights for blacks, functioned much like a pre–computer age Web site for racists, announcing publication, amid effusive praise, of the latest additions to the extremist canon. When the Liberty Lobby reprinted Cox's *White America* with an introduction by Carto himself, for example, the *Quarterly* informed readers of the reissue of "a classic book by this truly great man," calling the deceased Klansman's "greatest contribution . . . the proposal of a practical solution" to racial problems: the repatriation of blacks to Africa in order for "the United States . . . to remain White."[99] Gayre was especially enamored of works written by Northern League member H. B. Isherwood and published by the Racial Preservation Society, a British group that merged with the fascist National Front in 1967; Ray Hill, who had been a leader of the British Nazi movement before becoming an informant and antifascist, has described the society's efforts to convert anti-immigration sentiment into full-fledged Nazism. "Anything from [his] pen . . . must command scholarly respect," wrote Gayre in a review of one of Isherwood's pamphlets offering the usual dreary argument that "normal people" associated only with "their own racial kind" and singling out Jews as "by nature argumentative, . . . devious," and "possess[ing] an ingrained urge to tamper with the governments of the races they have settled amongst." Although Isherwood dismissed reports of the Holocaust as a tactic used "by the Jewish publicity apparatus for propaganda purposes," he pointed to other instances of genocide as an "object lesson" to those unable to see the folly in "mixing" races within the same nation.[100]

Nothing seemed too bizarre or too repugnant to receive the *Mankind Quarterly*'s stamp of approval. As a reviewer, Isherwood himself warmly recommended to the journal's readers a book by British author Géryke Young, arguing that only western Europeans were racially capable of the capacity for rational inquiry underlying not only all scientific research and the objective scrutiny of nature but also notions of human rights, which were "meaningless" to other races, and even the ability to appreciate "Western music," which was degraded when played by "non-Westerners." Lacking access to the "conceptual process" available to "the most stupid Westerner," the most intelligent "Easterners"—a term encompassing Asians, Indians, Turks, Arabs, and Jews—might be capable of copying what Europeans originated, but "under the skin" they were all "alien to constitutional government, the study of biology, the motorcar, or the Universal Declaration of Human Rights." As a consequence, declared Young, the East had "contributed nothing to our modern world, not even a single idea." Unlike the Eastern races, who, according to Young's analysis, had the *wrong* sort of consciousness for critical inquiry, blacks were dismissed as having no consciousness at all. And echoing the Nazi use of a similar metaphor, the "Western Jew" was described as a "germ plasm which for its sustenance feeds on a basically alien soma." Thus, Young concluded, the intrusion of "non-European peoples" into the intellectual and artistic disciplines would result in "jarring incongruities," and to absorb them into "our institutions" was a "logical impossibility"; Britain had to be "cleared of its multi-racial jungles, and be reconstituted as a homogeneous society." In the *Quarterly*, Isherwood recommended that this work be read by everyone "in authority" wherever there were attempts to "mix" different races in the same community.[101]

In addition to its promotion of the *Mankind Quarterly*, the IAAEE issued a number of its own pamphlets, printed by H. Keith Thompson, the Nazi agent, who recalled that the work had been "funded by a foundation set up by Col. Draper."[102] A reprint series offered individual articles that had already been published in the *Quarterly*, usually by IAAEE members, although there were a few exceptions. A coauthor (together with Swan) of one reprint on racial differences in the Wilmington, North Carolina public schools was H. M. Roland, a Citizens' Council employee and former superintendent of the Wilmington school system who had earlier produced a set of bulletins featuring photographs of small, cordially integrated groups, accompanied by the explanation that these smiling faces were part of a plot hatched in Moscow for the "speedy amalgamation of the races," a crime against white children "equal to . . . Hitler's Germany."[103]

The IAAEE also issued a much smaller series of previously unpublished monographs intended, more than the reprints, for a nonprofessional audience. The first monograph, authored by former professor of psychology Charles C. Josey, pointed out to "the average intelligent laymen" that racial prejudice was "essential to man becoming a free, rational, moral person," explaining, in elegant prose, that "if a person must hate, it is better to hate attitudinally persons who are remote than to hate aggressively one's intimate associates."[104]

A final IAAEE project in the 1960s, according to Swan, was frankly "designed to counter the UNESCO book": a compilation of statements on race drafted shortly after the war by conferences of internationally recognized scientists under United Nations Educational, Scientific and Cultural Organization sponsorship and intended as a response to the racially based policies of the Third Reich. One of these statements had declared that there were no innate differences in mental abilities between groups, maintaining that when races were "given similar degrees of cultural opportunity to realize their potentialities, the average achievement of the members of the group is about the same"; another had arrived at a more agnostic position, acknowledging the possibility "that some types of innate capacity for intellectual and emotional response are commoner in one human group than in another" but noting that "available scientific evidence" had not demonstrated any such conclusion. In both cases the scientists agreed that equality as an ethical principle concerning the rights to be enjoyed by all members of a society was not predicated on an assumption of equal endowment; as Thomas Jefferson had observed concerning blacks, "whatever be their degree of talents, it is no measure of their rights."[105]

To champion the linkage between political rights and putative biological facts was the very raison d'être of the IAAEE, which had planned, as one of its first activities, a collection of essays in response to the UNESCO statements. Swan, who was coordinating the effort before his arrest, explained to one of the prospective authors in 1960 that publication of the work would be funded by the Human Genetics Fund. The collection did not actually appear, however, until seven years later, delayed in part by Swan's legal problems but even more by the inability to find a publisher. "We have been trying for so long to have a commercial or university press bring out" the book, wrote an IAAEE attorney in 1966, but even "with a subsidy" no one was interested. Thus, he explained, "for this purpose we have set up the Social Science Press," an imprint that was also used for publication of Audrey Shuey's *The Testing of Negro Intelligence,* another book subsidized by both the Human Genetics Fund and Pioneer that no established press would accept.[106]

*Race and Modern Science*—its title intended to echo the UNESCO collection, which had been published as *The Race Question in Modern Science*—was eventually edited by Kuttner, who provided an introduction noting the book's contribution to a "fuller understanding" of the evolutionary value of "'race prejudice' . . . as an isolating mechanism favoring group survival and genetic variability." An "addendum" to the introduction provided comments by a number of other critics of the UNESCO statements, many of them former Nazi scientists; in support of laws prohibiting intermarriage, one German anthropologist wondered "which of the gentlemen who signed the Statement would be prepared to marry his daughter . . . to an Australian aboriginal." If the UNESCO statements were indeed "a veritable Bible for egalitarians," as they had been called by a scientist quoted by Kuttner, then the sixteen essays in *Race and Modern Science*—thirteen authored by IAAEE members, the other three by prominent contributors to Nazi race science during the Third Reich—had clearly been conceived to balance the scales, providing a bible for anti-egalitarians, a defense of racism as innate, inevitable, and of biological value.[107] Corrado Gini, the Italian sociologist and former scientific advisor to Mussolini who had replaced Gates as one of the *Mankind Quarterly*'s associate editors after the latter's sudden death in 1962, explained that Third Reich racial legislation was merely a natural "attempt to eliminate heterogeneous socio-cultural as well as anthropological elements" in the interests of "smoothing out existing differences" and "fostering the biological fusion of those remaining." Gregor pointed to the ubiquitous "repugnance to outbreeding" as proof that prejudice was "rooted in the nature of man," conceding, however, that certain "marginal" groups such as Jews and Communists had been taught to develop "anomalous response patterns" suppressing their natural tendencies toward racism in order to enhance their own "survival potential." And another contributor warned of the dire consequences of such suppression: "the rising number of racial and subracial crossings whose human products will increasingly present their unique problems to society."[108]

If the IAAEE's intention was truly to affect thinking about race in the academic world, then Draper's generosity was largely wasted. Except for a brief controversy in one anthropological journal triggered by the first issue of the *Mankind Quarterly*, the association's many projects exerted no noticeable intellectual influence and, aside from an occasional denunciation, were barely noticed by mainstream scholars.[109]

Judging by the fact that its efforts were advertised, and its publications distributed, exclusively by extremist sources, however, the association seemed to be more interested in providing scientific authority for a reemerging racist and Nazi movement than in having an impact on academic thought. For example, IAAEE membership was solicited in *Western Destiny,* where it could attract the attention of a readership also interested in how the Jewish Culture Distorters were destroying the white racial basis of Western civilization by peddling false notions about equal rights. The IAAEE reprints were available from the "Sons of Liberty" publication list, along with such learned works as *Christ Was Not a Jew,* an analysis of "Jewish parasitism and the Aryan deliverer"; *Jewish Ritual Murder,* which "documents the case proving Jewish ritual murder of Gentiles"; and *A Real Case against the Jews,* in which "a Jew tells . . . the real reason why the Jews should be hated." Even before its first issue, advance notice of the *Mankind Quarterly's* imminent publication was announced in Pearson's *Northern World* and subscriptions offered by Britons Publishing Company, a notorious specialist in anti-Semitic literature.[110] In the United States, subscriptions to the *Quarterly* could be ordered from a Liberty Lobby circular also offering subscriptions to *Northern World,* the "complete file back issues" of *Right,* and Francis Parker Yockey's *Imperium,* a particularly influential book in the neo-Nazi movement, dedicated to "the Hero of the Second World War," Adolf Hitler. *Race and Modern Science* also appeared on the lobby's Noontide Press List, together with the classic fraud *The Protocols of the Learned Elders of Zion, The International Jew, Hitler Was My Friend,* and a host of works "exposing" the Holocaust as an enormous hoax. And all the IAAEE publications regularly appeared on the list of recommended literature in the *Citizen,* the monthly publication of the Citizens' Councils. Swan and Gregor even toured the South, distributing copies of the *Mankind Quarterly* and the reprint series to state departments of education to encourage the use of scientific data "to counter the *Brown* decision" and the introduction in the high school curriculum of a course on race based on IAAEE materials. And in an internal dispute within the neo-Nazi movement, each side would claim that its position was based on IAAEE publications.[111] If the IAAEE's real purpose was to dignify hate groups and racists with academic support, then the Colonel's money probably was not spent in vain.

Whatever Draper's motivation, however, there is no doubt that he spent liberally. Without the relevant financial records—which may never be revealed, absent the unlikely event that Weyher chooses to do so—it is not possible to know exactly how much of Draper's resources were donated to the various IAAEE projects, but the amount was certainly substantial. In 1963, the only year for which some financial data are available, the IAAEE reported income of $23,210, all but $400 coming from "contributions and donations," undoubtedly Draper's money. The almost $22,000 ($133,00 AFI) of expenditures included $7,600 ($44,300 AFI) for "printing costs"—in a year in which neither *Race and Modern Science* nor any of the monographs was published—and $5,000 ($29,000 AFI) for the purchase of Avins's symposium on housing;[112] the fact that copies of the symposium were later distributed as part of the Liberty Lobby's campaign against a civil rights bill suggests that some projects carried out by Carto's organization, which had a number of prominent members in common with the IAAEE, probably were also funded by Draper. In any case, if the IAAEE spent this much money in a "slow" year, its expenses for the twelve years before Draper's death must have been sizable, including at a minimum the cost of publishing and distributing the reprint and monograph series, copies of which often were sent gratis to the 16,000 names on Swan's mailing list; the cost of publishing *Race and Modern Science,* copies of which were also sent gratis to many university libraries; the IAAEE's general organizational expenses; and the cost of the many individual projects of members of the association supported through Draper's Human Genetics Fund (which, of course, would not have been included in the 1963 organizational expenses). In total, the Colonel must have contributed hundreds of thousands of dollars to these efforts, the equivalent of probably five or six times as much in adjusted dollars. Indeed, during the nine years after Draper's death, when Pioneer became the acknowledged source of financial support for the IAAEE—further confirming the Colonel's earlier role—the association's much more modest activities, involving only a few small studies by Swan and others, received $82,000 ($207,700 AFI), including two years in which there were no grants at all.[113]

## Temperamentally Unsuited for Citizenship

While the IAAEE was pursuing its pseudoscholarly initiatives, another project supported by Draper and intended for a broader audience was being widely embraced by Southern politicians and educators: the writings of Carleton Putnam. Born to an established New York family prominent in law and publishing and descended from a distinguished line of New Englanders that included Israel Putnam, George Washington's first major-general, Carleton Putnam was a particularly well-connected member of the Episcopacy, counting numerous senators, judges, and appointed officials among his personal friends and acquaintances. After graduating from Princeton and then receiving a law degree from Columbia in 1932, he founded a small coastal airline in California, which quickly expanded throughout the nation until, two decades later, it merged with Delta to form the largest company of its type at the time, Putnam becoming chair of the board. After only a year in this capacity, however, he suddenly headed in an entirely new direction, channeling all his energy, despite having no training as a professional historian, into the first book of a projected four-volume biography of Theodore Roosevelt, which was published in 1958 and, according to the *New York Times,* "won the respect of later biographers." Instead of continuing with the Roosevelt project, however, once again Putnam abruptly changed course, abandoning the biography and dedicating the next decade of his life to the cause of racial segregation.[114]

According to his own account, Putnam had originally paid little heed to the *Brown* decision, preferring to leave "such a subject to the courts" until, in 1958, an editorial on school integration in *Life* magazine, which he found unprincipled and "wholly lacking in perception," provoked him to write to the one person who could do something "to correct the situation . . . the President of the United States." Speculating—no doubt disingenuously—that "perhaps, in the maelstrom of other problems and activities [Eisenhower] had overlooked the real significance of the desegregation cases," Putnam set out to demonstrate the "reasonableness" of segregation for the president, who could then "enlighten the nation." The resulting letter opposed "the right to equal education" for blacks, as well as all other forms of political and social equality, in part because it violated "the white man's right to freedom of association" but even more because equal treatment had to be "earned" through achievement, not legally mandated. And "any man with two eyes in his head," wrote Putnam, could see that blacks lacked "that combination of character and intelligence" necessary to civilization. Not even Lincoln, he pointed out, "to whom the Negro owes more than to any other man," was in favor of allowing blacks to vote, serve on juries, or hold political office, yet for the better part of the century the North, which did not have to deal with the problem, had been "trying to force the black man down the South's throat."[115]

In addition to sending the letter to the president, Putnam recounted how he had forwarded a copy of his letter to a confidant, the editor of a Virginia newspaper, who then not only offered it to his own readers a few days later as "eloquent testimony" that the case for segregation was making headway with "intelligent Northerners" but also sent copies to every editor in the United States. Whether or not this account was accurate, the letter was eventually republished in newspapers throughout the South, supposedly producing thousands of responses to Putnam from "sane and earnest" Southerners, all proclaiming him their hero: "College students . . . framed the letter and hung it on the wall. . . . Schools assigned it for class discussion. Editors of law journals asked to print it. Judges wrote . . . from chambers. Senators and Congressmen . . . requested permission to insert it in the Congressional Record." But when only a single, small Northern newspaper published the letter—and with an unfavorable comment—the Putnam Letter Committee, consisting of "distinguished public figures," was formed in Alabama to solicit funds for printing it throughout the North as a paid advertisement. Within a few months almost $40,000 ($245,000 AFI) had been collected— "mostly from hundreds of small contributions," according to Putnam—and the letter soon appeared in eighteen large dailies outside the South. Although Putnam claimed that 95 percent of the replies from Northern readers were favorable—demonstrating that "the man and woman in the street in the North" was really on the South's side—he professed greater interest in the hostile 5 percent, hoping to develop some understanding of the mentality behind the paper curtain. "The more I learned," he wrote, "the more startled I became."[116]

The common denominator among all those who failed to see the self-evident wisdom in Putnam's letter, he observed, was a conviction that "'modern' anthropology" had proven that racial differences resulted not from blacks' genetic deficiencies but from their unequal opportunities. Not until reading these replies did he supposedly realize how cunningly this "equalitarian" movement had proceeded, "infiltrating first the sciences that surround anthropology, moving next into the more strictly social sciences, enthroning itself at last in the Supreme Court's desegregation order." The nation, he concluded, had thus been deceived into adopting a social policy based on a "pseudoscientific hoax." This notion—that long overdue political equality was finally beginning to be extended to blacks only because of some "equalitarian" scientific conclusion—was patently inaccurate. Equal treatment under law is a normative ethical precept about rights constitutionally guaranteed to all members of the society, not an entitlement that is, or should be, predicated on some sort of biological or genetic evidence but a "truth" that is, in Jefferson's famous words, "self-evident." But the assertion that support for civil rights had been consciously predicated solely on the conclusions of modern science would become the basis for a campaign, spearheaded by Putnam, to shift public discourse from the ethical to the empirical.[117]

Putnam's account of the origin of his involvement was no doubt largely fanciful. The sudden "discovery" of modern, "equalitarian" anthropology only after reading the replies to his letter was certainly feigned naiveté on the part of someone who had earlier been a prominent invitee to the First General Meeting of the IAAEE and APFC, a gathering of activists selected precisely for their opposition to equalitarian science. And the claim that his efforts were funded by "small contributions" also strained credibility, but even if this were true at the inception of the campaign, Putnam, though hardly impecunious himself, would soon find his writings supported by Draper's money, becoming one of the few people in the racist movement, along with Weyher and Garrett, to be personally close to "our source of funds."

Although Putnam authored many publications for the cause, his most important contribution was *Race and Reason,* published in 1961. Originally titled *Warning to the North: A Yankee View,* the book had been scheduled to appear at least a year earlier, but the intended publisher suffered a sudden change of heart. "My New York group is thus starting the search . . . all over again," noted Putnam, but not even a number of subsequent rejections could deter "my financial backers [who] seem to grow in enthusiasm." The work was finally accepted by Public Affairs Press, a "soft-cover house," probably under the same terms that Draper offered a year later to Regnery Press, a similar publisher, as an incentive to consider a work on immigration that the Colonel had subsidized: In exchange for publication, Draper would contract to purchase a large number of copies, probably to be distributed to the names on Swan's lists. Whatever the conditions, the brief volume—actually a thirty-page essay followed by a number of questions and answers—was one of the movement's most successful publications, selling more than 60,000 copies within the first six months, although most of them probably were purchased by the "financial backer" for free distribution.[118]

Much of *Race and Reason* was devoted to exposing the insidious process by which "equalitarian" thought, "calling itself, here, Communism, there, Marxism, somewhere else, Socialism," had attained such vast influence in the United States. Offering the softcore version of *Western Destiny*'s obsession with the "Culture Distorter," Putnam identified the mastermind of this subversive conspiracy as Columbia University anthropologist Franz Boas, who had immigrated from Germany in 1886, and his many disciples, all members of the same "racial minority group" that though unspecified, included scientists named Klineberg, Weltfish, and Hershkovitz. In the late nineteenth century, he explained, immigration shifted from its traditional northern European roots, and "Boas' own minority group" arrived in the United States "in great numbers," seeking asylum after "centuries of failure" in their struggle for freedom. Not readily assimilated in their new homeland and "smarting from what they considered unjustified discrimination," they set out to demonstrate their own worth "by proving that *all* races were equal in their adaptability to our white civilization." Concentrating largely in Northeastern cities, where they bred prolifically, "not only in children but in ideas," these minorities, "not schooled in the Protestant Ethic upon which our nation was founded," had come to wield substantial influence in entertainment and mass communication and had "taken over" a number of important chairs in leading universities, as a result of which two generations of students had already been exposed to their influence.[119] Motivated by what Putnam elsewhere called the "double drive" of "out-group" resentment and left-wing ideology, these "white minority groups" had used their key positions, especially in the academy, "to advance what they conceive to be the interests of their special stocks" by deliberately promoting theories and policies "which are bound to weaken the white race as a whole."[120]

Although it was predominantly left-wing Jews who furnished the ideology,[121] Putnam explained, they did so on behalf of another danger: "the mulatto who was bent on making the nation mulatto," that unhappy soul whose disharmonic mixture of white ambition and black inadequacy made him frustrated with his own lot and a nuisance to everyone else. These two groups formed an alliance, that, Putnam observed, "had nothing in common save a belief that they had a grudge against society." To expect an impartial analysis of race from such people, he wrote, was like expecting an impartial analysis of prohibition from a saloonkeeper, yet somehow these groups had deceived the Supreme Court into believing that Jim Crow laws were the barrier to black achievement. In fact, he declared, blacks had been victimized not by political oppression but by biology: "It is what he is that makes the average Negro a second class citizen, not segregation." Putnam did acknowledge that there were some capable blacks, but he found these exceptions, invariably, to be the result of white genes, explaining that "a man may be as black as the ace of spades and still be a mixed blood with . . . relatively high intelligence, and other white attributes." In any case, he maintained, "a race must be considered as a race, there is no alternative to building the system around the average." And, for Putnam, the genetic inferiority of blacks as a race precluded not only integration but also any measure of social or political equality. Indeed, after passage of the voting rights act a few years later, he expressed horror at the dreadful proposal "to inject into the blood stream of the body politic . . . a virus of Negro votes . . . absolutely certain to undermine" the health of the society.[122]

In a joint introduction to *Race and Reason,* Gates, Garrett, Gayre, and George claimed to find themselves in an unaccustomed position, as scientists commenting on a social problem, but because of the importance of the issue they could not "dissociate [themselves] from the task." Managing to overcome their reservations, the four IAAEE authorities endorsed the book's "logic and common sense," commenting that "it probes to the core of an abscess, yet does so with a healing touch." In fact, George had not found it necessary actually to read the work before offering his name and endorsement in response to a request from Garrett. Already familiar with Putnam's published letter to the president, the anatomist "consider[ed] it improbable that he has said anything . . . that I would quarrel with. . . . I shall consider it a privilege to sign it."[123]

*Race and Reason* was launched with a massive publicity campaign, now sponsored by the New York–based National Putnam Letters Committee—a clique composed mainly of Weyher, Putnam, Trevor, Garrett, Swan, and a few others—which had apparently replaced the more parochial-sounding Putnam Letter Committee. A full-page advertisement appeared in the *New York*

*Times* book section, a mass mailing of form letters was sent to scientists and educators, and—in standard procedure for projects supported by Draper—10,000 copies were designated "for presentation to members of Congress, the higher federal and state judiciary, governors of states, churchmen and educators."[124] Thousands more were also donated to libraries and distributed gratis by Southern senators. Though considered a major participant in the Boasian equalitarian conspiracy, Columbia University geneticist Theodosius Dobzhansky nevertheless received a copy from Virginia Senator Harry F. Byrd, accompanied by a personal note of support, an indication that the book may well have been distributed, willy-nilly, to all the scientists on Swan's "basic mailing list," which included 14,000 members of professional associations in sociology, anthropology, psychology, and biology.[125] "Our source of funds" was certainly unstinting in his support.

And with good reason. Weyher's monthly tabulation of press clippings indicated that media reference to *Race and Reason* was overwhelmingly favorable: A year and a half after its publication, he reported that of 658 articles—including a handful in Britain, France, and South Africa—only 100 had been unfavorable, and one-third of these had appeared in "Negro papers." A more detailed analysis of the book's reception, also by Weyher, provided even greater reason to be optimistic. Within the first eight months, Putnam had been given the key to the city in Birmingham and New Orleans; the governor of Mississippi had proclaimed a "Race and Reason" day in the state, to be celebrated by "appropriate public functions . . . demonstrating the appreciation of people of our state for Mr. Carleton Putnam and for his splendid book"; and the State of Louisiana had purchased 5,000 copies of the book for required reading not only by students in many high school and college courses but also by educational officials. In addition, Putnam had appeared before a number of southern audiences; 10,000 copies of his speech in Jackson, Mississippi alone had been circulated by the Letters Committee.[126]

Encouraged by this favorable exposure, the National Putnam Letters Committee quickly moved to expand beyond the work of its namesake, adding the "George Report" to its offerings. While *Race and Reason* was in preparation, an attorney retained by the governor of Alabama "to represent him on racial litigation" had approached retired University of North Carolina anatomist Wesley Critz George with a request to conduct a study of the scientific facts of race.[127] Hardly a disinterested choice for the task, George was well known for his obsession with preventing any contact between the races even long before the *Brown* decision. During the war, for example, he had written to a local white clergyman who had opened his church to blacks, accusing the reverend of "furthering the work of the devil" by "aiding in the de-

struction of the white race" and "the civilization of America." Within three
days of the Supreme Court's action, he had written to the governor of North
Carolina, encouraging defiance of the ruling and declaring that preservation
of the public school system was not as important as "the protoplasmic integrity of the white race."[128] Other scientists might have lent their authority
to segregationist organizations; George led one, becoming president of the
Patriots of North Carolina, the state's major opponent of school integration.

Although the subsequent report bore only George's name as author, it was
in many ways a collective project, preliminary drafts of the study first undergoing substantial revisions suggested by Garrett and Putnam before being circulated by Weyher to other members of the IAAEE and the Pioneer
board for their comments. The final product, *The Biology of the Race Problem,* was submitted to the governor's office in September 1962.[129] It began by
framing the issue in the scientists' preferred manner: The Justices had "based
their decision in *Brown* . . . upon 'science,'" and thus the validity of the ruling was dependent on the validity of the science. This claim afforded George
justification for the crux of his report: evidence from a variety of physiological, psychological, and anthropological studies, all putatively demonstrating the innate intellectual inferiority of blacks. To demonstrate the dangers
of any social policy that would "convert the population of the United States
into a mixed-blooded people," he soberly described a study of cross-breeding among dogs in which the poor, confused hybrid exhibited the drooping
ears of its basset hound side but the excitable temperament of its German
shepherd ancestry. Like Putnam, George acknowledged the existence of some
"fine and able Negroes," but, he observed in stylish prose, just as "one swal-
low does not make a summer, . . . a few intelligent Negroes do not make a
race." Besides, insisted the anatomist, a "superior Negro" who sought entry
into "Caucasian social life" was not interested merely in "legitimate 'opportunity,'" but actually desired "racial amalgamation."[130]

George concluded the "impartial study" with his own description of the
Boasian conspiracy. (Indeed, despite Putnam's account of his startled discovery of this subversive network only after receiving responses to his published
letter to the president, more than two years before the publication of *Race
and Reason* George had written to the IAAEE, tracing the false ideas prevalent in the universities back to the influence of Boas.) Under equalitarian
influence, he observed in the report, many universities had devised manda-
tory courses "for wholesale indoctrination" of unsuspecting students. Even
in his own University of North Carolina, he found on reserve in the library
three full shelves of a reading required of all first-year students: an "integration tract" by Otto Klineberg, one of Boas's students, which George "judged

. . . to be without scholarly merit and without literary charm or virtue," assigned solely for its "considerable indoctrination value . . . in the hands of naïve youths."[131]

Although the George report had been prepared at the request of the State of Alabama, the Putnam Letters Committee was much more interested than the official recipient in exploiting the work as part of the larger struggle to preserve segregation. The plan devised by Putnam, Weyher, and William Simmons, leader of the Citizens' Councils, had been for Simmons, who had been in personal contact with the Alabama governor's office, to put "pressure on Montgomery" to publicize the report and make "mimeographed" copies for the press; "then we could take our time about finding a publisher for the printed edition," wrote Putnam.[132] But when the state was not particularly eager to do its part in this scheme, the Letters Committee had the report printed within a few weeks. However, there was some concern within the group over the propriety of distributing the State of Alabama's property, producing an internal discussion in which, as usual with an administrative matter, everyone forwarded their ideas to Weyher for a final decision. The work was eventually published, in accord with a suggestion from Putnam, as a "Report . . . Prepared by Commission of the Governor of Alabama," with a notation on the back cover stating that "This is one of a number of copies of Dr. George's report which has been purchased for distribution by the National Putnam Letters Committee."

When *The Biology of the Race Problem* was finally released to the public, Swan drafted an announcement, signed by IAAEE Executive Committee member Herbert Sanborn and distributed by the National Putnam Letters Committee; the two groups, controlled largely by the same clique, shared the IAAEE's mailing list and used as return addresses post office boxes at New York's Grand Central Station that were within arm's reach of each other, Swan probably being the ultimate recipient of mail in either case.[133] Both Putnam and Trevor recommended to Weyher that George's report be treated in the same way as Putnam's *Race and Reason*: advertised by the same firm and distributed gratis to "all the leaders of the Western World, including the top hierarchy in government, state and federal, on through religion, law, industry, banking, education, the press, movies, TV-radio, etc."[134] There was "no question," Trevor wrote to his fellow Pioneer board member, "that we could place from ten to fifty thousand copies of this book."[135]

Trevor had not exaggerated. Within a year, the George report had gone through four printings, producing "somewhere between 45,000 and 50,000 copies," according to an estimate by a Letters Committee staff member. Of this total, 13,000 copies were actually purchased, indicating that the Committee distributed more than 30,000 free copies. Trevor alone "offered the hardcovers to some 9,000 libraries on a complimentary basis throughout the U.S." Nor did the committee take gracefully to ungrateful recipients of its generosity. When, soon after copies of the report were sent to members of the American Philosophical Association, an apparently nasty, unsigned letter arrived from a particular college, George was informed that "our benefactor" desired an additional mailing be made in the near future; if one of the four members of the association at this school refused the new material, "we will be able to guess that he is the offender."[136]

Over the next half dozen years, the Putnam Letters Committee sponsored a number of other open letters written by its eponymous author as advertisements in major newspapers and published more than a dozen pamphlets. Most of the latter were speeches or articles by Putnam, although there were some notable exceptions. In addition to George's report, the committee also reprinted and distributed an article titled "The New Fanatics" that had originally appeared in the *Mankind Quarterly* in 1962, authored by someone previously unknown to the journal, William A. Massey, who had submitted an unsolicited manuscript that had to be "improved" by both Garrett and Putnam. Even then, there was apparently some controversy among the editors over whether it should be accepted, but Gayre eventually agreed under pressure from Garrett, "who would have liked something different," but "could not very well turn it down," a comment suggesting that someone else of significant influence—such as Draper or Weyher—had insisted that the article be published.[137] Distribution by the Letters Committee, rather than through the IAAEE reprint series, was an additional indication that the article enjoyed the Colonel's imprimatur; judging by his personal decision to have the Letters Committee publish a reply to Princeton sociologist Melvin Tumin's criticism of the scientific support for segregation, Draper appeared to play a more assertive role in determining what would appear in the Putnam series, intended more for the public, than in the "scientific" IAAEE literature.

"The New Fanatics" was one of the longest articles ever published in the *Mankind Quarterly,* its title referring to intellectuals who, according to the author, were using their influence as writers and teachers to manipulate an unsuspecting public into supporting integration and equal rights for blacks. Eschewing any discussion of empirical evidence, Massey found it "obvious that the Negro in the United States is an inferior group" and "may never make a good American citizen. Even if . . . of adequate intelligence he may be temperamentally unsuited for citizenship in a democracy." The nation was founded by a specific racial group for whom democracy was uniquely appropriate, Massey explained, and it was "not only the right but the responsibility" of this group "to restrict participation in the government," justifiably discriminating "against those races which are not felt suited." Of particular significance, "The New Fanatics" was republished almost verbatim some three decades later in a journal edited by Roger Pearson, who had by then become a major recipient of Pioneer grants.[138]

In 1964, after being approved for the position by Weyher, John J. Synon was named the director of the National Putnam Letters Committee fresh from his stint as director of the Coordinating Committee for Fundamental American Freedoms, a lobbying group also funded largely by Draper and dedicated to preventing passage of the Civil Rights Act of 1964. At about the same time Synon also took control of the Patrick Henry Group, another organization distributing literature, most of which had been originally published by the Letters Committee, together with works such as *Race and Reason* and *The Testing of Negro Intelligence.* That is, the Patrick Henry Group was essentially a clone of the Letters Committee, both organizations distributing material that had been published with Draper's support and administered by a person who had been paid with his money. Moreover, literature from the Patrick Henry Group eventually was ordered from a post office box in Kilmarnock, Virginia, just steps away from a box by then serving as the official location of the Letters Committee, which had been moved under Synon's directorship—further indication that the two organizations were practically synonymous.[139]

To its list of Letters Committee literature the Patrick Henry Group added five anti-integration pamphlets published by its own press, all of them authored by Garrett. In late 1965, the affluent suburbs north and west of New York City were flooded with thousands of copies of "How Classroom Desegregation Will Work," one of the least offensive of the five. Perhaps in deference to the more liberal sensibilities of a Northern audience, the pamphlet eschewed the usual hysteria over the imminent end of white civilization if schools permitted "race mixing," in favor of mere predictions of educational disaster, the spread of "Negroid culture," and the eventual decline of "intellectual and cultural assets" through intermarriage, the "primary goal of the integrationist." It also omitted some features that had appeared when the same pamphlet was published in the *Citizen,* the magazine of organized Southern resistance published by the Citizens' Councils, such as photographs of a smiling white schoolgirl amid a group of cheerful black playmates captioned "Will YOUR Child Be Exposed To THIS?" Apparently Garrett was concerned that such images might not be as terrifying to New Yorkers as they were in Mississippi at the time.[140] Within the next few months another half million copies of the pamphlet were sent to teachers throughout the nation.

In "Breeding Down," yet another Patrick Henry Group booklet distributed in huge numbers, Garrett explained that the civil rights movement's real strategy for blacks to attain equality with their betters was to make whites "Negroid" through mongrelization, mixing the descendants of Shakespeare and Newton with a race not "capable of rising above the mud-hut stage." Interviewed by *Newsweek* as a result of the pamphlets, Garrett denied being a racist or hatemonger, observing, in dubious support of his demurral, that blacks were "fine muscular animals when . . . not diseased, . . . but when they're frustrated, they revert to primitive savages"; presumably, segregated schools would relieve blacks from the discomfort of the former, so that whites could be protected from the consequences of the latter. Besides, he explained in yet another booklet, the *real* example of a "racist" was for a group to call itself the "Chosen People."[141]

## A Confession on the Part of the Negroes

From a practical viewpoint, the drumbeat of emphasis on blacks' intellectual inferiority not only was designed to influence public opinion about the dangers of integration but also was intended as the core of the legal strategy to overturn the *Brown* decision. Still clinging to the premise that the Supreme Court's ruling had been informed not by law or constitutional principle but by the factually erroneous claims of equalitarian scientists, the segregationists remained hopeful that a rehearing of the issue would produce a different outcome. Although the South's entire superstructure of racial conventions, formal and informal, had always been based on the implicit assumption that blacks were genetically inferior, the original Southern strategy in the courts had been to ignore the scientific testimony presented by the NAACP's expert witnesses as irrelevant to the central issues of states' rights and judicial precedents. In retrospect, this approach was considered a crucial error but one that could still be rectified though legal action. Despite what Putnam called "all the power of the educational establishment, all the massive and saturating influences of a vast Negrophile news and entertainment media, all the cunning of politicians" that he saw being "ruthlessly employed to deceive both our youth and the general public," the segregationist scientists believed that the "truth" would prevail if, in a new court proceeding, the "deceitful" evidence presented to the Supreme Court was exposed and valid scientific proof offered in its stead.[142]

Heading the legal team that would challenge the supposed factual basis of *Brown* was Georgia attorney R. Carter Pittman, a member of Liberty Lobby's advisory board and an ardent foe of integration: He had been named president of the first States' Rights Council and boasted of having made "the first attack . . . in the country" on the Supreme Court's ruling. To his colleagues in the legal profession Pittman argued that the signers of the Declaration of Independence had never really believed in the "perversion" of its most well-known phrase but had included the observation that "all men are created equal" solely to acquire an ally in the Revolutionary War by appealing to the sympathies of the French, who at the time were "saturated" with the ideas of "two half-demented philosophers . . . named Helvetius and Rousseau." For the public, presumably less interested in such intellectual arcana, Pittman authored essays such as "Communist Contribution to Equalitarian Dogma and Race-Mixing Turmoil," in which he insisted that the plaintiffs in *Brown* were all "mulattoes or near whites" and thus "not entitled to be considered as representative of the Negro." Obsessed with "mulattoes," like so many of the segregationists, Pittman demonstrated for one journalist the practice that had "become his trademark": Picking up a magazine article about successful blacks, he paged through the pictures, estimating the percentage of "white blood" for each individual from his or her appearance— "now this one, he's about seven-eighths white . . . and this one, he's got a lot of kink in his hair, so he's about 50 percent."[143]

Although Pittman was the segregationists' lead trial counsel, his most important legal contributions occurred before he entered a courtroom. First, he had to craft a strategy that would provide standing for his own appearance so that he could call the scientists as witnesses. During the early 1960s, the desegregation cases being litigated throughout the South generally involved black parents, represented by the NAACP as the plaintiffs, seeking to obtain a court order that would enforce the *Brown* decision, and a local school system as the defendant; Pittman and the scientists were not a party to any of these actions. And once granted standing, Pittman would have to convince a judge that his expert witnesses had relevant testimony to offer. The latter problem demanded not so much a legal strategy as a search for the right judge, one who would be sympathetic to the segregationists' "fact based" interpretation of the Supreme Court's ruling.

The first and most important challenge to *Brown* came in *Stell v. Savannah-Chatham County Board of Education*, argued before Judge Frank M. Scarlett.[144] In 1962, eight years after the Supreme Court's ruling, a group of black parents brought suit in federal district court against the Savannah-Chatham school board, which had instituted a "pupil placement policy" transparently designed to preserve segregation by assigning students to schools on the basis of a series of guidelines that made no mention of race but nevertheless did not place a single black student in a "white" school—nor, of course, the reverse. Yet despite this record of intransigence, the board "came into court prepared to surrender," according to William Simmons, head of the Citizens' Councils. But the board's place as defender of the current policy was immediately taken by a third party, a group of "intervenors" describing themselves as "Whites, sharing a common biological origin, cultural heritage and consciousness of kind," who maintained that the school board did not adequately represent their interests, making it necessary for them to have separate counsel—the pretext through which Pittman hoped to obtain standing before the court. The intervenors charged that their children would suffer educational harm if "forcibly compelled to associate with plaintiffs and others of their ethnic group" in the public schools, thus attempting to reverse roles with the NAACP: *They* would become the prosecutors and force the civil rights attorneys to act as defendants against the "scientific" evidence that would dismantle the presumed basis of the *Brown* decision.[145]

Although Pittman, the local Georgia attorney, had planned the legal strategy to attain standing, the substance of the case was left entirely to Weyher and the scientists under his direction. Indeed, Pittman had solicited comments on the draft of his motion to intervene from three other attorneys: his two co-counselors in the suit and Harry Weyher. The draft was also circulated for suggestions to the usual participants in projects funded by the Colonel: Putnam, Garrett, George, Gregor, and Kuttner. In addition to citing studies on racial differences in general, the eventual brief in support of intervention was based substantially on a study of the aptitude and achievement test scores for students in the Savannah-Chatham schools conducted by University of Georgia psychologist R. Travis Osborne, another recipient of regular cash gifts from Draper and a member of the IAAEE Executive Committee, as well as a Pioneer grantee. Much of the brief was actually written by Swan, who took charge of organizing both witnesses and evidence. The final product was submitted with three appendices written by the scientists: the George report and papers by Kuttner and Gregor.[146]

Judge Scarlett not only granted recognition to the intervenors but also agreed with their interpretation that the Supreme Court's decision in *Brown* had been based not on law but on empirical evidence concerning the detrimental effects of segregation on the education of black students. It was therefore appropriate, he ruled, to subject the plaintiff's request in *Stell* to similar scrutiny of the facts, which might be different in this case, and, overruling all the NAACP's objections, he decided to hear from the intervenors' expert witnesses. Pittman was understandably delighted in anticipation of the opportunity offered by *Stell*. "We have every reason to believe from our knowledge of the character, courage and reputation of . . . Frank Scarlett," wrote the attorney, that if the judge was persuaded by the facts, "we will win this case . . . [and] he will write an opinion that appellate judges will have great difficulty in ignoring."[147]

For Pittman and the official team of attorneys, this was not a legal case but a crusade, all of them contributing their services without compensation. "The only promise we have," Pittman noted in passive voice, "is that our expenses will be paid. We are assured also that funds will be made available to pay all of the expenses of expert witnesses and a reasonable expert witness fee." This was not a small amount, especially considering that, in addition to the costs associated with the trial itself, a month before the case was heard, a dozen segregationists were brought from different parts of the country to Atlanta for an all-expense-paid weekend strategy session at the posh Biltmore Hotel; in addition to the expert witnesses and other advisors, the attendees included William Simmons and Dan Shell from Mississippi, who were invited in anticipation of a similar case soon to be heard involving the Jackson, Mississippi school system. Pittman's promise that expenses would be paid was sent to Putnam, all the cooperating scientists, and his two co-counselors, but Weyher, who received a copy of every other relevant communication in the case, was not a recipient; "our source of funds" did not need to be reminded of his own commitment.[148]

In the weeks leading up to the trial the attorneys and scientists worked feverishly to craft a winning strategy. Gregor insisted that even compelling evidence of black genetic inferiority would be insufficient in the face of individual differences and wanted to stress the inevitable nature of racial conflict, which would be further exacerbated by integration, and the harm done to black students, even though the latter point had nothing to do with the interests of the intervenors. Putnam, who, as a well-connected Northerner, claimed to "know how these people think," worried that emphasis on racial conflict would only produce a call for more integration as a solution and repeatedly stressed the paramount importance of evidence on comparative brain physiology and differences in "evolutionary grade." "There is only one argument . . . that can defeat the environmentalist attack," he maintained, "and that is the argument from innate, genetic, inborn, hereditary limitations."[149] Eventually the segregationists decided on the kitchen sink approach, omitting nothing that might provide a reason to keep black and white students separated.

Trial in the *Stell* case took place in May 1963. In an unusual proceeding, neither the NAACP plaintiffs, seeking a court order to compel integration of the Savannah-Chatham public schools, nor the defendant school system presented evidence, and the bulk of the trial was taken up by the intervenors' expert witnesses, whose testimony was admitted over the objection of the NAACP's attorneys. First, Osborne, the only witness whose expenses were paid from an acknowledged Pioneer grant at the time, presented an analysis of test scores at different grade levels in the rigidly segregated Savannah schools, demonstrating that black students scored consistently below their white peers.

Garrett followed Osborne to the stand, testifying that "differences in educability" between the races were "inherent"; there was "no scientific possibility," according to Garrett, that differences of such magnitude "were either caused by or could be substantially altered by the students' environment." Next George appeared, supporting Garrett's conclusion that racial variation in intellectual ability was "innate" on the basis of demonstrable differences in "size, proportion and structure of the brain and endocrine systems." George also cited the work of the well-known University of Pennsylvania professor of anthropology Carleton Coon, who had recently concluded that blacks had crossed the evolutionary threshold into homo sapiens at a much later date than whites, suggesting that their lower intelligence was a consequence of the smaller amount of time in which blacks had been able to advance; reluctant to be publicly associated with the segregationists but sympathetic to their cause, Coon had been secretly providing advice to Putnam.

Ernest van den Haag, a professor of social philosophy at New York University and member of the IAAEE Executive Committee, then made the argument favored by Gregor, testifying that court-ordered integration would cause racial prejudice to increase, creating tensions in the classroom that would multiply disciplinary problems and harm the educational process for all students. In an integrated school, van den Haag explained, blacks, in particular, would suffer, developing a "collective neurosis" caused by the failure to establish an appropriate and healthy identification with their own group. And a reorganization of schools by educational achievement, in which only the superior black children would attend integrated classes, would be the worst policy of all, according to the expert witness, producing "pathological disturbance" in the few capable black students and intensified feelings of rejection among the rest, now deprived of their "natural leadership." Finally, Clairette Armstrong testified, confirming van den Haag's predictions of frustration for black students on the basis of her experience in New York City, where "one-third of all Negro truants gave inability to keep abreast of their school work as the reason for their running away from home."[150] Taken as a whole, the testimony of the intervenors' expert witnesses precluded any possible method for placing a black child and a white child into the same classroom.

Actually, the intervenors were prepared to call three additional scientists but withdrew these witnesses after the plaintiffs indicated that they had no intention to submit any evidence in response; indeed, the NAACP attorneys did not even bother to cross-examine the intervenors' experts on the correct assumption that the *Brown* decision, and the resulting petition for the court to order integration in Savannah, was based on constitutional principle, not empirical evidence. Simmons was elated; "They presented not one witness in rebuttal!" he exclaimed in the *Citizen*. However, Putnam was deeply disappointed at the failure of the plaintiffs to put on a case of their own. He had looked forward to seeing the equalitarians squirm when forced to confront the evidence of their "decades of deceit and chicanery" and interpreted their reluctance to respond as "a confession on the part of the Negroes" that cross-examination of their experts under oath was too dangerous to risk. However, the trial did provide him with a moment of great satisfaction. As George offered his testimony on "just *what it was* the Negro inherited," Putnam suddenly realized that Constance Baker Motley, the NAACP's "mulatto lawyer," was "weeping audibly."[151]

Having earlier concurred with the intervenors' contention that the *Brown* decision had been a finding of fact rather than a conclusion of law, Judge Scarlett's decision in their favor came as no surprise. Consistent with the "uncontroverted testimony . . . given as the unanimous opinions of conceded authorities open to cross-examination," he concluded that integration would "seriously injure both white and Negro students," thus leading him to deny the NAACP's request and dismiss their complaint. Of course, the Fifth Circuit Court of Appeals eventually overruled Scarlett, correcting his misinterpretation of the *Brown* decision, and the Supreme Court declined to hear the *Stell* case on appeal.[152]

Disappointed but undaunted, the segregationists made one more effort to have *Brown* overturned on scientific grounds when, a year later, the NAACP brought suit in Jackson, Mississippi, headquarters of the Citizens' Councils, again requesting court-ordered desegregation of the city's school system in the *Evers* case, named for the daughter of murdered civil rights leader Medgar Evers. Although this time the school district mounted a more aggressive defense than had been offered in *Stell*—including testimony by a congressman and a number of local educators—once again a group of "intervenors" was allowed to present its own expert witnesses by a sympathetic Southern judge. In addition to Pittman, the intervenors were represented by Dan Shell, a local attorney and chief counsel for the Jackson Citizens' Council, and George S. Leonard, a Washington attorney who had also participated in the *Stell* case. Once again, the scientists were called over the plaintiff's objections, Osborne, Kuttner, van den Haag, Garrett, and others taking the stand, although George was unable to appear because of an illness in the family, and his testimony from the earlier trial was entered into the record. Simmons, who attended as an observer, described in a letter to George how "the NAACP had some nigger parents on the stand," exulting in the confusion of a "fat mammy" who had become flustered during cross-examination.[153]

Judge Sidney Mize obviously wanted to issue a decision favorable to the defendants in *Evers,* but the reversal of Scarlett's ruling in *Stell* had rendered such an outcome impossible. Thus, although he considered it "contrary to the facts and the law," wrote Mize, "the Court feels that it is required" to rule in favor of the NAACP. Yet at the same time, he noted, the evidence that had been presented to the Supreme Court was "unworthy of belief"—a "misleading concealment" of the truth—and "the facts . . . 'cry out' for a reappraisal and complete reconsideration" of the *Brown* decision.[154] Even though black and white students would finally be educated together in Jackson—at least in the public schools—the Colonel's troops could at least take some satisfaction that a federal judge had agreed with their strange notion that the Supreme Court had been hoodwinked by the equalitarian conspiracy.

## Fact and Amount of the Gift to Be Kept Confidential

Although there was vigorous, often violent resistance to the civil rights movement throughout the South, only Mississippi could claim the oxymoronic accomplishment of making extremism the norm. In an ironic mirroring of the characterization of blacks that supposedly made them unfit for participation in white society, the Magnolia state had historically enjoyed a special reputation for savagery. As one historian points out, Mississippi led the South "in every imaginable kind of mob atrocity: most lynchings, most multiple lynchings, most lynchings of women, most lynchings without an arrest, most lynchings of a victim in police custody, and most public support for the process itself." Moreover, the reported cases tended to underestimate the actual number because authorities often did not bother to investigate "nigger killings"; as one local explained to a visitor in 1908, "when there is a row, we feel like killing a nigger whether he has done anything or not." The lynchings themselves were major social events, in equal parts theater and carnival, as huge crowds gathered—some in "reserved seats"—to enjoy refreshments while watching the victim be subjected to unspeakably horrible tortures before "death at the hands of parties unknown," as the local officials regularly claimed.[155]

In addition to these individual acts, brutality in Mississippi often was official policy, systematically planned and implemented at every level of government. Immediately after the Civil War, the Mississippi legislature enacted the infamous Black Codes, designed to reduce newly freed slaves to their former status by creating crimes such as "insulting gestures," applicable only to the "free Negro." A decade later, Mississippi's convict lease system began operation, in which many black prisoners, often sentenced for petty crimes, were essentially worked to death creating wealth for planters and industrialists. According to *Worse Than Slavery,* David Oshinsky's aptly titled account of the prison system, "not a single leased convict ever lived long enough to serve a sentence of ten years or more."[156]

Politicians in Mississippi regularly ran on a platform of white supremacy uncluttered by euphemisms. James K. Vardaman, Bilbo's predecessor in both the statehouse and the United States Senate, promised to treat the "coon problem" by abolishing education for blacks—which "simply renders [them] unfit for the work which the white man has prescribed"—and repealing, among other safeguards, the Fifteenth Amendment guaranteeing blacks the right to vote and the Declaration of Independence, which, according to Vardaman, did not apply to "wild animals and niggers." An exponent of lynching as an appropriate means of social control, Vardaman declared, after winning the governorship, that, had he lost, "we would have had to kill more negroes in the next twelve months in Mississippi than we had to kill in the last twenty years."[157]

These attitudes had changed little by the dawn of the Second Reconstruction. In an incident right out of *Huckleberry Finn,* a Mississippi clergyman and philosophy professor frankly recalled, three decades later, that as a seminarian in 1953 he had happened on a car overturned in a shallow river, its occupants drowning, only to have his horror turn to "relief" upon hearing that it was just "a car full of niggers." (A century earlier Twain's Aunt Sally asked of Huck, "Anybody hurt?" and received the reply, "No'm. Killed a nigger.") In another memory from the clergyman's youth, local farmers had speculated on whether blacks had souls, typically concluding that they were no different from animals, like "cows or mules."[158]

For more than a decade after the *Brown* decision, black life remained cheap in Mississippi and black rights nonexistent; attempts to obtain the latter often were met with vivid reminders of the former. In 1955, Reverend George Lee was murdered after encouraging blacks in Belzoni, Mississippi to register, and three months later Lamar Smith, who had committed a similar transgression in nearby Brookhaven, was assassinated on the courthouse lawn by a white man in broad daylight who was never identified although dozens of people watched the killing; even ten years later, not a single black was registered in this county, where blacks made up two-thirds of the 19,000 residents, and those who attempted to do so were photographed by the local sheriff.[159] Also in 1955, Emmett Till, a black youth from Chicago visiting his uncle in the Delta, had the temerity to flirt with a white grocery store clerk and was mutilated beyond recognition and murdered by her husband and a friend; the two men, who confessed to the crime, were acquitted by an all-white jury after an hour of deliberation "to make it look good." In 1958, four years before the widely pub-licized riots that attended James Meredith's entry into the University of Mis-sissippi, a black teacher had attempted to register for summer courses there, only to be committed to a mental hospital by state troopers on the grounds that "any nigger who tried to enter Ole Miss *must* be crazy." A year later, when a young black man who had studied at the University of Chicago insisted on attending Mississippi Southern College, he was framed for petty theft and sen-tenced to seven years in prison, where the demand that he work in the fields, even though seriously ill, led to his death.[160] In subsequent years more well-known names were added to the list of Mississippi martyrs—Medgar Evers, James Chaney, Michael Schwerner, Andrew Goodman, and Vernon Dahmer—making the state a synonym for racial hatred and violence.

In response to the rash of bombing and murder—forty such acts in the first six months of 1964 alone, according to a Federal Bureau of Investigation re-port—the Mississippi courts provided a brand of justice that protected the perpetrator and persecuted the victim. In a particularly Kafkaesque juxtapo-sition, three Klansmen who had confessed to the fire bombing of a black wom-an's residence were given suspended sentences on the same day that twelve civil rights workers were arrested—and later packed off to prison, where they were stripped naked and badly beaten—for cooking their own meals in a "Freedom House" without a health permit.[161] And in what amounted to acting as acces-sories after the fact, prominent Mississippians regularly attempted to shift the blame for serious crimes to agents provocateurs among the "integrationists." Senator James Eastland, for example, initially suggested that the disappearance of Schwerner, Goodman, and Chaney was a "hoax" perpetrated by a "Com-munist conspiracy." When the bodies were eventually scooped out of an earth-en dam, Medford Evans, a well-known former college professor and writer, maintained that either they were "killed by 'wet squads' on their own side" or "three stiffs from the morgue had been planted" in the mud. Evans also claimed that crosses were repeatedly "burned *by Negroes* on the property of segrega-tionist whites" to garner sympathy.[162]

Two groups led Mississippi's official resistance to civil rights, both of them eventual benefactors of Draper's generosity: the Citizens' Councils, a private organization founded in 1954, and the Mississippi Sovereignty Commission, a creature of the state established by legislative action in 1956. In practice, how-ever, the private and public efforts often were intertwined, beginning with the interlocking directorate that characterized the leadership of both groups. Of the twelve members of the commission—all but three of whom were high-ranking state officials—four were on the board of directors of the Citizens' Councils, and three others, including the commission's chair, Governor Ross Barnett, were prominent council members. In addition, the commission acted as a conduit for funneling monthly payments to the councils, which were used to finance the *Citizens' Council Forum,* a radio and television series that provided free programs—a number of them featuring Kuttner, Gayre, Putnam, and Garrett—to local stations in all fifty states; the practice was terminated in 1965 by Governor Paul B. Johnson, who succeeded Barnett, but not before the councils had received some $200,000 ($1.15 million AFI).[163]

The combined action of these two organizations converted Mississippi into a police state, if a somewhat paradoxical one—the public component functioning covertly and the private one publicly. The Sovereignty Commission ferreted out any deviations from segregationist orthodoxy, no matter how slight, using a cadre of paid investigators and a network of *informelle Mitarbeiter* similar in style if not size to the Stasi's.[164] A statement by the commission's public relations director explained that one of its major responsibilities was "to build a file on persons whose utterances or actions indicate they should be watched with suspicion on future racial attitudes." Before the commission was finally disbanded in 1973, it had amassed confidential files on 87,000 people, making it, according to one journalist, "the largest state-level spying effort in U.S. history."[165] In a typical report, one of the commission's paid investigators took down the license plates of all vehicles parked near the churches in which NAACP meetings were held "to determine the employers of these individuals," who were then notified so that they could "take steps to have such activity curtailed." An official from the commission even circulated a student directory from the University of Mississippi—at the time an all-white institution—to others on the campus who were asked to check off "the names of those who don't think right."[166] And when the bodies of Schwerner, Chaney, and Goodman were finally discovered, the commission (which had earlier circulated the civil rights workers' names and schedules to local officials, leading to their murder) initiated an investigation of the doctor representing the victims' families. As the *New York Times* observed in 1961, Mississippi was a state "in which neighbor informs on neighbor, where state-hired spies fill files . . . with information on suspicious characters, and self-appointed Junior G men scurry about . . . keeping the campaign of hate and suspicion fed to fever pitch."[167]

Conscientious members of the Citizens' Councils were naturally eager to do their part in conveying important information to the commission. William Simmons, for example, notified the state body of an "ugly situation": A friend told him that the friend's nephew, an eleventh grader, had heard at school of a white pastor allowing a black couple to be married at his church. Simmons, along with other alarmed council leaders, also requested an investigation of Jackson's University Medical Center Hospital, where "laxity in segregation" had been discovered in departments such as "Pediatrics Ward, Emergency Ward, . . . elevator service, . . . [and] Accounting Department."[168]

But the more important responsibility of the councils was enforcement, especially under the leadership of the man referred to as Governor Ross Barnett's "prime minister for racial integrity"; after Barnett's landslide victory, assisted by the all-out support of the councils, Simmons became, according to one journalist, the governor's "constant traveling companion," the author of many of his speeches, and an "observer" at meetings of the Sovereignty Commission, while the state legislature became "little more than a rubber stamp" for bills that enjoyed the councils' endorsement. Attracting to its ranks the community's most influential members—wealthy planters, bankers, businesspeople, editors, doctors, lawyers, and even judges—the councils relied primarily on social and economic pressure to correct deviant behavior on race.[169] Merchants and newspaper editors who refused to espouse white supremacy were forced out of business, and dissenters in politics, education, and religion were purged from their positions, many of them driven from the state.[170] When the federal Civil Rights Commission attempted to create a state advisory board in Mississippi, the Citizens' Councils announced that participants would be regarded as "traitors," Simmons declaring that anyone "so stupid . . . [as] to be used for betrayal" would face "well-deserved distaste, contempt and ostracism"; unsurprisingly, for more than a year no one accepted appointment. A white clergyman who eventually agreed to serve was accorded the treatment prescribed by Simmons: a barrage of hate phone calls, rocks thrown at his house, garbage strewn on his lawn, and his children attacked by their playmates. Shortly after signing a warrant against one of the rock throwers, the clergyman was arrested and taken to jail, charged with perjury for having made the accusation.[171] To help right-thinking Mississippians identify "The Enemy," Simmons also published a list of seventy-four organizations posing a threat to the South's way of life, including the Episcopal Church, Methodist Church, National Catholic Welfare Conference, American Jewish Congress, Young Women's Christian Association, four federal cabinets, and a host of American Federation of Labor–Congress of Industrial Organizations affiliates.[172]

Although as official policy the councils rejected lawlessness, there was no lack of support for individual members who found the approved forms of intimidation insufficiently effective. When NAACP organizer Medgar Evers was assassinated by Byron de la Beckwith, one of the most active members of the local Citizens' Council, a fund drive for the murderer's legal expenses was immediately launched by other members, one of whom called the shooting "a patriotic act." (The Sovereignty Commission screened prospective jurors to ensure a not-guilty verdict—an act that, when revealed three decades later, produced a new trial and a conviction.)[173]

Almost a decade after *Brown,* eight years after the Montgomery, Alabama bus boycott, and four years after the first lunch counter sit-ins, many Southern states were gradually, if grudgingly, accepting the inevitable: greater participation of blacks in the polity and the society. In Mississippi, however, not a single fissure had yet appeared in the segregationist wall. It was here, where the state legislature had recently considered secession—rejecting it only because impractical—and where its highest officials encouraged citizens to defy the law and stand up to Washington's "Red Army," that Draper chose to make the greatest commitment of his resources, eventually pouring millions of dollars into the Sovereignty Commission and the Citizens' Councils, Mississippi's twin pillars of white supremacy.[174]

In June 1963, Mississippi attorney John Satterfield headed for Washington, D.C., where Senator Eastland had arranged a meeting "with a very influential man . . . whose identity must remain off the record"; president of the American Bar Association the previous year, Satterfield had provided much of the legal expertise in Mississippi's struggle, drafting legislation for the Citizens' Councils and acting as counsel to the Sovereignty Commission. According to the commission director, who was also present at the Washington meeting, the unnamed man "gave us a plan and pledged his efforts . . . to make it effective."[175]

As a result of this meeting, the Mississippi Sovereignty Commission soon added a new project to its slate of activities: the Coordinating Committee for Fundamental American Freedoms (CCFAF), an initiative to discredit and defeat the civil rights bill then being considered by Congress. During the next year, the CCFAF, which received 80 percent of its financing directly from the commission, would become, according to the *Washington Post,* the "best-organized and best-financed lobby" up to that time, far outspending any other single group attempting to influence legislation in 1964. In fact, these contributions from the commission were themselves private donations made to a "special fund," the contents of which were passed directly to the CCFAF. As the director of the commission explained to a journalist, the money "represented donations from all over the United States and the Sovereignty Commission was merely the funneling agency."[176]

The records of the commission, released in 1998 after a thirty-year legal battle, show that hundreds of Mississippi's finest citizens did indeed contribute to the fight against the civil rights bill. This was a well-organized campaign: The checks, in amounts from $5 to $500, were first collected from their individual members by representatives of various business and professional associations—the Mississippi Bankers' Association, the Bar Association, the Restaurant Association, the State Medical Association, realtors, truckers, farm bureau organizations, and many others—who then forwarded them to the commission "to be credited to the special fund and not commingled with other funds." The executive director of the Bankers' Association even circulated a memo to individual banks, "suggesting" a donation of $1 for every $100,000 of resources.[177]

Dedicated as they were, these efforts produced a total of less than $35,000; the remainder of the more than quarter million dollars channeled to the CCFAF by the Sovereignty Commission arrived in the form of donations from an unnamed New Yorker. In late July 1963, less than a month after Satterfield's meeting in Washington, the commission received from an anonymous donor a Morgan Guaranty Trust cashier's check for $10,000 ($58,000 AFI) that was immediately forwarded to the new organization. Eight weeks later, a telegram arrived from a Morgan vice president, informing the commission of an "anonymous gift" of stock from a client valued at approximately $100,000 ($583,000 AFI), "fact and amount of the gift to be kept confidential." Governor Barnett and the director of the commission both responded immediately, instructing the Morgan official to sell the stock and deposit the money in a Mississippi bank, and promising to abide by the donor's wishes.[178] In January 1964, after a similar exchange of communications, another $105,400 ($607,000 AFI) worth of stock was sold and the proceeds deposited in the commission's account. The funds from both gifts, noted the director, were immediately "transferred to the Coordinating Committee for Fundamental American Freedoms to be used in the fight against the civil rights bills."[179] Altogether the anonymous Northerner donated more than $215,000, the equivalent, in 2001, of $1.25 million. Only a handful of trusted insiders knew that the money had come from Draper; the unidentified man with the plan in the meeting arranged by Eastland had almost certainly been Harry Weyher.

Even while taking great pains to preserve Draper's anonymity, the Sovereignty Commission exploited the fact that he was not a Southerner. In a speech to a Northern audience, the commission's director emphasized that he had received donations to oppose the proposed civil rights act from "people all over the United States," noting that "three-fourths of this money came from outside the south."[180] In fact, all by himself the Colonel accounted for

84 percent of the Sovereignty Commission's contributions to the CCFAF; without him, there really was no Coordinating Committee.

The CCFAF's composition further strengthened the impression that it was Draper's group. Although well-known conservative curmudgeon William Loeb, publisher of the Manchester, New Hampshire *Union Leader,* was the chair, he had been asked to serve in that capacity by Carleton Putnam, who was also a member, in order to have a New Englander nominally in charge. In addition to Putnam and Loeb, the CCFAF included George S. Leonard, an attorney who had been part of Pittman's legal team in the *Stell* and *Evers* cases and would represent other Draper funded organizations; Richard Arens from the Colonel's immigration committee; Satterfield, a member of the National Putnam Letters Committee and "the brains" of the CCFAF, according to one journalist; and as the organization's director, John Synon, who took over the Letters Committee operation immediately after passage of the 1964 civil rights bill led to the dissolution of the CCFAF.[181]

The CCFAF's failure to achieve its goal was not for lack of effort. Synon and his staff compiled a mailing list of 14,000 names, including "every editor, city editor, and editorial director in the nation," and sent thirty-five different press releases to these people alone. A series of twelve separate radio broadcasts was aired on a number of stations. In "critical" states, a "program of complete saturation" included full-page advertisements in all daily newspapers and mailings to all individuals "of particular influence": personnel directors, industry executives, attorneys, doctors, teachers, bank presidents, local officials, and other "thought leaders." In its one year of operation, altogether the CCFAF distributed 3.9 million pieces of literature opposing any abolition of the right to discriminate against individuals on the basis of race, color, or national origin. Although the majority of this material was crafted to defeat a specific piece of legislation, the CCFAF also distributed thousands of copies of pamphlets from the Liberty Lobby and the National Putnam Letters Committee, including *The New Fanatics,* with its reservations that blacks were even fit for citizenship.[182]

While the CCFAF was working to defeat the civil rights bill, Satterfield submitted to the governor of Mississippi a proposal, developed by Synon and Putnam, for a new, more ambitious organization, explaining that the same anonymous Northern donor had pledged $200,000 ($1.15 million AFI) toward its creation, provided that the state would contribute a similar amount; obviously the project had already been approved by Draper and Weyher. Unlike the CCFAF, which was temporary and specific, having been created solely to oppose a specific piece of legislation, the new organization was to be permanent and much broader in scope, designed to influence policy by convincing the public of "the completely different nature of Negro citizens and white citizens"; the nation had to be shown that the plight of blacks was not "due to environmental factors, particularly to mistreatment and 'discrimination,'" but to their own biological shortcomings. The CCFAF was "engaged in [a] battle," wrote Satterfield to the governor, but the new organization was necessary "to win the war."[183]

This project was the logical culmination of Draper's many efforts to keep blacks in subordinate status. The publication of *Race and Reason,* the pamphlets distributed by the IAAEE, the Putnam Letters Committee and the Patrick Henry Group, and the role of intervenors in the *Stell* and *Evers* cases had all been designed to exploit putative racial differences as a barrier to political equality. But the new proposal was of a far larger scale, a single, unified plan combining scientific research with public relations and legal components. As always for the Colonel's projects, "the base of the effort" was to be scientific documentation of racial differences, including "direct grants to educational institutions for . . . research projects"; work in areas other than "race differences" would be supported "insofar as they may be material to this basic problem." The results would then be circulated to newspapers, periodicals, wire services, syndicated columnists, and radio and television stations. In addition, a periodical "of our own," would be subsidized, though not published, by the new organization," and "fronts" would be created to distribute "more subtle writings, those which carry arguments *shaded* with our beliefs." The project's legal arm would engage in litigation and legislation. A final recommendation, "high on our 'must' list," according to the proposal, was to help some interest "ideologically attuned to our thinking" to acquire ownership of a radio and television complex.[184]

As evidence of his commitment to the project, Draper had Weyher again forward stock valued at $50,000 ($288,000 AFI) to the Sovereignty Commission, accompanied by the now standard instructions from Morgan Guaranty's vice president: "Fact and amount of the gift to be kept confidential." Once again, the stock was cashed and the money deposited with the Sovereignty Commission. The entire $200,000 in matching funds was quickly approved by the governor and included in the legislature's annual appropriation to the Sovereignty Commission but subsequently rescinded in the wake of national outrage over the murder of the three civil rights workers that occurred only weeks after receipt of the Colonel's latest display of generosity. In danger of becoming a pariah state, Mississippi was reluctant to begin another highly publicized effort at victim blaming. A year later, Satterfield sent Weyher a check for the exact value of the stock. "Since no matching funds have been made available," wrote the Mississippi attorney to his friend in New York, "we have . . . concluded that these funds should not be utilized."[185]

Although the project was never implemented by the State of Mississippi,

after Draper's death in 1972 Weyher converted Pioneer, which had been largely inactive while the Colonel was still alive, into the instrument envisioned
in Satterfield's proposal. In the subsequent thirty years the fund followed the
Satterfield blueprint fairly closely, providing the financial support for scientific evidence of racial differences, numerous front groups that would distribute the results, journals published by other organizations themselves
subsidized by Pioneer, and groups engaged in legislation and litigation on
race. And though not funded by Pioneer, Weyher even participated in the
effort to acquire a media complex suggested by Satterfield when he represented the Jesse Helms political machine in its unsuccessful attempt at a hostile
takeover of the CBS network.[186]

## Some Island of Segregation

Abandoning Satterfield's program did not mean that Mississippi would abandon the struggle; however, it did signal a change in direction as even the most
intransigent segregationists were forced to confront legal and political realities. Between the disappointing outcome of the *Evers* case in July 1964 and
passage of the Civil Rights Act in the same year, "the conquest of the public
schools by the Negro revolutionaries has been accomplished," wrote Simmons. Token, court-ordered integration of the Jackson, Mississippi school
system, headquarters of the Citizens' Councils, was scheduled to begin in the
fall of 1964, and as the group's leadership contemplated the unthinkable, the
sense of embattlement that had always characterized the segregationists' resistance blossomed into full-fledged paranoia. They saw "forces in this nation and internationally" that intended to "mak[e] us one race of a burnt
umber hue," blending white "brilliance and endeavor" with black "dullness
and idiocy" to create sterile minds that "might be trained and warped for
their purposes." Integration was thus not the real objective of demands for
black equality. "Disorder is the goal," declared a field director for the councils, "and integration is invoked to achieve it." In this view, black students
were being brought into "white" schools not to be educated but "to prevent
the education of the white students."[187]

    In the face of such powerful and sinister opposition, further attempts to
salvage the public schools were considered futile; as an article in the *Citizen*
observed, even the president had joined in "the jungle chant, 'We Shall Overcome.'" Instead of continuing their unsuccessful attempts to reverse the
"Black Monday" decision, the segregationists now sought a practical way
around it. The only remaining hope for preserving "the Southern way of life
against alien encroachment," they decided, was to provide "some island of
segregation" as an alternative to the public schools.[188]

Although planning for this new strategy had begun behind the scenes as early as March 1964 with the formation of a School Committee within the Jackson Citizens' Council, the first overt step occurred when the Council School Foundation was chartered in September 1964, at the beginning of the first school year in which a few blacks would attend formerly white schools in Jackson. Announcement of the intention to create a private school system for whites only was made at a meeting of the Jackson Citizens' Council, following an address by Garrett on the "intellectually inferior" nature of blacks. The School Foundation's board included Simmons as treasurer, shortly to become its president; Dan Shell as secretary, a member of the Sovereignty Commission, counsel (together with Satterfield) for the State's General Legislative Investigating Committee, and attorney for the intervenors in the *Evers* case; and J. Dudley Buford as counsel. Both Shell and Buford were also partners in Satterfield's law firm.[189]

In addition to protecting the racial integrity of its students, the private schools would also allow the council to implement the curriculum it had earlier recommended for the segregated public system. In the third and fourth grades, for example, students were to be taught that "God wanted the white people to live alone. And He wanted the colored people to live alone"; moreover, "White men built the United States so they could make their rules," but "some people want us [the races] to live together . . . [in order] to make our country weak." There would be no conflict between science and religion in the council schools: In the fifth and sixth grades, students would learn that "segregation is Christian" and that "God doesn't want races to mix"; "famous scientists" supported "God's plan," demonstrating that the races did not belong together because "the white man is very civilized, while the pure Negro in Africa is still living as a savage."[190]

In an astonishingly short period of time, the foundation created its own school system with its own superintendent. In early October 1964, the first council school, with 22 students in the six elementary grades, began operation, expanding by the beginning of the next school year to 110 students in all twelve grades. In September 1966, the foundation broke ground for its own modern educational complex, and three years later it controlled two racially segregated twelve-grade systems in Jackson with an enrollment of 3,000 students. By spring 1970 construction was under way for three new complexes, and the two existing systems were being enlarged. Nor did these projects offer merely essentials; each complex included an "auditorium-gymnasium, lighted athletic fields, and other related facilities." James J. Kilpatrick, who had been vice chair of the CCFAF, bragged that the classrooms were "carpeted, wood-paneled, air-conditioned, handsomely designed affairs," estimated to cost $4,000 ($18,000 AFI) each.[191]

This flurry of activity demanded a great deal of money for operating costs and capital construction. To assist with the former, in July 1964 the state legislature, largely controlled by members and supporters of the councils, quickly pushed through a bill authorizing payment of $185 per year to each child in a "nonsectarian" private school and allowing local governments to offer an additional amount. To defray construction costs the School Foundation solicited memberships at $100 per person, but by May 1966, only $9,000 ($50,000 AFI) had been raised, and, the president of the foundation lamented, "there were no large donors." However, income tax returns for 1964 and 1965 reported receipt of $55,700 ($321,000 AFI) in contributions the first year and $92,500 ($524,000 AFI) the second. Even allowing for the in-kind value of donated land—$4,000 in 1964 and $45,700 in 1965—the foundation still enjoyed cash gifts of more than $98,000 ($563,000 AFI) in its first two years.[192] Obviously it had found a source of funds in addition to its ninety paid memberships.

In this case again, Draper undoubtedly was the major contributor. According to his will, in the year before his death the Colonel made twenty-nine separate contributions of $1,000 ($4,400 AFI) each to private segregated schools, none of them in Mississippi.[193] It is hardly possible that, although he was donating to so many other schools throughout the South in 1971, Draper had contributed nothing to the development, a few years earlier, of the Council School Foundation's system. Not only was the Mississippi effort headed by "Billy" Simmons, his close ally in the fight for racial purity, but the Colonel had some particularly strong connection to Jackson, perhaps because it remained the unwavering locus of support for white supremacy. Although he was raised in New England and a long-time resident of New York, Draper's checking account at Deposit Guarantee National Bank in Jackson contained $179,000 ($765,000 AFI) at his death, almost three times the amount in his New York account; the Colonel also kept $450,000 in diamonds (almost $2 million AFI) in a safe deposit box at Deposit Guaranty, requiring Weyher, the executor of his will, to employ an armored truck to transport the gems back to New York for sale.[194]

In addition, Draper left $1.7 million ($7.26 million AFI) in his will to the Puritan Foundation, which had been incorporated in Jackson in August 1963 by Buford and Shell for unspecified charitable purposes. According to its charter, the nonprofit foundation was to receive investments, the proceeds from which it would then donate as "grants or gifts" to other nonprofit organizations "engaged in efforts to improve the conditions of mankind." That is, Puritan was formed to act as an intermediary, funneling money from unnamed donors to unspecified recipients. The true purpose of this vague document became somewhat clearer when an amendment, filed in March

1964—at exactly the same time that the Jackson Citizens' Council's School Committee was planning its alternative, segregated system—revealed that John B. Trevor Jr. was the Puritan Foundation's president and Harry Weyher its secretary, indicating that even before Draper's death the foundation had been one of Pioneer's unacknowledged activities. The participation of Buford and Shell in this laundering operation, both men members of the board of the Council School Foundation, suggested the ultimate destination of the Colonel's money in this case. Any residual doubt that Puritan had been Draper's method for funding segregated schools in Jackson was dispelled when, in 1978, the Puritan Foundation was merged into the Council School Foundation.[195] For practical purposes, there probably was never any real distinction between the two organizations.

Finally, Draper's will named Jackson's Deposit Guaranty as trustee for another $3.25 million ($13.9 million AFI). Although the ultimate recipient of these funds is unknown, they were also undoubtedly left for another operation intended to preserve "some island of segregation." The bank itself, where Simmons's father had been chair of the Executive and Trust Committees, had been notably sympathetic to the segregationists' campaign, providing substantial loans to the local Citizens' Council and its School Foundation for the five segregated schools in the Jackson area; disclosure of the loans in 1970 caused some embarrassment because, by that time, the chair of Deposit Guaranty's Executive Committee was also a member of an educational advisory committee set up by the Nixon administration to promote support for public schools in Mississippi.[196] Between the Puritan Foundation and the unnamed recipient of the Deposit Guaranty trusteeship, the Colonel had left just under $5 million ($21.14 million AFI) to the center of resistance to civil rights.

\* \* \*

With so much of Draper's assistance to the segregationist struggle shrouded in secrecy and obscured by intermediaries, there is no reason to believe that his support was confined only to the projects discussed here; although direct evidence of his contribution is lacking, there are numerous other organizations whose personnel and substantive position made them likely beneficiaries of the Colonel's generosity.[197] But although a complete list of recipients and amounts may never be possible, even before the bequests in his will, Draper clearly contributed millions of dollars to the campaign against civil rights, an amount equivalent to many times that much thirty-five years later. With no immediate family members, the racist cause was the central concern in the Colonel's life, and he had the independent wealth to back his convictions: At his death Draper's estate was valued at $25 million

($106 million AFI). Whatever the total, there is little doubt that "our source of funds" was the most important single financial resource for the struggle to maintain American apartheid.

Yet at the same time that Draper, Weyher, and Trevor—the three men who controlled Pioneer—were secretly providing financial and strategic support for attempts to deny to black citizens rights guaranteed by the Constitution, the fund itself made only five small grants. Like an accountant with two sets of books, only one of which was for public display, Pioneer later was able to portray itself as interested solely in assisting the pursuit of scientific knowledge.

When Draper died in 1972, the clandestine contributions, which had come directly out of his pocket, came to an end. With the insiders' books closed and the fund's image no longer in danger of being marred by secret connections to direct political campaigns waged by neo-Nazis and segregationists, Pioneer's true goal could enjoy an even more plausible deniability. But in the post-Draper era the fund became the instrument for carrying out the Colonel's agenda. His troops had lost every battle so far, but, just as Satterfield had advised, they looked to a new organization "to win the war." That organization was the Pioneer Fund.

# 4    They Are Not Like Us: The Pioneer Fund in the Post–Civil Rights Era

WANTING TO ensure that his fortune would continue to support his beliefs, both before and after his death, an aging Draper placed all his confidence in the president of his fund, giving Harry Weyher control of his resources and appointing the attorney trustee of his estate and executor of his will. The 1967 trust agreement also established a "Distribution Committee," consisting of Weyher and Draper, to carry on the Colonel's practice of selecting appropriate recipients for "substantial gifts" from the trust property while he was still alive. Although such gifts were naturally expected to abide by Draper's "preferences," Weyher was permitted to choose recipients by himself, provided he notified the Colonel within five days. This extraordinary confidence in Weyher was not an indication of any great friendship between the two men. During the probate hearings on Draper's will, his tax attorney—a member of the same firm as Weyher—testified that Weyher was not a "social acquaintance" of the deceased, "because Colonel Draper was a great loner." Rather, the decision to leave Weyher in complete control of the estate reflected Draper's faith that Pioneer's president shared his opposition to racial equality and would use the resources to pursue this goal.[1]

For his own part, Weyher was well aware of the expectations that accompanied control of Draper's estate: The Colonel's money was to be expended only on politically acceptable projects. Moreover, as Weyher had learned early in his association with the Colonel, the importance of this condition was not to be diminished in the least by Draper's death. In 1956, one of the attorney's first acts for his new client was to explore the establishment of some sort of long-term program to demonstrate the "dysgenic effects" of "potentially dangerous policies" such as the *Brown* decision. As he had explained to Wesley Critz George, Weyher was concerned that money left to a university or other institution might eventually "come under the control of people who would use it for purposes not entirely in accord with the purposes of the donor." Thus, even if Weyher did not enthusiastically share Draper's convictions, his appointment as trustee of the Colonel's money also brought with it what he perceived as a fiduciary obligation to use the funds in support of the Colonel's agenda. As Weyher stated to the Faculty Senate Committee at the University of Delaware during the 1989 controversy over Pioneer's grant to Linda Gottfredson, "I don't believe in changing somebody else's objectives or somebody else's targets if he is the one who paid for the whole thing."[2] Nor could there have been any doubt about what Draper's objectives were: not to *advance* science but to use it as a tool to support racial separation. As he had informed Frederick Osborn shortly before replacing him with Weyher, the Colonel insisted on research results that would "promote . . . ethnic homogeneity," and he would not aid "investigators whose . . . view points were markedly alien" to his own.[3]

After gifts were distributed and expenses paid—including, for Weyher, both an $80,000 ($342,000 AFI) gift and a $280,000 ($1.2 million AFI) fee as executor—the remainder of Draper's estate was divided into four unequal pieces. Approximately a million dollars—the smallest of the four pieces— was set aside to be divided among the many descendants of the Prestons and Drapers, each such relative receiving approximately $10,000 ($43,000 AFI). Having some idea of the nature of the groups that received the bulk of the estate, one of Draper's cousins stated that "the family was furious" that the Colonel had left such a "measly little bit" to his relatives, especially because so much of his fortune went to what many of them considered a "Hitlerite" cause. The remaining portions went to the trust supervised by Deposit Guaranty National Bank in Jackson, Mississippi; the Puritan Fund, which later merged with Simmons's Council School Foundation; and the Pioneer Fund, which received $2.6 million ($11.1 million AFI).[4] From Draper's viewpoint, these bequests were designed as different routes to the same end: The contributions to Mississippi were intended to help preserve segregation in practice, and the endowment for Pioneer was expected to provide the scientific evidence for the "completely different nature" of blacks that would justify segregation in theory.

Thus, while the Colonel was alive, Weyher distributed money directly from his account to scientific projects that met his criteria; after his death Weyher continued to distribute his money for the same purpose, Pioneer now replacing the Colonel as "our source of funds." It is instructive that in the two years after Draper's death, the fund distributed substantially more money than it had during the entire period from 1937 to 1972.

The subsequent appointments to Pioneer's board provided a clear indication that Draper's legacy would be continued under Weyher's control. To replace the Colonel, Weyher chose his mentor's favorite scientist, psychologist and tireless pamphleteer for segregation, Henry E. Garrett. Increasingly embittered by the nation's unwillingness to keep millions of its citizens in second-class status, by the late 1960s Garrett had begun to regard events that appalled others as signs of progress for the racist cause. "The Newark riots mean that there are 25 fewer Bantu for later," he wrote to George after blacks were killed during urban unrest in the summer of 1967.[5] Weyher's first appointment thus added to Pioneer's board a social scientist who had not only fought every attempt to extend equality to blacks but actually appeared to anticipate racial warfare in the United States.

When Garrett died only a year after being appointed to the board, he was replaced by attorney Thomas F. Ellis, like Weyher an insider in North Carolina politics and a long-time opponent of racial equality. In response to the *Brown* decision, Ellis had been an organizer of the campaign to "protect the people of [North Carolina] . . . from integration" and, in 1955, was appointed special counsel and executive secretary for the state's Advisory Committee on Education, which recommended that local officials be empowered to abolish public schools rather than integrate them; after George had sent his articles attacking the *Brown* decision to the governor's office, it was probably Ellis who forwarded them to Weyher, eventually leading to the anatomist's participation in the many activities funded by Draper. As the education committee's counsel, Ellis had declared that "the present integration movement in the public schools is but a part of a planned social revolution in the South, fostered, directed and financed by non-southern whites . . . [whose] eventual goal . . . is racial intermarriage and the disappearance of the Negro race by fusing into the white." He thus urged as official policy that "upon the integration of any school in a unit" in the state, "whether by voluntary action or court order, all appropriations, both state and local, for all schools in such unit be immediately terminated." A year later, at a time when the NAACP, the plaintiff in the *Brown* ruling, was beginning to seek enforcement of the court's mandate to end segregated public education, Ellis explored the possibility of enacting legislation to remove the tax exemption of black churches and other civic groups that allowed their property to be used for meetings of the association.[6]

Ellis went on to a career as a backroom political architect, becoming particularly well known for his use of race as a divisive tactic. In 1976, while serving on Pioneer's board, Ellis attempted to assist Ronald Reagan's campaign in the North Carolina presidential primary by circulating literature claiming that Gerald Ford, Reagan's chief rival, would name a black running mate

if nominated; although the tactic was disavowed by Reagan's staff, it appeared
to be successful, producing a victory in the state primary after Reagan had
been far behind in earlier polls. As the chief political strategist for North
Carolina Senator Jesse Helms, Ellis later crafted another tactic that rescued
a losing campaign: the "white hands" ad (which one journalist called "famous . . . in the annals of negative campaigning") in which the hands of a
white man crumple a rejection letter while a voice-over says, "You needed
that job and you were best qualified. But they had to give it to a racial minority because of a racial quota" supported, according to the ad, by Helms's
opponent, a black candidate.[7]

After service as a board member, Ellis himself became a Pioneer grantee
when the Coalition for Freedom, a tax-exempt foundation he created as an
outgrowth of Jesse Helms's National Conservative Club, received $195,000
($308,000 AFI) in the 1980s to support its goal of financing television pro-
grams with conservative political orientations. (According to the Washington Post, the IRS later revoked the coalition's tax-exempt status, charging that
the group had illegally participated in political activities by acting as a "cash
conduit" for the NCC and other conservative groups, activity that had occurred while it was receiving Pioneer money.) Ellis, in turn, employed Weyher as the attorney for Fairness in Media, which he cofounded, in its attempt
at a hostile takeover of CBS. Part of a multi-million-dollar political empire
of foundations and political action committees created by Ellis and Helms,
Fairness in Media was frank about its interest in the television network,
launching its bid not to make a profit but in pursuit of ideological goals.[8]

Another Pioneer board member appointed in 1973 was Marion Parrott, an
attorney and a relative of Weyher as well as a fellow resident of his home town
of Kinston, North Carolina. Parrott had been one of the state's directors of
the Southern Independent School Association, an organization headed by
Citizens' Council chief William Simmons and devised to circumvent the
Brown decision by creating an extensive system of private schools for whites
only throughout the South; indeed, Simmons had been chosen to lead the
association because, as president of Jackson, Mississippi's Council School
Foundation, he was already supervising the nation's largest segregated private school system.[9] Unlike Ellis, who served on Pioneer's board for only four
years, Parrott remained through the rest of the century, joining Weyher and
Trevor as its core. Thus even after Draper's death Pioneer's board continued
to be controlled by vigorous opponents of civil rights.

These were men who firmly believed that there was something fundamentally different about blacks, an otherness of which lower intelligence was a
part but certainly not the whole. There was something deeper about blacks

that defined their very nature, making it unthinkable for them to be full and equal participants in a society created by and for whites; they just did not fit in. The United States, Garrett had declared on television, was a "white man's civilization" where blacks were tolerated merely as "guests," enjoying no claim to equal status with their hosts, the permanent residents. Nor were exceptions to be tolerated in individual cases of outstanding ability. It was "unsound," according to Garrett, to treat "persons . . . strictly as individuals"; after all, he had argued in *Science,* "no matter how low . . . an American white may be, his ancestors built the civilizations of Europe," and "no matter how high . . . a Negro may be, his ancestors were (and his kinsmen still are) savages in an African jungle." As William Massey similarly observed in his *Mankind Quarterly* article republished by the National Putnam Letters Committee, even when highly intelligent, blacks were "temperamentally unsuited for citizenship." For Pioneer's board, science was not really necessary to demonstrate the existence of these differences, which, in Putnam's words, were obvious to "any man with two eyes in his head."[10] Empirical evidence thus was not an essential element of proof but only further confirmation of a conviction known instinctively to be the case, useful mainly in convincing *other* people. For Pioneer, black otherness was axiomatic, an article of faith long before becoming a conclusion of science.

The Colonel himself, of course, had been interested in science primarily as a justification for more practical measures. As Draper confided in 1947 to Malcolm Donald, his attorney and fellow board member, he had no real concern with research in genetics because "enough was known on the subject," and it was more important "to do something practical," such as "moving the colored race to Liberia." The advancement of knowledge was subsidiary to Draper's primary goal: a society uncontaminated by blacks and racially undesirable immigrants. In sympathy with the Colonel's objectives and charged with the responsibility of using his funds in a manner of which its founder would have approved, Weyher and his fellow board members found it necessary to reverse the Colonel's priorities for tactical reasons, placing the emphasis on science in the hope of recreating a climate of public opinion favorable to their cause.

The problem, from Pioneer's point of view, was that, primarily because of the Jewish-controlled media, the nation no longer shared their certitude about racial differences. An earlier era had harbored no such doubts. Not long ago, Garrett had observed, "the Negro was generally considered to be less intelligent and more indolent than the white, and to be somewhat lacking in the fundamental traits of honesty and reliability. This judgment was concurred in by most white Americans." But now that the society could no longer see what was so self-evident to the members of Pioneer's board, scientific investigations had become essential, not because there could be the slightest question about their outcome but in order to return public opinion to its earlier consensus, the necessary first step in redirecting social policy. Having spent the civil rights era on the wrong side of history, Pioneer turned to science, if not for a reversal of the extension of equal rights to blacks, then at least for vindication—to prove to the nation that it had made a mistake.

Yet even while preparing to continue the scientific assault on political equality, the key members of Pioneer's board had not lost sight of the larger picture. Still aware that the demand for equal rights for minorities was but one manifestation of the insidious Jewish penetration of media and government, Weyher and Trevor collaborated in the Colonel's last attempt to warn the public of this more serious, underlying problem. Almost two years before Draper's death, Weyher circulated to the usual insiders a manuscript by a pseudonymous author, "Wilmot Robertson," which was eventually published as *The Dispossessed Majority*. Considering the work a "really very fine exposition" based on "extraordinarily able research," Trevor asked Weyher's permission to forward the manuscript to one of his father's old friends in military intelligence; a copy of the request was also sent to "Col. Wickliffe P. Draper," one of the rare instances in which his name appeared in correspondence and an indication that he was once again the source of funds for its publication. This impression was further confirmed when Putnam noted, soon after the book's publication two and a half years later, that the "printing of 5,000 hardcovers was financed by a $20,000 [$85,000 AFI] grant from an individual who has since died."[11]

*The Dispossessed Majority* explained that almost all the nation's contemporary problems stemmed from the presence of "unassimilable minorities"—not just blacks but also Asians, Hispanics, Greeks, southern Italians, Arabs, American Indians, and Jews. These groups, estimated by Robertson at 30 percent of the population, were not entitled to the Bill of Rights and other constitutional protections because, he maintained, "rights *earned* by one [racial] group" could not be "*donated* to another." Moreover, the *Brown* decision had "kill[ed education] by destroying its binding force—the homogeneity of teacher and pupil." In particular, Robertson obsessed over "Jewish hegemony," writing that, as a result of "their fear and loathing of Western civility" and their "vendetta . . . against all things non-Jewish," Jews had set out "to bruise Western culture"—to undermine the intellectual disciplines and "divide and destroy the Western political and economic order"—through their leadership "of every divisive force in the modern era, from class agitation to minority racism, from the worst capitalistic exploitation to the most brutal collectivism, from blind religious dogma to atheism and psychoanalysis, from total dogmatism to total permissiveness." A good indication of their contribution to society, he suggested, was the condition of the city where Jews were most heavily concentrated: New York could "only be described as the greatest municipal catastrophe of the day—a scabrous pile of ugliness, tastelessness, and lawlessness." Noting that Jews had infected most of western Europe with the same "social diseases," Robertson observed that despite its severe defeat, Germany had emerged from the war as "the one large Western nation almost free of Jewish financial domination" and had become, as a consequence, "the most affluent and most stable nation in Europe." To put a stop to "the Jewish envelopment of America," he concluded, "history should not be repeated"; this time, "the operation ought to be accomplished with finesse."[12]

*The Dispossessed Majority* quickly became canonical in neo-Nazi circles. The most erudite of the Nazi activists, University of Illinois classics professor Revilo P. Oliver—who had been forced to resign from the John Birch Society after referring to the "beatific vision" that could be realized on Earth if only "all the Jews were vaporized at dawn tomorrow"—called it "politically the most important book published in this country since 1949— perhaps since 1917." In *The Mankind Quarterly* Robert Kuttner raved over the work, praising the "brilliance" of Robertson's "comprehensive" analysis, describing his "insights" as "original and penetrating" and "highly recommend[ing]" the "wealth of . . . material" that awaited "the careful reader."[13] (Although there was not the slightest doubt that Kuttner's enthusiasm was genuine, he had just received his last gift from the Colonel's estate when asked to review the book that had been posthumously published through Draper's support.)

Carleton Putnam, who had brought Robertson's manuscript to the Colonel's attention, was particularly enamored of the work, much to the surprise of Trevor, who "did not know that he had a good understanding of the broad spectrum of problems which face us—excellent as his views are" on the "limited area" of racial issues. In fact, Putnam well appreciated the larger perspective shared by some of Pioneer's board. He considered Hitler "the product of . . . a prior envelopment of German society by an aggressive, racially alien minority, which produced . . . a cancer," and *The Dispossessed Majority* now clearly demonstrated to him the "recommencement" of this pattern, "an ominous renewal of an envelopment, which may well create another cancer here in the United States unless it is checked and controlled." And he held "the Jew . . . responsible for our current Negro problem [and] the incitement of the Negro to insurrection against our White culture."[14] Putnam went on to take the lead in ensuring that *The Dispossessed Majority* was distributed

to "very influential people," those "near . . . to the controls of our society"—
"I do not say *at* the controls," he wrote to General Albert C. Wedemeyer,
another officer concerned with the Jewish threat, "because you and I know
who actually runs our society these days." In addition, he assisted Robertson in the formation of Howard Allen Press, which published a handful of
similar books on race, including a reprint of one of Garrett's pamphlets on
black inferiority.[15]

Pioneer's officially acknowledged grants concentrated primarily on race,
however. With the fund's portfolio well managed and enjoying the advantages of a steadily rising economy, Pioneer distributed close to $13 million
over the next three decades—more than $18 million adjusted for inflation.
Though not a large amount by foundation standards, the grants were carefully selected to support the fund's agenda. Especially throughout the 1970s,
Pioneer focused like a laser on "the completely different nature of Negro
citizens and white citizens," devoting almost every penny of its grants to
scientists ranging from nationally and internationally known researchers to
complete obscurities, all of whom, not coincidentally, had one belief in common: that blacks were genetically less intelligent than whites. And the fund
certainly enjoyed maximum exposure for its money, as Weyher, in keeping
with the strategy in the Satterfield proposal, exploited every opportunity to
pitch the work of recipients to the public, particularly to the media. Pioneer
also provided substantial resources for organizations created solely to publicize the work of grantees and other scientists with similar conclusions, in
some cases using the Colonel's tactic of choice for influencing opinion: circulating free books and articles to lists of influential people. Thus, although
many of the grants did go to support the work of various scientists, Pioneer
functioned in many ways more like a lobbying group.

Although Pioneer maintained this focus on racial differences in the 1980s
and 1990s, the fund also broadened its interests in a number of ways. It supported grantees who not only concurred that blacks were intellectually disadvantaged but found them similarly deficient in numerous indications of
morality. Taken as a whole, the conclusions offered by the fund's scientists
attempted to recreate the image of blacks that, according to Garrett, had been
the common-sense judgment "concurred in by most white Americans" decades before scheming Jewish "equalitarians" had duped the society: They
were unintelligent, indolent, dishonest, and unreliable. Many of these researchers also maintained that interracial hostility was natural (i.e., innate,
therefore inevitable) and necessary for evolutionary progress. In addition, as
the pattern of immigration changed in the late twentieth century, Pioneer
turned its attention and resources once again to the problem that had ob-

sessed the eugenicists of the 1920s, seeing the influx of newcomers—this time from the Third World rather than the less desirable parts of Europe—as a threat to the nation's well-being. Many of the fund's grantees frankly considered the United States a "white nation" and vowed to keep it that way.

An important exception to the focus on race was Pioneer's largest single grantee, Thomas Bouchard's Minnesota study of separated twins, which received $1.8 million ($2.6 million AFI) over a twenty-year period beginning in 1979.[16] Suggesting that many traits had high heritability, the Minnesota project was of genuine scientific interest, although, ironically, it was the sort of research that Draper would almost certainly have declined to fund in an earlier era, when a simplistic belief in the overwhelming influence of genes would have made the study's outcome too obvious to merit his money. In the zeitgeist of the 1980s, however, when an optimistic environmentalism had raised expectations over the likelihood of improving cognitive skills, proof of a trait's heritability had become a necessary (though hardly sufficient) element in the argument that differences between races were both immutable and genetic. As the Satterfield plan had indicated, work in areas other than "race differences" would be supported "insofar as they may be material to this basic problem."

Except for the grants made to the Minnesota study, Pioneer expended the bulk of its funds between 1971 and 1999 in five often overlapping categories:

—The coordinated efforts of Stanford's William Shockley and Berkeley's Arthur Jensen
—Nonprofit organizations devoted solely to publishing and distributing literature
—The work of Roger Pearson, one of the most important and enduring figures in the postwar Nazi movement, and his colleagues, including veterans of the battle against civil rights such as Kuttner and Swan
—A new group of scientists interested in race, many of whom furnished the intellectual justification for the far-right group American Renaissance
—A number of organizations opposed to immigration

These five areas accounted for almost 70 percent of the money distributed by Pioneer over three decades, and the Minnesota twin study received approximately another 14 percent. The remaining grants went to a variety of efforts, including work on racial differences by old allies such as Osborne, Gregor, and the IAAEE; eugenically oriented population studies; legal foundations pursuing conservative causes, such as the Center for Individual Rights, counsel for the plaintiffs in a number of attempts to overturn affirmative action; and various conservative projects such as Ellis's attempt to finance conservative television programming and the American Policy Institute, dedicated to reducing government regulation of business. No doubt as a ploy to enhance its image, Pioneer even gave token amounts—$1,000 ($1,700 AFI) and $3,000 ($8,200 AFI), respectively—to studies of Tay-Sachs disease and sickle cell anemia.

## The Shockley-Jensen Team

In 1965, just as it seemed that the segregationists were being routed by the civil rights movement's overwhelming moral authority, unexpected reinforcements suddenly arrived when Stanford physicist William Bradford Shockley entered the controversy over racial differences in ability, bringing with him the instant credibility of that ultimate scientific credential, the Nobel prize, which he had received jointly with two colleagues for invention of the transistor.

A prickly man accustomed to getting his way, Shockley was never hesitant to speak as an authority on issues far outside his area of expertise. In the early 1960s, he had become interested in world overpopulation, planning to encourage restraint in growth by submitting a statement signed by Nobel laureates to the Pope and the United Nations Secretary General.[17] Then, in 1965, invited as a laureate to address a Nobel conference on "Genetics and the Future of Man," Shockley chose the occasion to announce his concern with the problem of "genetic deterioration," caused by what he called "evolution in reverse": In place of survival of the fittest, the social programs of Lyndon Johnson's Great Society supposedly were promoting the disproportionate proliferation of genetic defectives. In an observation that must have delighted the officials of a fund based on a belief in the genetic superiority of "white persons who settled in the original thirteen states," Shockley subsequently proclaimed the first European inhabitants of the United States "the most competent population in terms of social management and general capacity for organization."[18]

Moreover, especially among blacks, according to Shockley, the least capable were producing the largest number of offspring, leading to their "genetic enslavement," an Orwellian phrase suggesting that blacks had overcome the chains of chattel slavery only to be shackled by the internal oppressor: their inferior genes. Not only were blacks less intelligent in this analysis, but attempting to improve their plight through social programs of any kind was a waste of taxpayers' money; the only real hope for improvement, according to Shockley, was not enriched education, better health care, or other environmental interventions but the systematic reduction of the black population through sterilization and other methods of birth control.[19] Earnest Sevier Cox's project had failed, but repatriation might not be the only way to decrease the number of blacks in the country.

In the subsequent decade, Shockley made ever more outrageous pronouncements about race, insisting, for example, that discriminatory treatment of blacks should not be considered prejudice because it was "based on sound statistics." The refusal to hire someone on the basis of race was defensible, he explained, because the "man-in-the-street has had experience and knows what to expect from blacks." Indeed, the physicist maintained, "nature has color-coded groups of individuals so that statistically reliable predictions of their adaptability to intellectually rewarding and effective lives can easily be made and profitably used" by others.[20] Personnel tests and other measures designed for appropriate job placement apparently were necessary only for employers who were color-blind.

Shockley's highly publicized statements on race and genetic deterioration immediately drew the attention of the Colonel's activists, and the Nobel laureate soon found himself the object of overtures from Weyher, Putnam, Garrett, Kuttner, and Osborne; the scientists who had opposed *Brown* often began their letters with the observation that they were writing at "Harry Weyher's suggestion," Draper's attorney continuing to be the coordinator behind the scenes. The physicist and the segregationists quickly formed an alliance, Shockley pleased to have a group of adoring supporters at a time when so many scientists were denouncing him as a racist and the Colonel's clique delighted at this unexpected appearance of a prominent ally, someone they previously had no idea was sympathetic to their concerns.[21]

Despite friendly warnings, Shockley immediately endorsed Putnam's work. Dwight J. Ingle, the University of Chicago physiologist who was sympathetic to Shockley's concerns and had earlier opened the pages of his prestigious journal, *Perspectives in Biology and Medicine,* to Garrett and Kuttner, feared that the association would be harmful to the cause. "If our efforts ever become identified or even slightly associated with those of Carleton Putnam," wrote Ingle to Shockley, "we will fail to gain support. . . . Putnam writes of love, but he hates Negroes and anyone who does not agree with him"; moreover, he "wants forced segregation of the races . . . [and] is . . . opposed to equal civil rights and opportunities." Even Kuttner, the neo-Nazi activist who explained to a Citizens' Council audience that the purpose of integration was to make it easier for black drug addicts "to catch a white girl," suggested to Shockley, out of concern for "diplomacy," that "reference to Putnam's works may be damaging"; according to Kuttner, Putnam was so outrageous that he had "embarrassed even the governor of Mississippi."[22]

Nevertheless when Putnam's next assault on equality appeared, in 1967, it bore Shockley's official endorsement on the dust cover, along with praise for the work from Satterfield, George, and a number of Southern newspapers. *Race and Reality* provided yet another account of the "equalitarian conspiracy" perpetrated by Jewish scientists to achieve unmerited rights for blacks and of its exposure in the *Stell* case. Not only were blacks to be educated in separate schools, insisted Putnam, but they had no right to the ballot: "The unlimited suffrage concept is marginal" even for "an advanced and experienced race like the Anglo-American," he wrote, but "to apply it to states or communities with high percentages of a retarded race is suicidal." Shockley's blurb on the book's jacket urged "thoughtful citizens to read Putnam's analyses . . . in the interest of replacing prejudice, prejudgment and bias with scientific method and objectivity."[23] (Ironically, while Putnam's book was again complaining about the suppression of scientific truth in court, he was resorting to the courts to suppress the truth about himself: His attorney was threatening Ingle to keep him from publishing "candid statements" Putnam made about race in letters written before he realized that Ingle was not "in full agreement with his views.") Putnam quickly produced a new pamphlet, distributed by both the National Putnam Letters Committee and the Citizens' Councils, noting the physicist's endorsement and pointing out how his views supported the segregationists.[24] In addition, Shockley sent unsolicited copies of the book, along with a lengthy letter repeating his endorsement, to leading members of Congress and well-known journalists such as Joseph Alsop. Now to the thousands of free copies of Putnam's book distributed to the usual recipients—religious leaders, the media, university presidents, the members of both houses of Congress, all state governors and attorneys-general, state superintendents of education, and justices at various levels from the circuit courts to the U.S. Supreme Court—could be added those that arrived with a cover letter from a Nobel laureate. (Ironically, one recipient of Shockley's letter recommending the book was well-known Cornell University geneticist Bruce Wallace, who had been hired during his graduate student days to teach Draper some elementary genetics and had been so repulsed by his employer's racist notions; "a person who recommends such rubbish," wrote Wallace about Shockley, was "inappropriate as a university lecturer.")[25]

To the segregationists, Shockley's emergence was a godsend, as if they had won the lottery without even having bought a ticket; after the media had largely ignored all their attempts to make black intellectual inferiority the central issue in discussions of race, a noted scientist had suddenly placed their favorite topic on the front page. Shockley immediately became their ultimate authority figure, regularly cited, with no objection on his part, to oppose racial equality. For example, John Synon, at various times director of the CCFAF, the National Putnam Letters Committee, and the Patrick Henry Press—all the Colonel's operations—suggested in his newspaper column that it was folly to ignore Shockley's warning and grant equal rights to blacks because, if the physicist was right, "the Black man is incapable, now or ever, of competing equally. . . . The Negro cannot stand the White man's pace." Shockley was also prominently featured in *The Citizen,* where he was contrasted with the "conglomeration of moral cowards" in the National Academy of Sciences who ignored his warnings.[26] The fact that Shockley had done no research on genetic differences was of no consequence; he was a Nobel laureate, saying what the Draper clique wanted desperately to hear and eager to proselytize, and they quickly set out to exploit the opportunity presented by Shockley's prestige through a public relations campaign in which the physicist was not only an enthusiastic participant but often the chief strategist.

From the outset, Weyher and his allies viewed Shockley as the latest component of their long struggle, his work to be coordinated with the larger effort against integration and the Jewish-controlled media. As Trevor informed Frank Mason, a career officer in military intelligence and his father's longtime comrade in the struggle against non-Nordic immigrants and Jewish influence, a "foundation set up by the usual benefactor is making substantial grants" to the physicist. The knowing reference to the Colonel indicated that, even nameless, Draper was immediately recognized as the standard source of funds for projects of interest in racist circles and that Pioneer considered the grants to Shockley a continuation of a campaign that had relied regularly on the usual benefactor's generosity.[27]

Shockley may not have initially appreciated either the larger picture or his role in it, although Putnam tried to enlighten him after receiving a request for funds from the physicist. "You may not realize," explained Putnam to his new scientific ally, "that you and I are fellow supplicants before the throne in New York. The National Putnam Letters Committee and my individual mailings and similar expenses in Washington are supported from that source." For further assistance, Putnam urged Shockley to direct his request to New York; Putnam had "no authority to divert funds" from his own efforts. It immediately became obvious who *did* have the authority. "Dear Harry," wrote Putnam to the Colonel's attorney and the disburser of his generosity, "let me say for the record that I would be happy to recommend a partial phasing out of funds going to the National Putnam Letters Committee and the transfer of these funds to Professor Shockley's budget."[28] That is, the money that had originally been allocated to Putnam for his campaign to preserve segregation and keep blacks out of "white" society would be redirected to Shockley so that he could provide what Putnam called the "essential ammunition," not only to support the segregationist cause but, more important, to help "break . . . the hold of politically motivated groups on the channels of communication." The issue of black inferiority was merely one aspect of the underlying problem, Putnam advised the segregationists' new authority; "it will be wise to keep in mind the nature of the war." To ensure that Shockley did not miss the point, Putnam sent him a portion of the draft of Robertson's *The Dispossessed Majority*—which was then being circulated to select insiders with Weyher's permission—documenting "the Jewish hold over the popular mind." When Robertson's book was eventually published three years later, Shockley recommended "its analyses of racial differences" and suggested people to whom Putnam should send copies.[29]

Actually, money from the "New York source" was channeled to Shockley through four different routes. Before Draper's death, the physicist found himself, as had George, Kuttner, Garrett, and others before him, the direct recipient of regular cash gifts, transmitted by Weyher on behalf of an unnamed client who wanted to provide the funds "as a token of his esteem" for Shockley's work. Shockley's gifts were more substantial than those for previous recipients, coming to more than $22,000 between 1968 and 1970 ($109,000 AFI). (Although there is no doubt that these checks came from Draper, neither of the gifts in 1969 or 1970 was noted on the list of gifts in the last three years of the Colonel's life contained in his estate papers, raising the question of whether there were other unacknowledged recipients of his generosity.)[30] In addition, other gifts in the form of securities from Morgan Guaranty Trust, totaling $76,000 ($370,000 AFI) between 1968 and 1971, were also sent to Stanford to be used for Shockley's "research," accompanied by telegrams from the same bank official who had forwarded the Colonel's contributions to the Mississippi Sovereignty Commission, requesting as usual that "the fact and amount of the gift be kept confidential."[31]

Finally, there were two types of acknowledged assistance from Pioneer. Between 1969 and 1976, the fund contributed almost $175,000 ($689,000 AFI) in grants to Stanford to support Shockley's "research into the factors which affect genetic potential." Pioneer also provided $54,500 ($169,000 AFI) to Shockley's own nonprofit organization to promote eugenics—the Foundation for Research and Education on Eugenics and Dysgenics (FREED)—which had begun with a $10,000 ($44,000 AFI) contribution from Weyher, probably another gift from the Colonel.[32] Although FREED was Shockley's idea, George S. Leonard, previously a member of the CCFAF and one of the attorneys for the intervenors in the attempts to overturn *Brown*, actually drafted the bylaws and executed the necessary paperwork for its creation. The organization's purpose, according to Leonard's bylaws, was to engage in activities designed to "further public understanding, legal utilization, and academic acceptance" of scientific information on differences in the "natures, capabilities, and potentialities of men."[33] In practice, FREED functioned as a publicist for Shockley, producing a newsletter with descriptions of his public appearances, his press releases, and copies of articles written by and about him. And like any good public relations operation, FREED sought to increase its base, requesting permission from recipients of the newsletter to have their written support for eugenics circulated "to other people who live in your neighborhood"; apparently Shockley was ready to organize a eugenics movement door-to-door.[34] Between the various gifts and grants, Shockley received $337,500 (almost $1.4 million AFI) altogether from the "throne in New York."

Little or no research was conducted with any of this money. Shockley *contemplated* a number of studies, many of them ethically questionable. For example, he planned to study the effect of heredity by hiring Pinkerton agents to carry out surreptitious investigations of the backgrounds of both randomly selected students and students who had been active in campus demonstrations to learn whether any had been adopted. In public, he requested blood samples from prominent black intellectuals to investigate whether the most capable "Negroes obtain their intelligence from white ancestors," and in private, he had Weyher ask a friend with influence at a New York hospital to obtain "blood samples from teenage negro mothers, whose children are illegitimate and who are on welfare" so that Shockley could have them similarly analyzed for any traces of Caucasian ancestry. Shockley also proposed research on the intelligence of black children adopted into white families and the use of physiological measures to assess reasoning ability.[35] Yet he never actually conducted any of these studies. Shockley did reanalyze and publicize data that had been collected by others. Indeed, his most important scientific contribution to the nature versus nurture controversy may have been unintended: It was Shockley who obtained from British psychologist Sir Cyril Burt information on the IQ scores of separated identical twins, which then helped to prove that Burt's study had been fraudulent.[36] However, none of these activities constituted original research, nor did they require substantial resources to undertake.

Instead of research, Shockley expended most of the money provided by Pioneer's multiple funding routes on a public relations crusade, conducting science by public pronouncement, press release, and mailing list. Obsessed with media visibility, he became a one-man publicity seeker and lobbyist for eugenic views. Nor did he feel any need for pretense about this purpose, candidly announcing, in typically freighted manner, his "intention to use significant members of the American press as the blocks or pulleys . . . and the First Amendment as a line upon which I shall endeavor to exert a force so as to deflect the rudder of public opinion and turn the ship of civilization away from the dysgenic storm that I fear is rising over the horizon of the future." In private correspondence, Shockley stressed that "our problem is too big for the standard Madison Avenue techniques" and that more dramatic measures were needed to gain attention.[37] Each new proposal on the physicist's part, often crafted to be deliberately outrageous, was unveiled through a press conference or news release; his "Voluntary Sterilization Bonus Plan," for example, proposed that people volunteering for sterilization be awarded a bonus of $1,000 for each IQ point below 100, with "bounty hunters" earning a portion of the award for persuading appropriate targets of the program to participate. Each lecture invitation was carefully orchestrated to achieve maximum coverage from the media, producing what one journalist dubbed a "traveling carnival of racism."[38]

To assist with what Shockley frankly called "my campaign," he used a portion of Pioneer's money, first to pay Kuttner as a "consultant" and then to bring the Liberty Lobby representative to Stanford for a year as a "research associate"; Shockley had earlier agreed to have copies of *Race and Modern Science,* the volume edited by Kuttner defending racism as innate and biologically valuable, sent to members of the National Academy of Sciences with an accompanying letter containing his recommendation of the book. Despite the title of his position, however, Kuttner carried out no more research than his employer; instead, as Shockley noted to R. T. Osborne, the new appointment was expected to "improve the correspondence situation enormously."[39] Now paid with Pioneer's money and writing on Stanford Electronics Laboratories stationery, among other communications Kuttner circulated copies of his decade-old articles in the neo-Nazi publications *Right* and *Truth Seeker,* warning of the population growth among "Africans and Asians with ambitious designs on the land and wealth of Caucasian peoples." Eager to keep up the campaign's momentum, he also encouraged Osborne's plans for a new, edited volume. "The time seems ripe to hit the public with more material," Kuttner wrote to his fellow expert witness in the attempts to overturn *Brown,* "saturation tactics"; even if there were a delay, "it at least keeps the attack going with more ammunition." It was important, Kuttner advised, to find some "different names" as contributors "so that it does not appear as if a very small group are airing a very narrow viewpoint." Anticipating difficulty in finding a publisher, Kuttner also suggested, as always, that "Harry Weyher ought to be approached."[40]

Shockley's campaign to sway public opinion also spent an enormous amount of Pioneer's money on copying and disseminating materials; like the source of his support, Shockley relied on the mailing list as a major lobbying tactic, distributing lengthy missives often accompanied by even lengthier photocopied articles that could run to hundreds of pages. Although the physicist was more selective in his choice of recipients—circulating his calls to action to hundreds of people at a time rather than to the thousands on the list that Swan had compiled for Weyher—he resorted to the lists just as often, churning out a constant stream of letters in response to events from the petty to the momentous. For example, Shockley attempted to stop the appointment of William D. McElroy as director of the National Science Foundation, urging his many contacts to write their senators in opposition to confirmation of the Johns Hopkins biologist because, at a meeting of the National Academy of Sciences (NAS), McElroy had moved to table Shockley's resolution on "hereditary aspects of our national . . . problems," a motion that passed by a vote of 200-10.[41] In another instance, after the Kerner Commission concluded in 1968 that the previous year's rash of civil disorders had resulted largely from "white racism" and recommended increased government assistance to expand Head Start, improve urban education, and provide job training and inner-city economic development, Shockley sent telegrams to the commission's chair, Illinois Governor Otto Kerner, and other members, insisting that "humanitarian" programs would lead to "genetic degradation." For years, he sent out one lengthy packet after another, regularly containing dozens of enclosures, to members of the NAS, the wire services, major newspapers, and smaller Southern papers that had supported segregation. There were specialized lists for specific purposes; for example, one group of sympathetic journalists Shockley dubbed "our dozen newsmen." Other recipients at various times included presidential candidates, senators, state legislators, and notable figures such as Pearl Buck and John Steinbeck. Shockley even once sent a thick packet of articles with a letter soliciting support to business executives randomly selected from *International Who's Who.*[42]

Shockley's most ambitious and most expensive mailing effort was designed to market the work of Berkeley educational psychologist Arthur Jensen in an attempt not only to sway public opinion about racial differences but also to bring pressure on the NAS to adopt his agenda. Although Shockley himself had conducted no empirical studies on cognitive abilities, he was instrumental in persuading Jensen, an active researcher in the field, that blacks were genetically less intelligent than whites and recruiting him into the Pioneer circle. Early in his career, Jensen had believed that racial differences in intelligence test scores were "due to environmental rather than to genetic factors," but his position changed dramatically after he spent the 1966–67 year as a fellow at the Center for Advanced Study in the Behavioral Sciences on the Stanford campus, where he engaged in regular discussions with Shockley, the two scientists working so closely together that, when Shockley was out of town, Jensen answered mail addressed to the physicist. The Draper clique considered the two scientists as working in tandem for the cause; as Putnam declared in his offer to transfer his own funds to Shockley, "the Shockley-Jensen team have been outstanding."[43]

In 1969, Jensen produced the article that would become the centerpiece of Shockley's campaign to impose his views on the NAS and the public. In this lengthy and inflammatory work—the longest publication in the history of *Harvard Educational Review,* taking up almost the entire winter issue—Jensen argued that minority schoolchildren were hampered neither by discrimination nor deprivation; their poor educational performance was a consequence of teaching methods that had been appropriate for white middle-class students but not for minorities, who did not respond to conceptual explanations because of the genetic limitations in their intelligence but who could nevertheless be taught by relying on their ability for association rather than understanding. Obviously reflecting the influence of his discussions with Shockley, Jensen also expressed concern that "misguided and ineffective attempts to improve [the] lot" of blacks through social programs would only lead—in the physicist's favorite phrase—to their "genetic enslavement" unless accompanied by "eugenic foresight." The conclusions of Jensen's article thus were both educational and social: rote memorization to improve the skills of low-IQ black children unable to appreciate abstract principles and some sort of eugenic intervention designed to reduce their numbers.[44]

Armed with the Jensen article, Shockley was ready for battle. Even a few weeks before the article's appearance, Shockley was already sending lengthy letters to members of the press he thought sympathetic, alerting them to the forthcoming publication, offering copies of the "nearly 200 manuscript pages," asking for their assistance in publicizing its contents, and requesting that their newspapers lobby the wire services for coverage. In 1968, he had appeared before the NAS, declaring that "American Negro shortcomings are preponderately hereditary" and urging the nation's foremost scientific body to undertake research in "dysgenics" to determine whether "our national Negro illness is caused by problems of evolutionary adolescence." This bizarre request had been ignored by his colleagues; as Joshua Lederberg, a Nobel laureate and member of Stanford's Department of Genetics, pointed out, "Scientists [who] have material questions . . . do not customarily demand the authority of the Academy to answer them: they devise critical experiments.

But it is all too evident that Shockley has answered all of his questions before the fact."[45] Two weeks before the next annual meeting Shockley sent to every one of the 800 members of the NAS a letter, along with twenty-three enclosures, comparing their actions to the complicity of Third Reich intellectuals with the Holocaust; then a few days later he distributed photocopies of the entire Jensen article, together with his own "Analysis and Recommendations" and a request for a telegram of support, to the 200 members of the engineering, physiology, psychology, and anthropology sections of the NAS. A month later he distributed 1,500 more copies—forwarded by Jensen but paid for by Shockley with Draper's money—to the rest of the NAS and to other scientists, politicians, and journalists. A batch also was sent to Putnam, which he mailed to "personal contacts," such as senators Edmund Muskie, Robert Byrd, Everett Dirksen, and Barry Goldwater; Vice President Spiro Agnew; J. Edgar Hoover; and three Supreme Court Justices.[46]

Still unable to persuade the NAS to do his will, Shockley sent Jensen's article to select members of Congress, asking them to pressure the NAS to adopt his agenda. When Emilio Daddario, a Democrat and chair of the Subcommittee on Science, Research and Development, responded, properly, that it was not "appropriate for me to interject myself into the affairs of the Academy," which was not a government body, Shockley tried to find "information on Republican or other opposition to Mr. Daddario." A few congressmen were more cooperative, agreeing to send to the president of the NAS a letter that Shockley had composed for their signature. Its true author not very subtly disguised, the letter asked the president to support a study "proposed . . . by Dr. William Shockley"—to find whether differences in children's cognitive skills were caused by the presence of a "Caucasian gene"—so that "national policies be based on sound scientific facts"; the letter actually was sent by some members of Congress. Leonard, who was providing legal advice to Shockley behind the scenes, inspected the draft, offering only one substantive comment: a reminder that racial mixture had already been investigated in "Race Crossing in Jamaica," Davenport's obscure study of the genetic disharmonies caused by miscegenation funded by the Colonel half a century earlier.[47]

With Shockley sounding the tocsin, "Jensenism," as a science writer for the *New York Times Magazine* later called it, immediately became a cause célèbre, producing such sensational headlines as "Born Dumb?" in *Newsweek* and "Can Negroes Learn the Way Whites Do?" in *U.S. News & World Report.* After the latter story was published—a highly favorable treatment of Jensen's claims in a magazine that had been particularly sympathetic to the segregationist scientists throughout the civil rights era—Putnam no doubt spoke for the whole group when he expressed to Shockley "utter delight" with the article "and what I assume to be your considerable connection with it."[48] The press's attention eventually produced yet another mass mailing as Shockley distributed hundreds of copies of the "Jensenism" article to his "general" and "professional" lists, asking recipients to write to the *New York Times* in support of the Berkeley psychologist.[49]

Of course, a public relations campaign was precisely what Pioneer desired from the Nobel laureate. In keeping with the plan outlined by Satterfield, the fund was paying not for science but for publicity, supporting the former only as a necessary expense to obtain the latter. Weyher showed no interest in the results of what little research Shockley actually conducted with the fund's resources because the physicist was not expected to find anything that Pioneer did not already know to be the case. However, the fund's president was obsessed with Shockley's press coverage, employing a clipping service, as he had done for Putnam, to monitor the effects of the campaign and forward to the physicist the evidence of his impact: articles in newspapers ranging from national publications to the *Bay City* (Michigan) *Times,* the *St. Albans* (Vermont) *Messenger,* and the *Littleton* (Colorado) *Arapahoe Herald.*

Exploiting his many contacts among media executives, Weyher worked as hard to get exposure for his prominent scientist as anyone at William Morris had ever done for a hot property in entertainment. "Dear Penelope," he wrote, to Penelope Wilson, host of the popular television show *The New Yorkers,* "you might be interested in trying to get Dr. William Shockley as a guest on your program," not to talk about physics, of course, but about his "current interests . . . in eugenics—for example, is our slum problem due to the people who created the slums, . . . and if [so], what should be done about it?" A few months later, Weyher plugged his star scientist to Wilson again, this time suggesting that the expert in eugenics could comment on "the current mess at Columbia," where Students for a Democratic Society had just taken over buildings in protest against the presence on campus of the Institute for Defense Analyses and the university's expansion into the surrounding Morningside Heights community. Weyher sent similar letters appealing for publicity for Shockley to "Dear Fritz," Frederick S. Beebe, chairman of the board at *Newsweek,* and "Dear Jack," John F. Dowd, editorial counsel of Time, Inc., publishers of *Time, Life,* and *Fortune.* A hand-carried note from Weyher also asked another "Dear Jack"—Jack Flynn, chairman of the board, editor, and publisher of the *Daily News*—to cover a "semi-private press conference" held by Weyher's "personal friend . . . Bill Shockley" in Washington, D.C.[50] Apparently, however, Weyher's connections were not strong enough to overcome the "equalitarian" control of the media. The lone national success in all these attempts occurred when his friend Vermont Royster devoted a column in the *Wall Street Journal* to Shockley's claims, observing that, if the physicist was correct, then public programs "for lifting up the disadvantaged are misdirected and possibly futile or even self-defeating" because they "cannot repair genetic damage." Unsurprisingly, Shockley was also given copious amounts of space in one local newspaper: The Manchester, New Hampshire *Union Leader,* published by William Loeb, who had chaired the CCFAF.[51]

Many of the financial details of Shockley's grants further strengthened the impression of a desire on Pioneer's part not to advance science but to collaborate in a public relations campaign. For example, Weyher paid for advertisements in major newspapers for Shockley's events and then asked Shockley to reimburse him, promising that a new grant would soon cover the cost of the reimbursement. Instead of the usual relationship between grantor and grantee in which the latter submits a description of prospective research, hopeful that it will fit the former's priorities, in this case it seemed taken for granted that Pioneer would bankroll a lobbying effort by a Nobel laureate seeking to raise the issue of black genetic inferiority. Even before distribution of the Jensen article, Shockley wrote to Weyher "to give some examples of the amount of correspondence and to say that we have succeeded in running through some $3500," adding that "I anticipate that we shall hit bottom" in another month; then just after the campaign the physicist informed the attorney that "the circulation of Jensen's article has depleted a bank account to nearly zero." These unsubtle hints would invariably produce another infusion of cash from the New York source. Sometimes, when his own budget was dwindling, Shockley sent material to Weyher with the instruction to "xerox and give wider distribution to the enclosures." In other uncommon practices, Shockley requested "a contingency reserve" in his grant to enable him "to take advantage of unusual opportunities," and he did not hesitate to run deficits, confident that Pioneer would eventually cover them. And when Weyher learned that Shockley was contemplating a sabbatical, fearful of the temporary loss of his major asset, he sent the physicist a special-delivery letter promising that Pioneer would ensure "no loss of income" during the leave if Shockley continued to focus on racial differences.[52]

Particularly instructive was the alleged distinction between the two types of grants that Pioneer provided for Shockley. Although the funds directed to Stanford were officially designated for research and the FREED money for public promotion of eugenics, in practice, Shockley acknowledged, "I have not found it easy to draw a sharp dividing line between the two"; "in fact," he added, "I have thought of nothing that would, of necessity, have to be done under Stanford's auspices [rather] than under FREED's." However, FREED was purposely drawn up by Leonard as a "non-private" organization, exempting it from any requirement to report the names of contributors, provided that at least one-third of the contributions came from "the general public." Thus, in one of his requests from Pioneer, Shockley merely asked for "as large an amount as FREED can accept from one source . . . without endangering its non-profit status." To justify the amount requested from a granting agency in such a manner was, to say the least, unusual.[53]

Unlike the spotlight-seeking Shockley, Jensen was more interested in pursuing his research program and was not as much the operator as his senior colleague; nevertheless, the psychologist did his part to organize favorable publicity. To journalists, Jensen claimed political naiveté, once telling a reporter for the *Times* of London that "I take a non-political view. I'm almost embarrassed by my lack of political involvement in this issue. That whole side of the thing is beyond me." Behind the scenes, however, he was much more calculating. Anticipating that his *Harvard Educational Review* article would generate controversy, the week before its publication Jensen wrote to the segregationists, suggesting that they make a contribution to the letters section of the next issue. And to a larger mailing list he sent out "Dear Friend" form letters encouraging them to submit responses "that take my side" to the *New York Times Magazine* after its feature story on "Jensenism."[54]

From Pioneer's point of view, of course, the publicity generated by their new authorities was but the essential first step, the means toward what was still the ultimate goal at the time: to overturn *Brown* through scientific evidence of black intellectual inferiority or at least prevent its further implementation. Even before the *Harvard Educational Review* article had made a previously unknown psychologist the most controversial social scientist in the country, Putnam had written to Illinois Senator Everett Dirksen, suggesting that he should "rise in the Senate and . . . request that the Supreme Court re-open the *Stell* case" on the basis of "Dr. Shockley's speech" at the NAS and "Dr. Jensen's findings"; there was no doubt that in a rehearing both scientists would join the previous experts for the intervenors. Weyher and Leonard also made plans to have Shockley join Garrett, McGurk, Osborne, and van den Haag—the latter all veterans of *Stell*—as an expert witness for the defendants in *U.S. v. Hinds County School Board,* one of a number of desegregation cases brought by the government in Mississippi school districts still relying on "freedom of choice" to dismantle dual educational systems.[55]

Although neither of these plans for judicial action came to fruition, there were also legislative attempts to use Pioneer's new experts to restore some form of the racial status quo, again orchestrated by Leonard, this time as counsel to the Foundation for Human Understanding (FHU), another Draper-funded organization; immediately after the Colonel's death, it became a Pioneer grantee. Acting on behalf of FHU, Leonard requested that the Senate Committee on Equal Educational Opportunity hear from a number of scientists who would explain that "racial differences in learning . . . are largely inherent . . . and would normally remain unchanged by programs for varying either the home or school environment"; given such innate differences, obviously the only realistic policy for true equal opportunity would be "special curricula and instructional methods for each major ethnic group." Along with the usual crew—Garrett, Osborne, Gregor, McGurk, and others—the accompanying list of potential witnesses included Shockley and Jensen.[56]

In addition, only weeks later the House Subcommittee on Education agreed to hear from the scientists during hearings on the Emergency School Aid Act, offering FHU another opportunity to use a similar strategy; the bill itself was designed to provide financial assistance to school systems actually undergoing integration. Still attempting to substitute empirically testable assertions for constitutional entitlement, the scientists maintained that, like the *Brown* decision, the act was premised on the belief that desegregation would produce educational improvement; this claim on their part could then be used to justify submission of the evidence of blacks' innate inferiority to demonstrate the faulty logic supposedly underlying the legislation by suggesting the real and unalterable cause of educational differences between the races. In particular, the scientists urged the subcommittee to use the act's evaluation component to "find out once and for all" whether integration improved the quality of education, clearly certain in their own minds, as Osborne noted in his statement, that to allow blacks and whites in the same school was "destructive" to the education of both races. Like the others, Shockley submitted a statement noting that the "deficit in Negro intellectual performance" was "hereditary" and suggesting that the proposed legislation be used to determine whether integration had any educational value. Jensen, one of the only two scientists (along with van den Haag) to appear personally before the subcommittee, joined in the chorus calling for investigation of the bill's "premise," although he too was certain of the result: Desegregation would be harmful because of blacks' genetic shortcomings. "The educational abilities and needs of the majority of white and Negro children are sufficiently different," he testified, implying that integrated schools would only harm both groups. Jensen was particularly concerned that in an integrated school many black children would *not* be placed in classes for the retarded where they belonged because they would be mistakenly "treat[ed] like the average white child." After listening to the witnesses, the subcommittee's chair eventually headed where the scientists were so eagerly pointing. If the

FHU experts were correct in their predictions of educational disaster caused by integrated schools, "was it possible," he wondered, "that this legislation conceivably could shoot down *Brown*?" Jensen made no comment.[57]

As the first Pioneer grantees outside of the faithful, Shockley and Jensen, two prominent scientists with no need for factitious presses created solely to publish their works, saved the fund from its otherwise exclusive association at the time with obvious racists still fighting to save domestic apartheid. Not wanting to alienate these new allies, the segregationists were even willing to tolerate a certain degree of ideological deviation; Shockley and Jensen certainly could not be expected to submit drafts of their writing to Weyher and Trevor for the collective vetting that had been common among Draper's scientists. Although neither grantee would publicly condemn integration, there was no repetition of the tactical error committed a few years earlier, when the segregationists' attempt to recruit Dwight Ingle "into our camp" had ended unhappily: Because Ingle was not sufficiently outspoken in his opposition to civil rights, Putnam had called the physiologist "a timid little academician with the intellectual conformity of a sheep," a comment prompting Gayre to complain that the goal should be "to win him over . . . not to punch him on the nose because he deviates on some points." Besides, it was probably not lost on Pioneer that the fact that Shockley and Jensen were not full-frontal racists, ranting that integrated schools would lead to the downfall of civilization, only made them *more* credible than the Colonel's other scientists. As Ingle pointed out to Shockley while pondering how to influence their colleagues, neither Garrett nor any of the other segregationists would be taken seriously by the NAS; "only Jensen could . . . do more good than harm."[58]

Eventually, however, Pioneer realized that Shockley's campaign came with one insoluble problem: Shockley. A thin-skinned nitpicker—so distrustful of other faculty that he proposed the use of polygraphs to "establish [their] actual views," so litigious that he wanted to sue every time someone called his views biased, and so wary that he taped his telephone calls—the nettlesome laureate managed to alienate even those who agreed with him. A simple invitation to debate, which was what Shockley sought, nevertheless became the preface to a set of negotiations over the conditions that could rival the Paris peace talks.[59] Trevor even contacted Frank Mason, his father's old ally in military intelligence, to seek assistance in changing Shockley's unappealing persona. Although "I am a fervent follower of your father's belief" that the national welfare depended on "maintaining . . . the homogeneity of the American people and avoidance of unnecessary dilution of the strains that made our country great," responded Mason, "deteriorating health forbids my taking on the Shockley problem." However, he did have some advice for Trevor on how Shockley could better "influence people," ranging from therapy to more well-focused lectures. "Harry Weyher and you know that what Dr. Shockley should do is simple," Mason observed; "I regret that I can't play a role in what you are both trying to accomplish."[60] Shockley's support from Pioneer thus ended for the same reason that it had begun: as a consequence of what Weyher and Trevor were "trying to accomplish." Funded not to conduct research but to "influence people," he was defunded for being ill suited to the task.

However, Jensen remained a Pioneer grantee for the next three decades, receiving close to $1.2 million (more than $2 million AFI) from the fund between 1973 and 1999 (whether he also received personal gifts "as a token of esteem" before Draper's death is unknown). Unlike the traditional method for funding an academically based scientist, though, in which the researcher's university is the official recipient, Jensen's grants were directed to the Institute for the Study of Educational Differences, a nonprofit corporation listing Jensen as president and his wife as vice president; represented by the ubiquitous attorney for the segregationists, George Leonard, the institute appeared to have no purpose other than to funnel Pioneer's money to its intended recipient without the bother of Berkeley's oversight.

Particularly skillful at avoiding public comment on policy—except for affirmative action, which he opposed on the basis that the genetically lower intellectual abilities of blacks *should* result in their disproportionate underrepresentation in higher education and the professions—while simultaneously hinting to the segregationists that he was on their side, Jensen was always careful not to bite the hand that financed him. Garrett clearly regarded Jensen as an ally in the struggle, considering him "the best of our young men," even though Jensen maintained a discreet silence before the congressional committee when asked whether his research could lead to the reversal of *Brown*.[61] Jensen ingratiated himself with Putnam too: Well aware of Putnam's efforts to deny political equality to blacks and his campaign to distribute *The Dispossessed Majority*, warning of the Jewish control of the media that had deliberately perpetrated the equalitarian hoax, Jensen wrote to the segregationist, praising "your writings and clear perceptions," which "pack a wallop," and "admir[ing] your forthrightness," although he never actually expressed agreement with anything Putnam said. In another activity that had doubtlessly been arranged by someone within the Pioneer clique, Jensen also collaborated with *Neue Anthropologie*, a German clone of the *Mankind Quarterly*, edited by neo-Nazi attorney Jürgen Rieger and dedicated to restoring *Russenhygiene; Neue Anthropologie*'s first issue honored Fritz Lenz, the doyen of racial geneticists in the Third Reich. The Berkeley researcher made regular contributions to the journal and served, along with Swan, on its "scientific board."[62] Again, this did not mean that Jensen agreed with the favorable reviews of anti-Semitic tracts or the tributes to racist scientists from the Nazi era that surrounded his own contributions, but the involvement of a well-known scientist gracing the list of neo-Nazis on the board certainly was a significant benefit to the journal's attempt to restore *Rassenhygiene* to respectability.

Most important of all from Pioneer's viewpoint, Jensen always remained faithful to their central concern. Although he also conducted research on other issues throughout his career, earning him a well-deserved scholarly reputation, racial differences in intelligence remained an obsession on his part. As well-known researcher on intelligence Yale psychologist Robert J. Sternberg observed in 1985, Jensen "is a competent scientist and scholar. . . . But I am at a loss as to why Jensen persists in studying the problem of black-white differences. . . . [He] has merely restated the same finding again and again. . . . I . . . wish Jensen would make better use of his considerable talents."[63] Though never a public supporter of segregation himself, Jensen was a valuable contributor to Pioneer's agenda.

## An Important "Monogram"

To ensure that the public was properly educated, Pioneer also financed organizations that, among other activities, distributed books and articles, many of which they themselves had published. The most important of these organizations was FHU, after Shockley and Jensen the next largest Pioneer grantee through the decade after Draper's death, receiving $349,000 ($764,000 AFI) altogether from the fund between 1973 and 1994. Directed, according to its incorporation papers, by Garrett and Osborne, FHU was actually run by its secretary-treasurer, Leonard, the attorney who had previously represented the intervenors and would soon appear before the Supreme Court as counsel for the Southern Independent School Association to defend its system of segregated private schools in the South, funded in part by money left by the Colonel. Though created, in the usual euphemism used by Pioneer-supported organizations, for "scientific and educational purposes related to . . . public understanding of the nature of man," in practice FHU was one more attempt on the segregationists' part "to win the war," arranging, for example, for Jensen, Shockley, and the scientists from *Stell* to offer statements to the House Subcommittee on Education.[64]

FHU's few attempts to sponsor research also were revealing. It forwarded Pioneer funds to FREED, for example, so that Shockley could work on "the rehabilitation of Sir Cyril Burt's studies," both the physicist and FHU apparently agreeing beforehand on what should be the appropriate outcome of his analysis of the Englishman's suspect data.[65] In a hilarious comedy of errors, the organization also recommended that Pioneer grant $5,000 ($14,700 AFI) to the University of California at San Diego (UCSD) to "complete and correct the work of Dr. Harry Munsinger," who had concluded, from his study of the transfusion syndrome affecting identical twins—in which, during gestation, one twin becomes essentially an involuntary blood donor to the other—that what little influence environmental factors exerted on the development of intelligence occurred in utero. Soon after publication of this result, Leon Kamin, the Princeton University professor of psychology who had exposed the fragility of Burt's data, showed that Munsinger's study was so riddled with errors and miscalculations as to be utterly worthless. Kamin's critique was circulated to the Pioneer clique long before it appeared in print, prompting Jensen to write an outraged letter to Munsinger denouncing his sloppiness and to withdraw an equally flawed article about to be published that he had coauthored with Munsinger. Shockley and Leonard quickly devised the plan for Pioneer to send money to UCSD in support of the research by Munsinger, who would then employ Shockley to perform the corrections. But when UCSD received Pioneer's money, accompanied only by a statement that it was to be used for study of the identical twin transfusion syndrome, the university immediately sent it to a professor in the School of Medicine, who was studying the same phenomenon in sheep pregnancies.[66]

However, FHU's main activity was to promote approved works. For example, it paid to have a favorable review of books by Jensen and Harvard psychologist Richard J. Herrnstein reprinted as a full-page advertisement in the *New York Times Book Review* section. When Herrnstein, who was not himself a Pioneer grantee, later published an article in the *Atlantic Monthly* claiming a media conspiracy to suppress the facts on genetics and intelligence, FHU paid for copies to be mailed to 8,000 daily and weekly newspapers. It also spent $27,000 ($53,000 AFI) for thousands of copies of *Straight Talk about Mental Testing* by Jensen to be distributed gratis to college presidents and admission officers around the country; in this "work for nonspecialists," as Jensen described it, the administrators who decided on the future of millions of applicants each year could read that the decline in the number of students with high SAT scores was attributable to a declining birthrate among the "ethnic groups" that had furnished most of the top scorers in the past. FHU also appeared to be the repository for all the segregationists' surplus publications. Among the 200 pamphlets available from the organization were works by Putnam, Simmons, Gregor, Garrett, George, Avins, and even the first scientific endeavor funded by the Colonel, the Davenport and Steggerda study.[67]

The bulk of FHU's budget was spent on publishing and distributing books that no press would accept. Just as Social Science Press had been created earlier to publish *Race and Modern Science* and *The Testing of Negro Intelligence,* FHU produced its own books; indeed, one of them was *The Testing of Negro Intelligence,* Volume 2. In some cases, it was obvious why a work had to be published in house. In 1979 and 1980, for example, FHU spent $45,500 ($104,400 AFI) on Osborne's book *Twins: Black and White,* a study purporting to go beyond mere racial differences on mental tests and demonstrate that the heritability of intelligence was the same for blacks as for whites; when the resulting data showed a number of huge differences in heritability, Osborne simply ignored them, proclaiming the "patterns of heritability ratios for blacks and whites . . . remarkably congruent."[68]

FHU's most appalling publication undoubtedly was *America's Bimodal Crisis: Black Intelligence in White Society* by Stanley Burnham, a book that offered a succession of racist canards as self-evident truths. As employees, the author declared, blacks "have cost their employers far more in theft, incompetence, and legal fees than they have contributed in their work productivity." The pseudonymous Burnham, for whom no background was provided, also claimed to know of numerous black Ph.D. candidates whose dissertations had to be largely rewritten "by a trained staff of secretaries and editors" because of poor mechanics, expressing his doubt, in a deliciously poetic irony, that "they has [*sic*] researched and written their own papers." Nor did it make sense to Burnham to "abide by Constitutional standards in a third-world situation"; the protection appropriate to "the white criminal simply does not apply to the underclass black criminal." Combining malapropism with megalomania, he declared his "monogram" so important that it "will be read and appreciated a century from now." Pioneer found Burnham's "monogram" of sufficient value to fund three editions between 1985 and 1994.[69]

Smaller grants also went to two similar organizations. The Testing Research Fund, which received $3,000 ($5,400 AFI) for the "distribution of research data on mental abilities," involved the usual participants: Garrett and Osborne as directors, Leonard as its counsel. Asked about his role in the organization, however, Leonard, the segregationist attorney, declared that "I am the Testing Research Fund," which was probably true of FHU as well. The Institute for Western Values, which later collaborated with some of the anti-immigrant projects supported by Pioneer, also received $12,000 ($22,200 AFI) to fund the publication of *Southern Horizons,* the autobiography of Thomas Dixon, who had glorified the Ku Klux Klan in his 1905 novel *The Clansman.* Apparently having been deemed consistent with Pioneer's purpose to disseminate information on "race betterment," Dixon's story recalled how slaves had lived happily in comfort and security, unhesitant to kill or be killed in defense of their own subjugation, until converted by Reconstruction into dusky Othellos, defiling Southern legislatures physically and morally and demanding their right to fair Desdemonas. Only the heroic Klan, noble and chivalrous, stood between these rampaging blacks and defenseless Southern maidens.[70]

In the 1980s and 1990s Pioneer's grants to these various "distributorships" decreased substantially, replaced in many ways by the fund's commitment to the ambitious publishing operation of Roger Pearson.

## Under Various Pen Names

Although scientific evidence of black intellectual inferiority had been the linchpin of the attempt to overturn *Brown* and although it remained an important element in the ensuing public relations campaign, it did not by itself provide justification for rigid separation of *all* blacks and members of other races. To safeguard the white purity that had been such an obsession for the Colonel and so many of his successors, to provide a basis for the United States as a "white nation," it was necessary to move beyond differences in intelligence—which were, after all, differences between individuals, not groups—and make race itself the issue. Of the many Pioneer grantees who argued that race and nation must be synonymous, that "biological homogeneity" was essential for nationhood, the most important was the British-born Pearson, whose entire life and career were dedicated to rationalizing racial separation in the name of Aryan purity. Perhaps the most important postwar exponent of the racial science that had characterized the Third Reich, Pearson is of additional interest as Pioneer's most enduring recipient, enjoying regular support from 1973 until the end of the century, and the grantee who provided substantive continuity with the Colonel's earlier interests, maintaining the linkage of support for both domestic apartheid and Nazi notions of racial hygiene.

From his earliest postwar writing to his numerous and often pseudonymous articles in Pioneer-funded journals throughout the last quarter of the century, the highly prolific Pearson has promulgated an ideology based largely on the thinking of notorious Nazi theorist Hans F. K. Günther, widely regarded as the Reich's official spokesperson on race; referred to by one German scholar as a "Rassenfanatiker," "Rasse-Günther," as he was called in the Third Reich, was awarded the Nazi Party's "science prize" in 1935 by Reichminister Alfred Rosenberg for having "laid the groundwork for the struggle of our movement and for the legislation of the National Socialist Reich."[71] In his own "cultural journal," *Northern World,* Pearson praised Günther as "one of the

world's greatest names in the field of raciology," publishing the latest rumi-
nations of the unapologetic Nazi expert, in which Günther explained how
the blond and blue-eyed ancient Greeks, honest and courageous, were sul-
lied by contact with "men of preponderantly hither-Asiatic race" (i.e., Jews),
characterized by "dishonesty, treachery, crafty calculation, corruptibility, and
betrayal." Pearson also attempted to publish new editions of Günther's work
from the Nazi era at his own expense.[72]

Like his role model, Pearson announced his firm belief at the time in the
biological superiority of the Nordic as the "symbol . . . of human dignity," an
aristocratic "world-conquering" race that had imposed its will millennia ago
throughout Europe, the Middle East, and North Africa, creating the great civilizations in Egypt, India, Greece, and Rome. But Pearson's version of Nordic
worship came encrusted in a thick layer of evolutionary gibberish and voodoo
genetics. The Nordic race, he explained, was "the very peak of evolutionary
progress—the highest form of life that Nature has ever produced" and the
furthest removed from "the ape-like appearance of our original ancestors
which . . . still characterizes Negroes and monkeys."[73] It was thus essential for
this superior group to be kept "pure" because, according to Pearson, "only like
can beget like," or "breed true," producing "healthy stock in their own like-
ness." It was impossible for "persons of impure stock . . . to reproduce their
own . . . kind," generating instead "only a confused mass of genetic qualities,
good and bad all mingled together, producing repeated failure, and unable to
eliminate these failures." Applying theory to practice, Pearson concluded that
if a group with "a superior set of genes mingles with, instead of exterminat-
ing, an inferior tribe, then it commits racial suicide, and destroys the work of
thousands of years of biological isolation and natural selection."[74]

As he surveyed the postwar world, however, Pearson saw the dwindling
Nordic aristocracy—the small amount of "true Nordic blood"—in danger
of contamination from eugenically unsound social policies, particularly
"modern political 'nationality' laws," which were no longer based on "common blood ties" but on "the accident of geographical location." Citizenship
in Nordic countries was thus being granted to alien races, Pearson complained, causing "racial chaos . . . playing havoc with our natural loyalties and
result[ing] . . . in mongrelisation at home and fratricidal warfare abroad,"
the latter a reference to the recently ended conflict between England and
Germany. In addition, he observed, because of high taxes on landholders in
Nordic countries, much of the aristocracy had chosen "to intermarry with
Jewish and other non-Nordic elements," thereby "sacrific[ing] their biological heritage . . . and renounc[ing] their real claim to nobility." Finally, Pearson worried that the newly invented process of artificial insemination could

be used to destroy "our race and our heritage." Unless the donor's background was investigated "through several generations"—necessary to ensure "pure stock" that would breed "racially true"—English mothers "could find themselves giving birth to Negro or half-Negro children."[75]

As a response to these conditions, Pearson founded the Northern League, encouraging Nordics throughout the world to restore racial order by thinking "in terms of ethnic and racial identity" rather than nationality or place of birth (the organization was thus the embodiment of the "traitorous" behavior of which anti-Semites have traditionally accused Jews: pledging loyalty to a supranational ethnic group). However, its monthly newspaper, *Northlander,* immediately made clear that the league was a vehicle for the postwar continuation of Nazi racial theory, the publication's early issues complaining of "Jewisprudence" in the judicial system and nominating Rudolph Hess, the Nazi official sentenced to life imprisonment, for a Nobel peace prize.[76] Moreover, shortly after the league's formation Pearson announced its partnership with Britons Publishing Company, an "old friend" that had "always stood solidly for the unity of the Nordic peoples—the true white peoples." Britons was well known for specializing in anti-Semitic literature, such as Henry Ford's *The International Jew,* and *The Protocols of the Learned Elders of Zion,* the infamous forgery purporting to document the Jewish conspiracy for world domination, which it had republished more than eighty times.[77] In addition to praising Briton's publications for revealing the "inside story" of the attempt to promote "internal hatred" among Nordics that had resulted in the two World Wars, Pearson also recommended the work of the "fine Nordic" Gerald L. K. Smith, who tells "the same story . . . on the American side of the water"; a notorious anti-Semite, Smith had authored works such as *Jews in Government,* a pamphlet on the "Jew Zionist" plot to acquire "world power and world control" through "Jew banking houses," the "Jew-controlled and Jew directed" KGB, and "Jew control" of the Roosevelt and Truman administrations.[78]

Unsurprisingly, the league quickly attracted former Third Reich notables as well as new adherents to Nazi thought. One early member was Franz Altheim, a former assistant to Heinrich Himmler; another was Günther himself, who had earlier suggested to Cox formation of a Nordic International, centered in either England or the United States to avoid suspicion.[79] Almost every prominent English neo-Nazi also joined, including Colin Jordan, head of the White Defence League and deputy leader of the World Union of National Socialists, whose wedding to perfume fortune heiress Francoise Dior was famously celebrated with an incision on the ring finger of the bride and groom, allowing a drop of their blood to fall united onto the blank forepage of their personal copy of *Mein Kampf,* followed by an exchange of rings engraved with swastikas. Also a member was John Tyndall, another leader in the White Defence League and co-founder with Jordan of England's National Socialist Movement, who, as part of the group's demonstration to "Free Britain from Jewish Control," provoked a riot in Trafalgar Square by declaring from the platform that "the Jew is like a poisonous maggot feeding on a body in an advanced stage of decay." Both Jordan and Tyndall subsequently received prison sentences for their paramilitary activities.[80]

Pearson was naturally eager to involve prominent racists from the United States in his pan-Nordic campaign. Just before formal creation of the Northern League, he had contacted Earnest Sevier Cox to suggest that the new organization reprint Cox's "highly esteemed publications" *White America* and *Teutonic Unity,* adding that "advertising through Northern World and the Northlander would be provided free." Pearson acknowledged that he had not even read these books at the time but had received "reports" of their great value, probably from Willis Carto, who had been organizing a campaign, centered around Cox's work, to stop the "niggerfication of America."[81] In 1959, Pearson spent five weeks in the United States, rallying neo-Nazi groups around the country to the Northern League banner, and a month later his transatlantic comrades returned the visit, attending the league's "moot"— an Old English term for a meeting of Anglo-Saxon freemen—held in Germany's Teutoburg Forest. The purpose of the moot was to commemorate the victory of Herman, the "Teutonic general" who had defeated the Roman legions in the forest during the first decade A.D., thus, according to Cox's featured speech, saving the Nordic race from mongrelization. Cox had even once suggested that "those of us who do not wish to deify a Jew" refer to calendar dates as "B.H. (before Herman) and A.H." The five-day event culminated with a ceremony in which Pearson's wife placed a wreath at the Hermansdenkmal, the memorial to their hero.[82]

Pearson eventually came to the United States, where, under pseudonyms, he edited two publications in succession. During 1964 and 1965, as "Edward Langford," he joined with Carto, who had established the Northern League's "American Alpha Group" in California, in producing *Western Destiny* as the continuation of *Northern World.* The new journal combined Pearson's biologically based racism with Carto's devotion to the thinking of Francis Parker Yockey, a mysterious right-wing figure who committed suicide while in police custody in Oakland in 1960. Yockey viewed Jews as "Culture Distorters," intent on destroying Western civilization; his book, *Imperium,* dedicated to "the Hero of the Second World War" (i.e., Adolf Hitler), has been called the bible of the contemporary Nazi community, "a neo–*Mein Kampf* for neo-

Nazis," and Carto bragged that he had himself contributed *Imperium*'s "brilliant Introduction."[83] Following Yockey's analysis, *Western Destiny* maintained that, since the "Fratricidal war," the true racial foundation of Western civilization had been suppressed by the Culture Distorter, "inherently unable to be in tune with our Western Culture" and, as a consequence, anxious to "destroy race . . . consciousness" among the youth of "our Race" by peddling cultural debasement and moral degeneracy. The only countries to resist this Jewish perversion, wrote Pearson in a *Western Destiny* editorial, were South Africa and, especially, Rhodesia, where, in an overwhelmingly black nation, the tiny English community, "untouched by the 'tar-brush'" and "purer in Race than . . . present day immigrant-swollen . . . Britain" still ruled, "enlightened and conscious of the truth about the Culture Distorter, openly and proudly declaring that they stand for White Civilization."[84]

Then, in 1966 and 1967, as "Stephen Langton," Pearson edited the *New Patriot,* an academic-appearing magazine describing itself as "a responsible but penetrating enquiry into every aspect of the Jewish question." As he acknowledged to General Pedro del Valle, a member of the *New Patriot*'s Editorial Advisory Board, Pearson was "the registered publisher and proprietor of the publication." Under his control, the journal offered an interpretation of history so bizarre that it could easily have been mistaken for parody. In the *New Patriot*'s topsy-turvy world, Jews had been the oppressors and Germans the victims in the war: It was the Jews who had carried out a "full scale . . . onslaught on Germany," and it was the Jews—motivated by hatred and envy of the German aristocracy, whose racial dignity and refinement were a constant reminder of their own "cultural inferiority"—who had demanded the complete "extermination or genocide of the German nation."[85]

In every issue for the two years of its existence, the *New Patriot* fulminated over the Jewish goal of world domination in pursuit of which Jews were determined to suppress Nordic culture and "destroy our people by planned . . . mongrelization." The "be-Jewing of modern art," the "spoliation" of music through vulgar and erotic rhythms composed by Jews," the "jungle style 'dances'" for which "the European form is inherently unsuited," but which "the Negro and the Jew can master"—all these "Jewish art forms," according to Pearson, "oppose any and every concept of human dignity, preferring always the perverted, imperfect, distorted and psychiatric" to "the tradition of Western or Teutonic-Aryan art forms."[86] And in the scholarly world, Jews eschewed the pure sciences in favor of psychology, where "the Jew is really in his element, for he loves nothing more than to enter other people's minds . . . and learn best how to shape them to his will . . . persuading others by glib lies and subtle insinuations" in words that "have no sanctity . . . except as tools to manipulate the minds of others." In fact, Pearson explained, the Jews' holiest prayer, the Kol Nidre, is an "advance notice, given in the secrecy of the synagogue, that no promise whatever shall be binding." Occasionally Pearson supported his own analysis with observations from other well-known theorists. An excerpt from the work of Alfred Rosenberg, for example, "translated specially for the *New Patriot,*" declared that "the Jew represents nothing but the negation of spiritual values, a blind will towards destruction . . . , [and] their aim . . . [is] to strip the world of its soul"; recognized as the Nazi Party's chief ideologist, Rosenberg was hanged at Nuremberg after being found responsible "for the formulation and execution of occupation policies in the Occupied Eastern Territories," where "his subordinates engaged in mass killings of Jews."[87]

In 1967, Pearson traveled to South Africa—where he had influential friends waging a more successful battle for white civilization—leaving his journal to be absorbed by *Thunderbolt,* the organ of the National States Rights Party (NSRP); the two publications were already linked by Pearson's ally Edward R. Fields, who served both as a member of the *New Patriot'*s Editorial Advisory Board and as *Thunderbolt'*s editor. A chiropractor by trade, Fields and his long-time associate, Atlanta attorney J. B. Stoner, who eventually served time in prison for the bombing of a Birmingham church, had founded the Christian Anti-Jewish Party, which they changed to the NSRP in 1958, drafting a constitution that began with the declaration that "Jew-devils have no place in a white Christian nation." Stoner, who considered Hitler a "moderate," stated that the party's aim was "to make being a Jew a crime, punishable by death"; Fields, the more tolerant of the two, maintained, "Every Jew who holds a position of power or authority must be removed from that position. If this does not work, then we must establish [the] Final Solution!!"[88] Although *Thunderbolt* did not share the *New Patriot'*s exclusive focus on Jews—who had to share the spotlight with the party's demand for the deportation of blacks—it was nevertheless an appropriate successor to Pearson's journal.

Upon his return to the United States, Pearson, now in possession of a doctorate in anthropology, began a transition to a more respectable, academic career, abandoning his image as an overt, fire-breathing Nazi. While searching for a position, he headed for Jackson, Mississippi, where the Englishman had clearly established connections before his departure for South Africa. Although the *New Patriot'*s letterhead had listed a post office box in Hollywood, California as its address of record, the journal had actually been published in Jackson, as was a reprint of Pearson's Northern League pamphlet, *Race and Civilization.* In addition, while in Jackson, Pearson was put up by

Elmore Greaves, a well-known opponent of integration who had just received campaign contributions from Draper for his unsuccessful bid for political office. The editor of a publication so extreme it labeled Senator James Eastland a leftist, Greaves had circulated a handbill after James Meredith was admitted to the University of Mississippi, calling for the student body "to keep the colored boy in a state of constant isolation . . . avoided for the NAACP leper that he is, . . . unwanted and . . . treated as if he were a piece of furniture of no value."[89]

Finding his houseguest "brilliant and charming," Greaves recommended Pearson to a friend on the faculty at the University of Southern Mississippi (USM), an institution regularly referred to on campus as Fort McCain after its president, William D. McCain. Having served in the regular Army and the National Guard, the president was addressed as General McCain—"Generalissimo" behind his back—and he ran the institution like a military base, unceremoniously firing liberal professors and resenting civilian authority. Called to testify in a criminal proceeding in which one of his deans was charged with embezzlement, McCain was fined $500 and given a thirty-day suspended sentence after threatening to "beat [the prosecutor's] damn brains out."[90] Also Adjutant in Chief of the Sons of the Confederate Veterans and Adjutant General of the Military Order of the Stars and Bars, McCain was still fighting the Civil War, maintaining that the Fourteenth Amendment was not legally part of the Constitution. A leader in the Citizens' Councils and a member of its "speakers' bureau"—the select group chosen to present the South's case in the North—McCain had been accorded the honor of introducing Carleton Putnam at the Jackson banquet to celebrate "Race and Reason Day," and in regular articles in *The Citizen* he reported the latest statistics that Weyher had privately compiled on the number of favorable reviews of Putnam's book.[91]

Naturally, the General was opposed to the prospect of having any black recruits at Fort McCain. Indeed, had James Meredith attempted to enter USM rather than Ole Miss, the outcome might have been very different. When Clyde Kennard, a decorated Korean veteran and Mississippi resident, had requested admission to USM two years earlier, McCain promptly notified the Sovereignty Commission, which launched an investigation into the applicant's friends and references, insisting that they dissuade him from such a foolish goal. Undeterred from applying, not only was Kennard personally rejected by McCain but, immediately upon leaving the president's office, he was arrested by local officials on the first of a number of charges so transparently trumped-up, with the assistance of campus security, that even the sheriff and prosecutor were shocked (although they did not intervene when

Kennard was sentenced to the hard time that led to his death three years later).[92] Two years after Meredith's enrollment, USM remained a white institution; when another black student applied in 1964, McCain was notified by the Sovereignty Commission that the applicant was a homosexual, so that the president could divulge the information to the press unless the application was withdrawn. Even after the university was finally forced to accept black students, McCain still did what he could to enforce segregationist orthodoxy, denying student government permission to have a black gubernatorial candidate or white liberals speak on campus while approving George Wallace and other defenders of segregation.[93]

Recommended by so reliable a source as Greaves and sharing the president's views on race, Pearson was hired at USM, beginning in fall 1971 as chair of the newly consolidated Department of Anthropology and Comparative Religious Studies, and he quickly set out to create openings for neo-Nazi scientists by eliminating many of the present faculty in the department. Finding that Cedric Evans, the chair of USM's Philosophy Department, had been raised in South Africa and had taught at Rhodes University, Pearson forwarded to McCain a letter he had solicited from a friend at Rhodes—a staunch defender of apartheid who had been convicted for shooting a black person—declaring that Evans had been a well-known agitator with communist sympathies, opposed to racial segregation. Evans was soon removed as chair and subsequently dismissed; Pearson became chair of an expanded department referred to on campus as CRAP: Comparative Religion, Anthropology and Philosophy.[94] Within a year he attempted to get rid of every nontenured member, failing only in the couple of cases where a professor had influential connections beyond the university.

In place of the fired instructors, all of whom had the appropriate doctorate and favorable teaching evaluations, Pearson hired Swan, an ex-convict who had never completed his doctorate and was unemployable elsewhere, and Kuttner, fresh from his Pioneer-subsidized position in Shockley's lab, a biochemist who taught anthropology at USM despite having no relevant training or qualification in the discipline beyond Willis Carto's observation that he was an "extremely valuable man for our side, and a racist to his toes." Although Kuttner had been working in Shockley's lab for only a few weeks at the time he applied for the USM position, he requested that the physicist recommend him on the basis of such scant knowledge because if Pearson did not submit a name to the dean, the administration "will advertise and hire a Left-Liberal"; Shockley dutifully forwarded a letter to USM stating that Kuttner "is adequately prepared to teach anthropology."[95] In addition, Pearson brought in Dietrich Luth, another ideologically acceptable appointment lacking a doctorate, whose major asset seemed to be unquestioning subservience to the chair; he was described by the dean of the faculty as Pearson's "loyal shadow Nazi." Pearson justified these personnel decisions largely on the grounds that the fired faculty members were not sufficiently conservative for USM; one professor, for example, had agreed to act as faculty advisor for the newly formed American Civil Liberties Union (ACLU) chapter on campus. However, even the dean—himself an ardent segregationist who once gave a speech on "Defense of the One-Party System in Mississippi" as necessary to prevent "competition for the negro vote [and] participation of the negro in state offices"—thought that Pearson had "used his post as an academic façade to bring in equal-minded fanatics."[96]

Although Pearson did not receive his first officially acknowledged grant from Pioneer until joining the faculty at USM, there is ample reason to believe that Draper had financed some of his earlier ventures. Many of the Englishman's publications emanated from Jackson, center of the Draper-funded resistance to civil rights. Other activists whose work in the campaign against civil rights had been supported by the Colonel were extensively involved in Pearson's projects. Kuttner had been a regular contributor to *Northern World* and then a contributing editor to *Western Destiny,* as were Garrett and Cox, and the first issue of the latter publication featured articles by Garrett and Putnam. And Pedro del Valle, a member of Pearson's Editorial Advisory Board for *The New Patriot,* had previously been a spokesperson for the American Coalition of Patriotic Societies, directed by Trevor and also funded by Draper. In addition, Pearson had access to substantial funds from unknown sources. For example, when he was sued by the Council on Foreign Relations for using a logo on the *New Patriot* almost identical to that on the council's well-known journal *Foreign Affairs,* Pearson quickly settled out of court for $3,500 ($19,300 in constant dollars). Moreover, Swan's mother recalled that he knew Pearson as early as the beginning of the *Mankind Quarterly* in 1960; indeed, she thought that her son became an assistant editor at the journal "through Pearson."[97]

A final and particularly important reason to believe that Draper may have assisted Pearson earlier was the striking similarity between the two men's beliefs; in many ways the Englishman was the Colonel reincarnate. More than those of the other scientists funded by Draper, Pearson's beliefs were a throwback to the thinking of Charles Davenport, Madison Grant, and other radical eugenicists from the era in which the Colonel's own opinions had been formed. Like Laughlin, Cox, and Draper, Pearson maintained that other races, especially blacks, should not even be present in "Nordic countries"; like Draper and his friends in military intelligence, Pearson saw Jewish Bolsheviks as the primary obstacle to social cohesion; and like Draper and other members of the Eugenics Research Association, who had looked to science in the Third Reich as a model, Pearson not only was a disciple of Günther, a leading Nazi scientist, but hinted at his own connections to the regime's inner circle. "I understand," he wrote to a frequent contributor to the *Mankind Quarterly*, "on good authority that in 1944, when his world was nearly in ruins, Hitler said 'Don't worry about the future of anti-Semitism—the Jews will take care of that,'" adding that "unfortunately, he spoke much truth."[98]

In particular, Pearson, like his predecessors in the 1920s, still considered Nordic superiority recognizable primarily not from IQ test scores—useful though such confirmatory data might be—but from physical appearance and heroic behavior, especially in warfare. Nordics were tall, blond, blue-eyed, large-skulled and fair-skinned, all signs of their natural aristocracy, and they were explorers, adventurers, and warriors, always the first to volunteer for battle. Obsessed with physical appearances, in the first issue of the *New Patriot* Pearson noted that "pictures of distinguished Aryans tend to raise the tone and prestige of a publication, [and] illustrations of members of the less favored races invariably lower the tone, even to the extent of creating, in extreme cases, a semi-pornographic appearance." In keeping with this sentiment, in publications financed by Pioneer he later offered page after page of facial drawings, often of soldiers, all blue-eyed and fair-haired, as evidence for "the belief that Nordic physical characteristics might be equated with nobility of social status, and even with an heroic, military or martial spirit," a view that, in a revealing comment by Pearson, had once enjoyed "widespread political significance in Germany" but had unfortunately been "shunned" since the end of the war. These had certainly been Draper's opinions as well. According to a cousin, the Colonel "loved beautiful blond people and wanted them to breed," and Pearson's conception of Nordic traits could have provided the template for Draper's own life, centered as it was on hunting, travel, and the military.[99]

Most significant of all, both Pearson and Draper were fixated on fighter pilots as the premier Nordic specimens. It was on the basis of this assumption that the Colonel, as one of Pioneer's first projects, had financed scholarships for the children of Air Force officers to encourage them to produce more offspring. In fact, years after Draper's death, when Weyher was once concerned that a Pioneer grant was not being used in accord with the fund's purpose, he produced a memo from the Colonel indicating that he had wanted to encourage greater reproduction among parents born in one of nine Southern states, with the father "required to be a Veteran or an ex-serviceman and either to have voluntarily made a free parachute jump or to have held a license to pilot aircraft." Pearson too frequently extolled the virtues of presumably Nordic aircrew, calling them—in another article filled with pictures of Nordics who had died in war "without issue"—"the chosen of the chosen." With extraordinary advances in genetic technology near the end of the century, he even offered the superiority of pilots as an example of the benefit to be realized from selective human cloning as a form of positive eugenics.[100]

But whether or not Pearson received any money directly from Draper, the Pioneer board certainly was familiar with who he was and what he had done at the time he became a grantee: He had conducted no research of any sort but had devoted himself primarily to publishing antiblack and anti-Semitic polemics, many of them appearing in blatantly Nazi periodicals that he edited. Nor did Pearson's receipt of funds from Pioneer, ostensibly designated for "research in heredity and eugenics," produce any substantial change in his work, further indication that he had been selected by the fund not despite his unsavory background but because of it. One of his first publications as a grantee appeared in two installments in *White Power: The Revolutionary Voice of National Socialism.* Just under the large swastika that served as the journal's logo, Pearson offered another paean to Nordic superiority, explaining that Rome had fallen because it permitted marriages between members of the Nordic ruling families and their inferiors from "an alien racial lower class," thus destroying the "class system based on race." Despite this lethal contamination of Nordic blood, Pearson praised Roman society for striving to implement the "eugenic ideal" by providing for the killing of "the weaklings and misshapen," an ancient version of the T-4 program initiated by the Reich.[101]

In 1973, either Pearson or Swan, now his colleague at USM, also received as a Pioneer grant a "gift of books on heredity and eugenics" valued at $8,000 ($32,200 AFI), which had been selected from the late Draper's personal library for someone at the university; Pioneer's tax form indicated that the value of the gift was appraised in October 1972, the exact same time that the Colonel's library was being appraised, according to his estate papers. Both Pioneer grantees had an interest in Draper's materials on racial hygiene acquired from the Reich. Fifteen years earlier as "Edward Langford," Pearson had announced an appeal by the Northern League for donations of rare books "of specifically Nordic interest," encouraging readers to "hunt through their own libraries" for such works; to an organization whose members thought the wrong side had won the war, this request was easily recognized as referring to works issued under the Nazis. Swan's similar collection was also well known; indeed, he made the decisions about distribution of the Colonel's library, selecting, according to Weyher, some works on eugenics to forward to Shockley for "use in . . . [his] research." But whoever initially received Draper's books, they eventually wound up in Pearson's possession. When Swan died in 1981, Pioneer provided $26,000 ($51,000 AFI) for the Englishman to purchase his celebrated, personal collection of Nazi literature and an additional $98,000 ($185,000 AFI) for a building to house it.[102]

Pioneer continued to fund Pearson's work through various institutions, providing $1.2 million ($1.9 million AFI) altogether between 1973 and 1999, as he moved from Mississippi to Montana for a year and then, in 1976, to Washington, D.C. The bulk of this money was provided to administer the Institute for the Study of Man, which he founded in Washington to investigate "the origins and nature of man in order that contemporary Western society and its pressing problems might be more clearly perceived." With his move to the capital, Pearson also endeavored to create a new, more respectable image as a mainstream conservative, eventually gaining membership on the editorial boards of such think tanks as the Heritage Foundation, the Foreign Policy Research Institute, and the American Security Council. At the same time, however, he made one more attempt to form a Nazi international, taking control of a new United States chapter of the World Anti-Communist League (WACL) after the old chapter renounced its membership, complaining, in an internal memo, that Pearson had filled the organization with "neo-Nazi, ex-Nazi, fascist, neo-fascist, and anti-Semitic groups," including former S.S. officers who had also been members of the Northern League. According to two journalists, the numerous ex-Nazi collaborators and war criminals directly recruited to the WACL by Pearson "represented one of the greatest fascist blocs in postwar Europe." Previous conservative groups that had been constituent members of the organization resigned, offended by its new direction.[103]

In 1978, the WACL gathered in Washington, D.C., for its annual conference with Pearson, head of the host chapter, as chair, assisted by a staff member at his institute, a former American Nazi Party stormtrooper, while Liberty Lobby members, who had helped to organize the event, distributed their literature. According to the *Washington Post,* one official delegation to the conference circulated materials calling a recent television show on the Holocaust "another campaign of Jewish propaganda to conceal their objectives of world domination." The French contingent came from Groupement de Recherche et d'Etudes pour la Civilisation Européenne (GRECE)—whose acronym formed a tributary pun on the homeland of Nordic culture—an organization with ideology identical to Pearson's, even the emphasis on pre-Christian societies in which "Aryans" ruled over the inferior races. GRECE's journal, *Nouvelle Ecole,* edited by Alain de Benoist (who, under the pseudonym Fabrice Laroche, had also been a contributing editor of *Western Destiny*), was a French version of the *Mankind Quarterly,* with Swan, director of the IAAEE, serving as its U.S. representative and Garrett, Gayre, Pearson, Kuttner, and Swan all members of the publication's Comité de Patronage. While at the conference, the GRECE delegation met with William Pierce (a former American Nazi Party functionary who eventually formed his own organization, the National Alliance, devoted to creating a "White living space" in which "Semitic and other non-Aryan values" have been "root[ed] out") because, Pierce explained, the French group was "working along lines very close to ours." As "Andrew MacDonald," Pierce was also the pseudonymous author of *The Turner Diaries,* the blueprint for right-wing terrorism that, according to prosecutors, inspired Timothy McVeigh, convicted of the bombing of a federal office building in Oklahoma City. Even in the midst of such a notorious gathering, however, Pearson was anxious not to tarnish his new image unnecessarily. When members of the NSRP attempted to distribute reprints from the *Thunderbolt,* the successor to Pearson's own *New Patriot,* he insisted that they leave. "Not that I'm not sympathetic with what you're doing," he was reported as saying, "but don't embarrass me and cut my throat." As they departed, Pearson asked the NSRP members to "give my regards" to party chief Ed Fields, his old comrade from the *Patriot's* editorial board.[104]

Pearson was soon forced out as head of the U.S. chapter of the WACL, naming as his successor Elmore Greaves, the Mississippi segregationist who had housed him some years earlier. Greaves did not last long either, quickly replaced by Major General John Singlaub, for years a Central Intelligence Agency specialist in terrorism and subversion who was subsequently a key figure in the Iran-Contra scandal, providing weapons, money, and training for the Contras. Nevertheless, "under Singlaub's leadership," commented a writer at the *New Republic,* the WACL "emerged from lunatic fringe obscurity to win new respectability."[105]

Twice foiled in his attempts to create an international organization for Nazis, Pearson turned his energies to directorship of the Institute for the Study of Man, where, generously supported by Pioneer for the next two decades, he presided over a small publishing empire of books and journals promoting his, and the fund's, agenda. In 1973, Pearson had founded the *Journal of Indo-European Studies,* followed, two years later, by the *Journal of Social, Political and Economic Studies,* and in 1978 he acquired the *Mankind Quarterly* after Gayre experienced financial difficulties. According to one of the Scottish editor's confidants, Gayre had been forced to "give up the ghost" after he had sued someone for calling him a "racist" and lost, requiring him to pay more than $50,000 in court costs. A decade later, Pearson began *Con-*

*servative Review,* an admittedly political journal in contrast to the others, which affected a scholarly image. Many of the institute's publications appeared under the imprint of the "Cliveden Press," a reference on Pearson's part to the Cliveden Set, the group of British aristocrats that had been aligned with Hitler; the name of the press eventually was changed to "Scott-Townsend." Pioneer quickly did away with the fiction that it was supporting research by Pearson, acknowledging that the annual grants to the institute were intended to support its "various literary activities."[106]

In the numerous journals and books published at the institute Pearson himself was the most prolific author, churning out dozens of articles, reviews, and edited volumes, most of them appearing under one of his many aliases. In a civil deposition in 1994, he was forced to admit under oath what had long been suspected: that many of the articles purportedly contributed by others to journals edited by Pearson actually were his pseudonymous work under the names "Alan McGregor," "J. W. Jamieson," "R. Peterson," and others. Sometimes he used one alter ego to praise another; as McGregor, for example, he reviewed a volume he had edited as Jamieson, calling it "an exciting work" and "a first class book." On a number of occasions he published the same work twice: the first time as a pseudonymous article, the second time as part of a book written under his own name. (It is instructive that none of Pearson's writing appeared in the one publication at the institute of acknowledged academic value, the *Journal of Indo-European Studies,* which he left to the control of respected scholars Edgar Polomé and Marija Gimbutas, both now deceased.)[107]

Pearson's numerous articles, most of them published in the *Mankind Quarterly,* hammered away at the same themes often in the same words with maddening repetition, like political commercials during campaign season, preaching a mixture of Güntherism with sociobiology. According to Pearson, "aristocracies" in pre-Christian societies arose among Indo-Europeans—the ancient Greeks, Romans, Germans, Teutons, and Aryans—because only these peoples recognized the importance of descent from ancestral heroes and thus instituted rigid rules ensuring that "noble" families remained genetically distinct from the rest of the population. In the Greek city-states, for example, the "eupatrids" were "descended from no less than nine generations of untainted noble stock," and "men chose their wives as they chose their horses, by the length of their pedigrees." In contrast to the rest of the world, Pearson maintained, only these early Nordic societies, through their eugenic breeding practices, created the conditions essential for evolutionary progress: genetically based hierarchies, in which an aristocracy of greater innate value enjoyed the right of command over their inferiors.[108]

Over the next two millennia, however, Pearson saw a number of factors threatening the Nordic elite that had been created by these biologically sensible principles. What first changed consciousness of the superior "blood line," he complained, was Christianity, "attacking the idea of pride of birth and human inequality" and preaching the misguided notion that "all peoples, nations and races [were] equal before God"; indeed, "the lower their level of achievement, the more deserving they were of sympathy and assistance." Thus, instead of acknowledging the racial superiority of their masters, the "heterogeneous mass of slaves and persons of low status," Pearson observed with chagrin, now had the temerity to seek "moral equality" with the aristocracy. Although Protestant northern Europeans made more of an attempt to preserve the pre-Christian emphasis on aristocratic breeding and Nordic racial purity, the Catholic church spread the genetically destructive idea of the universality of humanity.[109] In addition, Pearson claimed, the ranks of the aristocracy were depleted through the disproportionate losses in battle sustained by the heroic Nordic warriors, who always led both sides of the conflict, especially in the two fratricidal World Wars; "the self-image of those who prided themselves in their superior birth required that they expose themselves . . . to the dangers of the front line," in contrast to the cowardice of their racial inferiors, the meek who sought to inherit the earth after the brave had fallen. Yet another threat in the modern era was the use of "Western technology and Western medical science" to reduce infant mortality and increase life expectancy in Asia and Africa, thus "blunt[ing] Nature's pruning knife" and replacing fitness with fecundity as the basis for evolution.[110]

Pearson considered the eugenics movement in the first third of the twentieth century as the intelligent, scientific response to these threats. He regarded Davenport, Laughlin, Grant, McDougall, and others who had attempted "to ensure that the American gene pool would not be adulterated by inferior genes" from Italy, Poland, Russia, and Greece as leaders "inspired by a noble sense of public duty," even though, he observed sadly, "subsequent generations have not preserved the high level . . . to which they aspired." In particular, Pearson praised the work of Charles Conant Josey—one of Earnest Sevier Cox's earliest supporters and an author, four decades later, of an anti-integration monograph for the IAAEE—republishing his 1923 book under the Cliveden Press imprint. In *The Philosophy of Nationalism* (originally *Race and National Solidarity*) Josey had argued unabashedly for white "world domination" and the need to "impose our will on the world" so that the "backward races" might "serve our needs" and "their resources" be "turn[ed] . . . in our direction."[111] In response to the work of these pioneers, Pearson noted with obvious approval, many states enacted eugenics laws, providing for sterilization and "prohibiting miscegenation between blacks and whites" to avoid "the scrambling together of disparate gene pools." With these statutes in the United States serving as a model, he wrote, "it seemed probable that . . . all the leading nations of the West would eventually take steps intended to free their future populations from the dysgenic threat." There was great reason to be optimistic at the time, according to Pearson: "Morality would combine with science . . . and chart a rational course toward a happier future."[112]

But just as humanity was starting down this rosy path, it was led astray, in Pearson's account, primarily by a cabal of scheming egalitarian scientists, almost all of them Jewish and disciples of Boas, who saw eugenic progress in conflict with their desire "to demolish the unity and coherence of national units" by insisting on racial equality. This was the major reason for his lengthy history of anti-Semitic publications, he noted, in a letter written to a frequent contributor to the *Mankind Quarterly*. Acknowledging that he had "been responsible for a number of literary enterprises, under various pen names, which have been described as 'anti-Semitic,'" Pearson explained that his "main opposition to Jewish influence" stemmed from the "dysgenic" impact of "the policies of the more active members of the Jewish political organizations." These "race-mixing, dysgenic and Communist activities," he continued, "seem aimed at the destruction of all potential rivals to the Jewish community, in their apparent eagerness to obtain world power" and establish "rule over a vast subnormal mass of sub-humanity."[113]

The influence of these "biological egalitarians," combined with Christian universalist ethical concepts, produced what Pearson regarded as a horrifying "perversion" of altruism: Whites were aiding other races. The proper definition of altruism, in accord with its natural evolutionary function, he insisted, encompassed selfless acts performed by individuals to enhance the survival chances only of other members "of their own kind," members of "their immediate gene pool." Yet instead of properly limiting altruistic efforts to "their own genetic kinfolk," the Caucasoid populations of the West, much to Pearson's dismay, were providing assistance for "the most diverse members of the hominid species," thereby misdirecting their sympathies into "unnatural directions"—to "members of competing gene pools," a "reversal of the evolutionary process" that could result in "disastrous consequences."[114]

Worst of all, in Pearson's analysis, under the same malevolent influences society no longer appreciated the "evolutionary purpose of 'race prejudice.'" In the *Mankind Quarterly* "Alan McGregor" alone authored three articles on this theme between 1981 and 1993, although because large sections were reprinted verbatim each time, it would be more appropriate to state that "McGregor" published the *same* article on three occasions in Pearson's refereed scholarly journal. In each of these works, "McGregor" declared that racial prejudice was a biological necessity, "an honored quality" essential to evolutionary development, leading "healthy-minded people . . . to maintain a healthy reproductive distance" from other races in order to "maintain the integrity of the gene pool." The tendency to "distrust and repel" members of other races, "as well as to love and assist" one's own kind, was not only normal and "a natural part of the human personality" but "one of the main pillars on which civilization was built, and one without which civilization might well collapse." Unfortunately, according to "McGregor," the natural human tendency toward racial prejudice was "weakening under the pressure of human ideologies which are antithetical to biological realities." And the result of this breakdown, he observed with concern, was "heavily urbanized and intellectually distorted human beings," who, just like caged animals inappropriately attempting "to mate with animals of other breeds," exhibited numerous "perversions" of their natural instincts: "abnormal patterns of behavior ranging from homosexuality to a quest for abnormal erotic experiences including interracial sexual experimentation." Indeed, he complained, our appreciation of biological imperatives had so deteriorated that acts of racial prejudice had come to be considered, foolishly, as "immoral" or—worse yet—as "hate crimes." This same argument was regularly repeated, often in identical language, by "J. W. Jamieson" and by Pearson occasionally under his own name—nine times in all, five of which appear as sample articles on the *Mankind Quarterly*'s Web site, strongly suggesting that the rationalization and even the encouragement of racial conflict has been one of the main purposes of the journal.[115]

In fact, these articles were largely a reprise of ideas Pearson had promoted decades earlier in his Northern League pamphlets, where he had called "cross-breeding between separate sub-species [i.e., races] . . . clearly contrary to the normal laws of nature" and a "perversion of the natural instincts." Indeed, the article by "D. Purves" in the first issue of the *Mankind Quarterly* in 1960, advocating racial separation on the grounds that racism was an "instinctive feeling . . . rooted in man's nature" and served the "biological function" of protecting a group's "genetic integrity," sounded suspiciously like the work of Pearson, who was closely allied with Gayre, the journal's editor, in the Northern League at the time.[116] In any event, for the last four decades— in at least three of them with Pioneer's support—both Pearson and the *Mankind Quarterly* have been republishing at regular intervals essentially the same polemic, unadorned by research or data, arguing that people such as Lani Guinier and Tiger Woods represent evolutionary abnormalities and that racial prejudice is the natural, biological response to such "perversions."

In addition to publishing his own writing, Pearson's journals at the institute also provided a pseudoscholarly outlet for fellow Pioneer grantees and other authors with similar thinking on race whose work would have little chance of acceptance elsewhere. As Gayre had commented behind the scenes shortly after the *Mankind Quarterly* began operation, its purpose "was to provide our small group with the opportunity of being published," especially because "our views" were no longer tolerated in other outlets. The journals under Pearson's control continued to play this role. In the *Quarterly* and the *Journal of Social, Political and Economic Studies,* for example, he published more than a dozen articles by Ralph Scott, a professor at the University of Northern Iowa, who had collaborated on Pioneer-funded work with Swan and then received his own grants, some of which were used to organize antibusing conferences around the country under the name "Edward Langerton." Scott threatened a Delaware newspaper with "legal action" if revelation of his identity jeopardized his $2 million of federal grants; it turned out that he did not have any.[117] Under the same pseudonym, Scott authored *The Busing Coverup,* which once again declared that the Supreme Court had been "hoodwinked" by egalitarian scientists in the *Brown* case and called for a reversal of the decision; with or without busing, he did not seem to find the thought of blacks and whites attending the same school to be a pleasant prospect. (Amazingly, none of these activities prevented Scott from being appointed chair of the Iowa Advisory Commission on Civil Rights by the Reagan administration.)[118] Scott also reviewed Wilmot Robertson's *The Dispossessed Majority* for the Liberty Lobby newspaper, recommending the book as a "family must" for its "bright clear light" and "richly documented argument," especially the author's description of the "noble . . . attempt . . . to restrain the forces of hate after . . . World War II": the *prosecution* in the trials of Nazi war criminals. And after George Lincoln Rockwell had spoken at Northern Iowa, Scott defended the American Nazi Party founder's position in the campus newspaper.[119]

Almost every one of Scott's contributions to Pearson's journals was a variation of the same argument: School integration had handicapped white students while providing no improvement for blacks because of their genetic shortcomings. If nothing else, Scott certainly was persistent: Even decades after the *Brown* decision, he continued to attack the scientific testimony presented to the court (in 1998, forty-four years after the case, he was still attempting to organize a debate at professional conferences over the validity of the *Brown* evidence). Many of his articles were merely a verbatim republication of portions of his pseudonymous book, including the absurd charge that Kenneth B. Clark, the respected psychologist who had testified for the plaintiffs in *Brown*, had urged the use of "drugs and the electrical stimulation of certain brain areas" to alter the thinking of any researchers opposed to his social objectives and that the American Psychological Association supported this proposal.[120] A selection of Scott's articles eventually was published as a book by the institute, and the book was reviewed in the two journals where the articles had appeared, thus completing a cycle in which Pearson published these attacks on integrated education twice and then published a review of them—highly favorable, of course, and probably written by him.[121]

In another case Pearson reprinted almost verbatim in one of his journals an article opposing equality for blacks that had originally appeared in the *Quarterly* before his official involvement. "The New Fanatics" by William A. Massey had been first published in 1962 by Gayre at Garrett's urging and subsequently appeared as a pamphlet distributed by the Putnam Letters Committee. Declaring it "obvious" that blacks were inferior, Massey had maintained that even those "of adequate intelligence" were nevertheless "by inheritance temperamentally unsuited for citizenship," and he deemed it necessary and justifiable to discriminate against them, restricting their participation in government. In 1992, "The New Fanatics" by the same author reappeared in two installments in *Conservative Review*, one of the publications edited by Pearson at the institute. Although the three intervening decades had exercised no effect on the adjective in the title, the article was now phrased in a slightly less politically incorrect form, "crime-ridden minority welfare receivers" appearing in place of "Negroes" as the group that "may never make productive citizens" and was unsuited for citizenship even when sufficiently intelligent.[122] "Massey" probably was a pseudonym and may even have been Pearson himself, although it is difficult to be certain: No affiliation or identification was provided for Massey, and none of the standard abstracts or databases lists him as an author in the intervening thirty years, although in 1965 he was a contributor to *Western Destiny*, also edited by Pearson. In any event, despite the euphemistic revision, offering a slightly more selective definition of those unworthy of their constitutional entitlements, the updated article still proffered the same exclusionary ideology that Pearson had been promoting since formation of the Northern League: Nonwhites did not merit citizenship in Nordic countries.

Finally, the book series at the institute gave Pearson an opportunity to publish analyses even less subtle than those in his journals. In *Conscientious Evolution*, for example, reprinted by the institute eighteen years after its original appearance, professor of electronics Herbert F. Mataré maintained that notions of "human freedom or basic rights . . . within an advanced society are anti-evolutionary." Instead of equal rights for all, a more scientific system would provide "the better endowed" with "more votes than are given to less important citizens," and "low echelon beings" would be denied the franchise altogether. In addition, "the right to procreate should be rationed and controlled," the number of children allowed increasing with the number of votes. Nor did Mataré leave any doubt who would be relegated to the low echelons. "The Negro," he declared, "lacks all those properties that make for a successful member of a modern technocracy: logic, abstraction, analytical thinking, combinatory thought, inventiveness, [and] motivation to understand." Many of "these descendants of African tribes" have made a "reasonable effort," he acknowledged, but because "the Negro brain development is . . . 200,000 years behind the one of the white Europeans, it is useless to ask them to come up to the cultural level of the white world." During slavery, Mataré observed, an "ordered and friendly situation prevailed when the Negro was associated with the white master in a clearly defined form of servant." In contemporary society, however, "all one can do," not just for blacks but Mexicans and "Indians" as well, "is to provide . . . low skill occupations . . . and discourage their proliferation." The women who were allowed to reproduce would have little other role: "It is obvious," wrote Mataré, "that man and only man should have the more active role in life that is, that he should be the decision maker," while a woman should "be what she naturally tends to be: something for the man to take care of." Mataré's book was as much an assault on the English language as on the rights of blacks and women, filled with sentences such as, "With modern science reaching the dissolution of the once solid materialism, scientists have begun to feel uneasy about their basis, the ephemer materials point as a wave function amplitude of finite probability."[123]

In another typical volume issued by Pearson at the institute, Laszlo F. Thomay declared that "no special training in either sociology or political science is required to realize that people of different types never could live together in harmony and never will," a conclusion he elevated to an immutable "Natural Law of Race Relations" to be "accepted unquestioningly by everyone," no different from the law of gravity. Rather than futile attempts to defy the natural law, accompanied by "all-pervading propaganda" that different groups can live together peacefully, what was needed in the United States was "territorial separation" of minorities.[124]

Few, if any, of Pearson's activities during his three decades as a Pioneer grantee could be considered research; his numerous polemics on the importance of Nordic aristocracy contained little that had not been said decades earlier. Nor did his stewardship of the *Mankind Quarterly* or the *Journal of Social, Political and Economic Studies* suggest a less tendentious purpose; real scientific journals do not publish the same conclusions—indeed, sometimes substantially the same article—again and again. What Pioneer received for its almost $2 million investment, not in Pearson the anthropologist but in Pearson the activist, was largely a campaign for the United States to emulate the Nuremberg Laws, denying to nonwhites the benefits of citizenship. But he was not the only Pioneer grantee to pursue this goal.

## Americans Who Have Advanced White Interests

In the 1980s and 1990s, Pioneer added to its grantees another group of academics focused on race and intelligence, providing more than $5 million (AFI) to support seven new scientists, more than a quarter of all the money ever awarded by the fund. Only two of the seven conducted research on the actual racial differences, as opposed to their consequences: University of Western Ontario psychologist J. Philippe Rushton and University of Ulster psychologist Richard Lynn. Rushton proposed applying to differences between races a theory of reproductive strategies used in evolutionary biology to account for differences between species. At one extreme were organisms producing a large number of offspring to which they paid little parental attention; organisms at the other extreme produced very few offspring but lavished intensive care on each of them. According to Rushton, "Negroids" tended toward the former strategy, "Caucasoids" and, to an even greater extent, "Mongoloids" toward the latter. Moreover, he claimed that a number of other traits were systematically associated with these reproductive approaches. In comparison to the other races, Negroids had smaller brains, lower intelligence, greater sexual activity, shorter lives, and lesser degrees of altruism, law-abidingness, and social organization. In addition, Rushton, like Pearson, maintained that ethnocentrism had a biological basis, making "xenophobia . . . an innate trait in human beings," designed "to preserve the 'purity' of the gene pool."[125]

Lynn, an editor at the *Mankind Quarterly* even before its transfer to Pearson's control, had earlier maintained that Nordics were intellectually superior to "the other Caucasoid peoples inhabiting the more southerly latitudes" and, in a book on racial differences in personality, had concluded that Nordics were calm and well-controlled, in contrast to the anxious and hysterical races in eastern and southern Europe. As a consequence, he wrote, the Nordics, "easy going and prepared to co-operate," were more suited for constitutional government than the "abrasive peoples" in the Alpine and Mediterranean countries. In later work he shifted his attention to larger racial comparisons, concluding that "the Mongoloid peoples have slightly higher general intelligence than the Caucasoids," although he emphasized that both were far superior to Negroids: "The Caucasoids and the Mongoloids [are] the two most intelligent races and the only two races that have made any significant contribution to the development of civilization."[126] Interestingly, this judgment on Lynn's part produced one of the few trivial differences of opinion among Pioneer's scientists. Immediately following his article in the *Quarterly* were "Some Comments on Lynn's Thesis" by Pearson, who—obsessed, as always, with racial purity—hastened to explain that the "alleged 'white' average" was not an "accurate indicator of original unadulterated Caucasoid IQ" because it had been depressed in the United States by the inclusion of people with "partially Negroid or other racial ancestry" and in Britain by the presence of "Eurasians and other mixed blood immigrants." In addition, Pearson continued, in Asian areas with "some of the highest Mongoloid IQ scores," there had been intermixture with "Caucasoid Indo-Europeans," indicated, for example, by "members of the ruling classes in Japan [who] still often reflect a Caucasoid cast of features, sharply contrasting with the more Filipino-like features of the lower classes." Although creativity occasionally was found among Mongoloids, conceded "Jamieson," some time later, it was "Caucasoid Westerners [who] have transformed the world."[127] In any event, there was no disagreement about "Negroids": Both Pearson and Lynn agreed that they had contributed nothing of value.

The other new grantees were more interested in the social, political, and educational implications of racial differences. Well-known University of London psychologist Hans J. Eysenck was a long-time opponent of compensatory education for black children as well as all those other "Left-Wing" solutions: "Better Schools, Smaller Classes and More Teachers." He subsequently joined the editorial board of the *Mankind Quarterly*.[128] Johns Hopkins sociologist Robert Gordon found differences in IQ between blacks and whites to account for differences in such variables as poverty, criminality, belief in conspiracy rumors, and even opinions about the O. J. Simpson case. Linda Gottfredson, professor of education at the University of Delaware and codirector, along with Gordon, of the Project for the Study of Intelligence and Society, argued that socioeconomic inequality between races was the expected outcome of lower black intelligence and insisted that "much current social policy" was based on a "collective fraud," perpetrated by scientists who refused to acknowledge the intellectual inferiority of blacks. Neither Gordon nor Gottfredson was involved in any of Pioneer's more overtly discriminatory projects, both believing firmly that decisions in education and employment should be based on individual merit without regard to race; Gottfredson in particular pointed out a number of unprofessional practices in the construction of tests designed to redress racial imbalance in the hiring of police officers.[129] Their work was nevertheless useful to Pioneer's agenda; as the Satterfield plan had observed, the fund would support work "*shaded with our beliefs.*"

The last two grantees in this group had begun their academic life in fields far from the study of racial differences. Michael Levin, professor of philosophy at City College of the City University of New York, had previously been known for his work on the mind-body problem but came to Pioneer's attention after authoring two controversial publications: a letter to the *New York Times* in which he defended store owners who refused entry to young black males and an article on "The Trouble with American Education," which attributed the "malaise" in colleges and universities to the reduction in standards necessitated by the presence of intellectually inferior black students. As a recipient of the fund's support, Levin conducted no research but focused primarily on criminality, maintaining that blacks were genetically incapable of abiding by "white [behavioral] norms" and even suggesting that "free will" may be "correlated with race." As a consequence, he proposed a number of blatantly unconstitutional measures, including "searches of black males under circumstances in which searching white males would be impermissible," treatment of "blacks as adult offenders at an earlier age than whites," "race-based punishment schedules," and the requirement for "black males to ride in specially patrolled cars" on the subway.[130]

Finally, Glayde Whitney, a geneticist at Florida State University who had specialized in olfaction in mice, became a Pioneer grantee after fulminating over the "most successful disinformation campaign in the annals of modern propaganda," waged by "the egalitarian priesthood" to keep the public ignorant of the facts about race. Despite efforts to improve their cognitive skills and their morals, "blacks will be blacks," Whitney announced. Even when raised by white middle-class families, they displayed "evidence of maladjustment," behaving "like typical blacks raised under the usual conditions"; as he succinctly put it, "Pit Bulls raised by Cocker Spaniels grow up to be Pit Bulls." With the fund's support Whitney went on to point out other areas of research that had disappeared from "mainstream scientific literature" because of the egalitarian taboo, such as "hybrid incompatibilities between blacks and whites." Citing Madison Grant as an authority on "disharmonious combinations," Whitney explained that "crosses . . . between distant races can lead to genetic mixes that just don't work very well." As an example, he attributed the "very wide range of health problems" suffered by the African-American population, especially a high infant death rate, to the presence of incompatible white genes undetected because of the "one drop" convention, which

defined all "hybrids" as black. In another instance of neglected genetic analysis, Whitney suggested that the Kalenjin tribe in Kenya had furnished an
astonishing number of the world's best male distance runners because of
"natural selection for successful thievery" of cattle: Someone who could "run
far and get away with the stolen cattle" in this polygamous society "could af-
ford to buy many wives and thus make many little runners."[131]

As one of the featured speakers at the annual conference of the Institute
for Historical Review—the revisionist organization founded by Willis Carto, the patron saint of Holocaust denial—Whitney identified the source of
the egalitarian conspiracy, explaining to an audience filled with Holocaust
deniers and Nazi sympathizers that Jews were using the same tactics in science as they had used to invent the Holocaust: creating a "fake" to advance
their own interests. Jewish scientists, motivated by "bitter animosity" toward
gentiles, Whitney told the revisionists, had set out "to attack and subvert traditional European-American civilization" by "leveling the whites and blacks,"
a strategy that would "directly contribut[e] to the ascendancy of Jews, because if the whites could be convinced to accept blacks as equals, they could
be convinced to accept anyone." Whitney also authored the foreword to
David Duke's autobiography, comparing the ex-Klansman and neo-Nazi
activist to Socrates, Galileo, and Newton and warning that the NAACP and
other "front organizations" had been created "in furtherance of the Jewish
agenda": to preserve "Jewish distinctiveness . . . by eliminating distinctiveness among the non-Jews."[132]

Rushton, Lynn, Levin, and Whitney also provided the scientific authority
for another group enjoying support from Pioneer: American Renaissance.
Although the named recipient of the money was the New Century Foundation, which received $27,000 ($31,400 AFI) between 1994 and 1999, the foundation's major activity was to steward American Renaissance, including
publication of its eponymous monthly and administration of its biennial
conference. Jared Taylor, president of New Century, was also the editor of
American Renaissance, both organization and periodical dedicated to the ideal
of the United States as a white European nation.[133]

The basis for citizenship, AR regularly lectured, was not "the American
democratic faith," nor "the ideal of America as a country where advancement
is open to anyone," nor "allegiance to an idea that all people everywhere must
be free"; race was the essential ingredient of citizenship. Blacks and Third
World immigrants did not really belong in the United States and certainly
could not be "real" Americans.[134] As Taylor noted, John Rocker—the Atlanta Braves pitcher who had complained of all the "Asians and Koreans and
Vietnamese and Indians and Russians and Spanish people" in New York City,

demanding to know "How the hell did they get in this country?"—was "the one sane man in sports."[135] Indeed, *AR*'s favorite "scientific" quote, offered regularly by Taylor and other writers in the italics appropriate to its significance, was zoologist Raymond Hall's "biological law" that had appeared in the first issue of the *Mankind Quarterly* decades earlier: *"two subspecies of the same species do not occur in the same geographic area"* and, as a consequence, merely the thought of two races in the same society "on equal terms . . . is but wishful thinking and leads only to disaster and oblivion." A biology that mandated racial separation produced a moral philosophy to match. "All peoples practice a morality of loyalty to their own," proclaimed Taylor, and "suspicion or even hostility to outsiders"; white criminals "may be boobs," he observed, "but they're *our* boobs."[136] Another article in *AR* was even blunter, insisting on "a dual code of morality—one for one's own group and another for everyone else." After attending an American Renaissance conference, even well-known conservative Dinesh D'Souza labeled the group "racist"; a senior domestic policy analyst in the Reagan administration and hagiographer of the former president, D'Souza was first to sound the tocsin against political correctness in *Illiberal Education* and subsequently called for repeal of the Civil Rights Act of 1964, allowing employers, banks, and others to engage in what he called "rational discrimination."[137]

*AR*'s ideology seemed almost indistinguishable from Pearson's, but neither his name nor his institute was associated with the publication, although the two efforts obviously enjoyed some degree of collaboration. Not only were books issued by the Englishman's project regularly reviewed in *AR,* but the longest article ever to appear in *AR,* authored by "Edwin Clark," an "Indo-European writer living in Washington, D.C.," was vintage Pearson. "The Roots of the White Man" was a paean to Aryan superiority, which began in ancient Indo-European societies, where, according to Clark, "the higher ranks . . . [were] associated with the lighter-skinned Aryans, and the lower ranks . . . [with] the darker hues of the conquered non-Aryan races." The article went on to characterize Aryans, the forebears of contemporary whites, as natural nobility, uniquely suited to the limited democracy of "aristocratic republicanism," bold and adventurous conquerors of "non-Aryans," whose "passive proclivities and static tendencies render[ed] them easy to subjugate," and courageous loners who provided the models for contemporary comic book superheroes. The "Indo-European hero, fighting in single combat," was vanquished only by "treachery or trickery . . . by a non-Aryan," wrote Clark, citing David's victory over Goliath, an example that had been similarly used by Pearson's intellectual model, Günther.[138]

According to *AR*'s own survey of its subscribers, Jared Taylor himself ranked first on the list of "Americans Who Have Advanced White Interests," but also among the top fifteen "helpful to our cause" were David Duke, Wilmot Robertson, Nathan B. Forrest, the confederate general who became the first Grand Wizard of the Ku Klux Klan, Robert E. Lee, Arthur Jensen, William Shockley, and William Pierce, founder of the Nazi group National Alliance and author of *The Turner Diaries,* the fictional blueprint for race war used as a model by the neo-Nazi group The Order, which murdered Denver talk show host Alan Berg in 1984. Further down the list were George Wallace, Madison Grant, Carleton Putnam, Ed Fields, Pearson's old friend from the National States Rights Party, and the Colonel's old ally, Theodore Bilbo. By a large margin Adolf Hitler ranked first among "Foreigners Who Have Advanced White Interests" (although he also ranked first, just ahead of Karl Marx, among "Foreigners Who Have Damaged White Interests," no doubt because he has been such a public relations disaster for racists and anti-Semites). With the exception of Gerald Ford and Ronald Reagan, every president since 1932 was named among the "Americans Who Have Damaged White Interests," the first four persons on the list being Lyndon Johnson, Franklin Roosevelt, William Clinton, and Abraham Lincoln.[139]

*AR*'s interpretation of history was, to say the least, unique. In Taylor's view slavery may have been wrong, but the unappealing alternative was "Negro pandemonium." Besides, according to excerpts from oral histories published in the organization's monthly, blacks had overwhelmingly positive attitudes toward slavery. "Slavery was better for us than things is now," read one quotation; "niggers then didn't have no responsibility, just work, obey and eat." Another aging ex-slave looked forward to "be[ing] in heaven with all my white folks, just to wait on them and love them and serve them, sorta like I did in slavery time."[140] And once emancipated, explained Samuel Francis, a regular contributor to *AR* who was fired from the conservative *Washington Times* for his offensive views, the only "civil rights" to which blacks were entitled were "the right of personal security, the right of personal liberty, and the right to acquire and enjoy property." These essential elements of freedom, according to Francis, had absolutely "nothing to do" with "the right to vote, . . . to hold political office, . . . to attend the same schools, to serve on juries, to marry across racial lines, to serve in the armed forces, to eat at lunch counters, to ride on buses, to buy a house or rent a room or hold a job." None of these "phony 'rights,'" which had been "fabricated" for blacks "through the corruption of our" system, were entitlements, granted under the Constitution or the Declaration of Independence, whose observation that "all men are created equal" Francis called "one of the most dangerous sentences ever written, one of the major blunders of American history." For most of the nation's history, Taylor pointed out, there had been agreement with Theodore Roosevelt's observation that blacks were "a perfectly stupid race," and although blacks could "neither be killed nor driven away," no one expected "civilized white men" to work alongside them.[141]

Naturally, *AR* was appalled by the Second Reconstruction, providing a lurid description of the famous voting rights march from Selma to Montgomery as one long debauch in which drunken white clergy engaged in "public interracial copulation" while the good citizens of Selma and Montgomery displayed "astonishing . . . self-control" in the face of such degeneracy. It was not the segregationists' fault that some activists were murdered, according to *AR;* it was the disgraceful behavior of the Northern clerics "that prompted" the brutal clubbing of a Unitarian minister from Boston, and while he lay dying in the hospital, claimed the article, couples "fornicated during the services" called to pray for his recovery. In a different publication Taylor dismissed Viola Liuzzo, the Michigan woman who was shot and killed while transporting demonstrators, as a "Northern meddler . . . mentally unstable . . . [with] needle marks in her arms." And since the civil rights era, he complained, laws prohibiting racial discrimination had turned "common sense" into a "crime."[142]

The question regularly debated on the pages of *AR* was which of two possible strategies whites should follow to ensure their "racial survival" in the face of the colored threat. Maintaining that "short term palliatives like segregation and immigration restriction" were no longer effective, a number of contributors argued that it was necessary for whites to "accept partition" in the name of preservation and that they should "enter into serious dialogue with black and Hispanic nationalists who seek to establish racially based nations within the territory of the United States."[143] On the other hand were those, like Francis, who viewed separatists as lacking the "moral foundation for white supremacy" and, like the "egalitarians," reluctant to have "one race ruling another." To Francis, unplagued by any such doubts, the real solution was to exercise that "instinctual . . . proclivity . . . to expand and conquer" that was "biologically rooted in whites" and achieve a "reconquest of the United States," revoking the "phony" rights that allowed minorities to vote, hold office, and associate with their superiors, "sealing the border," and "imposing adequate fertility controls on nonwhites." Besides, he observed, racial partition would raise difficult definitional problems concerning eastern and southern Europeans, Jews, and even the Irish.[144]

On one point concerning nonwhites there was no disagreement: As Taylor succinctly put it, "They are not like us and will never be like us." This conclusion was regularly sanctified by Pioneer's scientific authorities, not just through scholarly articles that could be cited as support but through their frequent participation in AR's conferences and their contributions to its monthly. Although Jensen was never one of the conference speakers, in a lengthy published "conversation" with *AR*, he declared that the society's attempt to "build a multi-racial nation . . . is doomed to failure." Judging at least one quarter of all blacks "mentally retarded" and "not really educable," he insisted that "society has to protect itself from dangers within." He also expressed fears that a multiracial society would lead to the loss of "the great things of Western civilization" because of a population for which Beethoven, Goethe, and Shakespeare would be "meaningless," although he thought "Asians capable of preserving that level of civilization, once introduced to it."[145]

Other Pioneer grantees were not so coy, providing AR members, many of whom had actually complained in the survey that its monthly dedicated to white racial solidarity was "too tolerant," with ample justification for their instinctive beliefs about blacks and other minorities. As a contributing editor of *AR*, for example, Whitney authored a regular column, suggesting that different races did not belong to the same species and calling an organization "race destroyers" because it conducted a "Teaching Tolerance" program. Lynn also told the *AR* readership that "the rearing environment has no effect" at all on IQ scores and that the difference between whites and blacks was thus entirely genetic.[146] Rushton, too, often appeared at AR conferences. On one occasion, while an audience including David Duke and other white supremacists "listened in awed silence" according to a newspaper report, he explained that white women had larger birth canals than black women, allowing them to give birth to babies with larger brains. At another conference he declared that racial similarity was nature's basis for distinguishing "friend from foe." And in yet another presentation, later published in a collection of AR speeches, Rushton finally provided an example of "the fine idea" that Wesley Critz George had suggested to Weyher in 1963: to find a disease more prevalent among blacks, thus producing "alarm" among whites. The AIDS virus, he announced, "must be considered endemic to black populations." He also began this talk by endorsing the segregationist claim that *Brown* and the subsequent civil rights legislation had been premised not on blacks' rights as citizens but on the assumption that their "underachievement" could be "blamed . . . on prejudice and discrimination by white people"; although Rushton did not pursue the logic, his research claiming to disprove that assumption would thus produce a particularly appealing conclusion for this audience.[147]

Even more than the other academics, Levin did not mince words. "It is a matter of verifiable fact," he declared at one conference, "that the influence of whites dominates mankind"; on all the important criteria for evaluating a society's accomplishments, he continued, "whites come out on top." Indeed, he argued at another AR meeting that segregated schools for blacks in the South "were far superior to any educational institution ever created by a black society" and that in comparison "Jim Crow was a *stimulating* environment," one for which blacks should, no doubt, have been grateful.[148] In *AR* he stated bluntly that "whites are *right*" to discriminate against blacks because "the average black is . . . not as good a person as the average white." Traits such as honesty, self-restraint, and cooperativeness "did not have the same evolutionary value in Africa that they did in Eurasia," he wrote, so "individuals of Eurasian descent tend to be more moral than individuals of African descent." Perhaps "when this is more widely realized," he predicted hopefully, "whites will once again permit themselves" the freedom to discriminate, for good and rational reasons, "in favor of other whites in housing, employment, and the schools to which they send their children." As Taylor delightedly observed, Levin's work "leads to policies strikingly similar to those of the pre–civil rights era American South."[149] If AR could have its way, the South would indeed rise again.

Ironically, Levin, the most intemperate of Pioneer's academics to contribute to *AR*, caused the organization to temper its own anti-Semitism. There was no doubt that AR was a gathering point for many neo-Nazis. A journalist at the 2000 conference reported that when Taylor, speculating aloud on the reasons whites had lost so much ground during the last century, suggested that "maybe it is the Jews," there was a "burst of applause." *AR*'s survey revealed that next to Taylor and Francis, its readers' favorite nonfiction writer was David Irving, described by a British judge in a legal opinion as "an active Holocaust denier . . . associate[d] with right wing extremists who promote neo-Nazism"; also among the top dozen favorites were Wilmot Robertson, who viewed the defeat of Hitler, the "defender of the white race," as "shattering to Northern Europeans, both in Europe and America," and Revilo P. Oliver, who—in a book published by the press created by Robertson—argued that the Führer should be recognized as "a semi-divine figure."[150] And the most popular magazines among *AR*'s readers included five neo-Nazi publications: Wilmot Robertson's *Instauration,* Willis Carto's *Spotlight,* Ed Fields's *Truth at Last,* William Pierce's *National Vanguard,* and the *Journal of Historical Review,* dedicated to Holocaust denial.

Nevertheless, with Levin such a prominent contributor to "white interests," the publication for readers who looked to Hitler, Robertson, and Oliver as sources of inspiration and viewed Jewish intellectuals as intent on destroying the racial basis of Western civilization developed a sudden outrage over anti-Semitic attacks against *AR*'s favorite philosophy professor.

Despite their unsavory past, the journal observed, Jews were now "present in the foremost ranks" of opposition to "Third-World immigration and . . . government interference in race relations," their "energy and influence" helping to "save what is left of a beleaguered nation." Similar considerations had no doubt influenced Pioneer to support Levin and other Jewish academics such as Robert Gordon. Weyher and Trevor, who had earlier worked on the surreptitious publication of *The Dispossessed Majority*, which blamed Jews for "every divisive force" in the last century, also realized that some Jews could be useful to their agenda.[151]

## God's Plan for Humanity

To many of Pioneer's grantees, nonwhite immigration to the West became an increasingly important issue during the last decades of the twentieth century as a succession of more liberal federal statutes enacted between 1965 and 1990 did away with the national origin quotas that Draper and both Trevors had worked so hard to maintain, allowing a substantial influx of Asians and Hispanics. For those who believed that race should be the basis of citizenship, this was warfare without weapons, a reenactment of the early 1920s when H. H. Laughlin had feared "Conquest by Immigration," except that the Italians, Jews, Poles, and Russians then menacing the United States had now been replaced by new ethnic threats.[152] Pearson, for example, warned of "unarmed invasions conducted by migrant hordes" and complained that the society did not yet recognize the need "for the repatriation of biologically alien immigrants." Recalling the warnings of Enoch Powell, who had been denounced as a "racist" by his own Conservative Party in 1968 for claiming that newcomers would lead to "rivers of blood" in England, Lynn urged that "immigration . . . be reduced to zero"; unfortunately, he lamented, "the immigration of Third World people in the West is unstoppable, as long as we retain democratic structures," implying the eventual need for a change in the latter to eliminate the former.[153]

To have an effect on policy, however, it was necessary to support some more organized form of opposition to immigration, and between 1982 and 2000 Pioneer provided almost $1.5 million ($2.18 million AFI) to two lobbying groups dedicated to "immigration reform": the Federation for American Immigration Reform (FAIR) and the American Immigration Control Foundation (AICF). FAIR, the more moderate appearing of the two, was founded in 1978 by John Tanton, a Michigan ophthalmologist and environmental activist whose interest in conservation had led him to the view that some people, especially immigrants, were themselves a type of pollution; president of Zero Population Growth in the 1970s, he went on to create more than a dozen organizations concerned with population control and immigration. Tanton's knack for hiding bigotry behind patriotic-sounding slogans allowed him to attract mainstream public figures to an effort, who could then be offered as evidence of its respectability. U.S. English, for example, which Tanton founded in 1988 to promote English as the official language of the United States, could point to highly regarded journalist Walter Cronkite as a board member and as director the well-known conservative Linda Chavez, who had recently been the highest-ranking woman in the Reagan administration, serving first as head of the Commission on Civil Rights and then as Director of Public Liaison; both these high-profile members quickly resigned, however, when a memo surfaced in which Tanton suggested that Latin American immigrants threatened to corrupt United States institutions "with . . . the tradition of the *mordida* (bribe)," abolish the separation of church and state through their brand of Catholicism, and seize political power from the majority by being "simply more fertile."[154]

FAIR called for a temporary moratorium on immigration, during which there would be "a national debate" on the issue, leading to a "comprehensive immigration reform strategy." This moderate-sounding stance attracted to FAIR's National Board of Advisors such "distinguished citizens" as John V. Lindsay, the former mayor of New York City, and Eugene McCarthy, the antiwar candidate for the Democratic presidential nomination in 1968 and former senator from Minnesota. However, FAIR's publications suggested what sort of strategy the national debate should produce. *A Tale of Ten Cities,* for example, compared five cities with large immigrant populations to five cities with few immigrants, concluding that, on every social or economic indicator of "a good environment for family life," the presence of immigrants had a negative impact. According to FAIR's advertisement, the study demonstrated that "high immigration and the resultant population growth are destroying the American dream and quality of life for all Americans." (In contrast, a survey of "America's highest immigration cities" by the Alexis de Tocqueville Institution, including three of the five in the FAIR study, concluded that "immigration has had a positive impact.")[155]

Another FAIR publication, authored by Garrett Hardin, a Pioneer grantee and microbiologist at the University of California at Santa Barbara, promised, according to its foreword, to "spell . . . out . . . why immigration is a serious threat to the freedom of human beings everywhere." In *The Immigration Dilemma* Hardin not only called for the nation to reject what he called "Christian-Marxian ideals" and "reduce net immigration into the United States . . . to zero" but also insisted that "we should never send food" to any starving population unable to provide for itself, recommending "the gift of birth control information" as the only acceptable form of foreign aid in such cases. And domestically, in the same publication Hardin opposed the provision of the Universal Declaration of Human Rights that would leave "any choice and decision with regard to the size of the family . . . irrevocably with the family itself," maintaining instead that "coercion" was necessary to control the "freedom to breed."[156]

Although FAIR enjoyed the bulk of the money that Pioneer expended specifically on immigration, AICF receiving only $198,000 ($294,000 AFI), the financial support was more significant for the latter, which lacked the substantial support of multimillionaire Cordelia Scaife May, the largest donor to the former (as well as to U.S. English and other organizations linked to Tanton). In addition, it was AICF that was more reflective of the fund's thinking on race, FAIR receiving the lion's share of Pioneer's resources, probably because it was such an influential voice in discussions about immigration policy. Besides, according to FAIR's executive director, behind the scenes it was helping AICF to organize.[157]

But it was the AICF publications that insisted, like so many of Pioneer's other grantees, that citizenship should be based on race and that "xenophobia . . . and ethnocentrism" were "near-universals of human behavior" that had been genetically "'wired in' through evolutionary selection." Not only did the presence of nonwhite immigrants in the United States thus create inevitable ethnic conflict, declared the authors of one AICF monograph, but the resulting "ethnically-mixed population" was the "factor of overriding importance" in "America's apparent decline," substantially responsible for everything from "the first loss of a war in U.S. history" in Vietnam to economic problems and budget deficits that were more characteristic of "third-rate countries than . . . a dominant power." (The monograph was published in 1988 before the dramatic decrease in the deficit that occurred in conjunction with rising immigration.) Indeed, according to John Vinson, the president of AICF and editor of its newsletter, *Immigration Watch,* racial separation was even "part of God's plan for humanity" in which "the ethnic make-up of a nation is not an arbitrary human choice, but a reflection of divine providence," making it a violation of biblical principles to compromise national character by "practic[ing] multiculturalism." Also a familiar refrain among Pioneer recipients was Vinson's complaint that the descendants of certain, unnamed earlier immigrants had risen "to positions of influence in politics, business, media, education, and entertainment" and then "worked to lower the moral and spiritual level of American life."[158]

Although AICF, like a number of Pioneer grantees, equated citizenship with race, unlike the others it made little pretense that its position was predicated on principles of heredity or eugenics. There was the occasional reliance on the ever-useful Raymond Hall: One AICF publication included a substantial excerpt from his decades-old article warning that the presence of "Orientals" in North America was a "foolish . . . violat[ion of] every biological law." But in this case Pioneer's scientists waving their batch of IQ scores were of little value, having demonstrated that Asians had *higher* scores than whites, and AICF's many books and pamphlets made little attempt to demonstrate scientifically that nonwhite immigrants were less capable or less industrious than Americans of European background. In fact, the superior performance of some immigrants was offered as yet another reason for opposing their entry. One AICF study acknowledged that "America has lagged for years in producing native-born professionals in the hard sciences" and found that immigrants were "filling the gap," dominating graduate education in science and engineering with their "work ethic and technical competence" and providing sorely needed talent for the high-tech sector, while "the poor performance of U.S. students in science and mathematics" caused them to drift into the less demanding, "parasitic sectors of American society—politicians, bureaucrats, and trial lawyers." Instead of concern over the state of domestic education in the sciences, however, the study identified the problem as the "endless supply of foreign-born scientists," who were causing the "cycle [to] perpetuate itself." Yet another AICF pamphlet recognized that Vietnamese immigrants "outcompeted" their rivals in business by working "harder and longer," complaining that Americans should not "be forced to compete with quasi-slaves . . . in order to make a living." As Jared Taylor observed in *AR, "it doesn't matter"* whether some immigrants "build societies that are, in some respects, objectively superior to those of Europeans. It matters only that they are *different.*"[159]

Although AICF produced a lengthy list of books and pamphlets filled with charts and statistics to demonstrate that immigrants caused an increase in welfare, crime, disease, and unfair competition, its most notorious publication was not a factual analysis but an obscure French novel: *Camp of the Saints* by Jean Raspail was originally distributed in English by the Institute for Western Values (which had published the Thomas Dixon autobiography with Pioneer's funding) before being reprinted by a press controlled by Tanton and distributed by AICF. *Camp* described the progress from India toward the French coast of a huge armada of creaking, dilapidated ships, filled with a loathsome mass of human refuse from the Third World that would cause the Statue of Liberty to drop her torch and hold her nose. As if the author had systematically rooted through the thesaurus searching out every possible synonym for "repulsive," almost every page included a reminder of how vile was the cargo carried by these ships: Led by a "turd eater," they were "vermin" with "grotesque misshapen bodies," and "horrid, twisted limbs," contaminated with "some gangrenous rot," "complete with [an] assortment of pus, scab, and chancre," a horde of "ignorant Ganges monsters, misery incarnate, absolute zeros," a "sweating, starving mass, stewing in urine and noxious gases," "sleeping in dung and debris," turning the ocean into "one big festering sore," and creating a "horrible stench," as if "some rotting monster, jaws agape, were blowing its lungs out in huge fetid blasts." Inexorably, this ghastly assemblage, "in a welter of dung and debauch," pushed on toward the West, awaited knowingly by a fifth column of racial brethren: "kinky-haired, swarthy-skinned, long-despised phantoms; all the teeming ants toiling for the white man's comfort; all the swill men and sweepers, the troglodytes, the stinking drudges, the swivel-hipped menials, . . . the lung-spewing hackers; all the numberless, nameless, tortured, tormented, indispensable mass" that performed the essential tasks too unpleasant for Westerners to do for themselves.[160]

Yet neither of these odious throngs was the villain of Raspail's cautionary tale, a role reserved for the liberal quislings and antiracists in the church, state, and media and among the intelligentsia—some scheming, others merely naive—who had been "sucked in by all that brotherhood crap," ready to welcome the impoverished intruders, to "empty out all our hospital beds so that cholera-ridden and leprous wretches could sprawl between their clean white sheets, . . . cram our brightest, cheeriest nurseries full of monster children," and preach "universal mongrelization." The only heroic figures were the few intrepid defenders of Western culture and tradition who refused to succumb to feelings of guilt or pity and were instead prepared, with equanimity, to shoot down the unarmed intruders on sight in one last attempt to prevent the antiworld from destroying civilization. "Not a single refugee from the Ganges will set foot on South African soil," announced the President of the then-apartheid "white nation with eighty percent blacks," vowing, when the fleet neared his coast, "to open fire on defenseless women and children," the only response left to realistic whites "in this high minded racial war."[161]

When, finally, a handful of courageous Frenchmen—aided by the few blacks sensible enough to accept their role as servant to the West—was insufficient to hold back the wave of dark-skinned newcomers, nonwhites throughout the world saw their chance. In New York "the black tide," which had been waiting "caged like wildcats" while "praying like crazy for those goddamn ships," turned full force on whites, seizing their last refuges in the city's plush high rises. A social scientist had long before predicted this mo-

ment of "ultimate doom," when blacks' random, vicious assaults on passing motorists would escalate into wholesale revolt, advising the government
that there was "no hope . . . unless you kill them all, because you'll never
change them." And in London, the city was taken over by the "non-European Commonwealth Committee."[162]

More than any of its other publications, *Camp* suggested the ideology that
informed AICF. Of course, there was no science presented in the novel, nothing about measurable differences in IQ or any other trait, but only a relentless, visceral revulsion at the colored races' intrusion into the West. Chavez,
the member of the Reagan administration and a vigorous opponent of affirmative action, called the work "without doubt the most vehemently racist
book I have ever read."[163]

* * *

In keeping with the Satterfield plan's desire for maximum publicity, the different projects supported by Pioneer often functioned in a nicely coordinated
fashion, the fund's journals providing multiple sources of promotion for
work done by the fund's scientists. Jensen's book, *Straight Talk about Mental Tests,* for example, received effusive praise in reviews in both the *Mankind
Quarterly* and the *Journal of Social, Political and Economic Studies.* (However, true to Pearson's obsession with racial purity, in the former he complained
that Jensen's discussion of racial differences in IQ considered the correlation
between the test scores of blacks and their "estimated degree of Caucasoid
admixture" but neglected the effects "of black genes amongst segments of
the population classified as white"; the true racial difference was reduced not
only by blacks whose "white genes" raised their IQs but by whites whose
unrecognized "black genes" lowered theirs.) The reviews thus completed a
convenient cycle in which Jensen, a scientist whose work was supported by
Pioneer, wrote a book, which was then highly recommended in two journals
whose publication was funded by Pioneer and finally sent gratis to college
and university officials throughout the country by FHU, whose purchase and
distribution of the books was also paid for by Pioneer.[164]

*American Renaissance* also joined with Pearson's journals in highlighting
the work of Pioneer grantees. In 1997, for example, Richard Lynn published
*Dysgenics,* arguing that the eugenicists of the nineteenth and early twentieth
centuries had been correct in predicting the deterioration of Western civilization as a result of modern medical techniques and charitable assistance to
the poor, which had combined to allow the transmission of "defective" genes
and the reproduction of an underclass that was genetically less intelligent and
less moral. Between *AR* and Pearson's two journals, the book was discussed

at length four times, all these reviews agreeing that the West, burdened with its black population, was heading for a "genetic dead end" and certain that, as one reviewer put it, "some sort of 'compensatory meddling' will be required if human evolution is ever to return to its once healthy course."[165] The most obscure works supported by Pioneer, unlikely to be noticed elsewhere, received much attention in these interlocking outlets. When Charles Josey's eugenics-era book arguing for the necessity of white world domination was reprinted in 1983 by Pearson's Clivedon Press, for example, it was immediately recommended in the *Journal of Social, Political and Economic Studies* as an antidote to the recent "attempt to destroy . . . race consciousness . . . just at the time that we need a loyalty firmer than ever"; although *AR* was not even created until seven years later, it too reviewed Josey's tract, finding its "matter-of-fact statements" about white supremacy from the earlier, more enlightened era "refreshing" in contrast to the present "obfuscation" about race. Even Stanley Burnham's *America's Bimodal Crisis*, published by FHU—the pastiche of mangled English and proposals to deprive blacks of constitutional protections—received its due recommendation in *AR* as "an invaluable summary of . . . our most threatening problem."[166] And, of course, anything authored by Pearson was covered obsessively in his own journals and in *AR*, the reviews often contributed by some previously unknown writer whose style bore a suspicious similarity to Pearson's.[167]

Nor were the anti-immigration organizations left out of this loop. The authors of AICF publications were regular speakers at AR conferences and their books lauded in its journal for advocating that the children of immigrants born in the United States not be granted citizenship, which required "blood-kinship."[168] FAIR and AICF authors were also frequent contributors to the *Journal of Social, Political and Economic Studies*, which in turn praised both groups as opponents of immigration who "deserve recognition." Wayne Lutton, for example, whose work had previously appeared in the neo-Nazi *American Mercury* and Carto's *Journal of Historical Review*, contributed a number of anti-immigrant articles to Pearson's journal, coauthored in one instance by Tanton, who had founded FAIR, and in another by G. Palmer Stacy III, who had founded both AICF and the Institute for Western Values. Pearson then included one of these works—a tirade on the danger of Asian criminals, conveniently overlooking Rushton's conclusion that Asians were *less* inclined to criminal activity—in *Will America Drown?*, published by his institute's press and distributed by both the institute and AICF. The collection's editor, "Humphrey Dalton," and a number of the authors of individual articles probably were Pearson aliases.[169]

In addition to funding the work of a number of scientists, Pioneer has thus also supported an enclosed, sectarian world, a political subculture in which extremists recommend each other's latest fulmination against blacks and immigrants to other extremists and unabashedly discuss the need to violate widely accepted notions of constitutional and human rights. These interlocking Pioneer operations, all proposing similar policies of racial separation or racial exclusion and relying on similar rationales of white superiority and innate antipathy toward other races, have become the intellectual authority for other right-wing fringe groups, providing the canonical literature for the modern Nazi movement. The American Nazi Party's Web site, for example, includes among its "White Racist Links" the home pages for the Pioneer Fund, the *Mankind Quarterly,* and American Renaissance, along with an assortment of Klan organizations, skinheads, Holocaust deniers, and groups with names such as "Death to ZOG" ("Zionist Occupied Government"), "Better Than Auschwitz," and the "Adolf Hitler Message Board."[170]

Moreover, many publications produced with the fund's support are available almost exclusively from similar sources. Every Internet hate group offering publications such as *Death Penalty for Race Mixers* invariably also provides "the facts about miscegenation" and race in books by authors funded by Draper and Pioneer.[171] The Sons of Liberty's list of "Patriotic Books" includes articles by Swan, Kuttner, Pearson, Gregor, and other authors published by Pearson's institute along with hundreds of booklets with titles such as "Jewish World Conspiracy," "The Hitler We Loved and Why," "Jewish Ritual Murder," "Jewish War against the Western World," and "Today's Greatest Problem: The Jews." The "Truth at Last," an organization headed by Pearson's old friend Edward Fields, provides a host of recent publications issued by Pearson's institute along with many older Draper-funded racist classics by Garrett, Putnam, and Robertson, interspersed with such "educational material" as *The Protocols of the Learned Elders of Zion,* Henry Ford's *The International Jew,* and various works explaining that the Holocaust is a "hoax." Pioneer- or Draper-funded sources have also published more than half the fifty-four books on race offered by William Pierce's National Alliance, a group that, according to its editorial statement, "would like to see . . . all heterosexual White men and women on one side and all Jews, homosexuals, Blacks, Asians, and mestizos on the other. Then we would be ready for the shooting to start, and we would settle matters pretty quickly." The Alliance also cites specific passages from Pearson's writing as the authority for its claim that miscegenation is "the morality of death."[172]

Perhaps more than any of the other extremists, David Duke, the unabashed white supremacist and anti-Semite, has relied on the work of Pioneer's scientists to justify his political positions; the "Race Information Library" on

Duke's Web site is composed substantially of the full text of articles by Pioneer grantees, many of them from the *Mankind Quarterly*. A former Grand Dragon of the Louisiana chapter of the Klan and Imperial Wizard of the national organization, as well as a prominent member of the American Nazi Party, Duke later formed the National Association for the Advancement of White People, which advertised and distributed such classics of the Nazi movement as the *Protocols* and Francis Parker Yockey's *Imperium*, along with IAAEE publications and the *Quarterly*. Obsessed with his physical appearance, Duke also had his features Aryanized through a series of cosmetic surgeries, rearranging his nose and strengthening his chin through an implant, until he could probably qualify for inclusion as one of the Nordic faces in Pearson's articles. In 2000, Duke created the National Organization for European American Rights (NOFEAR), with himself as president, a capacity in which he also worked closely with the American Friends of the British National Party (BNP), founded by John Tyndall, Pearson's old comrade and Nazi activist from the Northern League four decades earlier.[173]

Indeed, it appears that Duke's interest in Pearson has not gone unreciprocated. Not only has the Nazi activist relied on Pioneer-supported efforts as his intellectual rationale, but Pearson, the fund's ideological point man, has used his institute to assist the Duke–Friends of the BNP joint venture. Books ordered from the institute's post office box address in Washington, D.C., arrive accompanied by a separate, hand-addressed packet of unsolicited material from the Friends of the BNP, the latter also bearing a post office box return address only steps way from the former. The unexpected brochures offer a videotape of Duke and other neo-Nazi activists speaking at a meeting of the Friends of the BNP, a "Supporters Application Form," and a literature list that includes *Camp of the Saints*, "published by American Immigration Control Foundation," a compilation of speeches from an American Renaissance conference, books published by FHU, and IAAEE reprints from forty years earlier.[174]

Whatever projects of scientific interest Pioneer may have supported—and there certainly are a few—it is also indisputable that the fund has continued to fill the role once played by its founder: to subsidize the creation and distribution of literature that could be used to support racial superiority and racial purity. Pioneer has indeed been scientific racism's keeper of the flame.

# Conclusion: Pioneer or Pamphleteer

The false charge of racism is simply a tactic to choke off rational discussion, a strategy of intimidation to silence expression.
—Sidney Hook, quoted in Harry Weyher, *Intelligence* (1999): 319

At present, I believe our best bet is to . . . make the white schools so unpleasant for them that the Negroes withdraw, or else boycott the school entirely.
—Henry E. Garrett to Wesley Critz George

Dr. Ward has a fine idea that might be very useful. . . . The venereal disease situation . . . might be the one for greatest alarm of parents who are forced to send their children to a heavily integrated school.
—Wesley Critz George to Harry Weyher

Putnam writes of love, but he hates Negroes.
—Dwight J. Ingle to William Shockley

During November and December of 1999, tens of thousands of social scientists in anthropology, psychology, and sociology unexpectedly discovered in their mail a "special abridged edition" of *Race, Evolution, and Behavior,* often accompanied by a card expressing the "compliments of J. Philippe Rushton," professor of psychology at the University of Western Ontario, the work's author; many of these academics received a copy of the work two or three separate times. Transaction Press, which had produced the original unabridged version of the book, was listed as the publisher, although, as Rushton later acknowledged, the cost of production and mass distribution of the abridged version had been paid from his Pioneer grant.[1]

In the preface to this small paperback Rushton promised to provide, in "a more popularly written style," an explanation for the public's personal experience: "Teachers in America know the races differ in school achievement. Policemen know the races differ in crime rates. And social workers know the races differ in rates of welfare dependency or getting infected with AIDS. They all wonder why." From Arab explorers in the eighth century to Europeans colonialists more than a millennium later, according to Rushton's account, all the visitors to Africa had agreed on the nature of blacks: They were like "'wild animals,'" naked, dirty, impoverished, the children often unaware of their father, but with "a natural sense of rhythm" and "oversized sex organs." Even "in the age of computers, fax machines, and the world wide web," he observed, "getting a dial tone in many African cities is difficult," the IQ for "Blacks living in Africa is the lowest ever recorded," and "neglect and decay are seen everywhere in Africa and much of the West Indies."[2]

As the genesis of this appalling condition of blacks everywhere, Rushton proposed his "Out of Africa" theory: Although modern humans first appeared in Africa, a split took place 100,000 years ago between the groups that remained in their continent of origin and those that headed north. The migrants, eventually evolving into whites and Asians, developed the larger brains and greater intelligence necessary to cope with the more "mentally demanding" tasks of "gathering and storing food, providing shelter, making clothes, and raising children during the long winters." These intellectual changes were "balanced by slower rates of growth, lower levels of sex hormones, less aggression, and less sexual activity," with the consequence that non-African races enjoyed longer lives and developed greater ability for self-control, planning, complex social organization, rule following, altruism, and family stability. The resulting "genetically-organized group of traits" reflected what Rushton called a "basic law of evolution link[ing] reproductive strategy to intelligence and brain development. The less complex an animal's brain, the greater its reproductive output." Non-Africans thus tended to invest time and effort in the care of their children rather than "the pursuit of sexual thrills"; in comparison with blacks, white and Asian men became, as Rushton succinctly put it, "'dads' rather than "'cads.'"[3]

The arrival of Rushton's unsolicited gift in its plain brown envelope provoked quite a stir in academic circles. Many social scientists were outraged at what they considered "racial pornography," one recipient calling the paperback "a wholly vile piece of work" and returning it to the publisher forthwith. A number of academics were exercised because the mailing label made it appear that the pamphlet had been distributed by their professional organization. In response, the executive officers of both the American Psychological Association and the American Sociological Association independently offered the same account: Their organizations had not sent out Rushton's paperback but had rented their respective mailing lists to a publicity agent employed by Transaction Press for the purpose of circulating a "flyer" advertising the unabridged edition, not for distribution of the work itself. Upon learning what had actually been mailed to their members, both professional associations announced that future requests from the press would not be honored.[4]

Transaction's editorial director, prominent sociologist Irving Louis Horowitz, acknowledged that the press had in fact given Rushton access to its advertising agency "to assist him in mailing his pamphlet" but had specifically forbidden him to claim any association with the press "to distance ourselves from what is essentially a promotional effort by the author to promote his ideas." Indeed, declared Horowitz, "we most emphatically are not . . . the publishers of the pamphlet, which, unlike the original work, was not subject to peer review or editorial discussion." Although Rushton complained that Transaction had "caved in to . . . pressure . . . to trash or suppress [the] book," he did not contest the press's demand for destruction of the remaining stock bearing its name: According to the *Chronicle of Higher Education*, he agreed to junk 60,000 copies.[5]

Queried about the process of distribution by a member of an Internet discussion group for social psychologists, Rushton posted the following reply: "I paid for the mailings from my research grant. There has been no misuse of any lists to my knowledge although perhaps some organizations are now trying to cover their asses for having sold their lists. Such is the power of vengeful political correctness that academics are scared of having other academics send them unpopular scientific views!"[6] Unmentioned in this extraordinarily pugnacious response was the apparent bait-and-switch from flyer to paperback, nor did Rushton seem to appreciate that many scientists rejected his ideas out of not fear but disgust. But particularly remarkable to many people, unfamiliar with Pioneer's nature and purpose, was that a granting agency putatively dedicated to supporting scientific research would fund the free distribution of some hundred thousand copies of a book, especially in the absence of any expression of interest in it by the recipients.

This campaign on Rushton's and Pioneer's part to distribute the "specially abridged edition" clearly was intended as a public relations effort, the latest attempt to convince the nation of the "completely different nature" of blacks and whites. Not only was the paperback written in a breezy style containing no references, but a tearsheet in the back of the book offered bulk rates "for distribution to media figures, especially columnists who write about race issues." In addition, the Charles Darwin Research Institute—founded by Rushton and used as a vehicle for his direct receipt of Pioneer money over and above the hundreds of thousands of dollars that the fund had allocated to the University of Western Ontario for his research—frankly announced that the abridged version had been published to "actively promulgate" his claims "about race and human variation to media figures, interested general readers, citizen groups with interest in these topics, and students, by mass mailings of the booklet, putting it on the internet and eventually perhaps by producing audio books and video tapes."[7]

Nor was Pioneer's campaign to retail Rushton's ideas to the public impeded by the need to destroy the huge supply of paperbacks paid for by his grant; indeed, it quickly gave the fund an opportunity for a new, ambitious effort, one having more in common with a public relations agency than a scientific endeavor. Six months after Transaction's demand, Rushton, together with three other Pioneer grantees—philosopher Michael Levin, sociologist Robert Gordon, and Jared Taylor, the editor of *American Renaissance*—appeared at a press conference at Washington's National Press Club to announce a "new, for-the-public version of Rushton's academic treatise": 100,000 more copies of the same "special abridged edition" of *Race, Evolution, and Behavior,* now copyrighted in the author's name, had just been published by Rushton's Charles Darwin Research Institute (i.e., once again by Pioneer). The "Four Senior Researchers," according to the "embargoed" press release, recommended the "New Book . . . on Genetic Races Differences in Crime and Intelligence," although the identical paperback had been widely distributed half a year earlier, and the unabridged and less tendentious version had been published half a decade earlier. The press conference produced the desired effect, however: In the next two days, many newspapers in the United States, Canada, and England carried stories on Rushton's claims.[8]

Missing throughout the controversy over Rushton's pamphlet was an appreciation of the historical pattern of which this campaign was merely the latest episode. Almost two-thirds of a century earlier, Pioneer's founder had paid for the republication of 1,000 copies of Earnest Sevier Cox's *White America,* which viewed blacks as a threat to civilization and called for their repatriation to Africa to preserve the United States for the white race. These books also had been distributed unsolicited, with the compliments of the author, to every member of Congress and to legislators in Southern states. These two events—the distribution of Cox's and Rushton's writing—were bookends encompassing more than six decades of similar attempts to affect public opinion by publishing material about racial differences and sending it to select groups. As the Draper-funded CCFAF had observed, its plan to defeat the Civil Rights Act of 1964 relied principally on the "distribution of pamphlets throughout the nation, particularly to persons of influence."[9] It is also instructive that, in the Colonel's earliest attempt to seek scientific assistance against the *Brown* decision, Weyher offered an unsolicited contribution from his client for the distribution of Wesley Critz George's pamphlets, shortly after the anatomist had declared that integration would "destroy our race and our civilization." Both before and after Draper's death, the mailing list has remained the Pioneer group's weapon of choice.

The materials distributed gratis over the years, first through Draper's resources and then through Pioneer's, have included, in addition to the writing of Cox and Rushton, such works as Carleton Putnam's diatribes against integration, *Race and Reason* and *Race and Reality;* George's similarly intended report, *The Biology of the Race Problem;* Henry Garrett's pamphlets, circulated to Northern teachers warning them of the evils in allowing blacks and whites to attend the same schools; William Massey's article "The New Fanatics," insisting that blacks were unfit for citizenship; Arthur Jensen's *Straight Talk about Mental Tests,* sent to college presidents and admission officers, and his *Harvard Educational Review* article, sent to journalists, congressional representatives, and members of the National Academy of Sciences; tracts by R. Travis Osborne, the intervenors' first expert witness in the attempts to overturn the *Brown* decision; and numerous other articles and books about race differences. Thus, although Pioneer may have funded some projects of scientific value, any results of genuine interest have been a salutary though incidental consequence of the fund's actual purpose: to provide ammunition for what has essentially been a lobbying campaign. As outlined in Satterfield's plan, research on racial differences was but the necessary first step in a larger strategy, producing results that could then be widely distributed as "scientific" support for policies designed to "win the war" against full participation of blacks in the society and the polity. In both its official and unofficial activities, Pioneer has been as much a pamphleteer as a source of support for scientists.

## Scientists' Rights

This is not to suggest that every grantee necessarily shares Pioneer's underlying agenda. Some recipients, such as Pearson, not only desire to recreate racial separation but also have devoted their lives to pursuit of that goal. Yet it is certainly possible that others may have no sympathy for such policies and want merely to use Pioneer's money to advance their own research and their academic careers. It is difficult to draw the more charitable conclusion, however, for grantees who exhibit such missionary zeal in their attempts to persuade not only their scientific colleagues but also the larger public or who appear before groups such as American Renaissance, providing its members—whose interest in science derives primarily from its instrumental value for the cause—with what they view as rational justification for their desperate desire to reconstruct an American apartheid. Although ideological compatibility is not a prerequisite for obtaining support from Pioneer, scientific heresy would be fatal. The fund provides assistance only to researchers who can be relied on to produce the appropriate conclusions about heredity and race. Should someone like Jensen undergo a sudden change of opinion about racial differences, his support would disappear faster than David Duke from the Apollo Theater.

Of course, neither the existence of an odious agenda on Pioneer's part nor the desire of some grant recipients to assist in promoting it justifies attempts to harass researchers, impede their work, or prevent them from obtaining support from the fund. The sort of treatment accorded to Rushton, for example, by both his own department and the administration at the University of Western Ontario has been nothing short of disgraceful: He was given an "unsatisfactory" rating in an annual review—the first step toward dismissal proceedings—despite being the recipient of a prestigious Guggenheim fellowship and having one of the most productive records of peer-reviewed publication in the department. Rushton appealed the rating, and it was eventually overturned. Other Pioneer scientists, such as Jensen and Eysenck, have undergone similar harassment for arriving at politically unpopular conclusions.[10]

Although such incidents are intolerable violations of academic freedom, there is an inescapable irony in the complaints of Pioneer grantees, so many of whom have demonstrated precious little concern that their conclusions have been offered, as part of a concerted campaign by the members of the fund that supports their research, to prevent some of their fellow citizens from attending school with whites, being allowed to use "white" public facilities, or being served in "white" establishments. Challenged to repudiate such misuse of his own work, Jensen has steadfastly refused to do so, claiming to be entirely apolitical, although he did not hesitate to appear before a legislative committee as part of a group of notorious opponents of civil rights seeking to halt school integration. Indeed, Jensen was fully aware that the source of his funds considered him part of the "team" providing the "essential ammunition" for maintaining educational apartheid. Pearson, who quickly cleared his department at the University of Southern Mississippi of faculty with liberal opinions so that he could replace them with unqualified neo-Nazis, authored an outraged book in 1991, lamenting the plight of Pioneer scientists harassed by the forces of political correctness, none of whom have lost their academic positions. Only months later, one of his pseudonymous articles in the *Mankind Quarterly* called for "modification of the 'Bill of Rights'" to deal with the problem of "uncontrolled immigration" and "ghetto welfare children."[11]

Rushton has not only contributed to American Renaissance publications and graced their conferences with his presence but also offered praise and support for the "scholarly" work on racial differences of Henry Garrett, who spent the last two decades of his life opposing the extension of the Constitution to blacks on the basis that the "normal" black resembled a European after frontal lobotomy. Informed of Garrett's claim that blacks were not entitled to equality because their "ancestors were . . . savages in an African jungle," Rushton dismissed the observation as quoted "selectively from Garrett's writing," finding nothing opprobrious in such sentiments because the leader of the scientific opposition to civil rights had made *other* statements about black inferiority that were, according to Rushton, "quite objective in tone and backed by standard social science evidence."[12] Quite apart from the questionable logic in defending a blatant call to deprive citizens of their rights by citing Garrett's less offensive writing—as if it were evidence of Ted Bundy's innocence that there were some women he had met and *not* killed—there was no sense on Rushton's part that all of Garrett's claims, whether or not "objective," were utterly irrelevant to constitutional guarantees, which are not predicated on scientific demonstrations of intellectual equality. Understandably and appropriately outraged at the violation of their own academic freedom, Pioneer grantees have found nothing objectionable in attempts, based on scientific conclusions that they have promulgated, to deprive others of their rights.

## The Campaign to Deny the Campaign

In the 1990s, after the controversy at the University of Delaware and the criticisms from Barry Mehler converted Pioneer from a source of support for controversial research into a part of the controversy, the fund mounted yet another campaign to influence public opinion not about race but about Pioneer. One tactic in this effort, often originating with Weyher, was to investigate critics' personal lives in search of information that might discredit them. (Putnam and others in the scientific clique opposed to civil rights had earlier used "friends" in the FBI to gather dirt on opponents, an option presumably no longer available three decades later.[13]) For example, noted behavior geneticist Jerry Hirsch was a vigorous critic of the fund and many of its grantees; in addition, he established a program in "institutional racism" at the University of Illinois, where he mentored Barry Mehler. Roger Pearson, in his book *Race, Intelligence and Bias in Academe,* suggested that Hirsch was too unstable to be taken seriously, noting that he had "become very emotional about race issues, and his former department chairman, Lloyd Humphreys, reports that on one occasion he had to be granted special leave on the recommendation of a psychiatrist." Hirsch sued both Pearson and

Humphreys, and in the subsequent deposition, Pearson testified that he had never met or spoken with Humphreys, who was also a Pioneer grantee, but had been fed the information about Hirsch by Weyher.[14]

William J. Frawley, a professor of linguistics who initially raised concerns about Pioneer at the University of Delaware, was accorded similar treatment. Describing Frawley as "an unusual figure for an academic," Pearson claimed that he had been arrested for threatening a "passerby" with a large knife, suggesting the image of a dangerous lunatic. In fact, the incident involved Frawley's confrontation with a man who had been stalking his wife, and as soon as the police learned the facts, all charges were immediately dropped.[15]

Pioneer also hired Beltrante Associates, a private investigation firm, to gather information on Mehler. One of Beltrante's investigators phoned the executive director of the Center for Democratic Renewal, a civil rights organization, stating that "Mehler, who claims to be associated with civil rights, is not what he appears to be, he may be associated with Communists." Then, when a student intern for the National Coalition for Universities in the Public Interest, called the fund to ask about its support for immigration restriction, Weyher asked whether the student had read Mehler's articles; upon receiving an affirmative reply, Pioneer's president claimed that Mehler was connected with the *Daily World,* successor to the old Communist Party newspaper the *Daily Worker,* and that he was "a nut." The attorney also repeated the information about Hirsch that he had allegedly received from Humphreys and described Frawley as an unbalanced person who had "gotten into fights at cocktail parties" and "threatened strangers with a kitchen knife." Shortly after the phone conversation with Weyher, the student intern received a call from a "researcher" supposedly studying Washington-based public interest organizations, who turned out to be another of Beltrante's investigators. Mehler's public statements were also audiotaped, either by Beltrante or someone else employed by Pioneer. Weyher sent a copy of one such tape to the University of Delaware as part of a lengthy personal attack on Mehler, and a Pioneer grantee quoted from the tape in an article critical of Mehler.[16]

In addition, Weyher attempted to intimidate critics through the threat of legal action. For example, after legal scholars Jean Stefancic and Richard Delgado published *No Mercy,* a book on conservative foundations in which they described some of Pioneer's activities, they received a letter from Weyher accusing them of having committed "libel against the Pioneer Fund and probably others" and warning that "should you republish this book, . . . we will not hesitate to bring an action against you personally as well as any publisher." Weyher also sent a copy of the letter to Temple University Press, which had published the book and was planning to issue a paperback version, and to the dean of the University of Colorado Law School, where Stefancic was a research associate and Delgado the occupant of an endowed chair. Although there were some minor factual errors in *No Mercy*, the notion that they were libelous—that is, that they harmed the reputation or lowered the standing of anyone connected with the fund—was an incredible stretch, especially considering that they occurred primarily in connection with the authors' account of Pioneer's history in the 1930s. Unfortunately, the letter had the desired effect: Although the law school was prepared to support its scholars, the press reacted fearfully, backing down from the paperback edition.[17]

In response to criticisms of Pioneer, a number of grantees also came to the fund's defense, providing an entirely erroneous image of its past that probably reflected not dishonesty as much as a naive belief in what Weyher told them. After Donald Swan's unsavory background had been briefly mentioned in an ABC news segment about Pioneer, for example, Johns Hopkins sociologist Robert A. Gordon sent the network a sixty-four page "provisional response." Calling Swan "the most obscure of the many persons ever" to receive a grant from the fund, Gordon implied that Weyher had no knowledge of his grantee's political inclinations and that, in any case, Swan had only "expressed an intellectual infatuation with Fascism, . . . unknown to all except those who maintain dossiers on such matters." Although Swan may have been an obscure figure to the public, his "infatuation" was certainly well known to Weyher, Trevor, and Draper, who relied on him as the most important single person behind the scenes in the IAAEE and the legal attempts to overturn *Brown*, both funded by the Colonel. Other than a raft of publications in the *Mankind Quarterly*, he had little record of scientific accomplishment before becoming an official Pioneer grantee, and as a recipient of money from the fund he published articles not only in professional journals but also in a segregationist newspaper and in the neo-Nazi *American Mercury*. Moreover, until his death in 1981, Swan remained one of Pioneer's insiders. When Trevor, in 1979, wanted to share some important observation, he sent it to the key grantees at the time, representative of the three components that the fund sought to combine: Jensen, the genuine scientist; Shockley, the publicity seeker; and Pearson and Swan, the neo-Nazi ideologues.[18]

Gordon's letter offered other revisions of Swan's past. The deceased grantee had merely ordered three books and some fruit by mail without paying for them—"personal eccentricities," according to Gordon, that were being used in an attempt "to embarrass Pioneer"—and had been "an avid book collector" who "corresponded widely with scholars around the world." The actual record on these activities is clear: Swan used multiple aliases for the fraudulent acquisition through the mail of products worth more than half a million dollars (AFI), he amassed a huge personal library of Nazi literature, and his foreign pen pals were members of the editorial boards of fascist journals in France and Germany, on which he served as a representative of the IAAEE. Pursuing the effort to sanitize Pioneer's image in the same manner as it had the campaign on racial differences, the fund sent Gordon's letter to 452 journalism schools.[19]

Another grantee to defend Pioneer was University of Delaware psychologist Linda Gottfredson, whose grant had been rejected by the institution, thus triggering much of the controversy and impelling her to seek legal assistance to reverse the decision. Gottfredson could have responded to the university's initial refusal by framing the issue solely as a matter of academic freedom, maintaining that it was her right to accept external support for her research regardless of its source. Instead, however, she chose to contest the decision on factual grounds, insisting that the characterization of Pioneer was inaccurate. "I would be greatly concerned if I thought the Fund was racist or anti-Semitic," wrote Gottfredson to the university president, and "surely would have nothing to do with it." And to the chair of the university's Faculty Senate Committee on Research she declared that "I personally would not accept funds from organizations that I considered reprehensible."[20]

Again probably passing on information furnished by Weyher, Gottfredson called the charge that Draper "promoted sending blacks back to Africa . . . simply false." She also pointed out, quite correctly, that Frederick Osborn, an earlier Pioneer president, had "turned against the racist and anti-immigrant claims that characterized much of the American eugenics movement," without realizing that this refusal to countenance racist policies had made him unacceptable to Pioneer's founder and had led to his replacement by the more ideologically reliable Weyher. Particularly absurd was Gottfredson's assertion that Roger Pearson—one of the most important figures in the postwar Nazi movement, who boasted of knowing "on good authority" Hitler's own words, created and published the *New Patriot* dedicated exclusively to anti-Semitic diatribes, and corresponded with leading figures in the American Nazi Party—had refused to have any further contact with Earl Thomas after learning that his devoted assistant had been a party member. And, according to Gottfredson, Pearson's *Mankind Quarterly*—in which his pseudonymous contributions regularly maintained that the tendency to "distrust and repel" members of other races was a biological imperative and that interracial marriages were a "perversion" of natural instincts—was merely "a multicultural journal" interested in "diversity . . . as an object of dispassionate study."[21] If Gottfredson's acceptance of support from Pioneer really was predicated on the accuracy of her beliefs about the fund's background, then there was ample reason for her to reconsider.

Naturally Weyher has been Pioneer's most intrepid defender, steadfastly disavowing any agenda other than the advancement of science. The five board members, wrote the fund's president in 1989, were "independent men of high ability and integrity and no personal, political or social aims conflicting with their objectivity."[22] These "men of integrity," unencumbered by any bias or underlying agenda according to Weyher, included Trevor, who had directed the American Coalition of Patriotic Societies while it campaigned against civil rights and for Nazi war criminals, and Weyher himself, who, together with Trevor, had spent years applying his "high ability" first to opposing the extension of political equality to blacks and then to perpetuating educational apartheid through a system of private, segregated schools, a project in which a third board member, Marion Parrott, was also active.

Weyher's defense of Pioneer often was artfully crafted to be factually accurate but highly misleading. To one university official, for example, the New York attorney observed, correctly, that the original charge of Draper's involvement in the repatriation movement had been made on the basis of unnamed sources and without interviewing Pioneer's founder, thus conveying the impression that the charge itself—which Weyher knew to be true, having personally arranged for the republication of Cox's essay on "Lincoln's Negro Policy" by Willis Carto's Noontide Press—was yet another of the "media's false stories."[23]

In another instance Weyher used the hint of legal action to pressure the *American Journal of Psychology,* which normally did not print letters from readers, to publish his "correction" of statements about Pioneer that had appeared in a book review in the journal. Weyher's letter made two points, in each case exploiting the flimsy distinction between the fund's official grants and the behind-the-scenes activities during the civil rights era. Pioneer had "never played a 'shadowy role,'" declared the fund's president in response to a charge made in the review, "since all of its grants are disclosed on its tax returns."[24] However, "shadowy" does not seem to be an inappropriate description for the extensive, surreptitious financial support provided by Draper and coordinated by Weyher to oppose equality for blacks. Indeed, more than three decades later Weyher was still reluctant to acknowledge the role that he and Draper had played. When a reporter for the *Wall Street Journal* contacted Weyher in 1999 to ask about the donations of stock to the Mississippi Sovereignty Commission, Pioneer's president at first claimed that he did not recall the transmission of some quarter million dollars' worth of the Colonel's assets to a campaign against integration in which he himself was intimately involved. Then, when revelation of the details of the transactions made his position untenable, Weyher pointed out that there had been nothing illegal in attempting to preserve de jure segregation in 1964, a position

that was encoded in law in many states at the time and supported by millions of citizens.[25] The same observation could once have been made about
the Nuremberg Laws.

In addition, maintained Weyher in his letter to the *American Journal of
Psychology,* the fund had "never given a penny directly or indirectly to . . . the
Liberty Lobby," another claim dependent for its veracity on ignoring the
unofficial activities financed by Draper and executed by his attorney.[26] Not
only had Weyher personally transmitted the Colonel's anonymous donation
to one of the intermediaries on the way to its ultimate destination with the
Liberty Lobby to pay for the posthumous publication of Cox's book, but the
IAAEE, funded largely by Draper, had purchased stacks of lobby attorney
Alfred Avin's symposium on the evils of nondiscriminatory housing, copies
of which were then distributed as part of the lobby's opposition to civil rights
legislation.

This tactic of calculated disingenuousness reached its height in Weyher's
response to a reminder of the *Mankind Quarterly's* past: that the journal had
once praised Earnest Sevier Cox as a "truly great man" for his proposal to
send blacks back to Africa and had published William Massey's "The New
Fanatics," insisting that even the intelligent "Negro" was "temperamentally
unsuited for citizenship." Pioneer's president claimed that he had checked
with the "present editors" and learned that "the quoted language has not
appeared in the journal since it moved from Scotland to the United States,"
where it first received the fund's support. "We do not know the quotes in
question and certainly had nothing to do with writing them," he declared,
describing any attempt to connect these sentiments to Pioneer as "guilt by
remote-remote association."[27] Once again, these statements by Weyher were
clearly designed to convey the false impression that he was both unaware of
the earlier opinions published in the *Quarterly* and unsympathetic to them.
In fact, Weyher had played an unacknowledged though certainly influential
editorial role during the journal's earlier years, circulating drafts of articles
for comment before publication, passing judgments on the merits of some
articles himself, informing contributors that a particular manuscript had
been accepted—although, he noted in one instance, it would have to be
"much edited before publication"—and promising a sympathetic scientist
such as George that the *Quarterly* "would like to have" an article he had submitted elsewhere. In addition, Garrett, Draper's chief scientific expert, had
insisted on publishing "The New Fanatics" over the reservations of Gayre,
the editor-in-chief, and it was later reprinted by the Putnam National Letters Committee, which was funded by the Colonel.[28] The suggestion that the
"present editors" had nothing to do with this article—implying, as it did, that

Pearson would not agree with its sentiments—injected yet another duplicitous note as Pearson had recently republished Massey's essay in a different journal under his control almost verbatim. Moreover, the *Quarterly*'s portrayal of Cox as heroic had certainly been shared by both Weyher and Cox's generous Northern friend, who paid for the postmortem publication of the Klansman's work as a "memorial to a zealous defender of our race and nation." It was unthinkable that Weyher did "not know the quotes in question" and did not wholeheartedly agree with them. Indeed, all the evidence suggests that he had been involved in their publication.

Weyher's campaign to discredit criticism of Pioneer culminated with his invited editorial in the professional journal *Intelligence,* much of it actually a verbatim reprint of an article he had authored elsewhere. According to the journal's introduction, this unusual invitation—for an attorney to address the readership of a scientific journal—was justified because "the Pioneer Fund . . . has been widely and unfairly attacked in the media, often with false charges." Weyher's lengthy editorial insisted once again that the fund "has no political agenda, and has taken no positions. It does not . . . publish literature. Its sole activity except for the Flanagan [scholarship] program in the 1930s has been to make hands-off grants to non-profit institutions for unfettered research on projects suggested by the institutions and for publication of the results." "To be unmistakably clear," the attorney added, "there are no cleverly focussed answers in this editorial, nor any dissemblances, nor any sophisms. I am saying flat out that Pioneer is not, and never has been, guilty of any of these allegations."[29]

This impassioned defense was again predicated on the captious distinction between Pioneer's official record and the long history of concerted, clandestine activity by the fund's directors in support of segregation and other reactionary causes, the latter projects treated as nonexistent in Weyher's analysis even though they involved the same Pioneer board members using money from the same source as the former. Indeed, Weyher himself apparently had difficulty distinguishing between the acknowledged and unacknowledged grants, his editorial noting that "Pioneer . . . had funded earlier research into the black-white intelligence gap . . . by Garrett."[30] However, there is no record of an official grant to Garrett, although his efforts in opposition to civil rights had been lavishly supported by the Colonel.

But even if the validity of this tenuous distinction between Pioneer's official and unofficial activities is granted, the latter still provides the critical context within which to consider the former. Pioneer was founded by a man who regarded Earnest Sevier Cox as a hero; who wanted "to do something practical" with his life, such as "moving the colored race to Liberia"; who could not abide a leading eugenicist as president of his board unless he professed support for segregation; who bankrolled the attempt to stop legislation granting equal rights to blacks; and who provided regular and substantial cash gifts to racists and neo-Nazis "as a token of appreciation" for their service to the cause. The fund was subsequently controlled by men who had supported the efforts of, among others, Henry Garrett, William Simmons, Wesley Critz George, and Carleton Putnam—all outspoken opponents of equal rights for blacks—and who collaborated to publish the work of Wilmot Robertson on the real problem underlying the civil rights movement: Jews. In the face of this history, largely undisclosed because the people involved have taken great pains to cover their tracks, it would take an astonishing degree of credulousness to accept that Pioneer is a politically disinterested organization that has funded studies of heredity and racial differences solely for the advancement of scientific knowledge.

Weyher's claim that Pioneer did not publish literature was similarly casuistic. Though not itself engaged in publication, the fund used proxy organizations to do so. Through his Charles Darwin Research Institute, for example, Rushton used Pioneer's money to print and distribute his "for-the-public" paperback. And the sole function of FHU, another organization created by the fund's veterans of the struggle to overturn *Brown,* was the publication and distribution of Pioneer-approved literature on racial differences. The creation of these intermediate layers gave Pioneer plausible deniability for the activities that members of the board had supported and probably planned, a continuation of the model that Draper had provided for his protégé. As Weyher had written to George in 1956, expressing the Colonel's interest in supporting dissemination of George's anti-integration screeds, his unnamed client wanted to contribute to an organization that would distribute the pamphlets "and not to directly finance such projects."[31]

A final indication of Pioneer's interest solely in science, according to Weyher, was the fact that the fund has supported "only the top experts." It was true that the fund could cite a list of distinguished researchers such as Arthur Jensen, Hans Eysenck, Linda Gottfredson, and others who could point to accomplishments besides their studies of racial differences. But there is an equally long list of other Pioneer grantees, including Robert Kuttner, Donald Swan, Roger Pearson, Ralph Scott, and Frank McGurk—all obscure academics lacking any major scientific achievements and notable primarily for their contributions to a string of racist and neo-Nazi causes. Indeed, Pearson, one of the most extreme recipients of Pioneer money, appears to be the closest to the fund. Not only does he have all the old IAAEE publications for sale, but he apparently enjoys access to "inside" information in Weyher's files:

Pearson's articles have quoted from "the collection of Shockley's personal papers in my possession" (despite his having no correspondence of his own with the physicist) and provided the innermost details of Pioneer's scholarship program from the 1930s, presented without reference of any kind.[32] As the Satterfield plan envisioned, the purpose of the former group of grantees has been to provide scientific conclusions that can be offered to dignify the policies advocated by the latter.

## The Last Gasp

Despite the attempts to sanitize Pioneer's image, it is undeniable that the fund was established to use science to pursue the goals of its founder: the preservation of white supremacy and white racial purity from the threat posed by blacks and undesirable immigrants, especially Jews. Nor is there any doubt that Weyher and Trevor were selected by Draper as trustworthy allies to carry on the cause. Indeed, there is no reason to believe that the clandestine activities described in the preceding pages—all discovered through hunch or serendipitous accident—were the only projects orchestrated behind the scenes by Draper and other board members. Although Pioneer has attempted, not always successfully, to maintain some distance from such overtly racist organizations in the post-Draper era, the fund has remained the vehicle originally designed to use science as a tactic in the war against civil rights.

The problem, from Pioneer's point of view, is that it has been losing on almost every front—not so much defeated as ignored, its favorite issues no longer of any great significance to either the scientific community or the public. Although an occasional event such as publication of *The Bell Curve* produces a temporary dustup over the old war-horse of racial differences in intelligence, very few researchers outside the Pioneer clique are particularly interested in a topic that has so little basic scientific value. And no matter how many pamphlets Pioneer prints and distributes, the public has exhibited little concern over an issue that has no tolerable practical application in a society based on individual rights. Perhaps the only area still generating some controversy has been the debate over affirmative action, in which, despite frequently overheated rhetoric, there are many people of good faith on each side and in which Pioneer's role has been limited to providing financial assistance to a legal foundation challenging preferential policies.[33] Thus the ultimate irony is that, having lost every battle to deprive blacks of their rights, the Pioneer board has finally found an issue enjoying broader and more respectable support by insisting that everyone should be accorded equal treatment independent of race—a principle to which scientific studies are, of course, irrelevant. This is not the camel's nose under the tent but the tail of a beast that once occupied the entire interior, now on its way out.

Although Weyher, Trevor, and Parrott may still pine for the segregated era that they struggled in vain to preserve, society has changed dramatically. The cultural truisms that were so common during their formative years—the unquestioned adherence not only to belief in white racial superiority but also to a whole system of racial etiquette prescribing the appropriate behavior of blacks toward their betters—is now regarded as the scourge of racism, a social pathology that must be exposed and eliminated. In perhaps the most devastating blow to the core members of Pioneer's board, what most of the nation regards as social progress represents their worst nightmare, the dreaded scenario pathologically feared by Draper, Cox, and every segregationist and offered decades ago by the scientists on the Colonel's payroll as the chief reason to oppose integration: that equal rights for blacks would inevitably lead to intermarriage, an assault on the "purity" of the white race. Not only do blacks now enjoy equal rights under law and the guarantee of civil liberties, but state antimiscegenation statutes have been struck down and interracial couples hardly raise an eyebrow. The 1967 film *Guess Who's Coming to Dinner,* considered so daring at the time for its portrayal of a young white woman who brings home a black fiancé to meet her chagrined, upper-middle-class parents, was characterized in a standard movie guide only two decades later as "quaint."[34]

Indeed, notwithstanding Raymond Hall's "biological law," at the turn of the century the United States included more citizens than ever of Asian, Latin American, and Middle Eastern background, and the nation is facing what demographers call "the beginning of the blend" as the exponential growth in interracial marriage begins to change the society's entire concept of race, blurring definitions and boundaries and calling old categories into question. A Princeton University study in 2000 estimated that 6 percent of the population was multiracial, and for the first time the decennial head count allowed respondents to choose more than one racial category as their self-identification. Furthermore, about 5 percent of all married couples were interracial, a statistic that will surely increase considering that it is composed disproportionately of younger people; almost half of all married blacks under twenty-five years old have spouses of another race, and in a 1997 survey of teens, 87 percent of the respondents either had dated or would date someone of another race. In 1998 *Mavin* began publication, a magazine that "celebrates the mixed race experience."[35] Whereas Pearson, Glayde Whitney, Jared Taylor, and other Pioneer grantees insist that it is natural and inevitable to dislike members of other races and rail against the destruction of the white race through intermarriage, most of the society finds Tiger Woods's racial mosaic a reason to celebrate. Indeed, the more common interracial relationships have become, the more frenzied have become the warnings from some of the fund's grantees that such relationships are neither possible nor desirable, the divisive rhetoric and undercurrent of hate behind their claims about the genetic nature of racism often seemingly designed to promote the dissension they claim to fear.

Pioneer represents the last gasp of an ideology whose time has gone. In 1937, when the fund was created, the notion that the United States was and should remain a "white" nation was not uncommon; neither the Colonel nor H. H. Laughlin, the first president of his board—both of whom believed that people of color did not even belong in the country—was considered much of an extremist at the time. Even almost three decades later, when Henry Garrett called blacks merely "guests" in a "white man's civilization," there was still some sympathy for such a sentiment among many conservatives reluctant to accept the inevitable outcome of the Second Reconstruction. By 2001, however, social and political equality for all citizens, no matter their race or creed, had become secular gospel in the United States, and even a conservative standardbearer such as George W. Bush declared, in his inaugural address, that "America has never been united by blood or birth. . . . We are bound by ideals. . . . And every immigrant, by embracing these ideals, makes our country more, not less, American."[36] Such platitudes are still opposed only by a tiny handful of people, among them a number of Pioneer grantees and various hate groups.

The fund created by Wickliffe Preston Draper in 1937 may not last much longer. The clock is ticking on Pioneer's board; Weyher, the youngest member, is over eighty, and Trevor is well over ninety. Perhaps mindful of the Colonel's concern, as Weyher once related to George, that his money not "come under the control of people who would use it for purposes not entirely in accord with the purposes of the donor," Pioneer's president has suggested that he may spend the fund out of existence rather than pass it on. Once the money is gone, he told one journalist, "we'll just quit."[37] If Pioneer is indeed soon to face dissolution, society will be the better for its demise. Research of genuine value can find sponsorship elsewhere. Whatever scientific progress the fund may have supported has hardly been worth the violence it has done to our social fabric.

# Postscript

THIS BOOK WAS ALREADY in production when a number of instructive changes occurred in the composition of the Pioneer board, beginning with the appointment of R. Travis Osborne. One of the recipients of cash gifts from the Colonel for his role in opposing the civil rights movement, Osborne had been the first witness to take the stand for the "intervenors" in their attempt to overturn the *Brown* decision. In an ironic reminder of the nation's racial progress, Osborne's name as professor emeritus still appears on the announcement for the University of Georgia's graduate program in psychology, but now followed immediately by what has become boilerplate language declaring the university's commitment to "equal opportunity" and its desire to "increase the number of minority students."

Then, on March 27, 2002, Harry Weyher died, and J. Philippe Rushton, the author of Pioneer's most ambitious recent attempt to persuade the public of blacks' evolutionary inferiority, was appointed the new president of the fund. At the same time Weyher's third wife, Michelle, was named a board member, as was Richard Lynn, a longtime editor at the *Mankind Quarterly* and recipient of numerous grants from Pioneer, one of which was forwarded at Lynn's request to an intermediary—the Atlas Economic Research Foundation—before being passed on to the Ulster Institute for Lynn's use, so that he could disguise its true purpose. In 2001 Lynn authored the fund's own bowdlerized account of its past—*The Science of Human Diversity: A History of the Pioneer Fund* (Lanham, Md.: University Press of America), with a preface by Weyher—making no mention of any activities opposing the rights of blacks.

The new board has announced its intention to "keep Harry F. Weyher's great legacy alive"; for the last three decades, of course, Weyher has performed the same function for Wickliffe Draper's legacy. It appears that his death will make no change in Pioneer's role as the chief source of support for scientific racism.

# Appendix: Archival Materials Consulted

John Beaty papers, Division of Special Collections and University Archives, University of Oregon, Eugene, Oregon

Theodore Gilmore Bilbo papers, University of Southern Mississippi, Hattiesburg, Mississippi

Carleton Coon papers, National Anthropological Archives, National Museum of Natural History, Smithsonian Institution, Washington, D.C.

Earnest Sevier Cox papers, Special Collections Library, Duke University, Durham, North Carolina

Charles Benedict Davenport papers, American Philosophical Society, Philadelphia, Pennsylvania

Wesley Critz George papers #3822, Southern Historical Collection, Wilson Library, University of North Carolina at Chapel Hill, North Carolina

Group Research Archive, Rare Book and Manuscript Library, Columbia University, New York, New York

John Marshall Harlan papers, Seeley G. Mudd Manuscript Library, Princeton University Library, Princeton, New Jersey. Material used by permission of Princeton University Library.

Institute of African Affairs archives, Duquesne University archives, Pittsburgh, Pennsylvania

Institute for the Study of Academic Racism (ISAR) files, Ferris State University, Big Rapids, Michigan

Paul B. Johnson papers, University of Southern Mississippi, Hattiesburg, Mississippi

Erle Johnston Jr. papers, University of Southern Mississippi, Hattiesburg, Mississippi

Harry H. Laughlin Collection, Picker Memorial Library, Truman State University, Kirksville, Missouri

Frank E. Mason papers, Herbert Hoover Library, West Branch, Iowa

George van Horn Moseley papers, Library of Congress, Washington, D.C.

Frederick H. Osborn papers, American Philosophical Society, Philadelphia, Pennsylvania

Regnery papers, Hoover Institution archives, Stanford University, Stanford, California

Charles Scribner's Sons archives, Manuscript Division, Department of Rare Books and Special Collections, Princeton University Library, Princeton, New Jersey. Materials used by persmission of Princeton University Library.

William Bradford Shockley papers, Stanford University archives, Stanford, California

Sovereignty Commission files, Mississippi Department of Archives and History, Jackson, Mississippi

Pedro A. del Valle papers, Division of Special Collections and University Archives, University of Oregon, Eugene, Oregon

Albert C. Wedemeyer papers, Hoover Institution archives, Stanford University, Stanford, California

Nathaniel Weyl papers, Hoover Institution archives, Stanford University, Stanford, California

# Notes

## Introduction: Keepers of the Flame

1. J. DeParle, "Daring Research or 'Social Science Pornography?'" *New York Times Magazine* (October 9, 1994): 50.

2. P. Brimelow, "For Whom the Bell Tolls," *Forbes* (October 24, 1994): 153. The two critical quotes come, respectively, from J. Jones, "Back to the Future with *The Bell Curve*," in *The Bell Curve Wars*, ed. S. Fraser (New York: Basic Books, 1995), 93 and O. Patterson, "For Whom the Bell Curves," also in *The Bell Curve Wars*, 208.

3. DeParle, "Daring Research," 51.

4. C. Lane, "The Tainted Sources of 'The Bell Curve,'" *New York Review of Books* (December 1, 1994): 14, 15; C. Lane, letter to the editor, *Commentary* (August, 1995): 16.

5. A. Miller, "Professors of Hate," *Rolling Stone* (October 20, 1994): 106–114; R. J. Herrnstein and C. Murray, *The Bell Curve* (New York: Free Press, 1994), 272.

6. L. Kamin, "Lies, Damned Lies, and Statistics," in *The Bell Curve Debate*, eds. R. Jacoby and N. Glauberman (New York: Times Books, 1995), 86; for Kamin's criticisms of earlier work, see L. Kamin, *The Science and Politics of I.Q.* (Potomac, Md.: Lawrence Erlbaum, 1974). See T. Samuel, "'Bell Curve' Trail Leads to an Outfit with a Racial Bent," *Philadelphia Inquirer*, November 27, 1994, E3; J. Mercer, "Fascination with Genetics," *Chronicle of Higher Education* (December 7, 1994): A28–29.

7. On the history of work by Jensen and Shockley, see W. H. Tucker, *The Science and Politics of Racial Research* (Urbana: University of Illinois Press, 1994), especially 182–233; see G. Lichtenstein, "Fund Backs Controversial Study of 'Racial Betterment,'" *New York Times*, December 11, 1977, 76.

8. B. Mehler, "The New Eugenics," *Science for the People* (May/June 1983): 21; B. Mehler, "Rightists on the Rights Panel," *Nation* (May 7, 1988): 640–641; B. Mehler, "Foundation for Fascism: The New Eugenic Movement in the United States," *Patterns of Prejudice* 23 (1989): 21.

9. Weyher did write a letter to the *American Jewish World*, denying any connection between the Third Reich and Pioneer's founders; see S. Kühl, *The Nazi Connection: Eu-*

*genics, American Racism, and German National Socialism* (New York: Oxford University Press, 1994), 10–11.

10. Pioneer's IRS records, which include its yearly grants, are available at the Foundation Center, Washington, D.C., and on the Web site of the Institute for the Study of Academic Racism, <http://161.57.216.70/ISAR/Institut/pioneer/pfspread/homepage.htm>. All adjustments for inflation provide amounts in 2001 dollars.

11. The beginning of the controversy was reported in M. Reed, "Group's Grants Assailed at U. of Del.," *Philadelphia Inquirer,* December 21, 1989, 1b, 6b. It was also described in Jack Anderson's syndicated column: J. Anderson and D. Van Atta, "Backing the 'Science' of Race," *Courier-Post,* November 16, 1989, 19a. Gottfredson's research appears in L. S. Gottfredson, "Societal Consequences of the *g* Factor in Employment," *Journal of Vocational Behavior* 29 (1986): 398–406. The letter from the Louisville School of Medicine is Wilson to Weyher, March 31, 1975, Shockley papers.

12. Indeed, very soon after the incident at Delaware, Smith College attempted to prevent Pioneer support for one of its faculty but eventually relented; see J. H. Blits, "The Silenced Partner: Linda Gottfredson and the University of Delaware," *Academic Questions* 4 (1991): 44.

13. "Report of the Faculty Senate Committee on Research on the Issue of Delaware's Relationship with the Pioneer Fund," University of Delaware, April 19, 1990, 11, 1, 6; the Faculty Senate Committee did observe (p. 10) that a faculty member could establish a center or program "independently of the University" through which to seek support from Pioneer "without directly involving the University." However, Gottfredson's co-researcher Jan Blits has suggested that the independent program approach might involve its own intolerable restrictions; see Blits, "The Silenced Partner: Linda Gottfredson and the University of Delaware," 43–44.

14. Reported in "Settlement at U. of Delaware," *Science* 256 (1992): 962; Mehler's charges were repeated in Kühl, *The Nazi Connection,* 10; the interview with Weyher appears in J. Sedgwick, "The Mentality Bunker," *GQ* (November 1994): 228–235, 250–251.

15. Weyher's letters appeared in *New York Review of Books,* February 2, 1995, 44; *Wall Street Journal,* January 19, 1995, A15; *New York Times,* February 21, 1996, A18. The "prodding" was noted in Weyher, "Contributions to the History of Psychology: CXII. Intelligence, Behavior Genetics, and the Pioneer Fund," *Psychological Reports* 82 (1998): 1354, and again in H. F. Weyher, "The Pioneer Fund, the Behavioral Sciences, and the Media's False Stories," *Intelligence* 26 (1999): 331; the letters eventually appeared in *Sacramento Bee,* March 9, 1996 and *The Independent on Sunday,* July 8, 1990.

16. "False Charges Against Pioneer" can be found at <http://www.pioneerfund.org/speak.html>; Gordon's letter, "How Smart We Are about What We Broadcast: An Open Letter to ABC News" appears at <http://www.pioneerfund.org/ABCletter.html>; Weyher, "Contributions to the History of Psychology," 1347–1374; Weyher, "The Pioneer Fund, the Behavioral Sciences, and the Media's False Stories," 319–336.

17. See Weyher's letter to the *New York Times,* February 21, 1996: A18, and his articles "Contributions to the History of Psychology," 1355, 1357, and "The Pioneer Fund, the Behavioral Sciences, and the Media's False Stories," 333.

18. For example, Arthur Jensen and British psychologist Hans Eysenck. See Weyher's letters to the *Wall Street Journal,* January 9, 1995, A15; the *New York Times,* February 21,

1996, A18; and the *New York Review of Books,* February 2, 1995, 44. Lane's apology is contained in his response, also in the *New York Review of Books,* February 2, 1995, 45.

19. Weyher, *New York Review of Books,* February 2, 1995, 44; see "False Charges against Pioneer"; the geneticist was quoted in R. W. May, "Genetics and Subversion," *The Nation* 190 (May 14, 1960): 421.

20. "False Charges against Pioneer"; see also Weyher, "Contributions to the History of Psychology," 1349, 1354, 1366. Weyher, *New York Review of Books,* February 2, 1995, 44.

21. Gordon, "How Smart We Are about What We Broadcast," 30; Weyher, *Wall Street Journal,* January 9, 1995, A15; Weyher, "Contributions to the History of Psychology," 1350.

22. From the Certificate of Incorporation of the Pioneer Fund (February 27, 1937), on file with the Department of State, State of New York.

23. Ibid.

24. From the Certificate of Amendment of the Certificate of Incorporation of the Pioneer Fund (April 30, 1985), on file with the Department of State, State of New York; quoted in "Report of the Faculty Senate Committee on Research on the Issue of Delaware's Relationship with the Pioneer Fund," 5.

25. Letter, Weyher to Tucker, December 2, 1985.

26. Quoted in C. V. Woodward, "Freedom and the Universities," *New York Review of Books* (July 18, 1991): 32.

27. See Tucker, *The Science and Politics of Racial Research.*

## Chapter 1: Our Northern Friend

1. E. S. Cox, *Let My People Go* (Richmond, Va.: White America Society, 1925), 34; on Cox's life, see Cox, *Black Belt around the World at High Noon of Colonialism* (Richmond, Va.: Mitchell and Hutchkins, 1963).

2. The quotation is from Cox to H. H. Howland, editor of Bobbs-Merrill, March 3, 1923. Among the other publishers who rejected his manuscript were G.P. Putnam's Sons, George H. Doran, D. Appleton & Co., Martin and Hoyt, Boni and Livright, Inc., and Charles Scribner's Sons, who had published Madison Grant's book; the correspondence between Cox and the publishers can be found in the Cox papers.

3. M. Grant, *The Passing of the Great Race* (New York: Charles Scribner's Sons, 1918). Grant to Perkins, November 7, 1924; Perkins to Grant, November 13, 1924; Scribner's archives, box 67. On November 14, 1924, Grant wrote back to Perkins, "I am afraid what you say about Mr. Cox's book is only too true."

4. E. S. Cox, *White America* (Richmond, Va.: White America Society, 1923), 300, 154, 299, 19.

5. Ibid., 72, 157, 161–162, 299.

6. Ibid., 237, 102, 119, 14, 19, 234, 311.

7. Ibid., 222, 189–190, 246, 190–191.

8. Ibid., 339–340. Even after their removal to Africa, blacks would remain subordinate to whites in Cox's scheme: "The United States, as sovereign power over the repatriated negro will be possessed of executive . . . status" and "may enforce beneficial measures." "It is to the negro's advantage," Cox maintained, "that the white extend influence over the negro, whether the latter dwell in America or Africa" (ibid., 353, 354).

9. E. S. Cox, *The South's Part in Mongrelizing the Nation* (Richmond, Va.: White America Society, 1926), 97, 29, 81, 53–54, 7–8; Cox, *White America*, 329–330.

10. Cox, *White America*, 357, 9, 61, 62; see W. H. Tucker, *The Science and Politics of Racial Research* (Urbana: University of Illinois Press, 1994), especially chapter 3. There are two letters from McDougall to Cox, both written on May 3, 1924; one is a personal response to Cox, the other a statement designed to be used for publicity purposes; Cox papers.

11. Ross to Cox, April 24, 1924 and January 27, 1925, Cox papers. "White America," *Eugenical News* 9 (1924): 3; though unsigned, the review was almost certainly written by the *News*'s editor, H. H. Laughlin.

12. The law is discussed in Plecker to Grant, June 18, 1931; the paper is enclosed with Plecker to Cox, May 19, 1932, soliciting his comments; Grant to Cox, June 11, 1930; Cox papers. On Günther, see Tucker, *The Science and Politics of Racial Research*, 115–117. Two years later, when the Swastika Press in the United States began publication of *American Guard*, it sent a complimentary copy to Cox as someone "interested in this Cause" (letter from the Press to Cox, June 24, 1932; Cox papers).

13. Campbell to Cox, March 6, 1936; Laughlin to Cox, March 18, 1936; Cox papers. The talk was published as E. S. Cox, "Repatriation of the American Negro," *Eugenical News* 21 (1936): 134.

14. Laughlin to Draper, March 18, 1936, Laughlin papers. Laughlin to Cox, June 1, 1936; Miller to Cox, June 4, 1936; Cox papers.

15. On the Preston and Wickliffe family histories, see R. Lawrence, *Draper, Preston and Allied Family Histories* (New York: National Americana Publications, 1954), 88–89, available in the Hopedale, Massachusetts Library; on General William Preston, see also his entry in *Dictionary of American Biography*, ed. D. Malone (New York: Charles Scribner's Sons, 1935), 205–206; quoted in C. B. Davenport, *Heredity in Relation to Eugenics* (New York: Henry Holt, 1911), 231.

16. Quoted in E. K. Spann, *Hopedale: From Commune to Company Town, 1840–1920* (Columbus: Ohio State University Press, 1992), 166.

17. T. W. Draper, *The Drapers in America* (New York: John Polhemus, 1892), v.

18. See the entry for Ira Draper in *Dictionary of American Biography*, ed. A. Johnson & D. Malone (New York: Charles Scribner's Sons, 1930), 437.

19. See Spann, *Hopedale*, 24, 86; also J. S. Garner, *The Model Company Town: Urban Design through Private Enterprise in Nineteenth Century New England* (Amherst: University of Massachusetts Press, 1984), 121.

20. Spann, *Hopedale*, 129.

21. See Garner, *The Model Company Town*, 167, 119; see Spann, *Hopedale*, xi, 131–134; also the entry for Ebenezer Daggett Draper in *National Cyclopedia of American Biography*, Vol. 23 (Clifton, N.J.: James T. White, 1933), 54–55.

22. Garner, *The Model Company Town*, 123; see also the entries for Eben Sumner Draper in *Dictionary of American Biography*, 435, and *National Cyclopedia of American Biography*, Vol. 23, 55–56, Vol. 14 (1910), 386. Although the Draper corporation closed down long ago and the family members have long since left the area, Hopedale still bears all the marks of their former influence: Draper Street, Draper Field, the Draper School, the Draper Gymnasium, and even the Draper Assisted Living Facility.

23. See the entries for William Franklin Draper in *Dictionary of American Biography*,

443–444, and *National Cyclopedia of American Biography,* Vol. 6 (2nd edition, 1929), 98–99, Vol. 32 (1945) 49.

24. Spann states that William Draper was ousted by his brothers because he was spending too much money on "research and development" (*Hopedale,* 176), and Garner hints that it was due to personal differences within the family. However, William Draper's grandson states that the brothers were irked at his absentee ownership; interview with William F. Draper, December 1998.

25. See the entries for Eben Sumner Draper in *Dictionary of American Biography,* 435, and *National Cyclopedia of American Biography,* Vol. 14 (1910), 386, Vol. 23 (1933), 55–56; also the description of Eben Sumner and George Draper in Lawrence, *Draper, Preston and Allied Family Histories,* 39–42; Garner, *The Model Company Town,* 127.

26. See M. Crawford, *Building the Workingman's Paradise* (London: Verso, 1995), 36, 79; on Olmstead, who was involved in such projects as New York's Central Park, Cornell and Yale Universities, the U.S. Capitol, and the National Zoo in Washington, see W. Rybczynski, *A Clearing in the Distance: Frederick Law Olmstead and America in the Nineteenth Century* (New York: Scribner, 1999). The studies are cited in ibid., 51; the awards are described in Garner, *The Model Company Town,* 205.

27. Sacco's participation in the strike is described in P. Avrich, *Sacco and Vanzetti* (Princeton, N.J.: Princeton University Press, 1991), 27, 29; Garner, *The Model Company Town,* 175.

28. See N. Lemann, *The Big Test: The Secret History of the American Meritocracy* (New York: Farrar, Straus, and Giroux, 1999); according to Lemann (p. 27), many Harvard students at the time did not even bother to attend classes, enrolling in special tutoring schools at the end of each semester to pass their exams. Draper's academic record, including his last year at St. Mark's, is available from the Harvard University Archives.

29. Draper's list of Harvard organizations appears in his entry in the *Harvard College Class of 1913 Class Album,* available from the university archives; the quote is from S. P. Stuart, *My First Cousin Once Removed* (New York: HarperCollins, 1998), 12.

30. On Draper's service during the war, see "Draper Is Wounded at French Front," *Milford [Massachusetts] Daily Journal,* July 19, 1917; "Draper Now Captain in U.S. Service; Is Veteran of France," *Milford Daily News,* December 4, 1917; "Thrilling Recital of Life as an Artillerist Given by Capt. Draper," *Milford Daily News,* December 5, 1917.

31. See Draper's entry in the *Harvard College Class of 1913: Twenty-Fifth Anniversary Report* (Cambridge, Mass.: Cosmos Press, 1938), available from Harvard University Archives; also the entry on Draper in the list of Pioneer directors posted on its Web page, <http://www.pioneerfund.org>; Draper's status in World War II is noted in "Indian Troops Praised," *New York Times,* September 11, 1941, 12.

32. The will is described in a number of articles in the *Milford Daily News:* "Summary of Bequests under the Will of George A. Draper," March 20, 1923; "G.A. Draper Est. Was Worth $10,757,332," April 7, 1924; "Large Trust Funds Left by Geo. A. Draper," December 3, 1925; "Geo. A. Draper Left Estate of $11,753,395.13," June 11, 1931. The will itself is included in the estate papers of Wickliffe Draper, Surrogate's Office, New York City. Although George Draper's will divided the estate equally between his son and daughter, the mix of trust funds and immediately available resources differed, Helen's share consisting almost entirely of the former, Wickliffe receiving substantially more cash and a smaller trust. This

decision may have reflected the veracity of rumors about her alcoholism. Helen's marital record is also detailed in the *Milford Daily News*: "Mrs. Helen D. Taft and N. F. Ayer Married at High Noon Today," May 24, 1924; "Mrs. Helen Taft Ayer Gets Divorce at Reno," September 9, 1930.

33. From Draper's entry in the *Harvard College Class of 1913: Twenty-Fifth Anniversary Report*.

34. On Limbaugh's rejection, see J. Knadler, "Celebdom's Gazillion-Dollar Digs," *Cosmopolitan* (July 1998): 128; Draper's residence and personal habits were described to me in an interview with William F. Draper, Wickliffe's second cousin.

35. See "Platoon of the Eighth Cavalry Is Winner in Rigorous 'War' Test of Unit Leadership," *New York Times*, January 7, 1929, 1.

36. See the list of "College Courses in Genetics and Eugenics," *Eugenical News* 1 (1916): 26, 34. Harvard's interest in eugenics, or at least in some aspects of it, did not last very long: Only a decade later, the university declined a $60,000 legacy from a prominent Philadelphia surgeon whose will stipulated that the money be used to support a course in eugenics that "shall be taught in all its branches, notably that branch relating to the treatment of the defective and criminal classes by surgical procedures"; see "Harvard Declines a Legacy to Found Eugenics Course," *New York Times*, May 8, 1927, 1.

37. W. McDougall, *Is America Safe for Democracy?* (New York: Charles Scribner's Sons, 1921); disenfranchisement is proposed in W. McDougall, *Ethics and Some Modern World Problems* (London: Methuen, 1925), 156–163; thoroughgoing segregation is proposed in W. McDougall, *The Indestructible Union* (Boston: Little, Brown, 1925), 162–164.

38. W. McDougall, *The Indestructible Union*, 135, 151; W. McDougall, *Ethics and Some Modern World Problems*, 38.

39. A. Chase, *The Legacy of Malthus* (New York: Knopf, 1977), 114. Actually Davenport was named secretary of the American Breeders' Association, which soon retitled itself the Eugenics Research Association to avoid the connection with livestock suggested by the former; at the same time the organization's journal was changed from the *American Breeders' Magazine* to the *Journal of Heredity*; see the announcement, "Breeders' Association Will Change Its Name," *American Breeders' Magazine* 4 (1913): 177.

40. C. B. Davenport, "Report of Committee on Eugenics," *American Breeders' Magazine* 1 (1910): 127; "Race Genetics Problems," unsigned editorial, almost certainly written by Davenport, *American Breeders' Magazine* 2 (1911): 231, 232; C. B. Davenport, "The Effects of Race Intermingling," *Proceedings of the American Philosophical Society* 56 (1917): 366, 367.

41. Davenport, *Heredity in Relation to Eugenics*, 219, 216.

42. Davenport to Madison Grant, April 7, 1925, quoted in C. E. Rosenberg, *No Other Gods: On Science and American Social Thought* (Baltimore: Johns Hopkins University Press, 1976), 95–96.

43. Grant, *The Passing of the Great Race*, 167, 228; J. W. Bendersky, *The "Jewish Threat": Anti-Semitic Politics of the U.S. Army* (New York: Basic Books, 2000), 3.

44. On the Committee on Eugenics and the IRL, see Chase, *The Legacy of Malthus*, 115; also M. H. Haller, *Eugenics: Hereditarian Attitudes in American Thought* (New Brunswick, N.J.: Rutgers University Press, 1963), 65. The quotation is from R. D. Ward, "Eugenic Immigration," *American Breeders' Magazine* 4 (1913): 101, 102.

45. In 1925, Cox and Francis Kinnicutt, an IRL leader, agreed to raise $250 each to distribute the books in the name of the White America Society; Kinnicutt thought it politically advantageous to keep separate the movements for immigration restriction and racial purity, although "of course," he acknowledged to Cox, "the two subjects have a direct relation"; Kinnicutt to Cox, January 20, February 6, and February 14, 1925, Cox papers.

46. See the obituary, "Madison Grant, 71, Zoologist Is Dead," *New York Times,* May 31, 1937, 15; the mammal named after him is the *Rangifer granti,* a caribou found only on the Alaska peninsula.

47. Haller, *Eugenics,* 73. Well aware of the advantage of being perceived as a scientist, Grant requested of his publisher that, "of all my degrees," only "the presidency of the Eugenics Research Association is worth mentioning" next to his name in a new edition of his book, *The Passing of the Great Race;* Grant to Perkins, September 18, 1922; Scribner's archives, box 67.

48. Grant to H. F. Osborn, March 9, 1918, in Davenport papers.

49. Grant, *The Passing of the Great Race,* 5, 89, 16, 18, 51; see S. Kühl, *The Nazi Connection: Eugenics, American Racism, and German National Socialism* (New York: Oxford University Press, 1994), 85.

50. Quoted in Bendersky, *The "Jewish Threat,"* 1; see chapter 5 in Bendersky for a discussion of the visitors to the Army War College.

51. T. L. Stoddard, *The Rising Tide of Color against White World-Supremacy* (New York: Charles Scribner's Sons, 1920), 129; Bendersky, *The "Jewish Threat,"* 261.

52. Bendersky, *The "Jewish Threat,"* 433; the officers are quoted in ibid., 38, 54, Patton on 357; the America First quote from Moseley appears in the photograph of his letter to the director of the America First Committee, between 222 and 223; the call for Jews to leave comes from G. Moseley, "We Need a Runnymede," Moseley papers, Library of Congress.

53. The book was promoted by General George E. Stratemeyer, Commander, Far East Air Forces; Marine General Edward M. Almond, Chief of Staff, Far East Command; General Pedro A. del Valle, Commanding General 1st Marine Division; and Navy Admiral T. G. W. Settle, Commander, Amphibious Forces in the Pacific; the poster with the recommendation from the four officers is reproduced in Bendersky, *The "Jewish Threat,"* among photos between pages 366 and 367; J. Beaty, *The Iron Curtain over America* (Dallas: Wilkinson, 1951), 77.

54. Theodore Roosevelt, for example, praised the book for Grant's "grasp of the facts our people must need to realize. . . . It is the work of an American scholar and gentleman, and all Americans should be immensely grateful to [Grant] for writing it"; quoted in *Eugenical News* 18 (1933): 111.

55. Davenport to Draper, March 23, 1923, January 13, 1926, Davenport papers; for details of the mission, see E. M. Augiéras, W. P. Draper, M. E. Gierzynski, M. V. Besnard, and T. Monod, *D'Algérie au Sénégal* (Paris: Société d'Éditions Géographiques, Maritimes et Coloniales, 1931). Although the Pioneer Fund's Web site (<http://www.pioneerfund.org>) calls Draper the "discoverer of Asselar Man," the skeleton was actually discovered by Besnard and Monod, two scientists and members of the expedition; see M. Boule and H. Vallois, "L'Homme Fossile D'Asselar (Sahara)," *Archives de L'Institut de Paléontologic Humaine,* Mémoire 9 (1932): 1; M. Boule and I I. V. Vallois, *Fossil Men* (New York: Dryden Press, 1957), 431.

56. Interview with William F. Draper, December 1998.

57. Davenport to Draper, March 23, 1923; Draper to Davenport, March 28, 1923; Davenport papers.

58. J. A. Bucher (Draper's agent at Guaranty Trust) to Davenport, March 11, 1925; Davenport to Draper, May 27, 1925; Draper to Davenport, January 12, 1926; Davenport to Draper, January 13, 1926; Davenport papers.

59. Draper to Davenport, February 5, 1926; Davenport to Draper, February 6, 1926; February 27, 1926; Davenport papers.

60. Davenport to Draper, March 15, 1926; Davenport to Steggerda, March 26, 1927, April 8, 1927; Davenport papers. The study itself is reported in C. B. Davenport and M. Steggerda, *Race Crossing in Jamaica* (Washington, D.C.: Carnegie Institute, 1929); see pp. 3–4 for the details of Davenport's trip.

61. Davenport and Steggerda, *Race Crossing in Jamaica,* 469, 472.

62. Ibid., 470–471; Davenport, "Is the Crossing of Races Useful?" November 12, 1929, Davenport papers. As geneticist William Castle pointed out at the time, however, the data actually collected by Steggerda indicated an average difference between blacks and whites on the length of each limb of half a centimeter, meaning that the misfit hybrid would be forced to reach an additional three-eighths of an inch for an object on the ground; W. E. Castle, "Race Mixture and Physical Disharmonies," *Science* 71 (1930): 604–605.

63. Davenport to Draper, September 29, 1928, May 25, 1928; Davenport to Steggerda, April 17, 1928; October 10, 1928; Davenport papers. On Fischer's contributions to Nazi race science, see Tucker, *The Science and Politics of Racial Research,* 128–129; and P. Weingart, J. Kroll, and K. Bayertz, *Rasse, Blut und Gene: Geschichte der Eugenik und Rassenhygiene in Deutschland* (Frankfurt: Suhrkamp, 1988), especially pp. 99–102, on his study of the "Rehoboth bastards."

64. Davenport to Grant, May 7, 1928; Grant to Davenport, May 15, 1928; Davenport papers.

65. "Eugenics Research Prizes," *New York Times,* June 10, 1928, 6. See also "Announcement of Prizes," *Eugenical News* 13 (1928): 78–79; "Offer of Prize on Causes of the Fall in Birth Rate," *Eugenical News* 14 (1929): 118; "Second Prize Contest," *Eugenical News* 15 (1930): 9; "Prize Contests for Research Essays on the Birth-Rate," *Eugenical News* 16 (1931): 84–85. The last of these announcements contains the data on the national origins of the submissions. The contests defined "Nordic" countries to include the Netherlands, England, Scotland, North Ireland, the Scandinavian peninsula, and the German states of Schleswig-Holstein, Mecklenburg, Hanover, and Westphalia (i.e., the northern provinces).

66. A memo on Eugenics Record Office stationery, appearing to relay a phone message, describes Draper's two proposals and asks for Davenport's reaction, October 10, 1932; Davenport to Draper, October 13, 1932; Davenport papers.

67. Davenport to Draper, October 28, 1972, Davenport papers. Details of the contest were given in "Prize Contest for Research in the Genetics of Mental Disorders," *Eugenical News* 18 (1933): 29–31; reference to the generous "patron" appeared in "The Twenty-First Annual Meeting of the Eugenics Research Association," *Eugenical News* 18 (1933): 55. Subsequent announcements of the contest were made in *Eugenical News* 19 (1934): 16; 19 (1934): 107; and 20 (1935): 10. Description of the winning entry appeared in "Probability of Institutional Commitment on Family History," *Eugenical News* 21 (1936): 9–10.

Because there were few papers "of serious merit" submitted as entries for the contest, only the first prize of $3,000 was awarded, and the remainder of the contribution was placed in the Eugenics Research Association's "Draper Fund." See "Suggestions for Publication and Researches in Connection with the Third Draper Prize Contest," n.d., and the financial statements of the "Draper Fund"—also referred to as the "Draper Account"—January 4, 1936, September 4, 1936, and February 25, 1937; Laughlin papers.

68. In 1947, for example, Cox received a check for $200 ($1,600 AFI) from Draper, which he accepted "as a token of your friendship" (Cox to Draper, November 18, 1947), and in 1954, he received, "as Colonel Draper's gift, the sum of $1,000 [$6,600 AFI]" (Vincent J. Malone, Draper's attorney, to Cox, June 16, 1954); Cox papers.

69. Plecker to Laughlin, June 8, 1936; Cox to Edgar H. Wells & Co., September 29, 1936; Cox papers. Decades later, in his only published description of this first meeting, Cox referred to his anonymous source of support simply as "a wealthy man"; E. S. Cox, *Lincoln's Negro Policy* (Richmond, Va., 1972), 79.

70. Draper to Cox, September 18, 1936; Cox to Draper, September 19, 1936; Maury (president of William Byrd Press) to Cox, September 28, 1936; Cox papers. Virginia's decision to memorialize Congress is described in Cox, *Lincoln's Negro Policy,* 45–53.

71. Quoted in *Newsweek,* July 15, 1946, 30; *Newsweek,* August 6, 1945, 39; *Time,* July 1, 1946, 22.

72. J. B. Stoner to Bilbo, November 18, 1942; Bilbo to Stoner, November 20, 1942; Bilbo papers. T. G. Bilbo, *Take Your Choice: Separation or Mongrelization* (Poplarville, Miss.: Dream House Publishing Company, 1947), preface.

73. On Bilbo's past, see R. G. Swing, *Forerunners of American Fascism* (New York: Julian Messner, Inc., 1935), 108–120; Bilbo to Cox, February 8, 1938, Cox papers.

74. The speech is reprinted in *Congressional Record* 75:3 (January 21, 1938), 872–896; the quotes appear on 890, 889, 873, 884, 881, 892, and 893. According to Cox, a number of other senators also made use of *White America* in the debate over the antilynching bill; Cox to Campbell, June 16, 1938, Cox papers.

75. Cox to Draper, February 16, 1938; Draper to Cox, March 12, 1938; Cox papers.

76. The speech is reprinted in *Congressional Record* 75:3 (February 7, 1938), 1533–1565; Bilbo to Cox, February 8, 1938, Cox papers.

77. The magazine that rejected Cox's submission was the *Saturday Evening Post.* Cox to Bilbo, February 2, 1938; Bilbo to Cox, March 22, 1938; Draper to Cox, March 30, 1938; Cox to Draper, April 3, 1938; Cox papers.

78. E. S. Cox, *Lincoln's Negro Policy* (Los Angeles: Noontide Press, 1968/reprint of the 1938 edition), 29, 57; Cox to M. L. Gordon, August 14, 1938, Cox papers. There was some initial confusion about which of Cox's writings was to be published at Draper's expense; both Bilbo (in a letter to Cox, February 26, 1938) and Draper (in a note to Cox, April 7, 1938) erroneously thought it was going to be "Let My People Go," a pamphlet written in 1925 and addressed primarily to blacks; see also the letter from J. A. Bucher, an official at Draper's bank, Guaranty Trust Company of New York, to Cox, April 7, 1938; Cox papers.

79. Cox to Bilbo, May 29, 1938; Cox to Draper, April 3, 1938; Cox papers. Although Lincoln did initially support the idea of colonizing blacks outside the United States, according to historian James M. McPherson, he retreated from this policy after 1862, moving toward assimilation of freed slaves as equal citizens; see J. M. McPherson, "Lincoln the

Devil" (review of *Forced into Glory* by Lerone Bennett Jr.), *New York Times Book Review,* August 27, 2000, 12.

80. Cox to Draper, June 12, 1938, Cox papers. The speech in favor of the amendment is reprinted in *Congressional Record* 75:3 (May 24, 1938), 7347–7371; the quotes appear on 7358, 7366–7367, 7363, 7359, and 7361.

81. Draper to Cox, June 14, 1938; Cox to Draper, August 14, 1938; Cox to Gordon, August 14, 1938; Cox to Bilbo, September 12, 1938; Cox to Draper, September 15, 1938; Earnest Sevier Cox papers.

82. E. H. Wells (bookseller) to Cox, September 17, 1938, Cox papers; H. J. Greenwall and R. Wild, *Unknown Liberia* (London: Hutchinson & Co., 1936), 11, 12, 122, 124.

83. Bilbo's speech and the text of the act are reprinted in *Congressional Record* 76:1, 4650–4676; Cox to Bilbo, March 19, 1939, Bilbo papers; Bucher to Cox, January 31, 1939, Cox papers; Cox's handwritten note at the bottom of the letter states that the check was returned to Draper.

84. Cox to Draper, May 4, 1939; Bilbo to Draper, May 4, 1939; Cox papers.

85. Draper to Cox, November 10, 1940; Cox papers.

86. Cox to Draper, July 10, 1949; Cox to V. J. Malone (Draper's attorney), July 17, 1953; Cox to Draper, July 27, 1953; Cox to I. Edwards (staff member for Senator William Langer), August 10, 1953; Cox papers.

87. Cox to Malone, March 16, 1954, March 17, 1954, March 22, 1954; Cox to Langer, January 6, 1954; Cox papers. Cox's first suggestion for reaching the black community—apparently unappealing to Draper because he made no response—was to "re-publish" the newspaper of the Universal African Nationalist Movement, the *African Times,* "which would give space to matters relating to Africa and the Langer bill" (Cox to Malone, November 21, 1953).

88. Cox to Malone, March 16, 1954, March 17, 1954; Cox to Langer, April 3, 1954; Malone to Cox, March 29, 1954; Cox papers.

89. Cox to Malone, June 17, 1954; Malone to Cox, July 9, 1954; Cox papers. E. S. Cox, *Unending Hate: Supreme Court Decision, a Milestone in the Federal Program to Break the Will of the White South in Its Dedicated Purpose to Remain White* (Richmond, Va.: Cox, 1955).

90. Draper to E. W. Nelson (co-executor of Cox's estate), July 16, 1966, Cox papers.

91. The characterization of Hitler's defeat appears in a letter from Carto, quoted in M. Ross, "Willis Carto: America's No. 1 Jew Hater," *Chic* (May, 1982): 58; although the recipient of the letter is not named by Ross, he is identified as Norris Holt according to C. H. Simonds, "The Strange Story of Willis Carto," *National Review* (September 10, 1971): 979. The comments on Jews appear in Carto to Holt, January 28, 1955, ISAR files.

92. Carto to Cox, March 29, 1954, February 2, 1955; Cox papers.

93. "Foreword to the Second Edition," of E. S. Cox, *Lincoln's Negro Policy,* 4, 5; the list of its books is available from Noontide Press, Los Angeles, California.

94. Nelson to Carto, April 19, 1867 [*sic*—obviously should have been "1967"]; see also Nelson to Carto, April 27, 1967; Cox papers.

95. Tribble to Weyher, June 8, 1967, Cox papers.

96. Cox to Draper, September 14, 1957, Cox papers.

97. Davenport and Steggerda, *Race Crossing in Jamaica,* 5; "Business Meeting," *Eugenical News* 23 (1938): 71.

## Chapter 2: Somebody Whose Views He Could Not Approve

1. All quotations from Certificate of Incorporation of the Pioneer Fund, Inc. (March 17, 1937), on file with the Department of State, State of New York. In 1985, the first purpose was legally amended, removing the word *white*, although the retention of the remaining language concerning "persons . . . in the original thirteen states" probably made the racial designation redundant; see Certificate of Amendment of the Certificate of Incorporation of the Pioneer Fund Inc. (June 14, 1985), on file with the Department of State, State of New York.

2. Ibid. The amendment also added to the second purpose the word "human" preceding "race betterment."

3. A copy of the bylaws is contained in the Osborn papers; Osborn to "Dear Frank" (no last name), September 10, 1975, Osborn papers; F. Osborn, "History of the American Eugenics Society," *Social Biology* 21 (1974): 122.

4. "White America," *Eugenical News* 9 (1924): 3, unsigned but undoubtedly written by Laughlin; H. H. Laughlin, "Outline of Proposed Specific Researches on Race Integrity in Southern and Eastern United States," n.d., Cox papers; Laughlin to Draper, March 18, 1936, and Laughlin to Draper, n.d. (events referred to in content of letter indicate that it was written in January or February 1936), Laughlin papers.

5. For the congressman's opinions, see A. Johnson, "The Outline of a Policy," *Outlook* 136 (1924): 140; Laughlin's statements before the committee appear in *Analysis of America's Modern Melting Pot: Hearings before the Committee on Immigration and Naturalization*, HR 67-3, November 21, 1922 and in *Europe as an Emigrant-Exporting Continent and the United States as an Immigrant-Receiving Nation: Hearings before the Committee on Immigration and Naturalization*, HR 68-1, March 8, 1924.

6. "Memorial on Immigration Quotas" (submitted to the president, the Senate, and the House of Representatives), January 4, 1927, reprinted in *Eugenical News* 12 (1927): 27–28; although the "memorial" listed more than thirty signers, including Davenport and Grant as well as Laughlin, its style strongly suggests that it was authored by the "expert eugenics agent."

7. H. H. Laughlin, *Immigration Control* (A Report of the Special Committee on Immigration and Alien Insane) (New York: Chamber of Commerce of the State of New York, 1934), 17–19; see also "Relaxing Quotas for Exiles Fought," *New York Times*, May 4, 1934, 7.

8. H. H. Laughlin, *Immigration and Conquest* (New York: Special Committee on Immigration and Naturalization of the Chamber of Commerce of the State of New York, 1939), 20, 21, 97, 92; Laughlin to Grant, November 19, 1932, Laughlin papers.

9. An early version of the model law appears in H. H. Laughlin, *The Legal and Administrative Aspects of Sterilization*, Vol. 2 of *Report of the Committee to Study and to Report on the Best Practical Means of Cutting Off the Defective Germ-Plasm in the American Population* (Cold Spring Harbor, N.Y.: Eugenics Record Office, 1914), 144–145; a later, more elaborate version appears in H. H. Laughlin, "Full Text for a Model State Law," in *Eugenical Sterilization in the United States* (Chicago: Psychopathic Laboratory of the Municipal Court of Chicago, 1922), 446–447. The plan for sterilizing the lowest 10 percent is described in Laughlin, *The Legal and Administrative Aspects of Sterilization*, 133.

10. Laughlin's testimony is reprinted in H. H. Laughlin, *The Legal Status of Eugenical*

*Sterilization* (Chicago: Municipal Court of Chicago, 1930), 16–17; *Buck v. Bell*, 274 US 200 (1927).

11. "Eugenical Sterilization in Germany," *Eugenical News* 18 (1933): 89–90.

12. Laughlin to Grant, January 13, 1934, Laughlin papers; the speech appeared as W. Frick, "German Population and Race Politics," *Eugenical News* 19 (1934): 33–38; the original version was published as "Ansprache des Herrn Reichsministers des Innern Dr. Wilhelm Frick auf der ersten Sitzung des Sachverständigenbeirats für Bevölkerungs- und Rassen-politik," *Archiv für Rassen- und Gesellschaftsbiologie* 27 (1933): 415–419.

13. "German Eugenics, 1934," *Eugenical News* 19 (1934): 140.

14. Laughlin to Schneider (dean, Faculty of Medicine), August 11, 1936, Laughlin papers; Dr. Brauss, Dortmund health officer, quoted in "Nazis Open Race Bureau for Eugenic Segregation," *New York Times*, May 5, 1933, 9; the annotated clipping is contained in the Laughlin papers. Two scholars in the field believe that the handwriting is clearly Laughlin's, although at least one well-known scholar disagrees; see S. Kühl, *The Nazi Connection: Eugenics, American Racism, and German National Socialism* (New York: Oxford University Press, 1994), 125, and R. Proctor, *Racial Hygiene* (Cambridge, Mass.: Harvard University Press, 1988), 101, 361. Although the neatly written notation on the article clearly reflected the sentiment at Eugenics Record Office, in my own opinion it has nothing in common with Laughlin's typically illegible scrawl.

15. Laughlin to Draper, February 24, 1937 and Laughlin to Draper, n.d., but sometime in January or February 1937, Laughlin papers.

16. On Osborn's background and life, see his entry in *Current Biography* (1941): 640–641; his obituary in the *New York Times*, January 7, 1981, B12; and the autobiographical manuscript in the Osborn papers.

17. Transcript of interview with Frederick Osborn conducted by Isabel Grossner, 1967, Osborn papers.

18. F. Osborn, "The Field of Eugenic Research," *Eugenical News* 15 (1930): 115; F. Osborn, "Memorandum on the Eugenics Situation in the United States," May 24, 1933. Osborn papers. "Confidential" is typed at the top of the memo, and a handwritten note just beneath says, "Written for Rockefeller interests." Ironically, the memo contrasts Laughlin favorably with Davenport, of whom Osborn is critical, and recommends that in the interests of progress, the Eugenics Record Office with Laughlin in charge be separated from Davenport's Department of Genetics at Cold Springs Harbor. In fact, although both men were highly prejudiced and unequipped by temperament to conduct disinterested research, of the two Laughlin was more the propagandist.

19. F. Osborn, "Implications of the New Studies in Population and Psychology for the Development of Eugenic Philosophy," *Eugenical News* 22 (1937): 106; F. Osborn, "Science Contributes," *Child Study* 16 (1939): 95; F. Osborn, "The Comprehensive Program of Eugenics and Its Social Implications," *Living* (1939): 33.

20. F. Osborn, "The American Concept of Eugenics," *Eugenical News* 24 (1939): 2; F. Osborn, "The Aims of a Eugenic Program," April 10, 1935, Osborn papers.

21. Osborn, "Science Contributes," 96; Osborn, "The Comprehensive Program of Eugenics and Its Social Implications," 37.

22. F. Osborn, "The Aims of a Eugenic Program," April 10, 1935, Osborn papers; Osborn, "The Comprehensive Program of Eugenics and Its Social Implications," 37, 33–34; F. Osborn, "The Basis of Eugenic Selection," *Eugenical News* 21 (1936): 69.

23. George A. Draper's will is available as part of the file containing Wickliffe Draper's will in Surrogate's Office, New York City; among other duties Donald made out the checks for Draper's contributions to the Eugenics Research Association; see Donald to Davenport, August 24, 1929, enclosing one of Draper's contributions; Davenport papers.

24. Donald to Collector of Internal Revenue, February 15, 1938; Osborn to Collector of Internal Revenue, February 18, 1938; J. R. Kirk (deputy commissioner, Treasury Department) to Pioneer Fund, c/o Frederick Osborn, March 8, 1938; D. S. Bliss (deputy commissioner, Treasury Department) to Pioneer Fund, c/o Frederick Osborn, April 1, 1938; Osborn papers. Osborn's letter enclosed the request from Malcolm Donald as the responsible financial officer, noting that he was acting as Pioneer's correspondent only because his office was more conveniently located should a personal meeting be necessary.

25. On Harlan's background, see the comprehensive biography by T. E. Yarborough, *John Marshall Harlan* (New York: Oxford University Press, 1992), 3–13; the quotation is from page 339.

26. W. F. Weyher, letter to the editor, *Wall Street Journal*, January 9, 1995, A15.

27. *Swain v. Alabama*, 380 US 202 (1965); for Harlan's position in this case and on public accommodations, see Yarborough, *John Marshall Harlan*, 235–236, 253.

28. *Brown* II was the Supreme Court's second opinion in the classic school desegregation case, a decree on the implementation of the decision in the original opinion; see *Brown v. Board of Education*, 349 US 301 (1954). Harlan's contribution was the assertion that "it should go without saying that the vitality of these constitutional principles cannot be allowed to yield simply because of disagreement with them"; see Yarborough, *John Marshall Harlan*, 235. For the antimiscegenation case, see *Loving v. Virginia*, 388 US 1 (1966).

29. Donald to Osborn, November 2, 1938; Harlan to Osborn, November 4, 1938; Harlan papers, box 584.

30. See Laughlin to Draper, March 15, 1937, in which he raises the possibility of Pioneer support for a survey he was conducting for the state of Connecticut; Draper to Laughlin, October 8, 1937; Laughlin papers.

31. Laughlin to Fischer, July 31, 1935; Laughlin to Draper, August 15, 1935; Draper to Laughlin, August 28, 1935; Laughlin papers. Fischer was one of the leading scientific anti-Semites in the Reich, maintaining, for example, that "the Jew is an alien," to be "warded off" as a matter of "biological self-defense"; quoted in B. Müller-Hill, *Murderous Science* (Oxford, U.K.: Oxford University Press, 1988), 36–37.

32. Announcement of the film's availability was made in H. H. Laughlin, "Eugenics in Germany: Motion Picture Showing How Germany Is Presenting and Attacking Her Problems in Applied Eugenics," *Eugenical News* 22 (1937): 65–66, although Laughlin misspelled the name of the Nazi office as "Aufklarungsamt für Vevolkerungspolitik Rassenpflege"; on both the Rassenpolitisches Amt and the Aufklärungsamt für Bevölkerungspolitik und Rassenpflege, see W. Benz, H. Graml, and H. Weiss (eds.), *Enzyklopädie des Nationalsozialismus* (Stuttgart: Klett-Cotta, 1997), 658–659. For an interesting discussion on the use of the term *Aufklärung*—"enlightenment"—in the Nazi bureaucracy, see R. Proctor, *The Nazi War on Cancer* (Princeton, N.J.: Princeton University Press, 1999), 48–49. On the propaganda campaign, see S. Kühl, *The Nazi Connection*, 48. An undated document in Laughlin's personal papers (Laughlin papers, Truman State University) titled simply "The Pioneer Foundation," projecting a budget and outline of work for 1937, notes that "the two German films referred to by Colonel Draper have been received," but no mention is

ever made again of the second film. It must have been either *Sünden der Väter* (*Sins of the Fathers*) or *Abseits vom Wege* (*Off the Beaten Path*), the only other films produced by the Reich's Office of Racial Politics by this time; see K. L. Rost, *Sterilisation und Euthanasie im Film des "Dritten Reiches"* (Husum, Germany: Matthiesen, 1987).

33. Laughlin, "Eugenics in Germany." Although Laughlin certainly had sterilization in mind, his words had an unintended irony: At the time, the Nazi government was formulating a more ominous "long time plan for the prevention . . . of hereditary degeneracy": the murder of "defective" children. See H. Friedlander, *The Origins of Nazi Genocide: From Euthanasia to the Final Solution* (Chapel Hill: University of North Carolina Press, 1995).

34. The plan to promote the film is outlined in "Opportunity for Possible Service in Eugenics," n.d.; Osborn papers. Its showing to Connecticut welfare workers is noted in a letter from Laughlin to Draper, March 15, 1937, Laughlin papers.

35. Laughlin, "Eugenics in Germany," 66; the original version of the article is contained in the Osborn papers. My translation; Rost, in *Sterilisation und Euthanasie im Film des "Dritten Reiches,"* 227, gives the original as "Das jüdische Volk stellt einen besonders hohen Huntertsatz an Geisteskranken" and "55-jähriger Jude. Hinterlistig. Hetzer."

36. On Campbell's popularity with the Nazis, see Kühl, *The Nazi Connection*, 34–35; also "Praise for Nazis," *Time*, September 9, 1935, 21, which observed that "the German Press quoted Dr. Campbell by the yard." The quotations from Campbell appeared in "U.S. Eugenist Hails Nazi Racial Policy," *New York Times*, August 29, 1935, 5, and in *Time*, September 9, 1935, 20–21.

37. "The Pioneer Foundation," n.d., Donald to Laughlin, February 19, 1937, Laughlin papers.

38. The board's resolution is recorded in the minutes of its meeting, April 27, 1939, Osborn papers; the terms and conditions of the grant were described in "Announcement of Educational Scholarships," n.d., circulated in 1939 to appropriate army officers; Osborn papers, American Philosophical Society; the expenditure is detailed in a memorandum to the board from J. H. Slate Jr., April 2, 1941, Harlan papers, box 584; the actual recipients are named in the treasurer's report for the period April 26, 1938–April 21, 1941, Osborn papers.

39. See D. Blackmon, "A Breed Apart: A Long-Ago Effort to Better the Species Yields Something Else," *Wall Street Journal*, August 17, 1999, 1, 8.

40. Lindbergh's attraction to eugenics is discussed in A. S. Berg, *Lindbergh* (New York: G. P. Putnam's Sons, 1998), 373; in retrospect in 1970, he even considered the war "in a broader sense . . . lost," because "we lost the genetic heredity formed through aeons" (C. A. Lindbergh, *The Wartime Journals of Charles A. Lindbergh* [New York: Harcourt Brace Jovanovich, 1970], xv); the quotes about Germany come from Berg, *Lindbergh*, 368, and Lindbergh, *Wartime Journals*, 36; C. A. Lindbergh, "Aviation, Geography, and Race," *Reader's Digest* (November, 1939): 66, 64.

41. Draper to Osborn, March 1, 1942; a letter from Homer N. Calver, Secretary of the American Museum of Health, to Osborn, dated December 12, 1941, refers to a "Pioneer Fund Study," conducted under the museum's auspices and involving a payment of $1,500, but no further details are provided; another document, "Preparation of Exhibit on Genetics, Populations Trends, Eugenics and Racial Differences," April 21, 1941, outlines the budget for an exhibit, also planned for the American Museum of Health, although there

is no indication that it was actually carried out; all in Osborn papers. According to the report filed at the end of 1947 by Malcolm Donald, by then Pioneer's secretary, the only expenditure since February 1943 had been $25.00 "for legal services," Osborn papers.

42. Donald to Osborn, July 11, 1947, July 22, 1947, October 21, 1947; Osborn to Donald, October 20, 1947; Osborn papers.

43. B. Wallace, review of S. Kühl, *The Nazi Connection: Eugenics, American Racism and German National Socialism,* in *Journal of Heredity* 85 (1994): 497.

44. Osborn to Donald, May 25, 1948, July 25, 1947, October 20, 1947; see also Osborn to Donald, May 28, 1948; the advisory committee is suggested in Osborn to Donald, May 20, 1948 and June 16, 1948; the other suggestions are outlined in a memo by Osborn, "Development in the Field of Improving and Increasing the Proportion of the More Homogeneous Stock of the Population of the United States," June 3, 1948; all in Osborn papers.

45. Osborn to Donald, June 16, 1948; "Request for Grant," May 8, 1951, asked for $24,000 over four years, which was granted, according to "Memorandum for Mr. Osborn" from Edward N. Sherry, member of Root, Ballantine, Harlan, Bushby, & Palmer (the law firm representing Pioneer), June 12, 1951; in a letter to Draper, June 24, 1955, Osborn thanks him "for the fund which you so generously provided in 1951 to be used over a four year period"; Osborn papers.

46. F. Osborn, "Memorandum" addressed to "Mrs. Hammons" (probably a staff member at the American Eugenics Society), August 10, 1954, Osborn papers.

47. W. Draper, "Notes to Eugenics Credo," August 10, 1954, Osborn papers.

48. "FO" [Frederick Osborn], "Memorandum for the Eugenic [*sic*] Society, December 16, 1954, Osborn papers.

49. Draper to Osborn, May 31 (no year given, but clearly written in 1956); Osborn to Draper, June 14, 1956, April 28, 1958; Osborn papers.

50. See Weyher's entry in *Who's Who in America (1999)* (New Providence, N.J.: Reed Elsevier, 1998), 4742. Along with other partners in his firm, Weyher was profiled in "Lawyers Who Try Not to Try Cases, *Life* (March 9, 1962): 80–86, which led to his censure for professional misconduct because at the time it was a violation of the Canons of Professional Ethics to use the media to engage in "indirect advertisements"; see 18 A.D. 2d 466 and 240 N.Y.S. 2d 126 (1963) and "Lawyers Censured on Article in Life," *New York Times,* May 16, 1963, 26.

51. See J. Sedgwick, "The Mentality Bunker," *GQ* (November, 1994): 228–235, 250–251; H. F. Weyher, *The Weyher Genealogy, 1600–1981: A Family History for the Children of Harry Frederick Weyher Jr. and Barbara Dore Mccusker Covering the Weyher, Parrott, Carter, Green, Mccusker, Duby, and Related Families* (New York: H. F. Weyher, 1981), 241; in the same work, see also the photos of pages from "letter of nobility of General Carl Weyher von Weyherfels."

52. Weyher to Jean MacArthur, February 25, 1986; Colonel Lyman H. Hammond Jr. (executive director of the General Douglas MacArthur Foundation) to Weyher, March 17, 1986. Weyher's paternal grandmother was the great-great-great granddaughter of a man whose sister was MacArthur's great-great-great grandmother; Prescott Bush to "Sylvia" (no last name), n.d.; all in H. F. Weyher, *The Weyher Genealogy: 1992 Supplement: A Family History Covering the Weyher, Parrott, Carter, Green and Related Families* (New York: H. F. Weyher, 1992).

53. Professor of English Thomas F. Gossett's landmark book *Race: The History of an Idea in America* (New York: Schocken Books, 1965) calls *The Clansman* "a literary source of the most sordid kind of racism" (p. 272). The autobiography, published through a Pioneer grant, was T. Dixon, *Southern Horizons: The Autobiography of Thomas Dixon* (Alexandria, Va.: IWV Publishing, 1984); the excerpt quoted by Weyher appears on pp. 135–137 and is reprinted in Weyher, *The Weyher Genealogy: 1992 Supplement,* 95–96. The quote refers to the Compromise of 1877, in which Democrats did not protest the transparently corrupt election of Republican Rutherford Hayes as president in return for a guarantee that Reconstruction would be terminated and control of the South returned to ex-Confederates.

54. Marion to Weyher, January 11, 1992; Helms to Weyher, February 16, 1992; in Weyher, *The Weyher Genealogy: 1992 Supplement.*

55. Cox's last book, finished by Smith, was eventually published as E. S. Cox, *Lincoln's Negro Policy* (Richmond, Va. [publisher not named], 1972), not to be confused with the pamphlet of the same name described in chapter 1, originally printed in 1938 and then reprinted as a memorial to Cox after his death by Draper; the "Details" pamphlet was published in 1966 by the National States Rights Party, whose bylaws declared that "Jew-devils have no place in a White Christian nation"; the bylaws are quoted in J. George and L. Wilcox, *Nazis, Communists, Klansmen, and Others on the Fringe: Political Extremism in America* (Buffalo, N.Y.: Prometheus Books, 1992), 384.

56. Nelson to Smith, September 28, 1966; Nelson to Carto, February 20, 1967; Cox papers.

57. On Trevor's background, see his obituary in the *New York Times,* February 21, 1956, 33; the colleague's observation comes from Mason to Alexander Trevor (Trevor Sr.'s grandchild), December 27, 1969, Mason papers, Trevor correspondence; on Trevor's role in military intelligence and influence on Congress, see J. W. Bendersky, *The "Jewish Threat"* (New York: Basic Books, 2000), xi–xii, 124–129, 158. Goethe to Laughlin, date not legible but probably written in 1937; Goethe, document headed "P.G.," n.d., but from references in text appears to have been written in 1934; Laughlin papers.

58. Laughlin to Draper, December 9, 1938, Laughlin papers.

59. For example, Trevor worked with William Kullgren, who distributed Nazi literature and sought to "awaken America to the diabolical Jew control"; see J. R. Carlson, *Under Cover* (New York: E.P. Dutton, 1943), 147–149, 196. Trevor was also one of the U.S. sponsors of *Communism in Germany* (Berlin: Eckart Verlag, 1933), a book published in the Reich to celebrate the victory of Nazism over "Jewish Marxist-Bolshevism"; on Trevor's role, see M. Sayers and A. E. Kahn, *The Great Conspiracy* (Boston: Little, Brown), 351–352. Miller is quoted in M. A. Lee, *The Beast Reawakens* (Boston: Little, Brown, 1997), 365; on the investigation of Trevor and his organization, see Bendersky, *The "Jewish Threat,"* 280.

60. Mason to Trevor, October 11, 1969, Mason papers, Trevor correspondence.

61. See the coalition's pamphlet "Resolutions" (adopted at its annual convention in the Mayflower Hotel, February 2, 1961), Group Research Archives: "American Coalition of Patriotic Societies" folder. See also the resolutions in the *Congressional Record* 87:1 (March 22, 1961), 4516–4519; del Valle's statement on the coalition's behalf appeared in the hearings of the House Committee on Foreign Affairs, July 24, 1962, 269–270, and the resolution he offered, opposing the purchase of United Nations Bonds, appeared in the *Con-*

*gressional Record: Appendix* 87:2 (August 7, 1962), 6036–6037; the del Valle quotations are taken from his letters to Colonel J. Beaty, author of *The Iron Curtain Over America*, July 1, 1960, May 22, 1960, Beaty papers, box 1.

62. On del Valle and *Common Sense*, see George and Wilcox, *Nazis, Communists, Klansmen, and Others on the Fringe*, 299–303; also G. Thayer, *The Farther Shores of Politics: The American Political Fringe Today* (New York: Simon and Schuster, 1967), 72–74. On del Valle's relations with the American Nazi Party, see G. L. Rockwell, "Confidential Report on the Campaign in Virginia," June 12, 1965; according to a letter of appreciation from Rockwell (Rockwell to del Valle, June 12, 1965), del Valle was one of eighteen people to make a contribution to the Virginia campaign and in response received a "Certificate of Faith" signed by the commander; the report, correspondence, and certificate are all contained in the del Valle papers, box 5.

63. The resolution on the Republic of South Africa appeared in the *Congressional Record* 87:2 (July 24, 1962), 14608–14609; the resolution on war criminals appeared in the coalition's pamphlet "Resolutions" (adopted at its annual convention in the Mayflower Hotel, February 1, 1962), Group Research Archives: "American Coalition of Patriotic Societies" folder; the call for Reder's release appeared in the Coalition's 1961 "Resolutions" and also in *Congressional Record* 87:1 (March 22, 1961), 4516. The details of Reder's crime were reported in "Victims' Kin to Vote on Pardon for Nazi," *New York Times*, July 14, 1967, 2 and "Town in Italy Rejects Nazi's Clemency Plea," *New York Times*, July 17, 1967, 2. In 1985, the ailing Reder was released on humanitarian grounds five months ahead of schedule; see E. J. Dionne Jr., "Italy Frees Nazi War Criminal 5 Months Early," *New York Times*, January 25, 1985, 1–2.

64. See *Congressional Record* 87:1 (April 13, 1961), 5869; *Congressional Record* 88:2 (February 19, 1964), 3128.

65. See the correspondence concerning republication of Cox's works: Lory (official with the American Coalition of Patriotic Societies) to Ellegood (Director of Louisiana State University Press), October 17, 1958; Cox to Lory, December 2, 1958; Cox to Ellegood, December 5, 1958; Ellegood to Cox, December 10, 1958; Cox papers.

66. Cox to Goethe, August 12, 1948; Dönitz to Cox, August 30, 1958; von Leers to Cox, May 21, 1955; Günther to Cox, September 27, 1955; Lory and Stephenson to Cox, November 5, 1962; Trevor to Cox, December 21, 1962; all in Cox papers. The speakers, Henry Garrett and Robert Gayre of Gayre, are discussed in chapter 3.

67. The budget for the second quarter 1964 lists the coalition's total receipts for the year as two gifts from Draper, one for $35,000 and one for $750, Group Research Archives, "American Coalition of Patriotic Societies" folder; Ravnitzky's statement, September 27, 1999, before the National Archives and Records Administration is available at NARA's Web site, <http://www.nara.gov/iwg/papers/ravnitzk.html>.

## *Chapter 3: Our Source of Funds*

1. *Brown v. Board of Education*, 347 U.S. 494 (1954).

2. The idea for a "Southern Manifesto" was conceived by Strom Thurmond; see *Time* (March 26, 1956): 25; the full text of the manifesto and the list of endorsers appeared in A. Shuster, "96 in Congress Open Drive to Upset Integration Ruling," *New York Times*,

March 12, 1956, 1, 6; on Maryland's rejection of the Fourteenth Amendment, see *Time* (April 18, 1955): 24–25; on replacing the public school system in Georgia, South Carolina, and Mississippi, see *Time* (January 3, 1955): 42. See also G. Oldfield, *The Reconstruction of Southern Education: The Schools and the 1964 Civil Rights Act* (New York: Wiley, 1969).

3. The best study of the organization is N. R. McMillen, *The Citizens' Council* (Urbana: University of Illinois Press, 1971); on membership numbers, see E. Townsend, "White Citizens [*sic*] Councils Flourish in South," *Christian Science Monitor*, May 11, 1956, and H. L. Mitchell, "On the Rise of the White Citizens Council," January 30, 1956, Group Research Archives, "Citizens' Councils" folder.

4. On North Carolina, see *Time* (September 16, 1957): 26; Tennessee, *Time* (September 23, 1957): 14–15; Autherine Lucy and Alabama, *Time* (February 20, 1956): 40, *Time* (March 12, 1956): 97, and P. Kihss, "Negro Co-ed Is Suspended to Curb Alabama Clashes," *New York Times*, February 7, 1956, 1; Little Rock, *Time* (September 16, 1957): 23–24, (September 23, 1957): 12–14; an excellent account of the riots at the University of Mississippi can be found in J. W. Silver, *Mississippi: The Closed Society* (New York: Harcourt, Brace & World, 1966).

5. For Rosa Parks's story, see D. Brinkley, *Rosa Parks* (New York: Lipper/Viking, 2000).

6. Formation of the federation is described in A. Lewis, "Segregation Group Confers in Secret," *New York Times*, December 30, 1955, 1, 12; the composition of the advisory committee is detailed in "Plans to Coordinate Conservative Activity," *Congressional Quarterly Fact Sheet*, March 2, 1956, 229–230, and in one of the federation's newsletters, describing the organization's history, n.d. but probably 1962; Draper's donation to Abbitt is noted in his estate papers, Surrogate's Office, New York City; Weyher to North Carolina Defenders of States' Rights, Inc., January 12, 1959, George papers.

7. The possibility of a third party and its principles is discussed in "Plans to Coordinate Conservative Activity." Barr eventually led a third-party movement to support T. Coleman Andrews for president as a states' rights candidate; see McMillen, *The Citizens' Council*, 118.

8. Smith's articles appeared regularly in the federation's newsletters, which were published undated between the late 1950s and 1962; some of the articles are available in the Group Research Archives, "Federation for Constitutional Government" folder; others are in the George papers.

9. On the federation's dissolution, see McMillen, *The Citizens' Council*, 117–118; an expanded version of Brady's speech was published as T. P. Brady, *Black Monday* (Winona, Miss.: Association of Citizens' Councils, 1955), 64, 7; C. Putnam, *Race and Reason: A Yankee View* (Washington, D.C.: Public Affairs Press, 1961), 35.

10. For details of the scientists' role in the *Brown* case, see W. H. Tucker, *The Science and Politics of Racial Research* (Urbana: University of Illinois Press, 1994), 141–151.

11. W. C. George, "The Race Problem from the Standpoint of One Who Is Concerned about the Evils of Miscegenation," was issued in 1955 by the American States' Rights Association in Birmingham, Alabama; W. C. George, *Race Heredity and Civilisation: Human Progress and the Race Problem* (London: Britons, 1962) was the published version of the essay that had been circulated in mimeographed form earlier.

12. Weyher to George, March 31, 1956; Weyher to George, August 31, 1961; George papers.

13. Putnam's remark is quoted in *New York Times,* December 2, 1961, 47; the characterization of Simmons as the "organization man" is quoted in McMillen, *The Citizens' Council,* 123; the characterization as an "extremist" comes from "Racists' Strategy," *New York Times,* September 28, 1962, 22.

14. George to Edward Moore, April 26, 1957, George papers.

15. Quoted in R. W. May, "Genetics and Subversion," *The Nation* 190 (May 14, 1960): 421.

16. On the composition of the "Draper Committees," see R. W. May, "Arens Received $3,000 a Year in Draper Grants," *Capital Times,* March 18, 1960; W. Unna, "Capitol Aide's Extra Job Attacked and Defended," *Washington Post,* March 13, 1960, B12; May, "Genetics and Subversion," 420–422; and H. E. Garrett, letter to the editor, *Science* 132 (1960): 685. The Eastland quote comes from his speech in Columbia, South Carolina, January 26, 1956, distributed by the Federation for Constitutional Government.

17. On Walter and HUAC, see D. Wesley, *Hate Groups and the Un-American Activities Committee* (New York: Emergency Civil Liberties Committee, 1962); on Fish and Nazi agent George Sylvester Viereck, see J. R. Carlson, *Under Cover* (New York: E.P. Dutton, 1943), 414–416. The quotation is from "Major General George Van Horn Moseley's Testimony Before the Dies [i.e., HUAC] Committee of Congress on June 1, 1939," distributed by Western Unity Research Institute, Chalmette, La.

18. On Draper's subsidization of Bouscaren's books, see letters from A. T. Bouscaren to publisher Henry Regnery, February 8 and February 16, 1962 (Regnery papers, "Bouscaren" folder), noting that "the Draper Fund . . . contracted to subsidize the printing of 1500" copies of *Security Aspects of Immigration Work* (Milwaukee: Marquette University, 1959) and asking Regnery to consider *International Migrations Since 1945* under a similar arrangement; although the introduction to *Security Aspects* acknowledges the author's debt to a number of people, including Richard Arens, there is no mention of Draper's financial assistance. *Migrations* eventually was published by Praeger in 1963. Another work on immigration that acknowledged support from the "W.P. Draper Foundation" was J. C. Messersmith, *Illegal Entrants and Illegal Aliens in the United States* (Carbondale: Southern Illinois University, 1958).

19. Arens's resignation was reported in "News Disclosures Forcing Walter Group Aide to Quit," *Gazette and Daily* (York, Pennsylvania), April 4, 1960, 1, 10; the reference to him as the person "in charge" of the immigration studies appeared in a letter from Weyl to Gayre, September 7, 1962, Weyl papers, box 12.

20. Garrett, letter to the editor, *Science* 132 (1960): 685; for a list of Pioneer's grants from 1954 to 1971, see H. F. Weyher, "Reply to Tucker: Defending Early IQ Researchers," *Psychological Reports* 84 (1999): 487.

21. M. M. Tumin (ed.), *Race and Intelligence* (New York: Anti-Defamation League of B'nai B'rith, 1963); Garrett to George, September 24, 1963, George papers. The reply was published as H. E. Garrett, *Race, a Reply to Race and Intelligence: A Scientific Evaluation by the Anti-Defamation League of B'nai B'rith* (Washington, D.C.: National Putnam Letters Committee, 1964); the composition of the mailing list was detailed in a "Confidential Memorandum," July 15, 1962, distributed by IAAEE treasurer Donald A. Swan, a copy of which is also contained in the George papers.

22. See letters from Weyher to George forwarding "the enclosed check," December 7,

1962, December 17, 1963, December 2, 1964, December 8, 1965, December 9, 1966, December 8, 1967, George papers; Draper's estate papers containing the list of gifts during the last three years of his life are available at the Surrogate's Office, New York City.

23. Putnam to Coon, April 20, 1964, Coon papers, box 10.

24. The bequest to Garrett is listed in Draper's will, included in his estate papers; Garrett's acknowledgment appears in his letter to the editor, *Science* 132 (1960): 685.

25. Gayre to Weyl, May, 27, 1964, Weyl papers, box 12; on the purpose of the study, see "An Ethnological Survey: A Study of the Racial Drift of the African Littoral," Institute of African Affairs archives.

26. The sources of support are also discussed in "An Ethnological Survey," Institute of African Affairs archives. Gayre to Weyl, April 24, 1962; on July 28, 1962, Gayre also wrote to Weyl that "I have spoken to Professor Garrett about your needs . . . and I think that you can put into him for a grant from the Human Genetics Fund with confidence"; the grant was approved judging from a letter to Gayre, June 22, 1962, in which Weyl refers to his "able assistant" who was performing the "cataloguing"; Weyl papers, box 12.

27. Shuey to George, September 22, 1958, George papers.

28. A. I. Guobadia to G. Grosschmid with copies to the Pittsburgh Press, president of Duquesne University, and KDKA TV news, June 1, 1964; on July 24, 1964, a university news release announced the withdrawal of support for the "'Gayre' expedition," together with a reminder of the many secondary schools, colleges, hospitals, dispensaries, and orphanages supported by the Holy Ghost Fathers, who operated Duquesne; Institute of African Affairs archives.

29. Gayre to Weyl, December 21, 1964, Weyl papers, box 12.

30. Garrett to George, October 15, 1967; Weyher to Swan, Garrett, Kuttner, and George, September 17, 1963; George to Weyher, September 21, 1963; George papers. The author of the paper on human infection was identified as Benjamin Ward. See also Weyher to George, February 16, 1962 and February 24, 1962, forwarding first the draft and then the footnotes of an article by Donald Swan.

31. Weyher to Garrett, February 16, 1962, February 24, 1962; Weyher to George, August 31, 1967; George papers.

32. W. C. George, *The Biology of the Race Problem* (Report Prepared by Commission of the Governor of Alabama, distributed by the Putnam National Letters Committee, New York, 1962); in his letter to George, August 14, 1962, for example, Weyher enclosed Trevor's comments on the report, along with a "suggestion from two other sources"; see also Weyher to George, August 1, 1962, in which Weyher called to George's attention an ambiguity that "someone pointed out to me"; George papers.

33. Weyher to George, October 4, 1962; George to Weyher, October 7, 1962; Weyher to George, October 2, 1962; George papers.

34. In his letter to Putnam, October 2, 1962, Weyher requested an estimate of the number of copies needed under each of two models for distribution, "since it would be cheaper to get the requisite number now . . . while the printer is still holding the type"; Weyher, "Memorandum to Mr. Le Vine," October 1, 1962; Pittman to Harbin, May 18, 1963; George papers. A subsequent misunderstanding arose between George and the Alabama Governor's office, which believed, apparently in error, that it would be getting hundreds of copies of the report gratis from the National Putnam Letters Committee; the situation was re-

solved when George notified the state that "one of our friends who has been largely instrumental in finding funds to finance the whole deal . . . [would] authorize the Putnam
Committee to forward 400 copies to Alabama without charge." Weyher, who was making all the other decisions at the time, probably was the "friend" who did the authorizing. See George to H. N. Cook (the governor's press secretary), November 6, 1962 and
November 10, 1962, George papers.

35. The lawsuits are discussed in detail later in this chapter.

36. Hepworth to George, June 14, 1963; Putnam to Weyher, August 31, 1963; Putnam to
Weyher, n.d. but probably written in 1964 from reference to the "Les Crain" [*sic;* correct
name is "Crane"] television show; George papers.

37. R. Kendall, *White Teacher in a Black School* (New York: Devin-Adair, 1964), 113, 122,
74, 99, 164, 34. Robert Kendall, the book's author, informed Putnam that Weyher was interested in the "picture project" and that Kendall was "sending him screenplay"; Kendall
to Putnam, January 24, 1968, Shockley papers.

38. Among other places, the ad appeared in the *New York Times,* February 11, 1964, 32;
Weyher to George, April 2, 1964, George papers; the George papers also contain the regular tabulations of the responses to Putnam's book, many of them unsigned though obviously done by Weyher; the first is dated June 30, 1961, followed by reports almost monthly
between January 1962 and January 1963.

39. George to Weyher, October 15, 1962; Weyher to George, October 22, 1962; George
papers.

40. Weyher to George, September 7, 1967; Kuttner to Weyher, September 7, 1967; George
papers. The article describing the study was R. D. Lyons, "Tests on Mice Find Mental
Activity Increases Size of Brains," *New York Times,* September 5, 1967, 23; Weyher's own
critique of the study, contained in his letter to George, suggested that he was involved in
some detail with the scientific strategy of the campaign, although he appeared to con-
found "phenotypic" with "genotypic."

41. J. B. Trevor Jr., "Segregation: An Old African Custom," *Citizen* (December 1962):
10. Two years later, Trevor reported on his latest trip, describing the enviable lot of blacks
under South African apartheid and contrasting that country's progress with the "lower
economic status" of neighboring Mozambique, where "persons of any ethnic background"
were allowed access to all public facilities; fortunately, however, the requirement of "suit-
able standards of . . . cleanliness and personal behavior" ensured that "only a small number of non-whites . . . are found in most hotels and restaurants"; J. B. Trevor Jr., "Fact vs.
Fiction in South Africa," *Citizen* (January 1965): 8–9.

42. George to Smith, February 15, 1962, George papers.

43. A. James Gregor, the IAAEE's secretary, quoted in a notice of the association's founding in *Eugenics Review* 52 (1960): 135–136.

44. On Garrett's background and career, see A. S. Winston, "Science in the Service of
the Far Right: Henry E. Garrett, the IAAEE, and the Liberty Lobby," *Journal of Social Issues* 54 (1998): 179–210; according to Winston, Garrett requested an appointment in Virginia's psychology department, only to be rejected because of his views on race, but was
then accepted by the education department, which was "pleased to have a person of such
prestige" (182).

45. H. E. Garrett, "The Scientific Racism of Juan Comas," *Mankind Quarterly* 2 (1961):

106; H. E. Garrett, letter to the editor, *Science* 135 (1962): 984; H. E. Garrett, *Race: A Reply to Race and Intelligence*, 8.

46. H. E. Garrett, "Klineberg's 'Negro-White Differences in Intelligence Test Performance,'" *Mankind Quarterly* 4 (1964): 222; H. E. Garrett, "Review of *Heredity and the Nature of Man* (by T. Dobzhansky)," *Mankind Quarterly* 6 (1966): 241; H. E. Garrett, letter to the editor, *Current Anthropology* 2 (1961): 320; interview with Garrett, *U.S. News & World Report* (November 18, 1963): 93.

47. Garrett to George, March 1, 1961, George papers.

48. H. E. Garrett, "The Equalitarian Dogma," *Mankind Quarterly* 1 (1961): 256. With some omissions the same article was also published as H. E. Garrett, "The Equalitarian Dogma," *Perspectives in Biology and Medicine* 4 (1961): 480–484, and the *Perspectives* version was then reprinted as H. E. Garrett, "One Psychologist's View of 'Equality of the Races,'" *U.S. News & World Report* (August 14, 1961): 72–74. Along with all overt references to Jews, the latter two versions also omitted the original's observation that "application of the equalitarian dogma, as in the school desegregation cases, inevitably foments dissention and bitterness on which the Communist thrives. Communists and their frontmen have served the cause of equalitarianism well: in government, in entertainment, in radio, and television"; readers of the *Mankind Quarterly* would have no difficulty in recognizing these areas as also an allusion to Jews on Garrett's part.

49. On the formation of the Northern League, see M. Billig, *Psychology, Racism & Fascism* (Birmingham, England: A.F. & R. Publications, 1979), 7; on the threat of "unhealthy stock," see R. Pearson, "Sir Arthur Keith and Evolution," *Northern World* (July–August, 1957), 4–7, which was also reprinted as "A Northern League Pamphlet." In a letter to Cox, June 22, 1957, Carto noted that "E.L. Anderson, Ph.D. is a pen name of mine," explaining that "since the American people have so much respect for titles and since they have lost the capacity to think for themselves, a Ph.D. is a good way to attract attention," Cox papers; according to journalist William W. Turner, the name was taken from the deceased uncle of one of Carto's assistants; see W. W. Turner, *Power on the Right* (Berkeley, Calif.: Ramparts Press, 1971), 152. In *Right* Carto had praised his alter ego for "mak[ing] history" with his new philosophy, calling "Dr. Anderson . . . the Mendel of cultural science"; editorial, *Right*, No. 57, June, 1960. Pearson acknowledged that he was the editor of *Western Destiny* in a letter to Cox, September 17, 1965, Cox papers.

50. Because *Western Destiny* was the successor to Pearson's journal *Folk*, itself the continuation of *Northern World*, its first issue was already the beginning of Volume 9 (June 1964); in a tactic frequently used by both Carto and Pearson, the letters-to-the-editor section on the same page noting "E.L. Anderson" as an associate editor included a submission from Willis Carto, praising the new journal and pledging to "count me . . . as a charter subscriber"; the description of the Culture Distorter comes from the first issue's editorial, *Western Destiny*, 9 (June 1964): 5.

51. Readers of *Western Destiny* were welcomed to its continuation as "the new *Mercury*" with a note that "they will see many of their friends on our new Board of Contributing Editors, so they should feel at home"; *American Mercury* (June 1966): 8; the "Hitlerian" characterization is from F. P. Mintz, *The Liberty Lobby and the American Right: Race, Conspiracy, and Culture* (Westport, Conn.: Greenwood Press, 1985), 105.

52. M. Roeder, "Germany Alive!" *American Mercury* (Summer 1975): 37; on Roeder's back-

ground, see R. Hill, *The Other Face of Terror: Inside Europe's Neo-Nazi Network* (London: Grafton Books), 190, 232, and K. P. Tauber, *Beyond Eagle and Swastika: German Nationalist Since 1945, Vol. II* (Middletown, Conn.: Wesleyan Press, 1967), 1251 (n.559). A. Hitler, "The Illogical War," *American Mercury* (Winter 1976): 32–35; K. Johns, "Otto Skorzeny, Soldier of the West," *American Mercury* (Winter 1974): 11–14; see also *Mercury*'s brief eulogy, "In Memoriam, Otto Skorzeny, 1908–1975" (Fall 1975): inside back cover; on Skorzeny and the coup, see M. A. Lee, *The Beast Reawakens* (Boston: Little, Brown, 1997), 4–5.

53. H. E. Garrett, "How Classroom Desegregation Works," *Citizen* (February 1966): 20; H. E. Garrett, "Scientist Explains Race Differences," *Citizen* (January 1968): 21; H. E. Garrett, "How Classroom Desegregation Will Work," *Citizen* (October 1965): 14; a videotape of Garrett's interview is available from the Mississippi Department of Archives and History.

54. "Jewized Gentiles," *Truth Seeker* 86 (September 1959): 131; C. S. [Smith], "A Proposed Resolution for a Congress of Freethinkers," *Truth Seeker* 84 (August 1957): 124. The publication defined "Jewize" as "to fit with Jewish verbal response patterns preventing the causal thought required for discriminatory protection" and explained that "slogans . . . such as 'We are all brothers' . . . are the means of *Jewizing*," *Truth Seeker* 84 (May 1957): 76.

55. R. Kuttner, "Biopolitics: The Theory of Racial Nationalism," *Truth Seeker* 86 (March, 1959): 41, 42; see also R. Kuttner, "Manifestoes and Resolutions on Race," *Truth Seeker* 84 (August 1957): 119, and R. Kuttner, "Biopolitics: The Validity of Racial Nationalism," *Truth Seeker* 86 (September, 1959): 129–131.

56. Kuttner's series in *Northern World* appeared as "The North European in Homeric Greece" 3 (July–August 1958): 8–16; "The North European in Ancient Rome" 3 (September–October 1958): 12–19; "The Early History of the Celt" 3 (November–December 1958): 12–19; and "The Early History of the Teuton" 3 (January–February 1959): 12–20. To *South African Observer* he contributed "Race and Democracy" (August 1957): 4–5; "Negro Leaders Set Precedent for Intra-Racial Marriages" (September 1959): 9; and "Forgotten Sciences" (July 1962): 12–13.

57. Carto to Cox, December 5, 1956, January 26, 1957, Cox papers.

58. "With this Sixtieth Issue, Right Discontinues Publication," *Right* (September 1960): 3, 4; R. E. Kuttner, "What Do We Owe the Negroes?" *American Mercury* (Spring 1967): 7, 8.

59. "Statement of Dr. Kuttner," in *Hearings before Subcommittee No. 5 of the Committee on the Judiciary on Miscellaneous Proposals Regarding the Civil Rights of Persons within the Jurisdiction of the United States,* HR 88-1 (July 19, 1963): 1964–1967, 1971.

60. R. E. Kuttner, "Race Mixing: Suicide or Salvation?" *American Mercury* (Winter 1971): 45, 48; R. E. Kuttner, "Integrated Living," *The Citizen* (October 1970): 16.

61. The address was reprinted in two installments as R. E. Kuttner, "Northern Light on Southern Scene," *The Citizen;* the quotes are from November 1972 (31) and December 1972 (24).

62. A. J. Gregor, "National Socialism and Race," *The European* 11 (1958): 286, 284. The differences with Pearson and Kuttner, which were hinted at in this article, were made explicit three years later when Gregor criticized *Northern World* for publishing unsigned, paraphrased excerpts from Günther's work in 1927 "without the least effort to bring them up to date." By 1939, these "fables," as Gregor called them, "were explicitly rejected by the

Head of the Rassenpolitischen Amtes of the NSDAP"; see Gregor, "Nordicism Revisited," *Phylon* 22 (1961): 352, 357.

63. Gregor to Weyl, March 28, 1963, Weyl papers, box 12.

64. A. J. Gregor, "On the Nature of Prejudice," *Eugenics Review* 52 (1961): 217, 219.

65. Armstrong's letter of opposition, dated April 20, 1939, was introduced into the record by John B. Trevor during congressional testimony; see "Admission of German Refugee Children," Joint Hearings before a Subcommittee of the Committee on Immigration, United States Senate, and a Subcommittee on Immigration and Naturalization, House of Representatives, 76th Congress, 1st Session, on S.J. Res. 64 and H.J. Res. 168, Joint Resolutions to Authorize the Admission into the United States of a Limited Number of German Refugee Children (April 20, 21, 22, and 24, 1939): 219. I am indebted to Keith Hurt for calling this testimony to my attention.

66. C. P. Armstrong and A. J. Gregor, "Integrated Schools and Negro Character Development," *Psychiatry* 27 (1964): 70, 71.

67. Interview of May Swan, Donald's mother, by Keith Hurt, October 29 and 30, 1987 and December 12, 1987, transcript in my possession.

68. H. K. Thompson, "I Am an American Fascist," *Exposé* (August 1954): 1, 4, 7; on Thompson and Remer, see Lee, *The Beast Reawakens.*

69. D. A. Swan, letter to the editor, *Exposé* (September 1954): 4.

70. See Swan's letter to Carleton Coon, April 23, 1960, attempting to interest the University of Pennsylvania anthropologist in contributing to the IAAEE's edited collection of essays, Coon papers, box 10; also Swan's letter to George, n.d., announcing the second annual meeting of the IAAEE on April 22, 1961, George papers.

71. Swan's various contributions to the *Stell* legal case are mentioned in a number of letters: Swan to George, April 15, 1963; Pittman to Swan, March 5, 1963; March 11, 1963; Pittman to Garrett, George, and Putnam, April 4, 1963; Putnam to Gregor, April 8, 1963; George papers. The comment on the falling out was made by Ernest van den Haag in an interview with Keith Hurt, December 6, 1987, transcript in my possession; in a publication discussing the role played by scientists associated with the *Mankind Quarterly,* Leonard did remark, however, that "much of the credit for collating and organizing the available data belongs to an Assistant Editor, Donald A. Swan"; see G. S. Leonard, "Ethnic Differentiation in the United States School Desegregation Cases," *Mankind Quarterly* 6 (1966): 144.

72. Garrett to George, September 24, 1963, describing Swan's role in combining and translating contributions of different authors, George papers.

73. See R. Walsh, "Probe PO Fraud, Find Arms Cache," *New York Daily News,* April 6, 1966, 5; also "Anti-Semitic Tracts Found at Home of New Yorker Arrested for Fraud," *Jewish Telegraphic Agency Daily News Bulletin* 33 (April 7, 1966): 4; Swan's use of an ethnic slur to the judge was mentioned by Robert Kuttner's wife, Kay, when interviewed by Keith Hurt, December 20, 1987, transcript in my possession.

74. In a letter to Stanford physicist William Shockley, January 25, 1973, Weyher explained that books intended for him from Draper's library "were selected by Donald Swan as being those of particular use in your own research," Shockley papers; Thompson is quoted in K. Coogan, *Dreamer of the Day: Francis Parker Yockey and the Postwar Fascist International* (New York: Autonomedia, 1999), 481; Pioneer's purchase of Swan's library is noted in the fund's IRS records; interview with May Swan by Keith Hurt.

75. On Viereck and the "Viereck circle," see Coogan, *Dreamer of the Day*, 102, 119, 256, 261, 428 and Lee, *The Beast Reawakens*, 105, and Carlson, *Under Cover*, 125–131, 414–416; Coogan's *Dreamer* is the best source on the mysterious Yockey. On Tansill, see "American University Dismisses Professor with Nazi Leanings," *New York Times*, March 9, 1937, 3; D. Perkins, "F.D.R. Gets the Blame" (review of Tansill's *Back Door to War*), *New York Times*, May 11, 1952, section VII, p. 3; Tansill's obituary in the *Washington Post*, November 13, 1964, C6; and *Time* (June 16, 1947): 49.

76. A. S. Winston, "Saving the Race: Herbert Sanborn and Neo-Nazi Movements, 1954–1967," paper presented at the annual meeting of the American Psychological Association, Boston, August 1999; the Sanborn quotation is from "Summum Jus, Summa Injuria," the enlarged manuscript of an article that appeared in the February 1963 issue of *The Cross and the Flag*, published by notorious anti-Semite Gerald L. K. Smith, head of the Christian Nationalist Crusade; the manuscript can be found in the Johnson papers.

77. See the "1st Interim Report" of the Emergency City-Wide Committee for the Preservation of Freedom of Choice by Gregor, February 28, 1958, and Swan to George, October 13, 1958, George papers. A copy of the "Announcement," February 15, 1960, signed by Swan and addressed specifically to Sanborn, is contained in the Herbert C. Sanborn archives, Vanderbilt University; I am indebted to Andrew S. Winston for giving me a copy of this document.

78. The "Certificate of Incorporation" (February 21, 1959), Queens County Supreme Court Justice J. I. Shapiro's "Memorandum" on the application (May 13, 1959), Avins's "Memorandum of Law in Support of Application" (June 3, 1959), and Shapiro's response, "Memorandum in Matter of Application" (July 9, 1959) are all on file in Supreme Court of the Borough of Queens, New York; see also Application of Association for the Preservation of Freedom of Choice, Inc.," 188 N.Y.S.2d 885–890 and "Charter Denied to 'Hate' Group," *New York Times*, July 15, 1959, 12. The characterization of Shapiro's ruling is from *Right* No. 47.

79. *Association for the Preservation of Freedom of Choice, Inc. v. Dudley*, 222 N.Y.S.2d 631; *Association for the Preservation of Freedom of Choice, Inc. v. Pickering*, 226 N.Y.S.2d 857.

80. A. Avins, "Anti-Discrimination Legislation in Housing: A Denial of Freedom of Choice," in *Open Occupancy vs. Forced Housing under the Fourteenth Amendment: A Symposium on Anti-Discrimination Legislation*, ed. A. Avins (New York: Bookmailer), 41–42; for Avins's testimony see his statements in *Hearings Before Subcommittee No. 5 of the Committee on the Judiciary*, House of Representatives, 89th Congress, 2d session and *Hearings Before the Subcommittee on Constitutional Rights of the Committee on the Judiciary*, U.S. Senate, 89th Congress, 2d session.

81. Gayre to Weyl, May 31, 1965, Weyl papers, box 12.

82. The "Statement of Aims and Objectives" appeared at the end of publications in the IAAEE reprint series. Garrett to "Dear Friend," n.d.; O'Keefe to George, April 10, 1965; George papers.

83. G. R. Gayre, *Teuton and Slav on the Polish Frontier* (London: Eyre and Spottiswoode, 1944), 30, 11, 33–38; see Billig, *Psychology, Racism & Fascism*, 13, and Coogan, *Dreamer of the Day*, 480, who speculates that Gayre may have been "a guiding light behind the NL's creation"; R. Gayre of Gayre, "Review of *The Religious Attitudes of the Indo-Europeans*," *Mankind Quarterly* 9 (1969): 143.

84. Gayre to Weyl, August 12, 1961, April 23, 1963, Weyl papers, box 12.

85. Gayre to Weyl, July 14, 1964, June 21, 1965, May 27, 1964, Weyl papers, box 12.

86. Gayre to Weyl, July 14, 1964, April 11, 1966, Weyl papers, box 12; for Gayre's contributions to the *South African Observer,* see R. Gayre, "Abuse of Anthropological Data" (May 1961): 13–14; R. Gayre, "Negrophile Falsification of Racial History" (November 1967): 8–10; no doubt with Gayre's assistance, the *Observer* also reprinted other articles from the *Quarterly,* such as H. E. Garrett, "The Equalitarian Dogma" (October 1961): 15. To obtain a South African passport, Gayre's strategy was first to acquire an Irish passport, an ironic plan in view of his opinion of the Irish as "a fractious belligerent quarrelsome, low grade, mentally-speaking, stock"; Gayre to Weyl, May 6, 1967, Weyl papers, box 12.

87. In a letter, July 23, 1947, Donald, Pioneer's treasurer described for Osborn, then its president, a meeting with Draper and Gates, in which the Colonel sought the geneticist's suggestions, Osborn papers; W. C. Boyd, review of *Human Ancestry: From a Genetical Point of View* by R. R. Gates, *American Journal of Physical Anthropology* 6 (1948): 386.

88. R. R. Gates, *Heredity in Man* (London: Constable, 1929), 329; N. A. Thompson, letter to the editor, *Eugenics Review* 27 (1936): 351.

89. Gates to George, April 29, 1952, George papers.

90. Gayre to Weyl, June 21, 1965, June 28, 1965; Weyl papers, box 12; D. J. Ingle, "Racial Differences and the Future," *Science* 146 (1964): 378; on Ingle and the "Dogma," see Tucker, *The Science and Politics of Racial Research,* 155–157. D. J. Ingle, "Comments on the Teachings of Carleton Putnam," *Mankind Quarterly* 4 (1963): 28–42; a typical editorial insertion (29) declared that "no amount of early training will make a terrier a sheep-dog"; in addition, Ingle's article was followed by an angry rejoinder, C. Putnam, "A Reply to Dwight Ingle," *Mankind Quarterly* 4 (1963): 43–48.

91. Morrison (private secretary to Gayre at *The Mankind Quarterly*) to O'Keefe (Executive Director, IAAEE), February 19, 1968, Weyl papers, box 12. Newby's book was *Challenge to the Court: Social Scientists and the Defense of Segregation, 1954–1966* (Baton Rouge: Louisiana State University Press, 1967); after protests to the press by the scientists, a revised edition was published two years later appending responses by Gregor, Gayre, George, and a number of others.

92. George to Gayre, November 15, 1960; Gayre to George, November 19, 1960; George papers.

93. Gayre to George, November 19, 1960; George to Gayre, November 28, 1960; George to Gayre, January 9, 1961; Gayre to George, January 17, 1961; George papers.

94. Garrett to "Dear Friend," n.d.; Garrett to George, April 10, 1965; George papers.

95. "Editorial," *Mankind Quarterly* 1 (1960): 4; D. Purves, "The Evolutionary Basis of Race Consciousness," *Mankind Quarterly* 1 (1960): 51, 53–54.

96. E. R. Hall, "Zoological Subspecies of Man," *Mankind Quarterly* 1 (1960): 118; the article had originally appeared in the *Journal of Mammalogy* 27 (1946): 358–364 and was recommended by Kuttner in "Manifestoes and Resolutions on Race," *Truth Seeker* (August 1957): 119.

97. Both the resignation and the reply are described in B. Skerlj, letter to the editor, *Man* 60 (1960): 172.

98. W. A. Massey, "The New Fanatics," *Mankind Quarterly* 3 (1962): 79–81; W. Arnold, "The Evolution of Man in Relation to That of the Earth, Part V," *Mankind Quarterly* 10

(1969): 86, 98. On this faction of postwar Nazi strategy, see Lee, *The Beast Reawakens,* especially the sections on Otto Ernst Remer; also Coogan, *Dreamer of the Day,* 167–181. The first word in the title of Yockey's book, *Imperium: The Philosophy of History and Politics* (Sausalito, Calif.: Noontide Press, 1962), was his term for a consolidated Europe.

99. R. Ford, review of *White America* by E. S. Cox, *Mankind Quarterly* 7 (1966): 118, 119.

100. R. Gayre, review of *Racial Kinship: The Dominant Factor in Nationhood* by H. B. Isherwood, *Mankind Quarterly* 17 (1976): 153; H. B. Isherwood, *Racial Kinship: The Dominant Factor in Nationhood* (Ladbroke, U.K.: Racial Preservation Society, 1974), 13, 28–30. Ray Hill's experiences with the Racial Preservation Society are described in his book, *The Other Face of Terror,* 29–38; also on Isherwood and the Society, see Billig, *Psychology, Racism & Fascism,* 12, 17.

101. G. Young, *Two Worlds—Not One: Race and Civilization* (London: Ad Hoc, 1969), 23, 73, 28, 44, 126, 115, 114, 127; H. B. Isherwood, review of *Two Worlds—Not One: Race and Civilization* by G. Young, *Mankind Quarterly* 11 (1970): 61.

102. See Thompson's statement in Coogan, *Dreamer of the Day,* 481.

103. See Bulletin #3, "Is *Force* the Christian Approach to the Brotherhood of Man," and Bulletin #4, "One Race by Amalgamation or Two Races as Divinely Created?" (n.d. but probably 1956); Roland's employment by the Citizens' Councils was mentioned in Garrett to George, November 11, 1961, bulletins and letter from the George papers. Roland's contribution to the series was IAAEE Reprint No. 14, H. M. Roland and D. A. Swan, *Race, Psychology and Education: Wilmington, N.C.* (New York: IAAEE, n.d.), which had appeared originally in *Mankind Quarterly* 6 (1965): 19–36.

104. C. C. Josey, IAAEE Monographs No. 1, *An Inquiry Concerning Racial Prejudice* (New York: IAAEE, 1965), 1, 21.

105. Swan to George, December 12, 1960, George papers; the UNESCO statements are reprinted in *The Race Question in Modern Science* (New York: Columbia University Press, 1961); T. Jefferson, *Notes on the State of Virginia* (New York: Harper and Row, 1964), 133.

106. Swan to Coon (who declined the invitation to contribute to the book), April 23, 1960, Coon papers, box 10; O'Keefe to Weyl, Weyl papers, box 12.

107. R. E. Kuttner, ed., *Race and Modern Science* (New York: Social Science Press), xx, xxv (quoting H. Weinert), xvii (quoting G. A. Heuse). One of the contributors, Friedrich Keiter, had authored works under the Nazi administration such as *Kurzes Lehrbuch der Rassenbiologie und Rassenhygiene* ["Brief Textbook of Racial Biology and Eugenics"] (Stuttgart: Enke, 1944) and *Rassenpsychologie; Einführung in eine werdende Wissenschaft* ["Racial Psychology; Introduction to a Growing Science"] (Leipzig: P. Reclam, 1941).

108. C. Gini, "Race and Sociology," in ibid., 270–271; A. J. Gregor, "Evolutionary Theory, Race, and Society," in ibid., 287, 279, 295; L. Gedda, "A Study of Racial and Subracial Crossing," in ibid., 123.

109. J. Comas, "'Scientific' Racism Again?" a response to the appearance of the *Mankind Quarterly,* was the lead article in *Current Anthropology* 2 (1961): 303–314, followed by twenty "Comments" from various scientists, including Gayre and other supporters as well as critics of the journal.

110. Copies of old Sons of Liberty book lists are available in the Group Research Archives, "New Patriot" folder; the announcement by Britons appeared in *Northern World* 4 (Yule 1959/60): 50.

111. Swan to Jones (Mississippi State Sovereignty Commission), June 12, 1961; Swan to Sumrall (Department of Education, Jackson, Mississippi), June 8, 1961; Sovereignty Commission Files. See also "Promotion of Race Study Sought," *Nashville Banner,* July 1961 (specific date not given), attached to letter, Swan to George, July 26, 1961, in George papers. For the internal dispute, see H. Singer, "National Ideology or Science?: Race under Discussion," *Mankind Quarterly* 11 (1970): 61–63 and the response, H. Kiesel, "Race, the 'Nation of Europe' and Ideology: A Critique," *Mankind Quarterly* 12 (1971): 111–115.

112. Group Research Archives, "International Association for the Advancement of Ethnology and Eugenics" folder.

113. The IAAEE received $2,000 ($8,000 AFI) in 1973, $2,000 ($6,300) in 1976, $13,800 ($38,300) in 1977, $13,500 ($37,000) in 1978, $25,500 ($62,700) in 1979, $21,500 ($46,600) in 1980, and $4,500 ($8,800) in 1981.

114. On the details of Putnam's life, see R. M. Thomas Jr., "Carleton Putnam Dies at 96, Led Delta and Wrote on Race," *New York Times,* March 16, 1998, B7, and T. R. Waring, Foreword to Putnam, *Race and Reason,* iii; the biography was C. Putnam, *Theodore Roosevelt, Vol. I: The Formative Years, 1858–1886* (New York: Charles Scribner's Sons, 1958). Among other personal contacts, Putnam's correspondence mentions "my classmate who was Eisenhower's special assistant," three Supreme Court justices, half a dozen senators, Vice President Spiro Agnew, and FBI director J. Edgar Hoover; Putnam to Shockley, July 23, 1968, April 23, 1969 (should probably be May 23 according to the postmark), Shockley papers.

115. The editorial, supporting the court's decision, was "Dabney vs. Dabbs on Integration," *Life,* September 22, 1958, 34; Putnam, *Race and Reason,* 1, 4–9.

116. Ibid., 10–14. The open letter, published as an advertisement, appeared in, for example, the *New York Times,* January 5, 1959, 19; although Putnam attributed great significance to the overwhelmingly positive nature of the responses, in fact the advertisement had specifically requested readers who "wished to aid in publicizing the Putnam letter" to reply.

117. Ibid., 15, 16.

118. Putnam to Coon, June 12, 1960, June 21, 1960, August 22, 1960, Coon papers, box 10; according to Putnam, the original publisher had been Devin-Adair, which later issued *White Teacher in a Black School* and was well known for right-wing literature but wanted to put off Putnam's book "three years to protect [its own] *The Case for the South*"; on the earlier agreement between Draper and a publisher, see note 18.

119. Putnam, *Race and Reason,* 16, 23, 47, 118, 85.

120. C. Putnam, *Race and Reality: A Search for Solutions* (Washington, D.C.: Public Affairs Press, 1967), 21; Putnam, *Race and Reason,* 48.

121. With questionable logic, Putnam wrote that, according to Garrett, who was at Columbia at the same time as Boas, "there is no question [Boas] had a communist cell whether or not he personally was aware of it," Putnam to Coon, August 1, 1960, Coon papers, box 10; the entry for Boas in the Myers G. Lowman archives (Hoover Institution), which kept track of the "affiliations" of suspect citizens, reports the usual evidence leading to an accusation of communist sympathies: Boas signed a statement in 1941 calling for solidarity against "Hitlerism" and participated in a number of other civil libertarian and antifascist activities.

122. Putnam, *Race and Reason,* 117, 28, 94, 92, 68; Putnam, *Race and Reality,* 172.

123. R. R. Gates, H. E. Garrett, R. Gayre of Gayre, and W. C. George, Introduction to Putnam, *Race and Reason,* vii–viii; George to Garrett, January 3, 1961, George papers.

124. One social scientist reported receiving two of the form letters; see D. C. Simmons, "A Yankee Looks at the Races," *New Republic,* September 10, 1962, 23. The quote on distribution is from Putnam to Coon, June 12, 1960, Coon papers, box 10.

125. See T. Dobzhansky, "A Bogus 'Science' of Race Prejudice," *Journal of Heredity* 52 (1961): 190.

126. "Memorandum," providing a summary of the clippings received through November 30, 1962, unsigned, though written by Weyher as the latest in a series of identical monthly reports that *did* bear his name; "Race and Reason," a report on the "reception" of the book, unsigned, though also written by Weyher, much of the language being identical to that in his signed summaries; a copy of the Mississippi proclamation is attached to the report; George papers. On the response in Mississippi and Louisiana, see also "Science and Segregation: The American Anthropological Association Dips into Politics," *Science* 134 (1961): 1868.

127. "Alabama Orders Study of Races," *New York Times,* November 3, 1961, 1.

128. George to [Rev.] Jones, March 23, 1944; George to Umstead, May 20, 1954; George papers. George's conflict with the clergy went on for some years. When a bishop, in support of combining white and black parishes, spoke of the church's interest in saving souls, George replied (George to Waters, June 2, 1953) that "it is men's bodies that you are bringing together. . . . There is no breeding in heaven, [but] . . . by . . . promoting the amalgamation of the . . . races we would be participating in the greatest sin of this generation."

129. In addition to the previously noted correspondence between Weyher and George, there are some twenty letters in George's archives, between December 1961 and August 1962, containing Garrett's and especially Putnam's detailed suggestions for revising the report, almost all of which George followed.

130. W. C. George, *The Biology of the Race Problem* (Report prepared by commission of the governor of Alabama, distributed by the National Putnam Letters Committee, New York, 1962), 1, 77–78.

131. George to Fox, September 12, 1959, George papers; George, *The Biology of the Race Problem,* 85–86. Boas had been the principal culprit and target of the racist wing of the eugenics movement since the Madison Grant era; see Grant to Perkins, March 7 (no year, but probably 1924), Scribner's archives, "Maxwell Perkins" file.

132. How best to exploit the report's submission was discussed in Putnam to George, July 12, 1962; Simmons to George, August 7, 1962 and September 10, 1962; George papers.

133. D. Swan, "Draft of Prospective Bulletin to Be Distributed by the National Putnam Letters Committee" (the final version of the bulletin was signed by Sanborn, a member of IAAEE's Executive Committee and professor emeritus at Vanderbilt), George papers. The IAAEE's return address was P.O. Box 3495; the National Putnam Letters Committee's was P.O. Box 3518.

134. In a letter to George, October 6, 1962, Weyher recounted IAAEE member Donald Swan's suggestion that the report be issued by "some . . . body in Georgia," probably a reflection of the involvement of Georgia attorney R. Carter Pittman, who would soon use it in a court case in that state; Trevor, in his response to Weyher, October 5, 1962, men-

tioned but then rejected the possibility that his own group, the American Coalition of Patriotic Societies, would sponsor distribution; Putnam's letter to Weyher, October 9, 1962, included the suggestion actually used in the publication; the suggestions to treat George's report in the same manner as *Race and Reason* appeared in Putnam to Weyher, October 9, 1962 and Trevor to Weyher, October 10, 1962; George papers.

135. Trevor to Weyher, October 5, 1962, George papers.

136. Bailey to George, December 9, 1963, September 20, 1963, George papers.

137. Garrett to George, November 12, 1964, George papers; Gayre to Weyl, March 23, 1964, Weyl papers, box 12.

138. W. A. Massey, "The New Fanatics," *Mankind Quarterly* 3 (1963): 79, 81; the article reappeared in two installments as W. A. Massey, "The New Fanatics: Part One," *Conservative Review* (November 1992), and W. A. Massey, "The New Fanatics: Part Two," *Conservative Review* (December 1992).

139. Synon's career as an activist is described in his obituary: H. Burchard, "John J. Synon, Fought for Conservative Causes," *Washington Post,* April 8, 1972, 10.

140. H. E. Garrett, *How Classroom Desegregation Will Work* (Richmond, Va.: Patrick Henry Press, n.d. but probably 1965); the photographs appeared in H. E. Garrett, "How Classroom Desegregation Will Work," *The Citizen* (October 1965): 13; distribution of the pamphlets was reported in M. Folsom, "Anti-Negro, Anti-Semitic Booklets Flood Suburbs," *New York Times,* December 19, 1965, 48.

141. H. E. Garrett, *Breeding Down* (Richmond, Va.: Patrick Henry Press, n.d. but probably 1966); Garrett was quoted in "Lesson in Bias," *Newsweek* (May 30, 1966): 63; his definition of "racist" was offered in H. E. Garrett, *Desegregation: Fact and Hokum* (Richmond, Va.: Patrick Henry Press, n.d. but probably 1965).

142. Putnam, *Race and Reality,* 66.

143. Pittman's associations are cited in McMillen, *The Citizens' Council,* 83–84; R. C. Pittman, "Equality versus Liberty: The Eternal Conflict," *American Bar Association Journal* 46 (1960): 874, 878; the story about Carter, by Margaret Shannon for the *Atlanta Journal-Constitution,* was reprinted in *Congressional Record: Appendix* 87:2 (June 14, 1962), A4423.

144. The best accounts of the *Stell* case are the decision itself, *Stell v. Savannah-Chatham Board of Education,* 220 F.Supp. 667–685, and R. C. Pittman, "The 'Blessings of Liberty' v. The 'Blight of Equality,'" *North Carolina Law Review* 42 (1963): 86–105.

145. Editorial, "A Good First Step on the Road to Reversal," *Citizen* (May 1963): 2; W. J. Simmons, "Reversing the 'Black Monday' Decision!" *Citizen* (December 1963): 17; the description of the intervenors and their claim are quoted in Newby, *Challenge to the Court,* 195–197.

146. Pittman to Bloch, Cowart, and Weyher (with copies to Swan, Gregor, Kuttner, Garrett, Osborne, and Putnam), November 21, 1962, George papers; R. T. Osborne, "School Achievement of White and Negro Children of the Same Mental and Chronological Ages," *Mankind Quarterly* 2 (1962): 26–29; Osborne's gifts are mentioned in Draper's estate papers; Pittman to Swan, March 5, 1963, alludes to the appendices and indicates that Swan assembled the evidence and prepared a "rough draft" of the "scientific" allegations; see also Pittman to Swan, April 29, 1963; George papers.

147. Pittman to Garrett, George, and Putnam (with copies to Osborne, McGurk, Swan, Kuttner, Gregor, Weyl, Bloch, and Cowart, April 4, 1963, George papers.

148. Ibid.; on the meeting in Atlanta, see Pittman to Garrett and fourteen others, April 15, 1963, announcing reservation of a block of rooms and the conference facilities at the Biltmore, George papers.

149. Gregor to Putnam, April 10, 1963; Putnam to Pittman, February 25, 1963, April 8, 1963, April 15, 1963; George papers.

150. See *Stell v. Savannah-Chatham;* Osborne mentions Pioneer's payment for his expenses as an expert witness in Osborne to Weyher, December 6, 1977, Shockley papers; on Coon's secret advice to Putnam, see Coon to Putnam, June 17, 1960, July 10, 1960, July 28, 1960, August 4, 1960, August 25, 1960, September 3, 1960, September, 1960, Coon papers, box 10. In ironic contrast to Coon's suggestion that blacks were less capable because they had evolved later than whites, two decades later J. Philippe Rushton, a Pioneer grantee discussed in chapter 4, found blacks intellectually inferior as a consequence of their *earlier* evolution; see J. P. Rushton, "Race Differences in Behavior: A Review and Evolutionary Analysis," *Personality and Individual Differences* 9 (1988): 1009–1024, and J. P. Rushton, "Do r-K Strategies Underlie Human Race Differences," *Canadian Psychology* 32 (1991): 29–42.

151. Simmons, "Reversing the 'Black Monday' Decision!" 18; Putnam, *Race and Reality,* 83.

152. *Stell v. Savannah-Chatham,* 684; for the appeal, see *Stell v. Savannah-Chatham,* 318 F.2d 425 (1963) and 333 F.2d 55 (1964).

153. *Evers v. Jackson Municipal Separate School District,* 232 F.Supp 241 (1964); "Bill" (Simmons) to "Critz" (George), May 22, 1964, George papers; for the segregationists' view of the Evers case, see *The Evers Opinion* (Washington, D.C.: National Putnam Letters Committee, n.d. but probably 1964).

154. *Evers v. Jackson,* 255, 250.

155. D. Oshinsky, *"Worse Than Slavery": Parchman Farm and the Ordeal of Jim Crow Justice* (New York: Free Press, 1996), 28, 25, 100, 101, 105. Oshinsky (102) quotes a description of a lynching, in which, in addition to other forms of mutilation, a large corkscrew "was bored into the flesh . . . and then pulled out, the spirals tearing out big pieces of raw, quivering flesh every time it was withdrawn."

156. Ibid., 21, 46. According to Oshinsky, many of the prisoners were children, sentenced to prison for crimes such as stealing some change from a store counter.

157. The observation about education is quoted in Silver, *Mississippi: The Closed Society,* 19; the other statements are quoted in Oshinsky, *"Worse Than Slavery,"* 89, 91; see also H. Dickson, "The Vardaman Idea," *Saturday Evening Post* 179 (April 27, 1907): 3–5.

158. C. Sullivan, *Called to Preach, Condemned to Survive: The Education of Clayton Sullivan* (Macon, Ga.: Mercer University Press, 1985), 142, 5; M. Twain, *Adventures of Huckleberry Finn* (New York: Oxford University Press, 1976), 280.

159. See McMillen, *The Citizens' Council,* 217, 218; R. Reed, "Mississippi Wants Goodwill, Governor Asserts," *New York Times,* February 17, 1965, 35.

160. S. J. Whitfield, *A Death in the Delta: The Story of Emmett Till* (Baltimore: Johns Hopkins University Press, 1991); Oshinsky, *"Worse Than Slavery,"* 231–233, 237–238.

161. The FBI report is cited in Silver, *Mississippi: The Closed Society,* 253; the Klansmen's verbatim statements of confession and allusion to the arrest of the twelve civil rights workers also appears in Silver (334–336), who suggests that the suspended sentence was

imposed by the judge in the belief that, even with signed confessions, a local jury would not convict the fire bombers; the civil rights workers' treatment by prison officials is described in Oshinsky, *"Worse Than Slavery,"* 234–236.

162. Eastland's speculations appear in C. Sessions, "Eastland Cites Ties," (Jackson) *Clarion Ledger,* July 23, 1964, 1b; M. Evans, "Mississippi: The Long Hot Summer," *American Opinion* (November 1964): 14, 18.

163. On the composition of the commission, see C. Sitton, "Mississippi Backs Citizens Councils," *New York Times,* March 31, 1961, 18; on the transfer of funds from the commission to the councils, see "Funds Vetoed for Mississippi Board That Fought Civil Rights," *New York Times,* April 22, 1973, 28; also, "Citizens' Councils: Origin, Organization, and Activities" (Library of Congress Report), n.d., Group Research Archives, "Citizens' Council Reports and Studies" folder.

164. As Peter Maass points out ("The Secrets of Mississippi," *New Republic,* December 21, 1998, 22), the East German apparatus relied on a staff of some 90,000 and another 100,000 "informelle Mitarbeiter," whereas the Sovereignty Commission employed only a handful of investigators, contracted some work out to private eyes, and received assistance from perhaps 100 informers.

165. Commission Director Erle Johnston Jr., quoted in Sitton, "Mississippi Backs Citizens Councils," 18; Maass, "The Secrets of Mississippi," 21.

166. Memo to "Members, State Sovereignty Commission" from Investigator Virgil Downing, June 1, 1961, Sovereignty Commission Files; J. Herbers, "Mississippi Purge Ousts Moderates," *New York Times,* November 3, 1963, 82.

167. See the memo from Erle Johnston Jr., director, Sovereignty Commission to file on "Autopsy of Slain Civil Rights Workers," September 4, 1964, Sovereignty Commission Files; the commission was exercised because the families' doctor had arranged for an independent autopsy by a New York pathologist; on the three civil rights workers, see "Funds Vetoed for Mississippi Board That Fought Civil Rights" and W. Rugaber, "Mississippi Agency Tells of Fight on Rights Drive," *New York Times,* July 29, 1968, 16; C. Sitton, "Methods of Citizens' Councils Stir Up Attacks in Mississippi," *New York Times,* March 30, 1961, 18.

168. W. J. Simmons to A. Jones, November 11, 1960; A. Jones, director (before Johnston), Memo to File on "Investigating Laxity in Segregation Customs Practiced in the University Medical Center Hospital, Jackson, Mississippi," November 9, 1960; Sovereignty Commission Files.

169. The characterization of Simmons appears in Silver, *Mississippi: The Closed Society,* 44; on the councils' influence with the governor and legislature, see H. Carter II, "Citadel of the Citizens Council," *New York Times Magazine* (November 12, 1961): 23. The councils often were perceived as a middle-class version of the Klan (see McMillen, *The Citizens' Council,* 359–360), an image that the organization consciously rejected; see "Citizens' Council No Place for Klan," *Citizens' Council* 1 (March 1956): 1.

170. Some details of the harassment during just the first year and a half after *Brown* are provided in H. L. Mitchell, "On the Rise of the White Citizens Council and Its Ties with Anti-Labor Forces in the South," January 30, 1956, Group Research Archives, "Citizens' Council Reports and Studies" folder.

171. Simmons was quoted in articles in "Rights Board Blasted," November 14, 1959, and

"State Citizens' Councils Are Challenged in Test," November 23, 1959, both in the (Jackson) *State Times*. He had earlier bragged to an investigator for the Sovereignty Commission that the Civil Rights Commission had been unable to find anyone to serve on the advisory board in Mississippi; see the memos from Z. J. van Landingham to Director, State Sovereignty Commission, March 18, 1959 and March 26, 1959, Sovereignty Commission Files. The clergyman was Rev. Tom Johnson; details of his experience appear in J. R. Salter Jr., *Jackson, Mississippi: An American Chronicle of Struggle and Schism* (Hicksville, N.Y.: Exposition Press, 1979), 25, 33, 47–48.

172. "Here Is the Enemy!" *Citizens' Council* 5 (November 1959): 4; the list was also described in "Citizens Councils List Their Foes," (Jackson) *Clarion-Ledger*, December 6, 1959, "Citizens Council Lists Enemies of Organization," *Jackson Daily News*, December 9, 1959; and "Council 'Enemy' List Brings Wide Comment," (Jackson) *Clarion-Ledger*, December 10, 1959, a smaller list of thirty-three organizations making up the "Leadership Conference on Civil Rights" was subsequently published as "Here Is the Enemy! Part II," *Citizens' Council* 5 (August 1960): 4.

173. On Evers and Beckwith, see "Civil Rights," *Time* 82 (July 5, 1963): 15–16, and Maass, "The Secrets of Mississippi," 23; the report investigating Beckwith's jurors is A. L. Hopkins, "Assisting Honorable Stanney Sanders, Defense Attorney for Byron de la Beckwith, Charged with Murdering Medgar Evans, c/m, in Checking the Background of Prospective Jurors," April 9, 1964, Johnston papers. Although the forty-two-year-old Beckwith had been a Mississippi resident for the previous thirty-eight years, having spent his infancy on the West Coast, the *Clarion Ledger* headlined its front-page story "Californian Is Charged with Murder of Evers" (June 24, 1963) to further the impression that all the state's problems were caused by "outside agitators."

174. The legislature's consideration of secession is cited in Salter, *Jackson, Mississippi*, 41–42.

175. The meeting is described in a memo from Director, Sovereignty Commission to Governor Ross Barnett and all members of the Sovereignty Commission on "Conference in Washington, D.C.," June 27, 1963, Sovereignty Commission Files. Satterfield drafted a bill that would allow local governments to provide public money for "educational" efforts by the Citizens' Councils, but it died in committee; see McMillen, *The Citizens' Council*, 335–336. Satterfield's work for the commission is mentioned in his letter to Erle Johnson [*sic*; should be "Johnston"], May 27, 1963, Sovereignty Commission Files.

176. J. E. Clayton, "Anti-Rights Bill Lobby Is Best-Financed Ever," *Washington Post*, March 22, 1964, A9; see also "Group Opposing Rights Bill Led 1964 Lobby List," *St. Louis Post-Dispatch*, August 18, 1965, and *Congressional Record-House* 88:2 (April 27, 1964): 9223; the "funneling" acknowledgment was made by commission director Erle Johnston Jr. to Sessions, May 4, 1964, Sovereignty Commission Files.

177. Many documents in the files from representatives of the various associations list the donations from their members; the quotations come from two letters by Leigh Watkins Jr., executive director of the Mississippi Bankers' Association: one to Johnston, the commission's director, September 19, 1963; and a form letter "To the Bank Addressed," September 11, 1963; Sovereignty Commission Files.

178. Telegram, A. W. Rossiter Jr. to Johnston, September 12, 1963; telegram, Barnett and Johnston to Rossiter, September 12, 1963; letter, Rossiter to Johnston, September 12, 1963;

letter, Johnston to Rossiter, September 16, 1963; Sovereignty Commission Files. The files also contain copies of the stock transactions, which, in this case, involved the sale of 2,000 shares of R.J. Reynolds Tobacco and 320 shares of Addressograph-Multigraph.

179. Telegram, Rossiter to Johnston, January 16, 1964, offering the proceeds from 360 shares of General Motors and 1,000 shares of Standard Oil; letter, Rossiter to Johnston, January 16, 1964; Johnston, Memo to File, February 4, 1964; Sovereignty Commission Files.

180. E. Johnston, "Talk to Be Delivered at Canton Lions Club," May 13, 1964, Sovereignty Commission Files. Interestingly, the only other substantial contributor was Roger Milliken, a South Carolina textile magnate, whose company replaced the failing Draper Corporation as the dominant loom maker by relying on superior and cheaper foreign machinery; Milliken's contribution is noted in Milliken to Johnson [*sic;* should be "Johnston"], December 9, 1963, and Satterfield to Milliken, January 27, 1964, Sovereignty Commission Files; on Milliken's conservative activities, see R. Lizza, "Silent Partner," *New Republic* (January 10, 2000): 22–25.

181. On Putnam asking Loeb to serve, see "Memorandum Concerning Cooperative Action Opposing the So-Called Civil Rights Act of 1963," n.d., Sovereignty Commission Files; Satterfield is called the "brains of the outfit" in L. Winfrey, "Anti-Rights Fight Costs $120,000," Memphis *Commercial Appeal,* January 30, 1964.

182. The CCFAF's activities are detailed in a number of documents, including "Final Report to Coordinating Committee for Fundamental American Freedoms, Inc.," June 15, 1964; "A Brief 'Resume' of Activities of the Coordinating Committee on [*sic*] Fundamental American Freedoms," n.d.; and "Project #5: New Hampshire," n.d.; Sovereignty Commission Files. An interesting political tactic suggested by the director of the Sovereignty Commission and used, unsuccessfully, by Southern senators attempting to defeat the bill was to propose amendments that would *strengthen* it so much as to elicit opposition from moderates; see Johnston to J. Stennis (Senator from Mississippi), February 17, 1964, and Stennis to Johnston, May 5, 1964, Sovereignty Commission Files. The amendment introduced by Stennis appeared in the *Congressional Record,* April 29, 1964, 9288.

183. Satterfield to Johnson, March 4, 1964, April 1, 1964, Sovereignty Commission Files.

184. Satterfield to Johnson, March 4, 1964; the accompanying plan, listing neither date nor author but, according to Satterfield's letter, drafted primarily by Synon on the basis of material prepared by Putnam and Satterfield, is headed "this presentation has been drawn to illustrate how a public relations program may be developed which would inform the public as to the differences between the races"; Sovereignty Commission Files.

185. Telegram, Rossiter to Johnston, May 25, 1964; letter Rossiter to Johnston, May 26, 1964, offering the proceeds from sale of 1,117 shares of Addressograph-Multigraph; Memo, Director, Sovereignty Commission, to W. Burgin (Chair, Senate Appropriations Committee) and J. Junkin (Chair, House Appropriations Committee), May 25, 1964; Memo, Director, Sovereignty Commission to H. Glazier (Administrative Assistant to the Governor), May 26, 1964; Satterfield to Weyher, June 16, 1965; Sovereignty Commission Files. See also the well-researched story on Draper and the CCFAF by D. Blackmon, "Silent Partner, How the South's Fight to Uphold Segregation was Funded Up North," *Wall Street Journal,* June 11, 1999, 1, 12.

186. On the attempt at a takeover of CBS, see T. B. Edsall and D. A. Vise, "CBS Fight a Litmus Test for Conservatives," *Washington Post,* March 31, 1985, A1, A16.

187. W. J. Simmons, "The Citizens Councils and Private Education," *Citizen* (February 1966): 10; C. L. Neill, "How to Start a Private School," *Citizen* (May 1966): 11; M. Evans, "The Future of Private Education," *Citizen* (April 1966): 18.

188. M. Evans, "As New as Childhood, and as Old as Truth," *Citizen* (July–August 1965): 15, 6; M. Evans, "This Manual Will Help You Get Started," *Citizen* (September 1964): 14.

189. W. L. Chaze, "CC Buys Residence for Use as School," Jackson, Mississippi *Clarion-Ledger*, September 12, 1964; the General Legislative Investigating Committee, for which Satterfield and Shell were counsel, had issued an official report on "The Occupation of the Campus of the University of Mississippi" blaming the riots in response to James Meredith's admission on the federal government's "take-over" through "raw political power."

190. The guidelines for grades 3 and 4 appear in the *Citizens' Council* (February 1957): 1, 4; the guidelines for grades 5 and 6 appeared over a number of issues: *Citizens' Council* (March 1957): 1, 4; *Citizens' Council* (June 1957): 3; *Citizens' Council* (July 1957): 3; and *Citizens' Council* (August 1957): 3.

191. On the rapid growth of the council schools, see D. H. Shell, "An Attorney's View of Private Schools," *Citizen* (June 1966): 7–9; "Work Underway on New Council School," *Citizen* (September 1966): 10; W. J. Simmons, "How to Organize a Private School," *Citizen* (January 1970): 5; and the Council School Foundation's "Notice to Prospective Patrons," June 28, 1970, vertical file, University of Southern Mississippi. The quote is from J. J. Kilpatrick, "Are They Carpenters, or Grave Diggers?" *Sunday Star*, March 1, 1970.

192. The tuition assistance is explained in Evans, "This Manual Will Help You Get Started," 10; Neill, "How to Start a Private School," 13; the Council School Foundation's income tax returns for 1964 and 1965 are available in the Group Research Archives, "Citizens' Councils" folder.

193. See Draper's estate papers.

194. See Draper's estate papers. A center of Confederate resistance, Jackson was burned down so often in the Civil War that, according to one long-time resident, it was called "Chimneyville" by the locals.

195. The Charter of Incorporation of the Puritan Foundation (August 14, 1963), the amendment (February 19, 1964), and the Certificate of Merger into the Council School Foundation (December 8, 1978) are all available from the State of Mississippi Executive Office, Jackson, Mississippi; also available from the same office is the Charter of Incorporation for the Council School Foundation (September 4, 1964) and its amendment (September 22, 1964).

196. On the activities of the bank and its chair, see R. Reed, "Mississippi Banks Assisting Segregated Schools," *New York Times*, August 27, 1970,

197. The Racial Studies Committee, for example, whose "Board of Endorsers" included Garrett, Putnam, and Simmons, distributed literature intended to demonstrate that blacks were not able to adapt to Western civilization; the committee's "primary package" offered Putnam's *Race and Reality*, the George report, and a pamphlet by Garrett, but also available were such works as the IAAEE reprint series, *Race and Modern Science*, and Audrey Shuey's *The Testing of Negro Intelligence*, all of which had been published with Draper's money; see L. H. Whitten, "Racists Aim at Youth," *San Francisco Examiner*, June 30, 1969, 2, and the list of "Books and Booklets Approved For Distribution," on Racial

Studies Committee letterhead, n.d., Group Research Archives, "Racial Studies Committee" folder.

## Chapter 4: *They Are Not Like Us*

1. Both the trust agreement and the "Examination of Attesting Witnesses" are included in Draper's estate papers, Surrogate's Office, New York City.

2. George to Weyher, March 26, 1956, George papers; "Report of the Faculty Senate Committee on Research on the Issue of Delaware's Relationship with the Pioneer Fund," University of Delaware, April 19, 1990, 6.

3. W. Draper, "Notes to Eugenics Credo," August 10, 1954, Osborn papers.

4. Interview with William F. Draper, December 1998. The dollar amounts come from Draper's estate papers. However, a book written by a major recipient of Pioneer funds, with the cooperation of Harry Weyher, states that Draper "bequeathed approximately $5 million" to Pioneer; see R. Lynn, *The Science of Human Diversity: A History of the Pioneer Fund* (Lanham, Md.: University Press of America, 2001), 18.

5. Garrett to George, July 20, 1967, George papers.

6. Ellis's desire to "protect the people" is from Ellis to Hastings, October 30, 1957, George papers. On the Advisory Committee's recommendations, see the committee's report, "The Pearsall Plan to Save Our Schools," and J. Batchelor, "Save Our Schools: Dallas Herring and the Governor's Special Advisory Committee on Education," M.A. thesis, University of North Carolina, Greensboro, 1983. The characterization of the integration movement is quoted in D. A. Vise and T. B. Edsall, "Battle for CBS Takes on Air of Mudslinging Contest," *Washington Post*, March 31, 1985, A16. Ellis's interest in the tax exemption status for churches, mentioned in his telegram to Mey [*sic;* the correct name is "Ney"] M. Gore, Jr., and Gore's letter of response, both dated July 18, 1956, Sovereignty Commission Files.

7. See "9 Senators Oppose a Reagan Nominee," *New York Times*, July 28, 1983, 17, and E. Tollerson, "Forbes Strategist Made Helms's Tough Ads," *New York Times*, January 27, 1996, 8.

8. T. B. Edsall and D. A. Vise, "CBS Fight a Litmus Test for Conservatives," *Washington Post*, March 31, 1985, A1, A16; Vise and Edsall, "Battle for CBS Takes on Air of Mudslinging Contest," A16; T. Locy, "Helms Breaks with Coalition Called a Cash Conduit by IRS," *Washington Post*, September 6, 1994, A8.

9. The Weyher and Parrott families were long-time friends in Kinston, Harry Weyher's grandfather and one of Marion Parrott's relatives, Clay Parrott, having moved to the town together in 1871; the grandfather married Clay's sister; see Weyher, *The Weyher Genealogy*, 81–82, 91–92. Parrott's involvement as one of the North Carolina directors of the Southern Independent School Association is noted in an undated press release from the association in the Sovereignty Commission Files.

10. H. E. Garrett, "'Klineberg's Negro-White Differences in Intelligence Test Performance,'" *Mankind Quarterly* 4 (1964): 222; H. E. Garrett, letter to the editor, *Science* 135 (1962): 984; W. A. Massey, "The New Fanatics," *Mankind Quarterly* 3 (1963): 79; C. Putnam, *Race and Reason* (Washington, D.C.: Public Affairs Press, 1961), 7.

11. Trevor to Weyher, July 30, 1970, contains the request; Weyher to Trevor, July 31, 1970, provides "my permission to send the Robertson manuscript to Frank Mason"; Weyher

to Mason, August 11, 1970, requests return of the manuscript because Weyher had just learned that a new version had been completed, which he promised to forward; Mason papers, Trevor correspondence. Putnam to Ochsner, September 18, 1972, Wedemeyer papers, Box 57, Putnam folder.

12. W. Robertson, *The Dispossessed Majority* (Cape Canaveral, Fla.: Howard Allen, 1981), 405, 301, 189–198, 365, 200–201.

13. Oliver's review was never published but was circulated privately; see the copy in Wedemeyer papers, Box 57, Putnam folder. His observation on Jews was quoted in B. R. Epstein and A. Forster, *The Radical Right: Report on the John Birch Society and Its Allies* (New York: Vintage Books, 1967), 113; R. Kuttner, review of *The Dispossessed Majority* by W. Robertson, *Mankind Quarterly* 14 (1973): 118–119.

14. Trevor to Weyher, July 30, 1970, Mason papers, Trevor correspondence, Herbert Hoover Library; Putnam to W. McCleery (editor, *Princeton Quarterly*), May 29, 1974, Wedemeyer papers, Box 57, Putnam folder.

15. Putnam to Wedemeyer, September 19, 1972, February 22, 1974; Putnam to Ochsner, September 18, 1972; Wedemeyer papers, Box 57, Putnam folder.

16. See T. J. Bouchard Jr., D. T. Lykken, M. McGue, N. L. Segal, and A. Tellegen, "Sources of Human Psychological Differences: The Minnesota Study of Twins Reared Apart," *Science* 250 (1990): 223–228.

17. The plan is discussed in Shockley to W. H. Draper Jr., March 21, 1963; W. Best to Shockley, December 3, 1962; Canfield to Shockley, December 5, 1962; and W. H. Draper Jr. to Shockley, February 15, 1963; Shockley papers. The papers also contain the resulting statement, "The Population Crisis vs. Peace and Prosperity," issued by Planned Parenthood.

18. The address is reprinted in J. D. Roslansky, ed., *Genetics and the Future of Man* (New York: Appleton-Century-Crofts, 1965), 70, 68; (D. Dickson) "Case for the Plaintiff," *New Scientist* (February 22, 1973): 436.

19. W. Shockley, letter to the editor, *Scientific American* 224 (January 1971): 6; see also W. Shockley, "Negro IQ Deficit: Failure of a 'Malicious Coincidence' Model Warrants New Research Proposals," *Review of Educational Research* 41 (1971): 245.

20. See the interview of Shockley in *Playboy* (August 1980): 82; W. Shockley, "Dysgenics, Geneticity, Raceology: A Challenge to the Intellectual Responsibility of Educators," *Phi Delta Kappan* 53 Special Supplement (January 1972): 307.

21. See Osborne to Shockley, March 6, 1969, Shockley papers. Among other critics, all seven members of Stanford's Department of Genetics, including Nobel laureate Joshua Lederberg, signed a statement calling Shockley's pronouncements a "pseudo scientific justification for class and race prejudice"; W. F. Bodmer, A. T. Ganeson, L. A. Herzenberg, J. Lederberg, E. C. Leventhal, E. M. Shooter, and S. Varon, letter to the editor, *Stanford M.D.* (October 1966), reprinted in *Congressional Record* (December 20, 1969): 40527.

22. Ingle to Shockley, September 22, 1966; Ingle to Shockley, January 10, 1967; Kuttner to Shockley, November 9, 1967; Shockley papers.

23. Putnam, *Race and Reality,* 132; Shockley's statement appears on the dust cover.

24. Ingle to Shockley, January 10, 1967, Shockley papers. C. Putnam, "Genetic Race Differences: The Findings of Dr. William Shockley" (n.d.), was issued by both National Putnam Letters Committee, Kilmarnock, Virginia, and the Citizens' Councils of America, Jackson, Mississippi.

25. For example, Shockley to Congressman Paul N. McCloskey Jr., February 26, 1969; Shockley to J. Alsop, April 14, 1969; Shockley papers. The Letters Committee's distribution list, April 8, 1969, is also contained in the Shockley papers. B. Wallace, "Genetics and the Great IQ Controversy," *American Biology Teacher, 37* (January, 1975): 12.

26. J. J. Synon, "The Liberals' Curse: Intellectual Dishonesty," *Sun Summit,* November 10, 1966, clipping contained in the Shockley papers. In the Citizens' Council journal, see J. J. Synon, "Dr. Shockley's Honesty Shocks Establishment," *Citizen* (January 1967): 6–7; and J. J. Synon, "Are Scientists Afraid to Face the Facts?" *Citizen* (July–August 1968): 10.

27. Trevor to Mason, September 25, 1969, Mason papers, Trevor correspondence.

28. Putnam to Shockley, October 31, 1969, December 9, 1969, Shockley papers.

29. Putnam to Shockley, December 1, 1969 and October 21, 1969, Shockley papers. The analyses in Robertson's book were recommended in W. Shockley, letter to forum members (Forum for Contemporary History, publisher of *Journal of the Forum for Contemporary History,* later to become *Skeptic*), April 23, 1973, disseminated by Foundation for Research and Education on Eugenics and Dysgenics, Stanford, California.

30. See the letters of transmittal from Weyher to Shockley: June 7, 1969 ($5,000), June 20, 1969 ($10,000), and June 19, 1970 ($7,200); Shockley papers.

31. See Weyher to Fuller (Stanford Trustee) ($20,000), August 6, 1968, and Cherry to Weyher, September 27, 1968, Stanford legal counsel's acknowledgement of receipt of the proceeds from sale of the securities; telegram, Rossiter to Meyer (associate general secretary, Stanford) ($46,000), December 29, 1969 (a second telegram sent the same day amended the stocks to be sold, which made no change in the amount of money to be forwarded to Stanford); Rossiter to Shockley ($10,000), December 22, 1971; Shockley papers.

32. Shockley originally intended to call the organization Foundation for Research and Education on Eugenics Recommendations (FREER) and submitted an announcement with that name to the *Wall Street Journal,* which refused to publish it; for a copy of the announcement, dated May 12, 1969, see Shockley papers.

33. Leonard to Shockley, November 4, 1969 and December 8, 1969, which enclosed the bylaws, Shockley papers.

34. W. Shockley, "Inquiry to Potential FREED Supporters," November 30, 1974, disseminated by the Foundation for Research and Education on Eugenics and Dysgenics, Stanford, California.

35. The investigation of students is discussed in G. A. Walden (assistant manager, Pinkerton's) to Shockley, April 8, 1969; on the study of blood samples, see Shockley to R. Wilkins (executive director, NAACP), August 10, 1973, disseminated by Foundation for Research and Education on Eugenics and Dysgenics, Stanford, California, and Weyher to Beekman, September 15, 1971; the other proposals are contained in Shockley to Weyher, January 6, 1968; Shockley papers. Shockley intended to analyze the blood samples for the presence of the Duffy gene, supposedly a marker of Caucasian background.

36. See Burt to Shockley, December 19, 1969, which contains a list of the scores, and Burt to Shockley, April 10, 1971, which provides additional information on the families of some of the twins; Shockley papers. On the controversy over Burt, see L. J. Kamin, *The Science and Politics of IQ* (Potomac, Md.: Erlbaum, 1974); N. J. Mackintosh (ed.), *Cyril Burt: Fraud or Framed?* (New York: Oxford University Press, 1995); and W. H. Tucker, "Re-Reconsidering Burt: Beyond a Reasonable Doubt," *Journal of the History of the Behavioral Sciences* 33 (1997): 145–162.

37. Quoted by L. F. Aarons in *Washington Post,* March 12, 1972, A11; Shockley to Leonard, January 18, 1976, Shockley papers.

38. Shockley, "Dysgenics, Geneticity, Raceology," 306; W. Shockley, "The Moral Obligation to Diagnose the American Negro Tragedy of Statistical IQ Deficit" (paper presented at New York University, April 7, 1974), 5. Shockley first mentioned the bounty hunter concept in an interview with the *National Enquirer,* but when the phrase did not appear in the published story, he presented it in a press release; see A. Goodell, *The Visible Scientists* (Ann Arbor, Mich.: University Microfilm, 1975), 339–340; the press release is contained in R. Pearson, *Shockley on Eugenics and Race: The Application of Science to the Solution of Human Problems* (Washington, D.C.: Scott-Townsend, 1992), 210–211. L. L. King, "The Traveling Carnival of Racism," *New Times* (December 28, 1973): 36.

39. Shockley to Satterfield, March 11, 1974; Kuttner to Bacon (associate director, Stanford Electronics Laboratory), December 23, 1970. Kuttner thanked Shockley for his recommendation of the book to the NAS in Kuttner to Shockley, November 9, 1967; see also Kuttner to Shockley, February 19, 1968; Shockley to Osborne, January 12, 1971. All in Shockley papers.

40. Kuttner to Munger, November 5, 1971, Shockley papers. The articles were R. Kuttner, "International Equalism Menaces Quality," *Truth Seeker* 91 (October 1964): 145–146, and R. Kuttner, "Overpopulation: A Corrected Perspective," *Right* 55 (April 1961): 1. Kuttner to Osborne, April 2, 1971, Shockley papers.

41. Shockley to E. M. Dirksen (senator from Illinois), June 22, 1969, is his own letter of opposition. As examples of other scientists who wrote letters at Shockley's urging in the attempt to block McElroy's confirmation, see Osborne to R. B. Russell and Osborne to H. Talmadge (senators from Georgia), July 9, 1969; and D. E. Faville to Dirksen and to A. Cranston and G. Murphy (senators from California), July 11, 1969; Shockley papers.

42. Telegram, Shockley to Governor Kerner, March 12, 1968 (also sent to, among others, mayor of New York John Lindsay and Vice President Hubert Humphrey); Shockley to E. Breech (TWA executive), October 7, 1968; Shockley to Kuttner, April 6, 1971; see Shockley papers for many other examples.

43. A. R. Jensen, "The Culturally Disadvantaged: Psychological and Educational Aspects," *Educational Research* 10 (1967): 10; by the time this article was published, however, Jensen had changed his position. Jensen has written that he first met Shockley "one Friday afternoon in 1967" (A. R. Jensen, preface to R. Pearson's *Shockley on Eugenics and Race*), although in a letter to B. Weinstein, December 2, 1966, Jensen noted that he "was writing on behalf of Professor William Shockley. . . . I have been consulting with Professor Shockley on topics related to individual differences in intelligence"; Putnam to Weyher, December 9, 1969, Shockley papers.

44. A. R. Jensen, "How Much Can We Boost IQ and Scholastic Achievement," *Harvard Educational Review* 39 (1969): 95, 115; see also A. R. Jensen, "The Culturally Disadvantaged and the Heredity-Environment Uncertainty," in *Disadvantaged Child,* Vol. 2, ed. J. Hellmuth (New York: Brunner-Mazel, 1968), 54.

45. For example, Shockley to L. Boccardi (Associated Press), February 15, 1969, Shockley papers; Shockley's statement to the academy is quoted in Pearson, *Shockley on Eugenics and Race,* 95; Ledcrberg to Bartley, May 19, 1972, Joshua Lederberg papers, available online at <http://profiles.nlm.nik.gov/BB/A/O/I/U>.

46. Shockley to "Dear Fellow Member of the National Academy of Sciences," April 15,

1969 and April 23, 1969; Shockley to R. B. Roberts, May 11, 1969; Mrs. W. Shockley to Mc-Connell, May 20, 1969; Shockley to Weyher, July 3, 1969, acknowledges that the bill for the copies of Jensen's article was sent to Shockley; Putnam to Shockley, dated April 23, 1969, but probably May 23, 1969, which is the date of the postmark; all in Shockley papers.

47. Daddario to Shockley, June 27, 1969; Shockley to Leonard, February 18, 1970, asks Leonard to inspect the enclosed draft, dated February 17, 1970; Leonard to Shockley, February 26, 1970. Shockley sent his request, together with the proposed draft of the letter, to Congressman George Bush (September 23, 1969), among others; those who actually sent the letter to the president of NAS included George E. Brown from California (September 2, 1969) and O. C. Fisher from Texas (October 1, 1969); Shockley papers.

48. L. Edson, "Jensenism, n. The Theory That IQ Is Largely Determined by the Genes," *New York Times Magazine* (August 31, 1969): 10–11, 40–47; "Born Dumb?" *Newsweek* (March 31, 1969): 84; "Can Negroes Learn the Way Whites Do?" *U.S. News & World Report* (March 10, 1969): 48–51; Putnam to Shockley, March 7, 1969, Shockley papers.

49. See "Dear _____ " form letters to members of the "general mailing list" and the "professional mailing list," September 11, 1969, Shockley papers.

50. Weyher to Penelope (no last name, but context of letter indicates that it is Penelope Wilson), January 31, 1968; Weyher to Wilson, May 10, 1968; Weyher to Beebe, May 10, 1968; Weyher to Dowd, May 10, 1968; Weyher to Flynn, June 11, 1971; Shockley papers.

51. V. Royster, "Thinking Things Over: The Lysenko Syndrome," *Wall Street Journal,* May 22, 1968, 18. Weyher was obviously pleased at the story because Royster sent "Harry" a note saying "delighted you enjoyed my column," June 3, 1968, Shockley papers. See Shockley's articles in the *Manchester Union Leader,* "Is Your Genetic Quality Higher Than an Amoeba's?" June 14, 1974, 28, and "Notes on the Life and Death of Tabby II," April 23, 1974, 24.

52. Shockley to Weyher, November 21, 1968, June 5, 1969, February 15, 1969; Weyher to Shockley, June 1, 1973; Shockley papers.

53. Shockley to Weyher, August 16, 1975; on FREED's tax status see Leonard, Memorandum for File: "FREED," August 30, 1971, Shockley to Leonard, December 15, 1972, and Leonard to Hume, December 22, 1972; Shockley to Weyher, August 11, 1974; all in Shockley papers.

54. Quoted in *Times* (London), September 19, 1974, 18; see Osborne to Jensen, March 11, 1969, Shockley papers; and Jensen to Weyl, February 24, 1969, and Jensen to "Dear Friend," September 11, 1969, Weyl papers, box 5.

55. Putnam to Dirksen, July 29, 1968; Leonard to Shockley, September 12, 1968; Shockley papers. The Court of Appeals in *U.S. v. Hinds County School Board,* 417 F. 2nd 852, rejected the school district's "freedom of choice" plan in Hinds and many other Mississippi counties as a method for disestablishing dual systems in view of the fact that "no white students had ever attended any traditionally Negro school in any of school districts and every district continued to operate and maintain its all-Negro schools."

56. Leonard to Mondale, May 8, 1970, Weyl papers, box 6.

57. See Leonard to Shockley, July 1, 1970, Shockley papers; for the testimony by Osborne, Jensen, and others, see *Emergency School Aid Act of 1970: Hearings before the General Subcommittee on Education and Labor on H.R. 17846 and Related Bills,* HR 91-2, June 29, 1970; the statements by Jensen and van den Haag are reprinted in *Congressional Record* (July 1, 1970): 22519–22526.

58. Putnam to Ingle, December 26, 1962, George papers; Gayre to Weyl, June 18, 1965, Weyl papers, box 12; Ingle to Shockley, February 13, 1967, Shockley papers.

59. Shockley to Weyher, August 16, 1975, proposes use of the polygraph; Leonard to Shockley, April 19, 1971, and Shockley to Weyher, July 17, 1971, attempt to dissuade Shockley from legal action in response to criticisms by other academics. Shockley's complaints typically backfired: When he demanded that Richard Lewontin, professor of comparative zoology at Harvard, retract remarks reported by the Harvard student newspaper, Lewontin responded with a new statement to the paper calling Shockley "a racist ideologue . . . abysmally ignorant of genetics . . . trading on his academic standing in electronics . . . to propagate his ideology by the use of fallacious pseudo-scientific arguments . . . [who] should be totally ignored"; Lewontin to Shockley, October 19, 1973. For negotiations after being invited to speak, see Shockley to Zimbardo, October 25, 1972, December 11, 1972, and December 15, 1972; Shockley papers.

60. Mason to Trevor, December 18, 1974, Mason papers, Trevor correspondence.

61. On affirmative action, see A. R. Jensen, "The Price of Inequality," *Oxford Review of Education* 1 (1975): 61–69; Garrett to Weyl, April 1, 1968, Weyl papers, box 12.

62. Jensen to Putnam, March 14, 1974; see Jensen's interview in the first issue, "Ist die Wahrheit verwerflich? Ein Gespräch von Alain de Benoist mit Arthur R. Jensen," *Neue Anthropologie* 1 (1973): 24–25. Rieger has been the neo-Nazi movement's chief legal counsel, a member of Pearson's Northern League described in detail later in this chapter, and organizer and featured speaker at a Munich conference titled "Eternal Penitence for Hitler?"; see M. Billig, *Psychology, Racism and Fascism,* Searchlight Booklet (Birmingham, England: A.F. & R. Publications, 1979), 20.

63. R. J. Sternberg, "The Black-White Differences and Spearman's *g:* Old Wine in New Bottles That Still Doesn't Taste Good," *Behavioral and Brain Sciences* 8 (1985): 244.

64. Incorporation records, available from the Recorder of Deeds, Washington, D.C.; on Leonard and the Southern Independent School Association, see *New York Times*, April 27, 1976, 14.

65. See Leonard to Draper, January 19, 1978, and Leonard to Shockley, January 27, 1978; Shockley papers.

66. The original study was H. Munsinger, "The Identical Twin Transfusion Syndrome," *Annals of Human Genetics* 40 (1977): 307–321; the critique was L. J. Kamin, "Transfusion Syndrome and the Heritability of IQ," *Annals of Human Genetics* 42 (1978): 161–171. Leonard to Weyher, July 13, 1977; Harvey (legal assistant at Pioneer) to Shockley, October 24, 1977; Benirschke (chair, Department of Pathology, UCSD School of Medicine) to Draper, November 28, 1977; Weyher to Johnson (vice chancellor, UCSD), January 27, 1978; Shockley papers. A draft of Jensen's angry letter to Munsinger, June 22, 1977, specifies neither the writer nor the addressee, but the context of the letter makes clear its author and intended recipient.

67. The ad appeared in the *New York Times Book Review,* September 1, 1974, 15; R. J. Herrnstein, "IQ Testing and the Media," *Atlantic Monthly* (August 1982): 68–74; A. R. Jensen, *Straight Talk about Mental Tests* (New York: Free Press, 1981), xiv, 49; the list of pamphlets available from FHU is contained in the Shockley papers Series III (enclosures).

68. R. T. Osborne, *Twins: Black and White* (Athens, Ga.: Foundation for Human Understanding, 1980), 178. Although some of the heritability ratios fit Osborne's claim, there were a number of glaring exceptions: On one test, for example, the ratios for blacks and

whites were .24 and 1.08 respectively; on another, .46 and 1.07. The handful of values greater than 1.00 in the analysis indicated another problem that drew no comment from Osborne: Because heritability is the ratio of genetic variance to total variance (i.e., of a part to the whole) by definition it must be less than 1. More than a decade earlier, Jensen had warned Osborne that such values were "theoretically meaningless"; Jensen to Osborne, February 15, 1968, Shockley papers.

69. S. Burnham, *America's Bimodal Crisis: Black Intelligence in White Society* (Athens, Ga:. Foundation for Human Understanding, 1993 [2nd ed.]), 91, 74, 75, 111, 16, 17.

70. Interview of George Leonard by Keith Hurt, November 22, 1987, transcript in my possession; T. Dixon, *Southern Horizons: The Autobiography of Thomas Dixon* (Alexandria, Va.: Institute for Western Values, 1984).

71. L. Segal, *Die Hohenpriester der Vernichtung: Anthropologen, Mediziner and Psychiater als Wegbereiter von Selektion und Mord im Dritten Reich* (Berlin: Dietz, 1991), 187; the language of the award is quoted in K. P. Tauber, *Beyond Eagle and Swastika: German Nationalism Since 1945. Volume I* (Middletown, Conn.: Wesleyan University Press, 1967), 583; see also the entry for Günther in R. S. Wistrich, *Who's Who in Nazi Germany* (New York: Macmillan, 1982), 114–115; and in Benz et al., *Enzyklopädie des Nationalsozialismus,* 841.

72. T. Swenson, "The Works of Professor Hans F. K. Guenther," *Northern World* 5 (Winter 1960/61): 7; H. F. K. Günther (translated by V. Bird), "Like a Greek God . . . ," *Northern World* 6 (Autumn 1961): 10. Pearson mentions his desire to pay for reprinting Günther's work in a letter to Cox, July 15, 1958, and Cox notes that Pearson is "negotiating with Dr. Gunther [*sic*] for right to publish his recent books in English," Cox to Ladewig, November 18, 1958, Cox papers.

73. "The Peoples of Europe," *Northern World* 5 (Winter 1960/61): 11; though unsigned, the article was written by Pearson because it later became a chapter in his book *Race and Civilization* (Jackson, Miss.: The New Patriot, 1966). R. Pearson, *Blood Groups and Race* (London: The Clair Press, 1966), 13–14; R. Pearson, *Eugenics and Race* (Los Angeles: Noontide Press, 1966), 11. Both the latter works were originally published in 1959.

74. Pearson, *Race and Civilization*, 3–4; R. Pearson, "Sir Arthur Keith and Evolution," *Northern World* 2 (July–August 1957): 7, 5. "Keith and Evolution" was reprinted as a part of Pearson, *Eugenics and Race*, 24–28.

75. R. Pearson, "Pan-Nordicism as a Modern Policy," *Northern World* 3 (March–April 1959): 6, 4, 5; Pearson, *Race and Civilization*, 122; R. Pearson, "Artificial Insemination: Curse or Boon?" *Northern World* 3 (July–August 1958): 7, 6. "Artificial Insemination" was reprinted as a part of Pearson, *Eugenics and Race*, 35–39.

76. Pearson, "Pan-Nordicism as a Modern Policy," 5; "News Review," *Northlander* (June–July 1959): 1; "Rudolph Hess for Nobel Peace Prize?" *Northlander* (April 1958): 4.

77. The association was announced in an editorial "Our Third Birthday," *Northern World* 4 (July–August 1959): 2; the company's booklist appeared in the same issue on pp. 41–47. On the history and ideology of *The Protocols*, see S. E. Bronner, *A Rumor about the Jews* (New York: St. Martin's Press, 2000).

78. "Sidelights on War and Peace," *Northern World* 4 (July–August 1959): 36, 37; G. L. K. Smith, *Jews in Government* (self-published, 1951), 2, 4, 5, 10, 12. Smith named "the secret three," the Jews who determined government policy behind the scenes, as Felix Frankfurter, Henry Morgenthau, and Herbert Lehman.

79. Altheim's membership is cited in J. Kaplan and L. Weinberg, *The Emergence of a Euro-American Radical Right* (New Brunswick, N.J.: Rutgers University Press, 1998), 41; Günther is referred to as "one of the first members of the League" in his obituary in *Northlander* (February 1969); Günther to Cox, September 27, 1955, Cox papers. Günther wanted to call the organization "Arcturus," probably after the star of that name, one of the brightest in the northern sky.

80. The affiliation of Jordan and Tyndall (and also fascist leader John Bean) with the league was announced in *Northlander* (January–February 1959): 4. Jordan's wedding was described in a brochure "Ancient Viking Blood Rite Revived" (Arlington, Va.: Stormtrooper, n.d.). Tyndall was quoted in R. Hill, *The Other Face of Terror: Inside Europe's Neo-Nazi Network* (London: Grafton, 1988), 80.

81. Pearson to Cox, November 9, 1957; Pearson to Cox, March 14, 1958; Carto to Cox, February 2, 1955; Carto called the short-lived organization the "Joint Council for Repatriation"; Cox papers.

82. Pearson's tour of the United States was described in the "New Review," *Northlander* (June–July 1959): 2. The moot was described in a brochure (undated but probably 1959) by "Edward Langford" (i.e., Pearson), "The Teutoburger Moot"; Cox's speech, titled "Herman's Brother," was published in a brochure (undated but probably 1959), "The Monument to Herman," Cox papers. The speech was also reprinted as E. S. Cox, "Herman's Brother," *Western Destiny* 9 (September 1964): 5–7, 18; the title refers to the brother who sided with the Roman invaders' attempt to "mongrelize" the northern European tribes. Cox proposed that the term "Herman's Brother" be used as a "more forceful" substitute for "scalawag" in his letter to the Northern League, February 18, 1960; the suggestion for calendar dates appeared in Cox to Carto, January 10, 1957, Cox papers. The wreath placed by Mrs. Pearson is mentioned in "Northmen Meet at Detmold," the *Truth Seeker* (September 1959): 135; Charles Smith, the editor of *Truth Seeker*, was also an invited speaker at the moot.

83. The best source on Yockey's shadowy existence with its multiple false identities is K. Coogan, *Dreamer of the Day* (New York: Autonomedia, 1999). To author his book Yockey used the pseudonym Ulick Varange, *Imperium: The Philosophy of History and Politics* (Sausalito, Calif.: Noontide Press, 1962); according to Coogan (p. 16), *Ulick* is an Irish word for "reward of the mind," and *Varange* refers to the Varangians, ninth-century Vikings who first brought Western influence to Russia, the two names together suggesting Yockey's desire for a united Europe. The characterization of *Imperium* is from J. George and L. Wilcox, *Nazis, Communists, Klansmen, and Others on the Fringe: Political Extremism in America* (Buffalo, N.Y.: Prometheus, 1992), 252–253. Carto's claim to have written the introduction appeared in an editorial, *Western Destiny* 9 (June 1964): 3, but some of his adversaries in the neo-Nazi movement maintain that it was actually written by right-wing intellectual Revilo P. Oliver.

84. See the editorials in *Western Destiny* 10 (November 1965): 3 and *Western Destiny* 9 (June 1964): 5.

85. The description of *The New Patriot* appeared on its cover; Pearson to del Valle, March 30, 1966, del Valle papers, box 5. Pearson also acknowledged that he was "Langton" in a sworn deposition in *Hirsch v. Pearson, Humphreys and Scott-Townsend Publishers,* Champaign County, Illinois, June 23, 1994, ISAR files. R. Bevan, "Analysis of the Hate-Germany Campaign," *New Patriot* 8 (December 1966): 48, 47, 51; the first year of publi-

cation was designated "volume 8" because the journal was a continuation of *American Reporter.*

86. Editorial, *New Patriot* 8 (June 1966): 3; R. Wagner, "Jewish Influence in Music," *New Patriot* 8 (March 1966): 37; editorial, *New Patriot* 8 (March 1966): 5; S. Langton, "Judaeo-Communist Influences in Western Art," *New Patriot* 9 (March 1967): 37, 34.

87. Editorial, *New Patriot* 8 (June 1966): 4; W. Fenn, "The Kol Nidre," *New Patriot* 9 (September 1967): 13; A. Rosenberg, "Jewish Materialism," *New Patriot* 8 (December 1966): 63, 65. The exact charges against Rosenberg are reprinted in L. L. Snyder (ed.), *The Third Reich: A Documentary History* (Chicago: Nelson-Hall, 1981), 579–580.

88. Stoner, Fields, and the NSRP constitution quoted in George and Wilcox, *Nazis, Communists, Klansmen, and Others on the Fringe,* 382–384.

89. Interview with Greaves (June 2000), who ran at various times for lieutenant governor and Congress; Draper's contribution to Greaves's campaign is noted in his estate papers. Greaves was editor of *The Southern Review;* the handbill is quoted in J. W. Silver, *Mississippi: The Closed Society* (New York: Harcourt, Brace & World, 1966), 56.

90. Interview with Greaves. On McCain's tyrannical rule at USM, see M. Piliawsky, *Exit 13: Oppression & Racism in Academia* (Boston: South End Press, 1982) and C. Sullivan, *Called to Preach, Condemned to Survive* (Macon, Ga.: Mercer University Press, 1985); McCain's courtroom outburst is cited in the latter, p. 210. The American Historical Association found that McCain, an archivist by training, had plagiarized a graduate student's master's thesis in his own journal article, an incident that passed without action by either the faculty at USM or the Board of Trustees; see Piliawsky, pp. 13–15.

91. McCain's service in the speakers' bureau is discussed in McCain to Johnston, August 27, 1987, Johnston papers; W. D. McCain, "History Is Being Made in Mississippi Now!" *Citizen* (November 1962): 6; W. D. McCain, "Who Is Carleton Putnam?" *Citizen* (November 1961): 11; W. D. McCain, "Who Is Carleton Putnam?" *Citizen* (March 1963): 54. McCain also attempted to have a pamphlet produced by his local council on the "Pseudo-Scientific Hoax" behind civil rights distributed at colleges throughout the state, an effort discussed in D. B. Red (secretary, Forest County Citizens' Councils) to A. Jones (director, Sovereignty Commission), February 18, 1961; Jones to McCain, March 16, 1961; Sovereignty Commission Files.

92. See the memos from the investigator for the Sovereignty Commission to (Governor) J. P. Coleman, August 27, 1959, September 14, 1959, September 21, 1959, and to director, State Sovereignty Commission, September 9, 1959; Sovereignty Commission Files. A building at USM was later named after Kennard.

93. Johnston to McCain, March 2, 1964, Sovereignty Commission Files. McCain's refusal to allow the gubernatorial candidate, Charles Evers—brother of assassinated civil rights leader Medgar Evers—to speak was reported in the USM student newspaper, *The Student Printz,* October 4, 1971, 1; when asked for a reason McCain was quoted as responding, "because I've said no." Other rejected speakers included Robert Kennedy and journalist Hodding Carter; see Piliawsky, *Exit 13,* 105.

94. The letter, from a Professor Bradshaw in the Fine Arts Department at Rhodes, was described in an unpublished manuscript by C. Evans, "Politics at Rhodes University, South African Style and Politics at the University of Southern Mississippi, Southern Style," 1999; I am grateful to Gail Evans, his widow, for providing me a copy. The acronym for the new

department is mentioned in Piliawsky, *Exit 13* and Sullivan, *Called to Preach, Condemned to Survive.*

95. Pearson's actions were covered by articles in the student newspaper: B. Boykin, "Problems Plague Philosophy Department," *Student Printz,* October 26, 1972, 1; K. Brehm, "More Firings Made in Philosophy Dept.," *Student Printz,* February 1, 1973, 1; see also Piliawsky, *Exit 13.* The adviser to the ACLU chapter was Sanford Wood. Two nontenured faculty members were able to save their positions after being fired by Pearson, whose decision was supported by McCain; in both cases the faculty members stated in personal interviews (May 2000) that they had helpful connections beyond the university. Kuttner to Shockley, March 31, 1971; Shockley to Pearson and Fike, March 30, 1971; Shockley papers. At Pearson's request, Shockley's recommendation was written on FREED letterhead because "the Stanford Electronic lab stationery would be too difficult to explain to the So. Mississippi administration."

96. Comments by the dean, Claude Fike, come from an interview conducted by Keith Hurt, October 17, 1987, transcript in my possession; a transcript of Fike's speech can be found in the Johnson papers. Pearson was so generally overbearing as chair—imposing textbooks for courses over instructors' protests and threatening to monitor classes to ensure conformity with school policy—that even other segregationists on the faculty, who had initially supported his appointment, turned against him. For example, William Scarborough, professor of history at USM, member of the Citizens' Councils, George Wallace supporter, and member of the "Board of Endorsers" of the Racial Studies Committee—another organization distributing IAAEE and Putnam Letters Committee literature—nevertheless became one of the most outspoken opponents of Pearson and McCain; Piliawsky calls Scarborough "one of the genuine heroes" at USM (*Exit 13,* 81). Fike called Pearson "like Mephistopheles, evil, attractive, and very suave." And another faculty member described him as "a snake in the grass" who would "smile at your face and then cut your throat"; interview with Clayton Sullivan, May 2000.

97. Pearson describes the settlement of the council's suit in his letter to del Valle, March 30, 1966, del Valle papers, box 5; interview of May Swan, conducted by Keith Hurt, October 29, 1987, transcript in my possession.

98. Pearson to Weyl, May 5, 1967, Weyl papers, box 113.

99. Editorial, *New Patriot* 8 (March 1966): 3. The drawings appeared in two almost identical publications—one a pamphlet, the other an article—both written by Pearson but published with a different pseudonym in each case: J. W. Jamieson, *The Nordic Face: A Glimpse of Iron Age Scandinavia* (Washington, D.C.: Cliveden Press, 1982); and A. McGregor, "The Swedish Face: A Glimpse into the Iron Age," *Mankind Quarterly* 22 (1982): 147–163; the quotation appears only in the former, on p. 5. Interview with William F. Draper.

100. "New York Plan," memorandum by Draper on the purpose of his bequest to Pioneer, July 1960; Shockley papers. A. McGregor (Pearson), "Altruism, War and Cultural Selection" (review of *War and the Breed*), *Mankind Quarterly* 28 (1987): 174. J. W. Jamieson (Pearson), "The Case FOR Cloning," *Mankind Quarterly* 39 (1998): 105. Other articles, all but one written under pseudonyms, in which Pearson cites the superiority of pilots are Pearson, "Devolution in Action," *Northern World* 2 (January–February 1958): 13; J. W. Jamieson, "Genetic Science, Social Morality and the Future of Mankind," *Journal of Social and Political Studies* 4 (1979): 195, 196; J. W. Jamieson, "Concerning Scientific Cre-

ativity: Hermann J. Muller and Germinal Repositories," *Mankind Quarterly* 33 (1993): 452; A. McGregor, "Scientific Change in Britain: The End of Eugenics?" *Mankind Quarterly* 28 (1988): 319. In an article on Pioneer's early Air Force project Pearson even converted Draper into a World War I pilot, probably an intentional error designed as a posthumous compliment; R. Pearson, "John C. Flanagan and the Development of Psychological Surveys: The U.S. Aviation Psychology Program," *Mankind Quarterly* 38 (1997): 85. Pearson's idolization of fighter pilots probably had personal roots; according to journalist Charles Lane, Pearson stated that his brother, a Royal Air Force pilot, had been shot down in World War II, which Pearson considered a meaningless conflict between racial brethren.

101. R. Pearson, "The Fall of Rome," *White Power* (August 1974): 1, and R. Pearson, "Ancient Greece," *White Power* (September 1974): 1. On the T-4 program, see H. Friedlander, *The Origins of Nazi Genocide: From Euthanasia to the Final Solution* (Chapel Hill: University of North Carolina Press, 1995); also G. Aly, P. Chroust, and C. Pross, *Cleansing the Fatherland: Nazi Medicine and Racial Hygiene* (Baltimore: Johns Hopkins University Press, 1994).

102. E. Langford, letter to the editor, *Northern World* 3 (November–December 1958). Six months later Pearson announced "formation of a League lending library, of books of Nordic interest"; Pearson, "Pan-Nordicism as a Modern Policy," 6. Weyher to Shockley, January 25, 1973, Shockley papers. Pearson's acquisition of Draper's personal library was yet another reason to believe that the two men had been linked earlier. Indeed, according to a colleague at USM, the Englishman moved from shabby quarters to a luxurious colonial house shortly after the Colonel's death, suggesting that Pearson might have been one of the ultimate recipients of the trust supervised by Deposit Guaranty; interview with Clayton Sullivan.

103. Articles of Incorporation of the Institute for the Study of Man, filed with the Office of Recorder of Deeds, Washington, D.C., May 5, 1976. The internal memo was quoted in C. Pyes, "Private General," *New Republic* (September 30, 1985): 11. For descriptions of some of the people who joined the WACL under Pearson, see S. Anderson & J. L. Anderson, *Inside the League* (New York: Dodd Mead & Co., 1986); the quote comes from p. 100.

104. P. W. Valentine, "The Fascist Specter behind the World Anti-Red League," *Washington Post*, May 29, 1978, C1–C2; the *Post* referred to the French group as "Nouvelle Ecole," which was actually the name of its journal. On GRECE, see I. R. Barnes, "The Pedigree of GRECE—I," *Patterns of Prejudice* 14 (1980): 14–24; I. R. Barnes, "The Pedigree of GRECE—II," *Patterns of Prejudice* 14 (1980): 29–39; and M. McDonald, "Le Nouveau Nazism," *Saturday Review* (February 1980): 13–16. On Pierce's group, National Alliance, see its Web site, <http://www.natvan.com>.

105. Greaves is named as Pearson's successor in Anderson and Anderson, *Inside the League*, 102; Pyes, "Private General," 11.

106. Weyl to Cattell, May 15, 1978, December 4, 1978, Weyl papers, box 12; the quote is from Pioneer's IRS records. Pearson was also the publisher of the *Journal of Indo-European Studies*, which he had founded while still at the University of Southern Mississippi.

107. Conceding that he could "not remember all of them," Pearson acknowledged a number of his pseudonyms in his deposition in *Hirsch v. Pearson, Humphreys and Scott-Townsend Publishers;* McGregor, "Altruism, War and Cultural Selection" (review of *War and the Breed*, edited by J. W. Jamieson), *Mankind Quarterly* 28 (1987): 178, 186. There are

many instances in which a pseudonymous article was later reprinted by Pearson, such as J. W. Jamieson, "Can a Mathematician Be a Social Scientist: The Case of William Shockley," *Mankind Quarterly* 30 (1989): 71–112, portions of which were later published as Pearson's introduction to *Shockley on Eugenics and Race: The Application of Science to the Solution of Human Problems* (Washington, D.C.: Scott-Townsend, 1992). Another instance is J. McGregor, "Race, Prejudice and a Guggenheim Fellow," *Mankind Quarterly* 29 (1988): 267–285, and A. McGregor, "Scientific Change in Britain: The End of Eugenics?" *Mankind Quarterly* 28 (1988): 301–324, both of which later appeared as chapters in R. Pearson, *Race, Intelligence and Bias in Academe* (Washington, D.C.: Scott-Townsend, 1991).

108. R. Pearson, *Heredity and Humanity: Race, Eugenics and Modern Science* (Washington, D.C.: Scott-Townsend, 1996), 12. See also Pearson's articles in the *Mankind Quarterly*: J. W. Jamieson, "Familial Charisma," 23 (1983): 356–364; J. W. Jamieson, "'Simple' and 'Advanced' Pastoral Societies Contrasted," 25 (1985): 419–433; and R. Pearson "The Concept of Heredity in the History of Western Culture: Part One," 35 (1995): 229–266.

109. A. McGregor, "Caring for Posterity," *Mankind Quarterly* 29 (1988): 187. Pearson, *Heredity and Humanity,* 118; R. Pearson, "Eighteenth Century Calcutta: Birthplace of Indo-European Studies," *Mankind Quarterly* 33 (1992): 100. See also J. W. Jamieson, "Early Christianity as a Missionary Religion," *Mankind Quarterly* 28 (1988): 414.

110. A. McGregor, "Scientific Change in Britain: The End of Eugenics?" 307; see also Pearson, *Race, Intelligence and Bias in Academe,* 69–70. The upper classes were always more courageous, according to Pearson; during the French revolution, he claimed, "the aristocracy walked bravely to the guillotine, not one of them deign[ing] to show fear," whereas the lower classes "showed extreme cowardice on the scaffold" (A. McGregor, "Eugenic Thought in France," *Mankind Quarterly* 30 [1990]: 338). A. McGregor, "Social Engineering in India and China: Contrasting Approaches to Birth Control," *Mankind Quarterly* 27 (1987): 480; J. W. Jamieson, "Intellectual Ability, Evolution and Eugenics," *Mankind Quarterly* 36 (1996): 386; see also R. Pearson, "The Concept of Heredity in Western Thought: Part Three—The Revival of Interest in Genetics," *Mankind Quarterly* 36 (1995): 97.

111. Pearson, *Heredity and Humanity,* 35, 43, 36; see also Pearson, "The Concept of Heredity in the History of Western Culture: Part One," 250. Josey to Cox, August 28, 1924, Cox papers. C. C. Josey, *An Inquiry Concerning Racial Prejudice* (New York: IAAEE Monograph No. 1, 1965). C. C. Josey, *The Philosophy of Nationalism* (Washington, D.C.: Cliveden Press, 1983), 61, 207, 210.

112. Pearson, *Heredity and Humanity,* 50–51; see also Pearson, "The Concept of Heredity in the History of Western Culture: Part One," 256–257.

113. Pearson, *Heredity and Humanity,* 58; see also R. Pearson, "The Concept of Heredity in Western Thought: Part Two—The Myth of Biological Egalitarianism," *Mankind Quarterly* 35 (1995): 346. Pearson to Weyl, May 5, 1967, Weyl papers, box 113.

114. Pearson, *Heredity and Humanity,* 139, 78–80; J. W. Jamieson, "Evolution and the Future of Humankind," *Journal of Social, Political and Economic Studies* 23 (1998): 297–298; J. W. Jamieson, "Biological Diversity and Ethnic Identity: Changing Patterns in the Modern World," *Mankind Quarterly* 36 (1995): 196–199.

115. A. McGregor, "Group Conflict: An Evolutionary Residual?" *Mankind Quarterly* 22 (1981): 43–48; A. McGregor, "The Evolutionary Function of Prejudice," *Mankind Quarterly* 26 (1986): 277–284; A. McGregor, "The Double Nature of Prejudice," *Mankind Quar-*

*terly* 33 (1993): 423–432. Verbatim portions of these articles also appear in Jamieson, "Evolution and the Future of Humankind" and Jamieson, "Biological Diversity and Ethnic Identity," as well as in R. Pearson, "Ecology Adaptation and Speciation," *Mankind Quarterly* 19 (1978): 103–118. See also the two books edited by Pearson (A. McGregor, *Evolution, Creative Intelligence and Intergroup Competition* [Washington, D.C.: Cliveden Press, 1986]; R. Pearson, *Ecology and Evolution* [Washington, D.C.: Mankind Quarterly Monograph No. 1, n.d. but probably 1979]) in which some of these articles were reprinted. The journal's Web site is <http://mankind.org>.

116. R. Pearson, "Devolution in Action," 33 and "Sir Arthur Keith and Evolution," 27, both in *Eugenics and Race* (collection of Pearson's articles from *Northern World*) (Los Angeles: Noontide Press, 1966). Interestingly, both these observations were insertions that had not appeared in the original articles in the journal: Pearson, "Devolution in Action" (January–February 1958): 12–16; and Pearson, "Sir Arthur Keith and Evolution" (July–August 1957): 4–7. D. Purves, "The Evolutionary Basis of Race Consciousness," *Mankind Quarterly* 1 (1960): 51, 53.

117. Scott's collaboration with Swan is acknowledged in D. A. Swan, G. Hawkins, and B. Douglas, "The Relationship between ABO Blood Type and Factor of Personality among South Mississippi 'Anglo-Saxon' School Children," *Mankind Quarterly* 20 (1980): 242; see P. Leo, "Name Revealed, Cover Blown for 'Busing Coverup' Author," *Wilmington (Delaware) Evening Journal*, June 14, 1976, 3.

118. E. P. Langerton, *The Busing Coverup* (Cape Canaveral, Fla.: Howard Allen, 1975); Howard Allen was the press created by Wilmot Robertson to distribute "Books That Speak for the Majority," among them Carleton Putnam's "Modern Classics on the Negro Problem." Scott's appointment as chair of the Advisory Commission was discussed in B. Mehler, "Rightist on the Rights Panel," *Nation* (May 7, 1988): 640–641.

119. R. Scott, "It's So Controversial, Newspapers Refuse Ads," *National Spotlight* (March 8, 1976): 7; Scott's defense of Rockwell was quoted in F. Santiago, "Rights Official Has 'Purity' Links," *Des Moines Register*, February 28, 1988, 9a.

120. Scott's articles in the *Journal of Social, Political and Economic Studies* include "School Desegregation: A Challenge to American Social Science?" 4 (1979): 67–79; "Private Foundations, Social Change and Tax Exemption," 6 (1981): 347–377; "Playing the Social Science Card: A New Option for Non-Activist Attorneys?" 10 (1985): 237–246; "Busing: The Remedy That Failed," 11 (1986): 189–199; and "'Push-Through' Educational Programs: Threat to Academic Integrity and to the Nation's Productivity," 12 (1987): 203–226. His articles in *Mankind Quarterly* include "Law and the Social Sciences: The U.S. Experiment in Enforced School Integration," 22 (1982): 275–310; "School Achievement and Desegregation: Is There a Linkage?" 24 (1983): 61–82; "Productive Factors for Increased Levels of Learning," 24 (1983): 243–291; "Desegregatory Effects in Charlotte-Mecklenburg County Schools: Longitudinal Demographics on Black Achievement and Middle Class Flight," 25 (1984): 47–69; "Sex and Race Achievement Profiles in a Desegregated High School in the Deep South," 25 (1985): 291–302; "Mandated School Busing and Student Learning: Achievement Profiles of Third, Fifth and Tenth Grade Black and White Students," 27 (1986): 45–62; "Racial Quotas in Public School Classrooms: The Newest Drive for 'Equity,'" 33 (1993): 309–319; "Untracking and Cold Fusion: Contrasting Research Demands in the Social and Physical Sciences and the 'Dumbing Down' of American

Schools," 34 (1993): 85–94; and "When Institutions Fail: Can Viable Social Policies Then Be Formulated?" 40 (2000): 435–472. The last of these (p. 447) contained the claim about Clark that had also been made in *The Busing Coverup* (p. 148).

121. The collection was published as R. Scott, *Education and Ethnicity: The U.S. Experiment in School Education* (Washington, D.C.: Council for Social and Economic Studies, 1988). The unsigned reviews appeared as "The Problem of Race and Ethnicity in U.S. Schools," *Journal of Social, Political and Economic Studies* 13 (1988):219–222; and "Education and Ethnicity," *Mankind Quarterly* 29 (1988): 427–431.

122. Massey, "The New Fanatics," 79; W. A. Massey, "The New Fanatics: Part One," *Conservative Review* 3 (October 1992): 28–35; W. A. Massey, "The New Fanatics: Part Two," *Conservative Review* 3 (December 1992): 34–41.

123. H. F. Mataré, *Conscientious Evolution* (Washington, D.C.: Scott-Townsend, 2000/ reprint of 1982 edition), 205, 108, 107, 190, 81, 102, 92, 111, 192–193, 56.

124. L. F. Thomay, *The Natural Law of Race Relations* (1993), 138, 4, 13, 140, 124. The book does not note a publisher, but Scott-Townsend, Pearson's imprint at the Institute for the Study of Man in Washington, D.C., offers it on a list of "books available direct from the publisher"; in addition, it is bound in identical fashion as other books published by Scott-Townsend.

125. J. P. Rushton, *Race, Evolution and Behavior* (New Brunswick, N.J.: Transaction Press, 1995); see, especially, chapter 10. Ironically, Rushton attributed these racial differences to the theory that blacks had evolved into *Homo sapiens* substantially *earlier* than other races; Carleton Coon, one of the segregationists' primary scientific authorities in their struggle to overturn *Brown*, had attributed racial differences to his theory that blacks had been the last to evolve. On ethnocentrism, see pp. 85–88 and J. P. Rushton, "Genetic Similarity Theory and the Roots of Ethnic Conflict," *Journal of Social, Political and Economic Studies* 23 (1998): 477–486.

126. R. Lynn, "Ethnic and Racial Differences in Intelligence: International Comparisons," in *Human Variation: The Biopsychology of Age, Race and Sex,* ed. R. T. Osborne, C. E. Noble, and N. Weyl (New York: Academic Press, 1978), 269. R. Lynn, *Personality and National Character* (New York: Pergamon Press, 1971), 176; see also R. Lynn, "National and Racial Differences in Anxiety," *Mankind Quarterly* 11 (1971): 205–214. R. Lynn, "The Evolution of Racial Differences in Intelligence," *Mankind Quarterly* 32 (1991), 107, 116–117.

127. R. Pearson, "Some Comments on Lynn's Thesis by an Anthropologist," *Mankind Quarterly* 32 (1991): 181–182, 188, 186–187; J. W. Jamieson, "Concerning Scientific Creativity: Hermann J. Muller and Germinal Repositories," *Mankind Quarterly* 33 (1993): 450, 448.

128. H. J. Eysenck, "The Dangers of the New Zealots," *Encounter* 39 (1972): 81. Weyher may have distributed Eysenck's book, *The IQ Argument* (published in England as *Race, Intelligence and Education*), having once inquired from the publisher about purchase of 1,000 copies; see North (director of marketing, Library Press) to Weyher, July 29, 1971, Shockley papers.

129. See R. A. Gordon, "Everyday Life as an Intelligence Test: Effects of Intelligence and Intelligence Context," *Intelligence* 24 (1997): 203–320. L. S. Gottfredson, "Societal Consequences of the *g* Factor in Employment," *Journal of Vocational Behavior* 29 (1986): 398–406; L. S. Gottfredson, "Egalitarian Fiction and Collective Fraud," *Society* 31 (1994): 55, 53. On the criticisms of test construction, see "Testimony of Linda S. Gottfredson on the

Department of Justice's Involvement with the 1994 Nassau County Police Entrance Examination," Constitution Subcommittee, Judiciary Committee, House of Representatives, May 20, 1997, available at <http://www.ipmaac.org/nassau/gottfredson6.html>.

130. See M. E. Levin, *Metaphysics and the Mind-Body Problem* (New York: Oxford University Press, 1979); M. Levin and M. Levin (Margarita, his wife), letter to the editor, *New York Times*, January 11, 1987, section IV, p. 32; M. E. Levin, "The Trouble with Higher Education," *Quadrant* (January/February 1988): 19–23; M. Levin, "Race Differences: An Overview," *Journal of Social, Political and Economic Studies* 16 (1991): 209, 214, 213; M. Levin, "Responses to Race Differences in Crime," *Journal of Social Philosophy* 23 (1992): 9, 24.

131. G. Whitney, "Professor Shockley's Experiment," *Mankind Quarterly* 37 (1996): 45, 49, 51, 52; G. Whitney, "On the Races of Man," *Mankind Quarterly* 39 (1999): 330, 329, 327.

132. Whitney's speech to the 2000 meeting of the Institute for Historical Review can be heard at <http://www.ihr.org/conference/13thconf/schedule.html>; G. Whitney, Foreword to D. Duke, *My Awakening* (Covington, La.: Free Speech Press, 1998).

133. Taylor's full name was Samuel Jared Taylor, leading him to use Samuel as the author of some articles and Jared of others.

134. J. Taylor, "To Each His Own," (review of *The Disuniting of America* by Arthur M. Schlesinger Jr.), *American Renaissance* 3 (April 1992): 11; L. Auster, "Multiculturalism and the War against White America," *American Renaissance* 5 (August 1994): 4; "George Bush on America," *American Renaissance* 2 (September 1991): 9.

135. Quoted in J. Pearlman, "At Full Blast," *Sports Illustrated* (December 27, 1999): 60; Taylor is quoted in J. Tilove, "White Nationalists Seek Respectability in Meeting of 'Uptown Bad Guys,'" Newhouse News Service, at <http://www.amren.com.newhous.htm>.

136. Though unacknowledged, the quote came from R. Hall, "Zoological Subspecies of Man," *Mankind Quarterly* 1 (1960): 118; for examples of its use, see Taylor, "The Myth of Diversity," *American Renaissance* 8 (July–August 1997): 8, and M. W. Masters, *American Renaissance* 6 (July–August 1995): 5. J. Taylor, "The Seeds of Conflict," *American Renaissance* 10 (1999): 4; the "boobs" observation was quoted by D. D'Souza, "Racism: It's a White (and Black) Thing," *Washington Post*, September 24, 1995, C2, and in D. D'Souza, *The End of Racism* (New York: Free Press, 1995), 389.

137. M. W. Masters, "How Christianity Harms the Race," *American Renaissance* 8 (September 1997): 3. D'Souza characterizes American Renaissance as "racist" in "Racism: It's a White (and Black) Thing," C1, and in D'Souza, *The End of Racism*, 396; in the latter work (545) he proposes repeal of the Civil Rights Act. The attack on political correctness was D. D'Souza, *Illiberal Education: The Politics of Race and Sex on Campus* (New York: Free Press, 1991); for the Reagan hagiography, see D. D'Souza, *Ronald Reagan: How an Ordinary Man Became an Extraordinary Leader* (New York: Free Press, 1997).

138. E. Clark, "The Roots of the White Man (Part I)," *American Renaissance* 7 (November 1996): 3, 8, 7, 5; E. Clark, "The Roots of the White Man (Part II)," *American Renaissance* 7 (December 1996): 3. Günther described how Goliath "comes forward . . . for single combat" in Nordic fashion—"a choice . . . full of unknown terrors to the Jews"—only to be "brought down to his death by the stone flung from afar"; H. F. K. Günther, *The Racial Elements of European History* (Port Washington, N.Y.: Kennikat, 1970 [1927]), 129.

139. The survey was published as J. Taylor, "Who Reads *American Renaissance?*" *American Renaissance* 8 (July–August 1997): 8–11.

140. Taylor was quoted in D'Souza, *The End of Racism,* 387 and in D'Souza, "Racism: It's a White (and Black) Thing," C2; G. Braun, "Forgotten Black Voices," *American Renaissance* 4 (September–October 1993): 10. Although these quotations probably were accurate, as historian George M. Fredrickson points out ("The Skeleton in the Closet," *New York Review of Books,* November 2, 2000, 63), interviews with ex-slaves were conducted by whites in the 1930s, and "blacks at the height of the segregation era in the South would have been reluctant to express their true feelings about how their inquisitors' forebears had treated them"; even with this "inherent bias," noted Fredrickson, the interviewees' accounts of whipping, which was "virtually omnipresent," indicated that "slavery was legalized brutality."

141. S. Francis, "Race and the American Identity (Part II)," *American Renaissance* 10 (January 1999): 6; S. Francis, "Prospects for Racial and Cultural Survival," *American Renaissance* 6 (March 1995): 7; S. Francis, "Race and the American Identity (Part I)," *American Renaissance* 9 (December 1998): 4; J. Taylor, "The Racial Revolution," *American Renaissance* 10 (May 1999): 3.

142. M. Evans, "Selma to Montgomery, 30 Years Later," *American Renaissance* 6 (May 1995): 6, 3; J. Taylor, "The Many Deaths of Viola Liuzzo," *National Review* 47 (July 10, 1995): 38; Taylor, "The Racial Revolution," 1, 5.

143. R. McCulloch, "The Preservationist Imperative: Why Separation Is Necessary for Survival," *American Renaissance* 6 (June 1995): 3; M. Schiller, "Separation: Is There an Alternative?" *American Renaissance* 6 (February 1995): 4; see also Michael Hart's speech to an American Renaissance conference, published as "Racial Partition of the United States," in *The Real American Dilemma: Race, Immigration and the Future of America,* ed. J. Taylor (Oakton, Va.: New Century Foundation, 1998), 107–118.

144. Francis, "Prospects for Racial and Cultural Survival," 5, 6, 7, 3.

145. S. Taylor, "A Reply to Father Tacelli," *American Renaissance* 6 (January 1995): 7; "A Conversation with Arthur Jensen (Part II)," *American Renaissance* 3 (September 1992): 3, 4, 5.

146. Taylor, "Who Reads *American Renaissance?*" 11; G. Whitney, "Diversity in the Human Genome," *American Renaissance* 8 (March 1997): 8; G. Whitney, "What Is the Role of the Family?" *American Renaissance* 9 (May 1998): 5; R. Lynn, "Research That Was to Prove Jensen Wrong Proves Him Right," *American Renaissance* 5 (March 1994): 4.

147. T. Samuel, "When White Supremacists Gather, Their Talks Can Get Very Detailed," *St. Louis Post-Dispatch,* April 6, 2000, A6; J. Lubinskas, "Another Successful AR Conference," *American Renaissance* 9 (October 1998): 3; J. P. Rushton, "The American Dilemma in World Perspective," in *The Real American Dilemma,* 22, 11.

148. M. Levin, "Is There a Superior Race?" *American Renaissance* 10 (February 1999): 4, 5; M. Levin, "Recent Fallacies in Discussions of Race," in *The Real American Dilemma,* 83.

149. M. Levin, "The Evolution of Racial Differences in Morality," *American Renaissance* 6 (April 1995): 5, 3; J. Taylor, "Why Race Matters," *American Renaissance* 8 (October 1997): 6.

150. Tilove, "White Nationalists Seek Respectability in Meeting of 'Uptown Bad Guys'"; Taylor, "Who Reads *American Renaissance?*" 9; the judge's opinion, delivered as part of a verdict for the defendant whom Irving had sued for libel, is quoted in S. Lyall, "Critic of a Holocaust Denier Is Cleared in British Libel Suit," *New York Times,* April 4, 2000, A1, A6; W. Robertson, *Ventilations* (Cape Canaveral, Fla.: Howard Allen,

1974), 76; R. P. Oliver, *Christianity and the Survival of the West* (Cape Canaveral, Fla.: Howard Allen, 1973), 75.

151. Taylor, "Who Reads *American Renaissance?*" 9; E. Blair, "Swift Punishment for Heretics," *American Renaissance* 1 (December 1990): 6; S. Hornbeck, "Cherchez le Juif," *American Renaissance* 10 (March 1999): 11; Robertson, *The Dispossessed Majority*, 198. In a risible non sequitur, two scholars concluded that "the claim of anti-Semitism dissolved when it was learned that several of the Pioneer Fund's grantees were Jewish"; A. C. Kors and H. A. Silverglate, *The Shadow University: The Betrayal of Liberty on America's Campuses* (New York: Free Press, 1998), 137. Similar logic would suggest that Mississippi's Sovereignty Commission was not racist because it gave some money to blacks.

152. On immigration laws, see N. H. Montwieler, *The Immigration Reform Law of 1986: Analysis, Text and Legislative History* (Washington, D.C.: Bureau of National Affairs, 1987); "Immigration Act of 1990, Public Law 101-649," issued by the National Archives and Records Administration, Office of the Federal Register (1990); and *IIRAIRA: Selected Legislative History of the Illegal Immigration Reform and Immigrant Responsibility Act of 1996* (Washington, D.C.: AILA Publications, 1997).

153. J. W. Jamieson, "Migration as an Economic and Political Weapon," *Journal of Social, Political and Economic Studies* 24 (1999): 347; Pearson, *Heredity and Humanity*, 103; Powell's "rivers of blood" speech was reported in A. Lewis, "A Top Tory Fears Black Dominance," *New York Times*, April 21, 1968, 1, 4; R. Lynn, "The Racial Transformation of Britain," *American Renaissance* 11 (August 2000): 1; the "unstoppable" statement was quoted in Tilove, "White Nationalists Seek Respectability in Meeting of 'Uptown Bad Guys.'"

154. See R. Conniff, "The Right Calls the Shots," *Progressive* (October 1993): 22, 23, and J. Crawford, *Hold Your Tongue: Bilingualism and the Politics of "English Only"* (Reading, Mass.: Addison-Wesley, 1992), Chapter 6, "Hispanophobia."

155. On FAIR's policy and national board, see its Web site, <http://www.fairus.org>; L. Bouvier and S. Garling, *A Tale of Ten Cities: Immigration's Effect on the Family Environment in American Cities* (Washington, D.C.: Federation for American Immigration Reform, 1995), xvi; the advertisement appears on FAIR's Web site; P. Peters, "Immigration: The View from City Hall—A Survey of Mayors and Officials in High Immigration Cities," issued by the Alexis de Tocqueville Institution, Arlington, Virginia, 1996.

156. C. T. Munger, foreword to G. Hardin, *The Immigration Dilemma* (Washington, D.C.: Federation for American Immigration Reform, 1995); Hardin, *The Immigration Dilemma*, 39, 121, 72, 119, 23, 27, 30.

157. Crawford, *Hold Your Tongue*, chapter 6, and Conniff, "The Right Calls the Shots," 26.

158. G. A. Elmer and E. E. Elmer, *Ethnic Conflicts Abroad: Clues to America's Future?* (Monterey, Va.: AICF Monograph Series, 1988), 9–10, 43; J. C. Vinson, *Immigration and Nation, a Biblical View* (Monterey, Va.: American Immigration Control Foundation, 1997), 2, 19, 5, 13.

159. A portion of the Hall article is reprinted in B. A. Nelson, *American Balkanized* (Monterey, Va.: American Immigration Control Foundation, 1994), 94–95; J. S. Robb, *Affirmative Action for Immigrants* (Petoskey, Mich.: Social Contract Press, 1995), 61, 71, 62, 73, 63–64. L. Auster, *Huddled Clichés* (Monterey, Va.: American Immigration Control Foundation, 1997), 28, 29; J. Taylor, "If We Do Nothing," *American Renaissance* 7 (June 1996): 4; see also J. Taylor, "Race and Nation" in *The Real American Dilemma*, 45.

160. The book was reprinted twice in English. The first English edition—J. Raspail, *Camp of the Saints* (New York: Charles Scribner's Sons, 1975)—was paid for by Cordelia Scaife May and distributed by the Institute for Western Values, according to Crawford, *Hold Your Tongue,* 160; the second edition, identically paginated, appeared as J. Raspail, *Camp of the Saints* (Petoskey, Mich.: Social Contract Press, 1995). Some advertisements name AICF as the publisher. The quotes are from 107, 260, 215, 218, 263, 259, 152, 109, 294–295.

161. Ibid., 261, 53, 266, 126.

162. Ibid., 285, 19, 18, 286.

163. Quoted in Conniff, "The Right Calls the Shots," 24.

164. The reviews appeared in *Mankind Quarterly* 22 (1982): 260–263 and *Journal of Social, Political and Economic Studies* 7 (1982): 183.

165. The book was R. Lynn, *Dysgenics: Genetic Deterioration in Modern Populations* (Westport, Conn.: Praeger, 1997); the quotes are from T. Jackson, "The Descent of Man," *American Renaissance* 8 (April 1997): 8, and M. Van Court, review of *Dysgenics: Genetic Deterioration in Modern Populations, Journal of Social, Political and Economic Studies* 23 (1998): 228; the other two reviews were E. M. Miller, "Income, Intelligence, Social Class and Fertility," *Journal of Social, Political and Economic Studies* 22 (1997): 99–121, and K. Lamb, "Intelligence and Fertility," *Mankind Quarterly* 37 (1997): 335–339.

166. Josey's book was discussed in a review of *The Philosophy of Nationalism* in *Journal of Social, Political and Economic Studies* 8 (1983): 473–476, and T. Jackson, "The White Man's Burden," *American Renaissance* 3 (August 1992): 6–8; Burnham's book was reviewed in T. Jackson, "Facing the Gorgon," *American Renaissance* 4 (April 1993): 8.

167. Pearson's *Heredity and Humanity: Race, Eugenics and Modern Science* (Washington, D.C.: Scott-Townsend, 1996), for example, was reviewed in G. Whitney, "Whatever Happened to Eugenics?" *Mankind Quarterly* 37 (1996): 203–215; E. M. Miller, "Review and Extension of *Heredity and Humanity,*" *Journal of Social, Political and Economic Studies* 21 (1996): 349–360; and J. Taylor, "The Future of the Species," *American Renaissance* 8 (July–August 1997): 16–17. Pearson's *Race, Intelligence and Bias in Academe* was reviewed in *Journal of Social, Political and Economic Studies* 16 (1991): 251–254 and again in the same journal, probably by Pearson himself as "Jonathan Makepeace," "'Anti-Hereditarianism' in the Groves of Academe," 16 (1991): 369–384.

168. See L. Richards, "The Late Great United States," *American Renaissance* 2 (August 1991): 3–5, which reviewed Lawrence Auster's *The Path to National Suicide: An Essay on Immigration and Multiculturalism;* Auster spoke at the 1994 AR conference; Wayne Lutton, another AICF author, also spoke at the 1996 conference. The "blood-kinship" quotation comes from T. Jackson, "Two from the Social Contract Press," *American Renaissance* 7 (January 1996): 8–9, a review of *The Immigration Invasion* by Lutton and Tanton.

169. D. D. Murphey, "The World Population Explosion and the Cost of Uncontrolled Immigration," *Journal of Social, Political and Economic Studies* 19 (1994): 481; G. P. Stacy and W. Lutton, "The U.S. Immigration Crisis," *Journal of Social, Political and Economic Studies* 10 (1985): 333–350; J. Tanton and W. Lutton, "Immigration and Criminality in the U.S.A.," *Journal of Social, Political and Economic Studies* 18 (1993): 217–234; H. Dalton (ed.), *Will America Drown? Immigration and the Third World Population Explosion* (Washington, D.C.: Scott-Townsend, 1993). More than a dozen articles in the *Journal of Historical Review* were authored by Charles C. Lutton, who seems to be the same person as Wayne

Charles Lutton, the anti-immigration activist; the two men have identical educational backgrounds, specialize in the same historical areas, and have been members of the same tiny faculty at Summit Ministries in Manitou Springs, Colorado.

170. See the party's Web site at <http://www.americannaziparty.com>.

171. *Death Penalty for Race Mixers* is available from the Christian Research Dispensary (<http://sharpwebpage.com/CR/C>) along with George's *Biology of the Race Problem*, Putnam's *Race and Reason* and *Race and Reality* (the latter providing "the facts about miscegenation"), and a compilation of speeches given at an American Renaissance conference.

172. Sons of Liberty books can be ordered from Arabi, Louisiana; the full list appears at <http://home.inreach.com/dov/cdlbook1.htm> and at <http://www.cdlreport.com/patrioticbooks.htm>; the books available from The Truth at Last are listed on the group's Web site, <http://www.stormfront.org/truth_at_last>; the National Alliance editorial, "Dividing the Race," comes from its periodical, *National Vanguard Magazine* (November–December 1995); Pearson is cited as the authority in "Miscegenation: The Morality of Death," *National Vanguard Magazine* (March–April 1997); both articles are available at the National Alliance Web site, <http://www.natvan.com>.

173. Duke's Web site contains the Race Information Library at <http://www.duke.org/library> and his new organization, NOFEAR, at <http://www.duke.org/nf>. On Duke's background, see T. Bridges, *The Rise of David Duke* (Jackson: University Press of Mississippi, 1994); his surgical makeover is described, together with before-and-after pictures, in L. N. Powell, "Read My Liposuction," *New Republic* (October 15, 1990): 18–22.

174. This packet was received by my son, who had never previously requested literature from any right-wing group, after he ordered materials from the publisher of Pearson's journals and books.

## Conclusion

1. See *Chronicle of Higher Education*, January 14, 2000, A24.

2. J. P. Rushton, *Race, Evolution, and Behavior* (Special Abridged Edition) (New Brunswick, N.J.: Transaction Press, 1999), 10, 9, 15, 17–18, 48. Rushton is quoted as acknowledging Pioneer's support for the paperback in *Chronicle of Higher Education* (January 14, 2000): A24.

3. Rushton, *Race, Evolution, and Behavior* (Special Abridged Edition), 85, 25–26, 89, 24.

4. C. Mayer, review of *Race, Evolution, and Behavior* (Special Abridged Edition), posted on <http://www.feist.com/cdmayer/book.htm>. A statement from the Executive Officer of the American Sociological Association was posted on the group's Web site at <http://www.asanet.org/footnotes/mar00/exec.html>; L. Michael Honaker, the deputy chief executive officer of the American Psychological Association, made a statement by e-mail circulated on the Society for Personality and Social Psychology listserv.

5. I. L. Horowitz, letter "To Our Friends, Readers, and Subscribers," *Society* 36 (January–February 2000): inside front cover; *Chronicle of Higher Education*, January 14, 2000, A24.

6. The e-mail response was posted on the Society for Personality and Social Psychology listserv.

7. See the institute's Web site, <http://www.charlesdarwinresearch.org>.

8. A copy of the press release, dated July 11, 2000, is also available at the institute's Web site; stories on the press conference and Rushton's claims appeared in J. Gatehouse, "Rushton Has Supporters at U.S. Book Launch," *National Post* (Canada), July 11, 2000, A2; H. Daniszewski, "Rushton Relaunching Reviled Race Theories, *London Free Press,* A1; and R. S. McCain, "Professor Cautions AIDS May Spread in U.S. Like Africa," *Washington Times,* July 12, 2000, A14.

9. Johnston to Puckett, January 23, 1974, Sovereignty Commission Files.

10. See "Rushton Fails Review of His Academic Work," *Globe and Mail* (Canada), May 19, 1990, A17. In response, a number of distinguished researchers wrote on Rushton's behalf to the University of Western Ontario. Although many of them were other Pioneer grantees, some—such as Jack Block from Berkeley and James Flynn from the University of Otago in New Zealand—were well-known critics of Rushton's work.

11. R. Pearson, *Race, Intelligence and Bias in Academe* (Washington, D.C.: Scott-Townsend, 1992); J. W. Jamieson, "Malthus Revisited," *Mankind Quarterly* 32 (1992): 433.

12. See W. H. Tucker, letter to the editor, *Society* 34 (July–August 1997): 4, and Rushton's response in the same issue, 4–5.

13. Putnam refers, for example, to having "my friends in the F.B.I. track down" information about someone; Putnam to Coon, August 1, 1960, Coon papers, box 10. Nathaniel Weyl, a frequent contributor to the *Mankind Quarterly,* also attempted to use such connections, writing to J. G. Sourwine, general counsel for the Senate Internal Security Subcommittee (of the Committee on the Judiciary), chaired by James O. Eastland, to request "significant adverse information" on someone with suspect politics, although Sourwine, to his credit, refused; Weyl to Sourwine, August 20, 1963, and Sourwine to Weyl, September 16, 1963, Weyl papers, box 10.

14. Pearson, *Race, Intelligence and Bias in Academe,* 155; deposition of Roger Pearson in *Hirsch v. Pearson, Humphreys, and Scott-Townsend Publishers,* June 23, 1994, 6th judicial circuit, Champaign County, Illinois, ISAR archives.

15. Pearson, *Race, Intelligence and Bias in Academe,* 257; phone interview with Frawley, November 3, 2000.

16. Notes of the phone conversation in December 1989 between Bob Durant, an investigator for Beltrante and Associates, and Danny Levitas, executive director of the Center for Democratic Renewal; notes of the phone conversation in January 1992 between Dan Kiss, student intern at the National Coalition for Universities in the Public Interest and Weyher; both in the ISAR archives. In his letter to the editor of the University of Delaware student newspaper, *The Review* (October 29, 1991, p. 6), Robert A. Gordon, a Pioneer grantee from Johns Hopkins University in Baltimore, quoted from a tape of Mehler speaking in Urbana, Illinois.

17. Weyher to Stefancic and Delgado, January 15, 1998, ISAR archives; phone interview with Delgado, November 8, 2000. The book was J. Stefancic and R. Delgado, *No Mercy: How Conservative Think Tanks and Foundations Changed America's Social Agenda* (Philadelphia: Temple University Press, 1996); Pioneer is discussed on pp. 13 and 34–44.

18. R. A. Gordon, "How Smart Are We about What We Broadcast: An Open Letter to ABC News," posted at <http://www.pioneerfund.org/ABCletter.html>. D. A. Swan, "Differences in Races Are Not Just Skin Deep," *Pulse* in two parts: January 20, 1973, 20, and January 27, 1973, 18; reprinted as D. A. Swan, "Racial Differences Are Not Just Skin Deep,"

*American Mercury* (Spring 1978): 30–34. Trevor to Jensen, Shockley, Pearson, and Swan, February 5, 1979, Shockley papers.

19. R. A. Gordon, "How Smart Are We about What We Broadcast"; Weyher, "The Pioneer Fund, the Behavioral Sciences, and the Media's False Stories," *Intelligence* 26 (1999): 329.

20. Gottfredson to Trabant, November 14, 1989; Gottfredson to Nees, March 18, 1990; ISAR archives.

21. Gottfredson to Trabant, November 14, 1989; Gottfredson to Nees, March 18, 1990; ISAR archives.

22. "The Pioneer Fund—Media Attacks," memo attached to Weyher to MacFarlane (dean, Graduate School of Journalism), February 7, 1989, ISAR archives.

23. Ibid.

24. The "shadowy" comment appeared in T. F. Pettigrew, "The History of 'Research' on Alleged Racial Differences in Intelligence," *American Journal of Psychology* 109(2) (1996): 331; Pettigrew was reviewing W. H. Tucker, *The Science and Politics of Racial Research* (Urbana: University of Illinois Press, 1994). According to Weyher ("The Pioneer Fund, the Behavioral Sciences, and the Media's False Stories," 331), "Pioneer filed a formal complaint" with the American Psychological Association's Office of Ethics against both Pettigrew and the editor of the journal, and, "after separate negotiations," persuaded the journal to publish a letter, which appeared as H. F. Weyher, letter to the editor, *American Journal of Psychology* 110(2) (1997): unnumbered page following 314.

25. See D. A. Blackmon, "How the South's Fight to Uphold Segregation Was Funded Up North," *Wall Street Journal,* June 11, 1999, A1, A8; H. F. Weyher, letter to the editor, *Wall Street Journal,* June 22, 1999, A23.

26. Weyher, letter to the editor, *American Journal of Psychology.*

27. The reminder of the *Quarterly*'s past occurred in W. H. Tucker, letter to the editor, *Society* 35 (November/December 1997), 4. Weyher submitted a response from which the quotes are taken: a letter to the editor, November 11, 1997, which *Society* declined to publish on the grounds that the exchange had gone on long enough, although the editor notified Weyher that he had "passed on your letter to Professor Tucker for his personal reaction"; Horowitz to Weyher, November 18, 1997; both letters in my personal possession.

28. Weyher to Garrett, February 24, 1962; Weyher to George, August 31, 1967; George papers.

29. Editor's introduction to Weyher, "The Pioneer Fund, the Behavioral Sciences, and the Media's False Stories," 319; the quote is from ibid., 331; the earlier article was H. F. Weyher, "Contributions to the History of Psychology: CXII. Intelligence, Behavior Genetics, and the Pioneer Fund," *Psychological Reports* 82 (1998): 1347–1374.

30. Weyher, "The Pioneer Fund, the Behavioral Sciences, and the Media's False Stories," 323.

31. Weyher to George, March 31, 1956, George papers.

32. Ibid., 333; R. Pearson, Introduction to *Shockley on Eugenics and Race: The Application of Science to the Solution of Human Problems* (Washington, D.C.: Scott-Townsend, 1992), 26; R. Pearson, "John C. Flanagan and the Development of Psychological Surveys: The U.S. Aviation Psychology Program," *Mankind Quarterly* 38 (1997): 85–97.

33. The Center for Individual Rights, recipient of $40,000 ($49,000 AFI) from Pioneer between 1992 and 1996, has represented plaintiffs in *Hopwood v. Texas,* 78 F.3d 932, which struck down affirmative action in Texas, Louisiana, and Mississippi, and in two suits challenging the race-conscious admission system at the University of Michigan—one at the undergraduate school (*Gratz v. Bollinger*) and one at the law school (*Grutter v. Bollinger*); on the undergraduate suit, see J. Wilgoren, "U.S. Court Bars Race as Factor in School Entry," *New York Times,* March 28, 2001, A1, A18.

34. The Supreme Court declared antimiscegenation statutes unconstitutional in the appropriately named case *Loving v. Virginia* 388 U.S. 1 (1967), although Alabama still did not officially repeal its ban on interracial marriage, the last state to do so, until an amendment to its constitution was passed by referendum in November 2000; M. Martin and M. Porter, *Video Movie Guide 1989* (New York: Ballantine, 1988), 558.

35. On the Princeton study, see "Census Tally of Mixed-Race Americans Fuels Debate," *Courier-Post* (N.J.), December 10, 2000, 12A; on the statistics of interracial marriage and dating, see "Interracial Marriage. VitalSTATS, August 1997," Statistical Assessment Service, available at <http://www.stats.org/newsletters/9708/interrace2.htm> and K. S. Peterson, "Teen-Age Dating Shows Racial Barriers Falling," *Detroit News,* November 3, 1997, available at <http://detnews.com/1997/nation/9711/03/11030094.htm>. *Mavin* is published in print and online at <http://www.mavinmag.com>.

36. George W. Bush's inaugural address is posted on the White House Web site, <http://www.whitehouse.gov/news/inaugural-address.html>.

37. Quoted in J. Sedgwick, "The Mentality Bunker," *GQ* (November 1994): 251.

# Index

library of, 87, 169–170; military service and, 21–22, 56; Nazism and, 5–6; as observer in India, 21–22, 56; private school funding, 128–129; research conducted by, 29–30; Third Reich and, 63
Draper, William F., 19
"Draper Committees," 71–78
Draper Company, 19–21
Draper Fund, 31, 32–33, 44. *See also* Pioneer Fund
*Drapers in America, The* (Draper), 17, 59
D'Souza, Dinesh, 183
Duke, David, 182, 184, 186, 195–196, 202
Duquesne University, 74–75
Dutcher Temple Company, 19
*Dysgenics* (Lynn), 193–194

Easterners, 97
Eastern Psychological Association, 79
Eastland, James, 67, 71, 119, 122, 165
Eisenhower, Dwight D., 51, 66, 102
Eliot, Charles William, 23
Ellis, Thomas F., 69, 133–134, 139–140
Emergency School Aid Act, 153–154
Episcopacy, the, 21, 22, 101
equalitarian anthropology, 103–106
ERA. *See* Eugenics Research Association
*Erbkrank* (*The Hereditary Defective;* film), 52–54
*Eugenical News,* 15–16, 33, 41, 44, 46–47, 53
eugenics movement, 3, 5–7, 23–42; control over births and, 46, 50, 189–190; ethnic essentialism and, 23; immigrants and, 24–27, 45, 138–139, 193–194; intermarriage and, 23, 24, 25, 27; Jews and, 25, 28–29, 174; mongrelization and, 11, 24, 35, 70, 71, 111, 162, 163; Pearson and, 173–175; racial policy and, 14–16
Eugenics Record Office, 31, 48–49
Eugenics Research Association (ERA), 15–16, 24, 30–33, 47, 52, 53, 54, 61, 167–168
Evans, Cedric, 166
Evans, Medford, 119
Evers, Medgar, 116, 119, 121–122
*Evers v. Jackson Municipal Separate School District,* 116, 124, 125, 126
evolutionary biology, 179–180
*Exposé,* 86
Eysenck, Hans, 180, 202, 210

FAIR. *See* Federation for American Immigration Reform

Fairness in Media, 134
Far Eastern Military Tribunal, 88
Faubus, Orval, 66
FBI. *See* Federal Bureau of Investigation
Federal Bureau of Investigation (FBI), 63, 119, 203
Federation for American Immigration Reform (FAIR), 188–190, 194
Federation for Constitutional Government, 67–68, 72
feminism, 14
FHU. *See* Foundation for Human Understanding
Fields, Edward R., 164, 171, 184, 187, 195
Fifteenth Amendment (U.S. Constitution), 118
financial aid to children, 6, 7, 43, 54–56
Firestone, 37
Fischer, Eugen, 32, 52
Fish, Hamilton, 72
Florida State University, 181
Flynn, Jack, 150
*Folk,* 91
*Forbes,* 1
Ford, Gerald, 133–134, 184
Ford, Henry, 161, 195
*Foreign Affairs,* 167
Forrest, Nathan B., 184
Fort McCain, 165
*Fortune,* 150
Foundation for Human Understanding (FHU), 3, 152–153, 156–159, 193, 194, 196, 210
Foundation for Research and Education on Eugenics and Dysgenics (FREED), 144–145, 151–152, 156
Fourteenth Amendment (U.S. Constitution), 51–52, 65, 165
Fourth Reich, 70
Francis, Samuel, 184–185, 187
Frawley, William J., 204
FREED. *See* Foundation for Research and Education on Eugenics and Dysgenics
French Institute of Human Paleontology, 29–30
Frick, Wilhelm, 46–47

Galton Society, 27
Garrett, Henry E., 71–75, 79–81, 93, 105–111, 115, 116, 197, 210, 213; Jensen and, 155–156; pamphlets of, 110–111, 138, 201, 203; on Pioneer Fund board, 133, 135

WILLIAM H. TUCKER is a professor of psychology at Rutgers University (Camden) and the author of *The Science and Politics of Racial Research,* winner of the Anisfield-Wolf Book Award, the Ralph J. Bunche Award (from the American Political Science Association), and the 1994 Outstanding Book on the Subject of Human Rights in North America (from the Gustavus Myers Center).

The University of Illinois Press
is a founding member of the
Association of American University Presses.

University of Illinois Press
1325 South Oak Street
Champaign, IL 61820-6903
www.press.uillinois.edu